MAKING THE GRADE
Grades 7–8

By the Staff of SCORE!

Simon & Schuster

This series is dedicated to our *SCORE!* parents and children— thank you for making these books possible.

Published by
Kaplan Educational Centers and Simon & Schuster
1230 Avenue of the Americas
New York, NY 10020

President, *SCORE!*: Robert L. Waldron
Series Content and Development: Intentional Educations
Assessment Pull-Out Section Authors: Preeti Shah and Dr. Paul Glovinsky
Author of Chapter 4, "How Can I Help My Child Prepare for Standardized Tests?": Hannah Rubenstein
Educational Content Editor: Julie Landsman
Project Editor: Eileen Mager
Resources Section: Eileen Mager, Amy Arner Sgarro, Doreen Beauregard
Production Editor: Maude Spekes
Managing Editor: Dave Chipps
Executive Editor: Del Franz
Layout Design and Desktop Production: Krista Pfeiffer, Christopher Mattox
Desktop Publishing Manager: Michael Shevlin
Illustrations: Lorie Park and the Wild Goose Company

Special thanks to: Ruth Baygell, Jay Johnson, Kevin Rockmael, Ed Stanford, Barry Tonoff

Library of Congress Cataloging-in-Publication Data is available.

Manufactured in the United States of America
Published Simultaneously in Canada

Second Edition, October 1999

7 6 5 4 3 2 1

ISBN: 0-684-86897-0

CONTENTS

About Kaplan

Pull-Out Section: The Home Learning Quizzes

Foreword

Good grades can be encouraging and satisfying, and we at *SCORE!* are always pleased when the children who attend our educational centers do well on their report cards. Even so, we want so much more for our children than straight A's. Many of us were honors students ourselves, so we know that "making the grade" is only the beginning. What we really want for our kids are good grades and everything that good grades are supposed to represent.

- We want our kids to master the key communication systems that make civilization possible: language (spoken and written), math, and music.

- We want them to build their critical thinking skills so that they can understand, appreciate, and improve their world.

- We want them to continually increase their knowledge, and to value learning as the key to a happy, successful life.

- We want them to always do their best, to persist when challenged, to be a force for good, and to help others whenever they can.

We know these are ambitious goals, but our children deserve no less. Our mission at *SCORE!* is to create great opportunities for learning and development for kids across the country. We've already helped thousands of children through programs in our centers, and we're eager to reach thousands more with this series of books designed for parents of first through eighth graders.

SIMPLE PRINCIPLES

We owe the remarkable success of *SCORE!* Educational Centers to a few simple principles, and we would like to highlight these points as you consider working with this book to create great Learning Adventures with your child.

Making the Grade

• We expect every child to succeed.

• We make it possible for every child to succeed.

• We reinforce each instance of success, no matter how small.

Such simple principles are easily understood, but understanding them is simply not enough. The purpose of this book is to help you put these principles into practice in order to support and enhance the academic development of your child. As a parent facing ever growing demands at work and at home, you need useful, practical answers now. We'd like to share what we've learned in our work with thousands of children across the country. We'd like to show you how to put these principles to work.

ASSESSING YOUR CHILD

Just as a good physician performs a thorough diagnosis before prescribing treatment, we recommend starting with a thorough assessment of your child's academic status. At *SCORE!*, we have learned that excellent grades don't always indicate academic excellence. As standards have eroded, more and more children get A's and B's in school. We often come across "straight-A students" whose actual skills lag behind national standards by a full grade level or more. And if your child's grades are poor, you will probably find it useful to improve your understanding of exactly what that means.

One helpful approach in assessing your child's skills is to ask yourself the following questions, especially as they relate to what you were capable of at your child's age:

1. How much is my child reading? At what level of difficulty?

2. Has my child mastered appropriate language arts skills, such as spelling, grammar, and syntax?

3. Does my child have the ability to express appropriately complex thoughts when speaking or writing?

4. Does my child demonstrate adequate mastery of all age-appropriate math skills, such as mastery of addition and subtraction facts, multiplication tables, division rules, etc.?

These questions are a good starting place and may give you new insights into your child's academic situation and how things have changed since you were a child. At the same time, the subjective assessment guidelines included in this book will help you to understand how your child is grasping school material, homework, and key concepts in language arts, math, and science. You will probably be surprised by the results, no matter what grades your child is earning at school!

WHAT'S GOING ON AT SCHOOL?

Teaching is a noble profession, and we have made the acquaintance of many fine teachers in the communities where our educational centers are located. Unfortunately, we have found a tremendous amount of disarray in those same teachers' school districts. No one seems to agree on what parents and students should expect of schools, and we are a long way from reaching a national consensus. In the meantime, many districts are striving to be all things to all people. Until we refocus our public and private institutions on excellence in learning, we can expect uneven results and knowledge gaps for children at every ability level, no matter how "good" the school district.

Parents will always need to monitor the situation at school and take responsibility for their children's learning. Even if your children attend the best school in the country—public or private—you should find out what your child should be learning at each grade level and match that against what your child actually learns. If knowledge gaps develop, you can work with your child's teacher to see that they are filled. Because class sizes are mostly too large and teachers are mostly overworked, parents need to take responsibility for this challenge. With the appropriate tools, you can catch and correct learning gaps before they become a problem.

ENCOURAGING YOUR CHILD TO LEARN AT HOME

There is so much you can do to enrich your child's opportunities for learning at home. This book is full of fun Learning Adventure activities you can do with your child that will help to build an understanding of key concepts in language arts, math, and science. Judging by our experience at *SCORE!*, the more kids understand, the more they enjoy learning. Each small experience of success reinforces confidence, brick by brick. As you help your child learn, please bear in mind the following observations drawn from experiences in our centers:

• Positive reinforcement is the key. Try to maintain a ratio of at least five positive remarks to every negative one. If you're not sure how you're doing, keep a tally for a day or two. The patterns you see may not be as positive as you would expect.

• All praise must be genuine. This is easy when children are doing well, but even when they are having difficulties you need to find something to honestly praise. For example: "That was a good try," "You got this part of it right," or "I'm proud of you for doing your best, even though it was hard."

• When a child gets stuck, giving the answer is usually not the most effective way to help. Try asking open-ended questions or rephrasing the problem, such as: "Maybe there's another way to do that," "I wonder what made you think of doing it that way," or "What would happen if you changed...?" (Questions that begin with "Why" should be avoided, since they will probably make your child feel defensive.)

• Remember to be patient and supportive. Children need to learn that hard work pays off.

FOR PARENTS OF UNUSUALLY BRIGHT CHILDREN

In the case of unusually bright children, you may need to seek out the kind of academic challenges they may not be getting in school. Gifted children are at risk of assuming that all learning is easy and boring. We often find that such children become extremely upset when faced with a challenge they cannot immediately conquer. When children face a difficult problem, they run the risk of making mistakes or being wrong, a prospect that can be quite scary for kids who depend on being right all of the time.

Consequently, a bright student can actually feel more threatened by a challenge than a weaker student would. We believe that it is healthier for children to come face to face with such challenges at an early age, because they can be taught that making mistakes is okay, that nobody is expected to be perfect all the time, and that hard work and perseverance are more important attributes than the ability to guess an answer right away.

We come across far too many children who have done very well in math through prealgebra, only to fail miserably as they begin algebra itself. Typically, such children rushed through their "boring" and "easy" math homework during the early years. As a result, they did not actually master the material. They also may not have learned patience and perseverance. The solution requires a complete review of math basics, followed by intensive encouragement to overcome angry outbursts and bad attitudes (these usually indicate significant fear of failure). We often are successful in getting such students back on track, but problems like this can be avoided entirely when they are addressed early on.

PARENTS ARE KEY

In many ways, especially as regards motivation, parents are not so very different from their children. At *SCORE!*, we often come across parents who need some encouragement. We are happy to offer it. In our experience, we have found that parents are uniquely suited to helping their children learn. Our simple principles apply to parents too, and you'll find lots of support in this book:

• We expect every parent to succeed.

• We help make it possible for every parent to succeed.

• We reinforce the success of each parent-child team.

We are doing our best to open new *SCORE!* centers across the country. Since we may not have arrived in your neighborhood yet, we invite you to look to the encouraging anecdotes, home learning resources, and useful hints throughout this book. We hope to share our discoveries with you and encourage your efforts to accelerate your children's learning.

THERE'S MORE TO LIFE THAN ACADEMIC EXCELLENCE

Most parents recognize that academic excellence is just one of many things they would like to ensure for their children. At *SCORE!*, we are committed to developing the whole child, and that is another key component of "making the grade." We emphasize:

• Academic skills and critical thinking

• Positive reinforcement to build confidence and a love of learning

• Extensive experience with setting and achieving goals

• Great role-model relationships with positive, admirable adults

SCORE! instructors are known as "Coaches," and for good reason. Great coaches instruct, lead, motivate, and serve as role models. Most importantly, they share responsibility for the performance of each team member. Likewise, our Coaches guide, inspire, and cheer on the children under their care and take ownership in the outcome. If there is one thing we at *SCORE!* have learned about children, it is that they rarely get too much positive attention from people who care about them. And every time we pay attention to a child, we get so much more than we give.

—From the Coaches at *SCORE!*

How Do You Foster Your Child's Interest in Learning?

In preparing this series, we surveyed scores of parents on this key question:

- "Even though I always buy my children books, we still continue to borrow books from the library because they have access to a better variety of books that interest them."
- "I've never forced reading. My oldest son had difficulty learning to read, and the struggle made him hate it. The thing that worked was to have him focus on reading sports books—that interested him. Now he avidly reads the sports section of newspapers, sports-related magazines, and sports-related nonfiction books."
- "I model good reading habits for my children by reading and belonging to a book group."
- "I put books and magazines in every bedroom and bathroom and in our living room so my daughter and I stay in the habit of reading."
- "Talk about the characters and discuss the stories that you've just read together."
- "We do many things together as a family. We give a lot of praise and positive feedback."
- "We keep the TV locked up. That thing only encroaches on learning."
- "No Nintendo™! And no TV in the morning or until homework is done."
- "When her home workbooks are completed, we share them with her classroom teacher."
- "The most important thing we do is not give an immediate answer to homework questions. We try to use books, the computer, and other resources to discover the answers and information together."
- "Our seventh grader wasn't interested in reading his science book and doing science homework. Finally, my husband found out that he didn't understand what he was reading. We started reading the science book with him every day, and now he is very much interested in science."
- "We make homework low key, but non-negotiable—it's something that must get done."
- "We have a membership to a local museum that we all like to visit."
- "We take our children on many trips and outings. They cultivate their curiosities."
- "We like to expose our seventh-grade son to other people's lives and ideas, so we take him places."
- "I put my children in the environment of what I'd like them to learn so they experience it firsthand!"
- "Our daughter often bakes and prepares desserts with her dad."
- "We do a lot of experimenting when we cook with our children. We love to do science experiments in the kitchen together."
- "Sports are a great way for our kids to learn about life—cooperation, teamwork, leadership, goal-setting . . . ."
- "Music—music lessons, attending concerts, involvement in children's symphonies and music groups—adds a great learning dimension to our kids' lives."
- "Walks are perfect learning experiences. You can really enjoy conversation and observation with your children."
- "We get together as a family for regular dinners."
- "We sit down together as a family and make a family mission statement."
- "I feel that parents should take all the little questions kids have seriously and answer them truthfully."

How to Use This Book

You want to do all you can to foster and support your child's successful progress through school—those important years in which learning and growing should reward the effort and enthusiasm your child invests.

The nature and amount of effort and enthusiasm children bring to their school work directly affect each child's educational rewards. But your child's effort and enthusiasm also depends significantly on the effort and enthusiasm you provide at home. You already knew that or you would not have purchased this book. What you want to know is how to best use this book to help fulfill your goal of promoting your child's enjoyment of learning and success at school.

The core of this book lies in Section III, where the "Learning Adventure" activities that you can do with your child show you ways to take advantage of time you spend together learning and developing valuable skills. The two sections that precede those activities provide a context that you will find valuable in observing and thinking about your child as he experiences his school years.

THE BIG PICTURE

Because being a parent sometimes feels like being entangled in an infinite web of questions, we focus *Making the Grade* around some very basic questions that all parents ponder as they worry about how best to contribute to their children's education.

Get Your Bearings—the Opening Sections

Section I—"What Should My Child Be Able to Do?"—focuses on your growing child, how he develops, how he learns, how schools look at his progress, and how a parent can fit into his educational world. Section II—"What's Being Covered in School?"—gives you a look at what schools are likely to be expecting your child to learn by the completion of his present grade.

Making the Grade

We have kept these opening sections as brief as possible; their purpose is to give you useful background and guidance for what you do with the Learning Adventure activities. We recommend that you read Section I in order to easily and quickly gain a useful perspective on factors that affect your child's learning and school experience. We expect you'll read this section initially and return to browse through it from time to time later on as you enjoy watching and participating in your child's learning.

We expect that you'll use Section II primarily for reference, to look up information about school expectations in specific areas of learning for your child at the appropriate grade level, and to review for yourself, as needed, specific school content that you may not have thought about for many years! To provide for convenient, quick access, we present each of the three content areas—Language Arts (which includes Reading), Math, and Science—separately. Each content area provides an outline of expectations for 7th grade and then for 8th grade, followed by a sort of bird's-eye view of the content covered during those two years of schooling—descriptions or explanations of the concepts and skills listed in the two grade outlines.

If your child is presently in grade seven, you can simply skip the grade eight outline and save reading it for next year. If she is in grade eight, there's no reason to read the grade seven outline unless you're interested in seeing what she probably should have learned in the previous year. We expect parents to use Section II of the book in widely different ways. You may find reading through the content a fascinating trip down memory lane where you might discover new learnings that were not offered during your school years. Or you may simply dip into the content sections only when you feel a need to brush up on something. Maybe it's a spelling or punctuation rule (how to use apostrophes to show possession in plural nouns) or the meaning of a concept (like *erosion*), or both (the concept of *perimeter* and how it is calculated).

Know Your Way Around

Sprinkled throughout the book are sidebars and short features containing tips, strategies, stories, and advice from our *SCORE!* Coaches, teachers, and parents from around the United States. You'll also find the latest research to help you make your child's 7th and 8th grade years true Learning Adventures. Look for these icons to help you know who is giving you information and why:

 Whenever you see the "house" icon, expect "learning at home" advice.

 The "blackboard strategy" icon offers thoughtful, sometimes inspiring tips and approaches for parents on learning and parenting.

 Parents and students have a lot to juggle every day! Our "juggler" icon signals practical "try this at home" tips and activities.

If it has anything to do with the Internet, computers, software programs, or learning technology, you'll find it under our "computer" icon.

 The "book" icon yields learning-related excerpts from recommended books and authors, as well as reading and other bookish matters.

 Finally, the *SCORE!* logo signals insights from *SCORE!*'s Coaches and stories from our national educational centers, intended to give you everyday insights you can use at home with your children.

The Heart of the Book—Learning Adventure Activities

The bulk of the book consists of learning activities and hundreds of "What's More" activity ideas geared specifically to the 7th and 8th grade curricula and tailored for learning enjoyment at home. These are activities designed for parents to do with their children.

Time—Your Most Precious Resource. Money, property, and the best connections in the world cannot come closer to the value of time you spend with your child. We are convinced that the best way for parents to promote their children's educational success is for them to spend time with their children; the more time spent, the better the payoff! Our activities are offered as ways to help you focus that time on enjoyable learning.

Perhaps most often the time may involve your helping to get the Learning Adventure activity started and then taking a back seat, checking in, remaining interested, supportive, and inquisitive about what your child is learning. Several activities feature games you play together, where your involvement continues actively throughout the activity. Many activities can expand to include other family members or friends. You may be surprised by how many of the activities suggest valuable ways to use "down time" together, ways to take advantage of time you normally don't even realize you have available—driving time, waiting time, meal prep time, clean-up time.... You'll soon discover all kinds of time just awaiting your educational use. And most of these activities offer attractive alternatives to TV-viewing time.

In short, the core of this book contains ways parents and children can enjoy doing things together that contribute to school success. At the same time, they contribute to building a foundation of memories that secure your youngster's confidence in himself and in the parental support that encourages him to reach forward and learn more.

How to Use the Activities. You can use these Learning Adventures in any of a variety of ways—the rule is suit yourself, or more to the point, suit your child. There is no required order. (You can even jump into an activity from the next grade, or last grade, if it seems appealing to and appropriate for your child.) Select activities to build further upon strengths and interests you observe your child to have. Also select activities to assist your child where he may be having trouble or to augment work being done at school. Of course, you should also select activities simply because they appeal to you—they look like something you and your child can enjoy together.

Don't worry if you and your child do activities that "she doesn't really need" or that you've done before. Enjoyable repetition provides practice that reinforces and consolidates your child's learning. One of our authors recalls with special pleasure the endless games of Twenty Questions played with her family at Sunday supper and on almost any long car ride.

To provide an organizational structure and accommodate parents who wish to select activities according to subject area and grade, the activities are grouped accordingly. Thus, you can pick out a science activity related to any particular core area of the grade seven curriculum. The "At a Glance" section of each activity will tell you which core area or areas the activity addresses, the main skills it promotes, the materials needed to carry it out, and approximately how much time it will take. The rest of the activity provides step-by-step instructions to help you do the activity. Of course, you can augment and adjust the steps as best suits you, your child, and your home environment. Each activity concludes with three or more suggestions of further activity ideas—the "What's More" sidebars—that you and your child can pursue.

Link Up with Learning. As you can see, choosing and carrying out activities should be linked to keeping in touch with what your child is doing at school and how she feels about it. Nothing beats talking with your child; in addition, use the strategies discussed in the essay in Section I called "How Are Children Evaluated?" and in the Section IV questions under "The Parent-School Partnership," as well as the materials in our pull-out "The Home Learning Quizzes" to help you assess what your child knows and can do, along with charting her progress and your own home learning knowledge and awareness.

More Support—Questions and Resources

The last section responds to the concerns most parents have and indicates where you can obtain further resources for promoting your child's educational development and pleasure.

We expect you'll browse among the questions out of curiosity, as well as consult them when particular questions or issues become important in your child's school life. We hope the resource listings will lead you to specific materials to contribute to activities you choose to do with your child, and give you avenues for enlarging your own learning.

Last, but Essential—The Home Learning Quizzes

Our book concludes with what we view as an invaluable tool for you and your child—your assessment materials. By using the strategies for learning about your child (and—surprise—probably a bit about yourself while you're at it), you will maximize the benefit (and pleasure) you and your child will experience.

Parents' Pages. The Parents' Home Learning Quiz (pages 1–8 of the pull-out) enables you to teach yourself more and more about your child, how he learns, and what he is learning. As your child's learning coach, taking this quiz and reading the introductory material enables you to periodically assess your own knowledge and awareness of your child's progress, and discover more about how to maximize your child's education. You'll also be able to assess your own style of interaction with your child. Enjoy these new insights!

Your Child's Pages. The Kid's Home Learning Quizzes (pages 9–16 of the pull-out) are meant to be fun "How much do I know?" questions taken right out of the grades seven and eight curriculum in language arts, math and science.

Much like the popular *BrainQuest*™ series, these are sometimes easy, sometimes challenging at-grade-level questions for your child to tackle. Approach the quizzes like a game of trivia or one of the Learning Adventure activities: "See how many of these you can get right..." Then congratulate your child on each right answer! There's no grading or scoring, just the good feeling of being able to have your child point out to you how much he knows.

While not a scientific tool to measure your child's grade-level abilities, the tougher problems and wrong answers will give you and your child good indications of where more learning needs to take place. (Or they may cover skills your child hasn't been taught yet in school.) Use outside resources and appropriate Learning Adventure activities from Section III to help practice and reinforce the skills. See if your child can answer the quiz questions correctly after having more practice with the skills. And so the learning fun and quizzing continues....

Communicate with *SCORE!*

And last but not least, we want to hear from you. We consider the parents who use our books to be invaluable resources. We want to hear your assessment of activities, your ideas, your success stories, and the questions that you want us to address in the future.

The "About Kaplan" pages at the back of the book give you a variety of ways to contact Kaplan and our *SCORE!* centers. Write, call, or e-mail us with your feedback and experiences. If you're online, subscribe to *SCORE! Edge,* our free electronic newsletter for parents and for students. Receive great home-learning advice, tips and contests, and plug into new language arts, math, and science activities. Subscribe to *SCORE! Edge* at www.ScoreLearning.com. Turn the *Making the Grade* experience into a lifetime of enjoyable learning for your family.

What Should My Child Be Able to Do?

CHAPTER 1

How Do Children Develop?

Children develop sporadically, surprisingly, rapidly, unexpectedly.... You can add just about any adverb you want, or any *ten*, and still not have the complete picture. Parenting can sometimes feel a lot like coping with cooking. Just as you've got the onions browning nicely, the rice boils over; while you're cleaning up that mess and cutting up the broccoli, the onions start to burn. It's just that children *never* stay the same. Their lives, their bodies, and their abilities are in continuous change. Sometimes the changes are steady and easily measured, and sometimes they are sudden and surprising. When it's not exhausting, it's exhilarating to be around children. In those moments when we surface for a breath above the sea of soccer, socks, and successes, we can appreciate what a privilege it is to witness the young human being in our care growing toward adulthood.

And as we fret about our own children, it is reassuring to remember that children throughout the world (along with their parents) are moving through the same developmental stages and have been doing so for countless generations.

Anxiety-Free Thinking About Your Child

We all have our worries about our children; are they too tall, too short, not enough of this, too much of that? Society, schools, grandparents and in-laws, and our own internal monitors all seem to be waiting to judge our children's performance (and ours as well). We've put some topics into this section to help you think about your child as the wonderful and unique person that she is, and to put to rest some of the anxiety you may feel.

HARD WORK = SUCCESS

What we ought to borrow from the Japanese—and communicate to every student and parent in this country—is the belief that success in school comes from hard work, not native intelligence, and that all children, if they are given instruction that is not only supportive, but appropriately demanding, can learn what they need to know to be educated and competent members of society.
—from *Beyond the Classroom* by Laurence Steinberg, Ph.D. (Simon & Schuster, 1996)

GRADE EXPECTATIONS

There are oftentimes two different kinds of parents. One is determined to get her child in line with the skills needed for a certain grade level. For instance, "By a certain grade, my son needs to learn to read well, or he has to have certain division and multiplication skills." And then there are the parents who are less interested in their children's having attained certain skill levels but are more concerned with what skills their children do have. I tell parents that I'm not into gearing their child into being a "typical 8th grader" because there is no typical 8th grader—they're all over the spectrum. Students should be given the freedom to move ahead, catch up to their grade level, or whatever keeps them motivated and excited to learn.

ALL KINDS OF MINDS

Try reading *All Kinds of Minds* by Dr. Mel Levine (Educators Publishing Service, 1993) with your child. It's a sympathetic, light-hearted, and extremely intelligent presentation of learning issues of all kinds—great for students and parents alike.

There's no such thing as an average child. As you consider your child's development through the school years, it's helpful to remember that "average" is a statistical term and not the description of a person. The unit called *average* is arrived at by lumping together all of something and finding the mathematical mean. The average of anything is nothing more than the abstract quality of the middleness. Some aspect of each child's being may happen to fall on the mark called average, but it's unlikely. Each child is going to be more of this and less of that. Your child is a unique individual.

He got that from your side of the family! In the academic world, this topic is called "nature versus nurture." Much study has been devoted to this topic, but as far as this book's approach to parenting is concerned, there is no *versus* at all. Both elements, our own combination of genes and our environment, play their roles together in how we grow into adulthood.

For parents concerned with how development affects their children, however, the most significant differences among school age children are those of developmental timing, for instance, the more than six-year range between the earliest normal onset of puberty for girls and the latest beginnings for normal boys!

Some people with political agendas make endless efforts to prove that there are racially significant differences in intelligence. There is no valid scientific evidence for genetic inferiority or superiority in intelligence. There is, however, extensive evidence that children with the loving support of their families and the society around them will do better in school.

Theories of Development
In earlier times, folks didn't think about human development much. There were occasional introspective geniuses (St. Augustine is one example) who left autobiographical records of their childhood and gave thought to education and development, but children were generally thought of as little adults who just got bigger and (most of the time) smarter.

The growth of science in the eighteenth and nineteenth centuries changed how we viewed ourselves. The knowledge and techniques of study learned from the natural sciences were applied to human beings, and the result was the growth of psychology and the study of human nature. Sigmund Freud, Erik Erikson, and Jean Piaget are the three most notable recent thinkers in this area. People may agree or disagree with their particular theories, but we all owe them a debt for stepping in to take a closer look at how the curious creatures we call human develop.

The theorist who has had the most influence on education is a Swiss scientist, Jean Piaget, who devoted much of his life to carefully examining how children think. Most contemporary western educational programs are built on aspects of his findings and theories. His observations of children led him to conjecture that our intellectual abilities increase through qualitatively different stages from infancy through adulthood. The infant who begins life by putting together only the simplest and most immediate or tangible facts grows through several intellectual stages into an adult capable of building and using powerful abstractions.

Seeing the Whole Child

No matter what particular theory of development rings truest to you, there is an important lesson to be learned from child psychologists, developmental specialists, and scientists of human behavior and learning like Piaget. This lesson is that thoughtful observation is the basis of understanding. In the case of the experts, it has led to understandings about large patterns of human nature. In the case of you, the parent, it is your understanding of an individual, your child.

All of us get caught up in the trap of comparing our child to other children (after all, Mozart was only three when he started to compose). Our parents probably did it to us and we know we shouldn't do it, but there we go again! One way to short-circuit this pointless exercise is to keep in mind that developmental age and chronological age are two different things!

At any particular age, any three children can be at three very different stages of mental and physical development within

THINKING ABOUT DEVELOPMENT

Jerome Brunner, Robert Coles, Herbert Kohlberg, and Carol Gilligan are among the many contemporary specialists in different aspects of child development who are worth looking into. Their insights into the development of thinking, moral development, and values are fascinating. In this speculative field, there are no absolutes and lots of controversy and excitement.

FROM THE VERY FIRST DAYS

Learning begins in the first days of life. Scientists are now discovering how young children develop emotionally and intellectually from their first days, and, therefore, how important it is for parents to begin immediately talking, singing, even reading to their infants.
—from the 1997 State of the Union Address, President Clinton

a general range. Given our wildly different genetic makeups and the different timetables those genes set for our physical development (and don't forget to throw in the role that different environments play) there's really no accurate way to compare children on a point-by-point basis. The best that we can do is observe closely, try to understand, and do the best we can to support our children's own growth and development.

"I need new sneakers!"

First, let's talk about your child's physical growth and development. Human bodies don't grow at a sedately slow and steady pace. Different parts of us grow at different speeds and at different times. Our heads and the brains inside grow very rapidly until sometime between the ages of four and six and then continue to grow, but more slowly, until adolescence. Our height and weight increase tremendously from birth until around age three and then slow down until puberty when there is a second growth burst. Our lymphoidal tissue (the tonsils, adenoids, and parts of the intestines) grow quickly through about age ten and then taper off, still growing, but at a slower rate until maturity. Our reproductive organs grow very slowly until the onset of puberty and then grow rapidly. The muscles and our skeletal frame develop a little unevenly; feet, hands, and head reach adult size before the rest of us, and our legs lengthen before our trunk stretches out. (Hey, look! He's wearing high waters!) Kids outgrow their pants before they outgrow their shirts.

Quiet! Child Thinking

Mental development in children alternates between incremental growth and great leaps. Whereas the physical and emotional changes that our children experience can't be missed, mental growth can be less obvious. Ankles erupt out of pant legs, hairs sprout, doors slam, and last year's obsessions suddenly become little kid stuff. Mental growth appears to be just as obvious at first. There is a clear, measurable increase in how much your kid knows. Vocabulary grows (not always the words we want!), skills increase, and children acquire more factual information.

These are quantitative differences and they are substantial, but there are changes in your child's mental ability that are subtler and much more profound.

From Collecting Facts to Spinning Theories. Students of human development have come to realize that, as we mature, the very ways in which we do our thinking change. The differences between a toddler and an adult are much more than size of vocabulary and the accumulation of factual information.

Children start school being very specific, concrete thinkers. Their thinking is based on the manipulation of objects and immediate events and the relationships among them. In the later elementary and early middle school years, this kind of thinking is mixed with a more abstract ability. In this middle stage, they are able to generalize. They can consider a group of objects and think about them in terms of an abstraction that sums them all up. In late middle school and high school, they make a third transition. They become able to take generalizations and conjectures and think about them quite separately from real objects. They can theorize about tyranny, democracy, and relativity, and they can argue (and they do love to argue) about the general advantages and disadvantages of either of the former or the philosophical fallout of the last.

Characteristic Questions. If you were to characterize children at different levels of mental development in a rough-and-ready way, you might separate them by the kinds of questions they ask. *What* is the question that belongs to the earlier years. *How* is the question for the middle school years. *Why* and *What if* are the questions of adolescence and beyond. Of course, these questions get asked at all ages, but the ability to fully understand them and appreciate the answers grows and unfolds as we mature intellectually.

There is no exact timetable for development. No one can say, "At seven-and-a-half years of age your child will be able to do thus and such or think in this or that way." In fact, developmental specialists are very careful to make a distinction between developmental age (the age at which certain things generally happen) and chronological age (the

MISTAKES 101

If I tell kids often enough, "This mistake is an opportunity to learn something, so you can go forward from it," then I also learn that I can build on any experience or craziness in my own life to make myself a better person. We help students take a proactive approach to when things hit the fan.

IT TAKES A LOT

I admire any parent out there because it's such a tough job. There are times I think I want to have ten kids because kids are the greatest, then I see how much work parents have to put into their children and I think, Whoa, can I do that? It's a lot to be a successful parent and raise happy kids!

LEARNING RESOURCES

There are many great resources available for parents to help their children learn at home. Near the back of this book, check out our suggestions—by no means complete, but a good place to begin your search—for parenting, language arts, math, and science resources. While interviewing parents for this book series, we heard a variety of specific resources listed by name. Here is a sampler:

- *Living Books* software
- *BrainQuest*™ card series
- *Math Workshop* software
- Games like Skip-Bo™, Rummy Cubes™, dominoes (for building strategy and number concepts), checkers, Sorry™, Monopoly™, Scrabble™, and Tic Tac Toe
- Super Solver software series
- *National Geographic* specials and TV series
- *Body Adventure* CD-ROM
- The Discovery Channel
- *GeoMath, GeoSafari* software
- *Positive Discipline* by Jane Nelson (How to talk so kids will listen . . .)
- *Kid-Pix* software
- *Encarta* CD-ROM

actual age). Every child develops in her own way and at her own pace depending on environmental factors and her own genetic nature.

Looking at it Another Way. If children were squirrels, in grades two, three, and four, they'd be gathering and sorting nuts and enjoying the climb; they'd spend their next three years finding more trees of similar types and organizing nuts (while worrying, of course, about whether they were wearing the same thing as the other squirrels); and in grades six, seven, and eight, our squirrels would be planning storage facilities, worrying about how many nuts to set aside, and wondering how many could they eat right now because they're really hungry.

"Leave me alone!"

When it comes to emotional and social development, we also find varying rates of growth. You could speculate that this is nature's way of keeping parents on their toes. You get used to your child's behavior during a nice period of consolidation—life is going smoothly, your kid looks and acts the same from day to day (ignoring sudden external changes in fashion and hairstyle). Then, just when you were feeling relaxed, comfortable, and like maybe you were doing a good job as a parent, suddenly you're faced with a whole different person. It may be that the teddy bear gets demoted to a spot in the closet, or a certain food is only for babies, or you'll hear, "I'd never wear that," about yesterday's favorite garment. Whatever it is and at whatever the age, you scramble to quickly learn the habits and customs of what almost seems like a whole new species.

7th and 8th Graders—A Snapshot

We've called this section a *snapshot*. It has to be a bit blurry, however, because the subject of the picture is always in motion! Development, whether physical, mental, or emotional, is a process. There is no moment at which everything comes to rest and you can describe the static moment and the particular child and say that this is exactly how it is.

No snapshot can accurately catch the qualities of each child, because every child is unique. Within any group of children, there is an enormous range of development. Since children at any one chronological age stretch across the entire range of what is normal and appropriate for each particular stage of growth, we have tried to provide a general picture knowing that you will flesh out the portrait through observation of your child's own individual details.

At School. As you might expect, the wide spread of physical, mental, and emotional development in this age group is reflected in their school work. Young adolescents are capable of more intellectually demanding work and have bursts of real achievement. Deep feelings and complicated thoughts can appear in their writing and artwork. Most of them have begun to use more mature forms of thinking (questioning is widespread) and have begun to work in areas of science and mathematics that involve more complicated conceptual thought. At the same time, some kids at this age withdraw into daydreams, become heavily involved with escapist reading, or have to be prodded along to get anything done.

Physical Development. Most girls are into puberty at this point and some have already gone through it. Some boys have begun puberty, but at the beginning of grade seven, most are just starting their growth spurt. It is not unusual for an 8th-grade class to have three fourteen-year-old boys at three completely different stages of development, one at the beginning of puberty, one smack in the middle, and one already on the other side. The same is true for girls, but this tends to occur two years earlier. Three girls, all chronologically twelve, can be at three different places in their physical development. Because of the transitional state of most of these young bodies, adolescents in these grades have often been described as having *twitchy* responses, showing erratic body control, and, more simply, as being just like big puppies.

SUCCEED IN SCHOOL

Parents of 7th and 8th graders should check out a learning resource that their child can grow into, Kaplan InterActive's *Succeed in School* CD-ROM program (Simon & Schuster Interactive, 1996). This program is based on the latest accelerated learning techniques to help kids improve their study habits, self-esteem and attitude, reading speed, note taking skills, and writing. Resources and self-tests help students pinpoint their learning strengths and weaknesses. For ordering information, call (800) KAP-ITEM.

DETERMINED MOTHER

We wouldn't have had children if we didn't want to try to do the best job we could to make sure that they're secure, in an environment that's conducive to learning, and where they can flourish—but not to the point where we won't let our children take their own falls.

Mastering skills is a continuum, without a real end point. Children are taught something in school, but they might still be mastering the skills as adults.

MAIN EVENTS

SCORE! emphasizes learning as an "event." For instance, "We learned the times tables today," and boom—we have a learning event! We hear many children say, "This is division, and I can't do division," and they categorize what they're not comfortable with. We help teach kids that they can "do division," and it's a revelation to them. It becomes this event for kids. "Oh wow, I just did division!" They feel like they just ran the 100-yard dash in under 10 seconds.

Learning moments between parents and children should become learning events. "We're going to practice 5 times 5," and make it an event at home. Then when your child masters 5 times 5, it's like it's up on a billboard for kids: "This is what I can do!" When your child can say, "I get this science assignment," that should become an event too. And so on and so on.

Social and Emotional Concerns. Watching children during these years is a lot like watching a river running into the ocean. The river flows one way, the tide pushes the other way, and a strong breeze is blowing across the whole bay. The results are choppy waves and strong currents going every which way. Seventh and eighth graders are children who are launched on their way to adulthood, not sure of what that means, eager to get there (wherever it is), and, although they won't always admit it, more than a little scared. Unpredictable mood swings, tears, frustration, and wanting to be independent while still needing to hang on to family (but often too embarrassed to say so) are all characteristic emotional responses at this age. Sometimes all of them happen at once.

By this age, some children have become interested in relationships based on sexual attraction, although they may not admit it; and some are not, although they may not admit that either. As with most aspects of this time of life, confusion reigns. Interests in other activities such as sports, reading, friendships, and games can be very intense, but sometimes short-lived.

A strong concern for physical appearances, the desire to look great and, at the same time, exactly like everyone else (only better), couldn't occur at a more frustrating time than this. When you put the differences between the sexes and between individuals within the sexes together, add a dash of shaky self esteem, and stew them in the pot of peer approval, you can understand why this is such a tumultuous period.

A Group Portrait and a Last Thought

Imagine a 3rd grader, a 5th grader, and an 8th grader playing a game of Monopoly. You see their obvious differences in size and physical maturity, and, by being observant, pick up on the less obvious differences in their interests and abilities. The 3rd grader is fascinated with all the houses and hotels, eager to get the right token, attentive to collecting and stacking the money and (although deeply interested in the rules and fairness) mightily concerned with winning. Meanwhile, the 5th grader loves to be the banker, is zealous about the rules and how they affect fair play, and makes quick moves without a lot of planning. And there's the 8th grader—knowing exactly the best property to own (and will argue with you about it), thinking in terms of strategy, and, although playing steadily and seriously for most of the game, occasionally exploding in tears or anger and remonstrating with the other players about being unloved and not respected.

It's almost as if they were playing three different games. In one way, they are. Although they are playing together, each child plays a game appropriate to that child's own developmental level. As they mature, they will pass through new stages and enter new versions of the game, just as we have done.

PRACTICE PRACTICING

Success for children can take any form: sports, academics, playing an instrument. Whatever the passion is, use it to create an academic goal. Ask your child if it's always fun at soccer practice. The answer is, no, of course not. Sometimes it's raining and your child would rather be inside eating macaroni and cheese. Or your child would rather be anywhere else than at practice because she is making so many horrible mistakes. But rather than thinking, "I don't want to be doing sprints any more," your child needs to be thinking, "Sprints will really help out my game!" Practice really does make perfect—in sports, studies, and life. So practice practicing academics at home, and bring some excitement to your child's mastery of a skill by celebrating the learning that takes place.

CHAPTER 2

How Do Children Learn?

Have you ever heard these comments before? "Kim is so good with her hands, but she just doesn't enjoy reading." "Jack remembers every little thing he reads, but he's not real well coordinated or good at sports."

CUSTOMIZE

Not every child understands from the same learning approach. There are several different approaches for each child. It's finding the way to teach the material to the child that's key for parents in helping their children learn. There are many ways to teach a concept, and parents will have to experiment with approaches and find one or more that work.

"Even when she was a baby, Julia could sing along with the radio, right on key." "Martin is a real people-person. He just knows how to get along with everyone, from the kids in his Scout troop to the cranky guy in the apartment upstairs."

For generation after generation, parents have been having those kinds of conversation about their kids. And although they weren't trained educators, these parents had made an important discovery: People learn in different ways!

Many Kinds of "Smarts"

It's not just kids. People in general have multiple intelligences—ways of perceiving, knowing, and understanding the world. Recently, experts have identified "seven kinds of smarts"—seven different types of intelligence. And, as people have always sensed, in most people, one or two or more of those intelligences are usually stronger than the others. That blend of traits makes each person unique. But the experts also point out that everyone can work on developing the other kinds of intelligences as well.

Your child's learning style—just like your own—makes it easier for him to learn and do certain kinds of things, from reading novels to doing gymnastics to playing the guitar. With your help, your child can also develop some of the other ways of learning that will be useful both in school and in real life.

MAKING PROGRESS

I see all types of parents. Some are really strict and totally into the academic progress their children are making. Some parents really push their kids hard. I personally like to see parents allowing children to work at their own pace, knowing that the progress will happen without pressure. The parents who really monitor their kids so closely tend to freak out their kids a lot; if they miss even one problem on a lesson, it becomes a very stressful event.

HE'S ALLOWED

It was a real success for me as a parent to realize that my challenging son is not going to necessarily "like" school, but he can still succeed in school. I believe in supporting his school and his education as much as possible, while at the same time letting my son find his own way.

Learning Styles in School

Most traditional school courses, such as math or science or language arts, do draw on specific types of intelligence—mainly verbal, visual, and logical. In the classroom, skills in reading, writing, analyzing, computing, thinking critically, and learning from books are emphasized. The kid who is naturally strong in those kinds of intelligence may have an advantage in the classroom.

Modern textbooks, however, usually try to give teachers suggestions for activities and approaches that will help children who have other styles of learning. And, as the experts note, children (with the help of their parents) can also work to strengthen the specific learning styles that are emphasized in school. That is what many of the activities described in this book are designed to help you accomplish with your child.

Seven Ways of Learning

How does *your* child learn? Look for the characteristics described here and apply them to what you've already noticed about your child. What are her strengths? Her weaknesses? What types of intelligence are stronger in your child? What types need encouragement?

Take note of some of the general approaches mentioned here to encourage the development of each kind of intelligence. Then look through the specific Learning Adventure activities described in Section III of *Making the Grade*. These will help you work with your child to strengthen the kinds of intelligences that are needed to be successful in school, while still keeping the unique blend of traits that make up your child's personality.

Verbal/Linguistic. If your child is strong in this kind of intelligence, he may have started to talk early and in complete sentences. Probably he learned to read early and easily, too, and has a wider vocabulary than many kids his age. He likes books, puns, word games, and puzzles and probably enjoys writing. He may have more trouble taking in spoken information, such as from a lecture, than he does, for instance, in reading printed directions. This is the kid "whose nose is always in a book," who may ignore the scenery during a car ride and read a book instead.

Verbal/linguistic intelligence is one of the ways of learning that is very important in many school courses. You can encourage your child's verbal/linguistic intelligence by making reading and its associations fun and pleasurable. Many kids who are good readers and writers learned by imitating their parents, so show that you enjoy reading.

Make reading material—books and magazines—easily available at home. Encourage trips to the library and take an interest in the books your child likes. (You may be surprised to find how enjoyable some so-called kids' books can be.) For younger children, storytelling, poetry, and reading aloud are especially important.

Logical/Mathematical. Logical/mathematical intelligence goes beyond being "good at math." Perhaps your child has a good dose of this kind of smarts. Strength in this type of intelligence includes thinking in clear, logical ways and liking to analyze problems and situations. These kids are good at finding patterns and sequences, and they may frequently point out logical flaws in other people's actions. They are curious about new ideas and developments in science and may enjoy "brainteasers" that demand logical solutions. They can reason their way to solutions and think abstractly.

Most kids who are strong in this type of intelligence like science and most kinds of math. You can encourage logical/mathematical intelligence by giving your child a chance to use these skills outside school. Learn about science by star watching or hiking in the woods. Build "what if" experiments, math computation, or logical problems into everyday situations. For instance, ask your child to figure out (with mental math) the comparative

POWER AND COMFORT

Parents can tell their children that they're soon going to be a "published author!" Kids love to write stories, type them up, add a byline and artwork—and parents can collect writings that they've done over the year and make it a fun home project to bind them together. And there are so many writing games that parents can use at home. There are travel games related to poetry, reports, and stories, and many other games kids can play with to help build a more powerful vocabulary and comfort with the language.

PRAISE FOR PARENTS

I love working at *SCORE!*. The program is great, but every child who succeeds here does so because of their parents. The parents make a commitment to their child's education. Without that commitment, nothing will succeed.

Allow your children to keep learning throughout the summer so they can jump right in at the beginning of the school year.

CONCERNS

Support your teacher's plan for your child's learning, but if you see a problem, discuss your concerns with the teacher—but not in front of your child, at least to begin with. A parent and teacher may view a child differently. Be patient, but up front with your concerns and questions.

DO SOMETHING

We do not allow a lot of sitting-around time at home. We stress "do something." As a family, we go to the beach, we go on hikes, we go for walks, we go to bookstores, we go to the library, we go to the pool and do swimming together. We spend a lot of family time together, especially on the weekends. That's the way we foster a learning atmosphere for our child.

price per ounce of two different brands of breakfast cereal in the supermarket. Or when you are buying gas, ask, "Can you figure out how many miles per gallon we got with that last tank of gas?"

Visual/Spatial. This intelligence includes both artistic vision—sensitivity to color and imagery—and a sense of space and spatial relationships. These kids often likes to draw and doodle and they have a good visual imagination. If your child is strong in this kind of intelligence, she may enjoy jigsaw puzzles. She's likely to be good with maps and location and can probably find her way around unfamiliar places. In math, she'll probably think geometry is fun, but may have more trouble with algebra, which is more symbolic and abstract.

Encourage visual/spatial intelligence by supplying your child with tools and materials: a camera or camcorder, drawing and painting equipment, and well-illustrated books. A younger child will enjoy manipulatives and design blocks. Give your child a taste of good art and design, not just by visiting art museums and galleries but also by looking at buildings and surroundings, and sharing an interest in good architecture, furnishings, cars, gardens, and houses.

Body/Kinesthetic. People as varied as athletes, inventors, and dancers have this type of "hands-on" intelligence. They are aware and confident of their own movements and physical self and are generally well coordinated. This characteristic also makes them restless—this is the kid who "can't sit still for a minute."

Since action and activity are so important to this kind of child, parents need to make sure these kids have a chance to do what they are good at. A child like this is likely to want to spend time actively outdoors or to work at handicrafts and activities such as pottery or woodworking. He may be interested in sports, hiking, dance, or gymnastics. Remember that this is a child who learns best by doing—by practicing an activity rather than just watching or reading about it. Children who are not strong in this kind of intelligence can be encouraged to develop their physical skills and abilities.

Musical/Rhythmic. Your child's musical/rhythmic intelligence can show itself in different ways and to different degrees. Even very young children show a good sense of rhythm and an ability to sing along or imitate a song they have just heard. They may hum to themselves, tap out rhythms, or make up their own songs and tunes.

In many schools today, music and art programs have been eliminated or cut back because of budget cuts. You can make up for this problem to some extent at home. No matter what her musical ability or formal training, you can help your child enjoy and appreciate different kinds of music through tapes, CDs, radio and TV, and live concerts or performances.

If your school system offers instruction on musical instruments, you'll be doing your child a favor by enrolling her. Music as recreation can bring immense pleasure to people throughout their lives, even if they do not have the skill or inclination to perform professionally. Real involvement in music has even been shown to enhance acquisition of traditionally academic skills such as mathematics, literature, and writing.

Interpersonal. Interpersonal intelligence includes "people skills," the ability to get along, communicate, and work together. While hard to quantify, these skills are usually quite obvious. Your child may be the one who almost always gets along with others, whether in school or at play. He likes to be involved in social activities or group sports and is often a leader or the center of a group of friends.

If your child is strong in this type of intelligence, you will not have to work at encouraging him to be active and sociable. In fact, you may have to work to keep him from becoming overscheduled. He may need to develop the ability to enjoy his own company and solitude. For a shyer, less outgoing child, one who has less of this kind of intelligence, it is important to encourage and support social activities while not pushing too hard.

CREATIVE WAKE-UP

When my son was younger, part of my morning routine with him was to get up, put on some fun music, and color and paint with him. He still loves to do it.

REACHING GOALS

My husband and I love *SCORE!* from the standpoint that they give kids goals. It's not just this fun place where kids go and play on the computer. They learn, but it gives them an educational, fun format where they can reach and attain goals and be commended. Kids love that! Kids love to be patted on the back. They like being told, "That was great! Good job. Look how hard you worked." They might not be getting this praise somewhere else, and if they're not, what a great experience for them to get it here. Our daughters love it, and they tell us, "I'm almost to my goal!" "I got a *SCORE!* card!" "I've got 25 *SCORE!* cards and I'm going to get a gold one." This has been a healthy, good, fun experience for our girls.

TOOLS TO SUCCEED

Give your children the tools to succeed. My mother bought me a blank journal. It said "My Book" on the outside of it, and every day I wrote a poem in it. This was like a little assignment that my mother and I did together each day. A year later, I had a full book of poems that I can't imagine having done on my own without my mother's encouragement. But she gave me the tools to express myself to do it.

Intrapersonal. While interpersonal intelligence looks outward, intrapersonal intelligence looks inward. Children strong in this kind of intelligence are likely to be thoughtful, and they are generally more aware of their feelings and emotions than children for whom this is not a strong intelligence. Not necessarily a loner, this child is probably self-reliant and independent and enjoys solitude and her own company. She is likely to have a firm idea about what she believes and what her goals are. She is self-directed and will explore ideas on her own.

Keeping a journal is one way for your child to develop intrapersonal intelligence and self-awareness. A child who is already strong in this type of intelligence may need encouragement to reach out to new friends and join in group activities.

Playing to Your Strengths

Your child is a unique blend of different intelligences—and so are you. Your own interests and ways of learning will inevitably have an influence on the kinds of activities that you can and want to do with your kid. Not surprisingly, it will probably be easiest to encourage the kinds of activities and approaches that you yourself are most comfortable with.

After you've analyzed your child's different kinds of smarts, take a look at your own. You may want to make a checklist for both of you.

• What are the areas in which each of you are strong?
• Do your strongest learning styles differ much?
• Do you share weaker learning styles?
• Or do your areas of weakness and strength complement one another?
• Which are the kinds of smarts that are the easiest for you to work on with your child?
• Which kinds are the hardest?

"We're so different!" After thinking about the seven kinds of smarts, you may come up with this conclusion. One of the challenges parents face in helping their kids do better in school occurs when there are differences in their learning styles. Just because you and your child belong to the same family, you aren't necessarily alike in interests or learning styles. If you have more than one child, chances are that they're not exactly alike, either.

Before you can cope with these differences, you have to recognize them. Think of things you've noticed in everyday life—you love sports, your child thinks they're boring. Your kid is a whiz at math; you can't balance your checkbook without a calculator. You work on a dozen different handcraft projects; your child would rather read.

Paradoxically, it can be hardest to help your child develop the kinds of smarts that you already have. For instance, if you're very verbal and a great reader, it's easy to become impatient and critical with a child who isn't. You may find it hard (even frustrating) to understand just why this stuff is hard for her.

On the other hand, you have an advantage because you like and appreciate books and reading or the constant discoveries of science. Here you have an opportunity to pass on some of that appreciation to your child. It just may take a little more patience. And remember, she may never be the book lover or science whiz that you are. But you can be a terrific role model.

"That's not what the book says." Another pitfall of being skilled or knowledgeable in a certain area or way of learning is that you may try to explain things to your middle-school child in college-level terms. If you're an engineer or accountant, for instance, your math skills and knowledge are much greater than what your child needs to know—for now, at least. A too-rich explanation could make things harder for him.

PROBLEM SOLVER

There are at least ten different strategies for your child to use to solve math, word, and other homework problems (from *The Problem Solver* by Shirley Hoogeboom and Judy Goodnow). Every parent should know them and teach them to their children—they're not necessarily going to be covered in school!

1. Act out or use objects.
2. Make a picture or a diagram.
3. Use or make a table.
4. Make an organized list.
5. Guess and check.
6. Use or look for a pattern.
7. Work backwards.
8. Use logical reasoning.
9. Make it simpler.
10. Brainstorm.

Bring your family together to work on a "family mission statement." Every parent and child has goals. Write them all down, then work together to make them all happen.

CONCENTRATION

Relaxation induced by specific music leaves the mind alert and able to concentrate. The music found most conducive to this state is baroque music, like that of Bach, Handel, Pachelbel, and Vivaldi . . . . Most baroque music is timed at 60 beats per minute, which is the same as an average resting heart rate.

—from *Quantum Learning* by Bobbi DePorter (Dell, 1992)

When trying to help, check out what kinds of solutions or answers the textbook or homework assignment is actually asking for. Give your child just the help that's needed. Think back to when you were first learning these facts and processes. Then use the Learning Adventure activities in Section III to work on the skills he needs to know this year.

Learning Together. On the other hand, through family ties and influence, you and your child probably have some similar learning styles, along with similar areas in which you're both less comfortable. You may both be good musicians and athletes, not so good at verbal or visual skills. As a result, you may both have to work in areas of less strength, rather than avoiding them.

Maybe mathematical/logical intelligence isn't your strongest area—or your child's, either. But as you help your child to make the grade, you may find yourself developing new kinds of smarts yourself. As you work through activities in math and science together, for instance, you'll find that both of you are building new skills and strengths.

CHAPTER 3

How Are Children Evaluated?

From the moment of birth, we start measuring and sizing up our kids. At first we have only their physical characteristics (birth weight and length are just the beginning) to work with, but right away we begin to compare them to some norm. How is my child doing compared to others? We keep asking ourselves this question. As kids begin to walk and talk and learn—the hundreds of little skills they do before entering school—the comparisons fly. All through the toddler and preschool years, we watch, we read, we talk, and we wonder, Is my kid doing okay? Before we know it, our baby is off to school and this evaluating stuff goes big time. When schools judge how well your child is doing, the process is called *assessment*.

Assessment Is . . .

Few topics on the school reform agenda have generated as much discussion and scrutiny as assessment has—after all, how well your child is doing has been at the core of the school experience since the beginning of time, hasn't it?

Simply put, assessment is the systematic and purposeful method of looking at where students are and where they should be going in their classroom and in their school system. The measurements are made about all development aspects of your child—emotional, social, cognitive, physical, and intellectual. The results can be used for several purposes:

MAKING PROGRESS

When kids are behind in a subject, they're not fully aware of how far behind they are. They may have started out being a year behind and maybe they work up to only three months behind, but in their mind, they're still behind. They don't realize they've made much progress. Parents can help out so much just by encouraging students and pointing out how far their child's hard work is carrying them.

For education to be a priority for a child, it must also be one for the parent.

HAVE FAITH

I have a video of Mary Lou Retton, the Olympic gymnast, working out before the 1984 games. She was doing a switch from the parallel bars, and she was doing a very tough move. She missed it twenty times in a row. She got back up and kept trying. That's physically and mentally exhausting to do, but she kept getting up and trying again. She got it on the twenty-first try, and went on to big achievements in her sport. Parents need to help children be patient and persevere. And parents need to have faith, to give their children the space to fail and encourage them to keep trying and learning until they finally understand.

CLICK FASTER

Conceptualization starts with the imagination! Expose children to as many artistic and colorful activities as often as possible. Weave the imagination into any educational activity and it will click faster for your child.

- To tell you and your child how she is doing
- To give teachers information to plan what and how to teach your child
- To provide school districts with the data they need to see how well they are doing their teaching job

Changes Underway

Along with the many current efforts to make schools more relevant to kids, educators are making some big changes in how they assess kids. They are:

- Moving away from something that teachers do to students towards more of a partnership between teachers, students, and their parents
- Moving away from a single letter grade on a quarterly report card towards a more continual process involving a series of tests, observations, and work samples
- Moving away from single events treated separately from the learning process ("Stop what you are learning and take this test . . . .") to an activity that is interwoven into the lesson plans

As a parent, you need an understanding of these kinds of assessment. Here's a closer look at some of the old and the new ways schools are evaluating children's educational growth.

Traditional Assessment

Remember the joys of this kind of testing! You'll recall that it:

- Is mostly paper-and-pencil based
- Is given formally—every child has to do the same thing at the same time
- Usually involves a multiple-choice format that emphasizes memorizing facts
- Is almost always subject specific (ah, those weekly spelling tests, reading pop quizzes, and history unit tests)
- Involves comparison of a child's progress to that of other students

- Is based on what a child is able to remember at the time of the test
- Often is required by the district or state (as in the case of a standardized test like the California Achievement Test, or CAT)

You'll learn more about the traditional assessment tool of **standardized tests** in the next chapter, in which the test prep experts at Kaplan discuss the different types of standardized tests and how you can help your child prepare for them. You can even see which tests your child will be taking at different grade levels, from Kaplan's new state-by-state listings of standardized test requirements.

Alternative Assessment

A wide variety of other ways of evaluating students' progress is now available. Alternative (as opposed to traditional) assessment is more of a process than a single event. It puts the emphasis on your child's progress over time rather than on individual test scores. Alternative assessment:

- Is an ongoing picture of the work a child does in a variety of contexts
- Is focused on a child's work compared to his own previous work
- Is meant to show how kids apply what they know, not just facts they memorize
- Is able to show progress not just in single subjects but also in interdisciplinary projects (where subject matters, like reading in social studies, are combined)
- Is often conducted informally through observation or conversation
- Is commonly referred to as *portfolio assessment*, since the notes and work samples are usually kept in a manila folder

MEASURING KIDS

Remember that all tests have their limitations. They are not perfect measures of what your child can or cannot do. They are at best one entry in the overall picture of your son or daughter.

Some tests may not measure just what we think they do. For example, in an assignment to copy spelling words from the blackboard, we may learn this about students:

- How well they can print
- How well they can copy
- How long they can sit still
- How quickly they can work
- How willing they are to do work that may seem meaningless to them

---

"Not everything that counts can be counted and not everything that can be counted counts." —*Albert Einstein*

Here's a look at some of the specific types of portfolio assessment. Notice how these methods typically include much more information than what a child writes on paper.

Performance Tasks. These are assignments (whether student-initiated or teacher-planned) that are designed to measure your child's skill in a certain area; for example, being able to write a persuasive essay or to follow written directions to build a specific kind of birdhouse. Looking at the entire process rather than just the end result takes into account each child's individual learning style.

Observation. By paying attention to how students approach a problem, interact with other students, or use their free time, teachers and parents can build the complete picture of your child's success in learning. Teachers may take notes in checklist form or in more of a narrative, anecdotal fashion.

Self-Evaluation. When children are encouraged to make thoughtful evaluations of their own work, they begin to accept responsibility for their own learning—a key element in their educational growth.

What's a Parent to Do!

The ways you can help your child succeed in school are changing, too. It used to be that test scores and grades were sent home without much explanation. But now it's increasingly possible for parents to talk with teachers about what certain grades and scores mean. In these discussions, you can also contribute to your child's success in schoolwork by helping the teacher get the big picture of the your child. These are opportunities for you to offer unique information about your child's likes, dislikes, and way of doing things that are important for the teacher to know.

Supporting Your Child in the Assessment Process. Do you remember how your folks reacted to your report cards? Your attitudes about test taking and report cards send a message to your kids that can help or hinder their school progress. You can help your child by:

- Not being overly anxious about scores or grades
- Not judging your child on the basis of a single score
- Using mistakes as a focus of discussion rather than reasons to punish
- Using all modes of reports as opportunities for discussion (along with praise and encouragement)

Staying in touch with teachers about your child builds partnerships for the benefit of your child. These partnerships are important to help your child get the best education possible.

How You Can Use Assessment

Assessment is not for schools and teachers alone—you and your child should get involved too! *Making the Grade* includes a special pull-out section, "The Home Learning Quizzes," because the whole point of assessment is to use it as a learning tool. Our parents' quiz provides strategies for you to use to learn about how your child is doing—what he knows and can do, what is difficult for him, what helps him progress, and so forth. It also provides a way for you to discover what you know about home learning and how aware you are of your child's progress, growth, and habits. Use the kids' quizzes to help you choose appropriate home learning resources and Section III activities to fill in your child's knowledge gaps. But, above all, use the home learning quizzes to have fun with your child and develop a "big picture" of your child's progress. Self-assessment is important to everyone's learning, and so the pull-out section encourages you and your child to see what you already know and explore some new ground.

WITHIN REACH

Many parents say negative things around their children. It destroys the confidence and motivation of children with each utterance of "He can't do this," or "She can't read that." Parents should rethink their delivery to express a concern about the level of their children's academic work. Try saying "This concept is very challenging right now." That way, kids recognize that the tough lessons are at the moment not achievable, yet they're not permanently out of their reach.

MONEY MATTERS?

America's schools spend more per pupil than virtually any of the countries that routinely trounce us in international scholastic comparisons.
—*Beyond the Classroom,* Laurence Steinberg, Ph.D. (Simon & Schuster, 1996)

CHAPTER 4

How Can I Help My Child Prepare for Standardized Tests?

Standardized tests . . . the term conjures up images of impersonal classrooms, hard bucket seats, and the fast-moving hands of a looming black clock. What could be more fun? Well, all we can say is that

ASK THE TEACHER

- Are the test results consistent with my child's performance in the classroom?
- What do the test results mean about my child's skills and abilities?
- Are any changes anticipated in my child's educational program?
- What can I do at home to strengthen my child's skills?
  —"What Should Parents Know About Standardized Testing in Schools," by Carolyn B. Bagin and Lawrence M. Rudner. Published by ERIC. Accessed online at www.accesseric.org/resources/ parent/testing.html.

it's got to be better than this, because as a school-aged student of the new millennium, your child will be taking quite a number of these tests.

Fortunately, contemporary educators, teachers and test makers alike, are a dedicated and sensitive lot. They've chosen their profession because they like children and want to help them thrive. Most are quite creative in their teaching methods.

As dedicated as these educators are, your child will benefit enormously from your thoughtful participation in the test-taking process. You can help your child prepare for standardized tests in a variety of ways, from attending to the basics (getting enough sleep and eating well before the test), to helping him become a "testwise" test taker. But first, just what is a standardized test?

What is a Standardized Test?

Standardized tests provide a common measure of student performance. A standardized test contains the same set of questions and is given under the same conditions to

CHILDREN WITH SPECIAL NEEDS

Children with special needs can arrange to take standardized tests under conditions conducive to them. They might take the test as if it were a regular in-class test, alone, or perhaps at home. Time and other requirements may be altered depending on the child's individual needs.

None of this will be possible, however, if your child has not been officially diagnosed by the school's Individualized Education Program (IEP) as having a learning disability. In other words, you may not simply decide that your child is learning disabled and request special testing conditions. Your child must first receive a battery of tests by the IEP, which then decides, along with your child's teachers (including any special education professionals assigned to him or her), upon an official evaluation.

different groups of people. The answers are scored in the same manner. Standardized tests are designed by commercial publishers or state committees, or by a combination of the two. These tests use as their foundation the curriculum your child is studying.

What Kind of Standardized Tests Will My Child Take?
The standardized tests your child will take are usually of two general types. One is called the *norm-referenced test.* Norm-referenced tests measure your child's skills and knowledge against a representative sample, or "norm," of other children. That sample may be drawn anywhere, from the third graders in local Hebrew day schools to the national population of third graders. Tests in this category include the TerraNova, the Stanford Achievement Test, and the Iowa Test of Basic Skills.

The other test type is called a *criterion-referenced test.* Criterion-referenced tests also measure your child's skills and knowledge, but rather than gauge little Leopold's skills against other children, criterion-referenced tests assess his grade-level mastery. Most criterion-referenced tests are developed by state-appointed committees, who define the number and types of questions that should be answered correctly to demonstrate this mastery.

While norm-referenced tests remain the most commonly administered of standardized tests, criterion-referenced tests are gaining ground in many states, as politicians and educators at the state level want to know how strong or weak the teaching (and learning) is at their schools. Most states have adopted initiatives set forth in the *Goals 2000: Educate America Act.* This federal legislation, passed in 1994, calls for content and performance standards in the core disciplines. Criterion-referenced tests are meant to chart this progress within the various individual districts. Norm-referenced tests usually align themselves with national standards.

As you can see in the state-by-state listings starting on page 44, some states, such as Connecticut, mandate only that students take the state's own criterion-referenced test, such as the

Connecticut Mastery Test. (Individual school districts, however, may administer other tests as they see fit.) Other states, such as Idaho, rely on the nationally administered, norm-referenced Iowa Test of Basic Skills (ITBS). A quick glance at the chart reveals that many states are moving towards a combination of state-developed criterion-referenced tests and nationally administered norm-referenced tests.

What's New and Different About Standardized Tests?
The standardized tests you may remember from your own school days—norm-referenced tests that were largely, if not exclusively, multiple-choice—are changing their stripes. While today's tests continue to contain ample numbers of multiple choice items, they also rely on several types of open-ended questions (see sidebar), writing exercises, and other higher-order thinking activities. The belief is that these testing formats offer a more accurate assessment of students' knowledge and skills.

Today's standardized tests are actually more difficult than those of previous years. Rather than focusing on the memorization of rules and procedures, the newer generation of tests require your child to use her critical thinking skills and to write more. In the math portion of some tests, she'll be asked to explain how she arrived at her answers. In the language arts portions, she'll find a type of open-ended item called a constructed response question, which might ask her to explain an author's statement, or perhaps diagram an article's main event and supporting details.

Many tests now include extensive sections on written communication, including prewriting, composing, and editing exercises. These *performance assessments*, increasingly favored by educators, require students to demonstrate their knowledge and skills, including the process by which they solve problems. For example, your child may be asked to spend 45 minutes writing a story based on a short "prompt" or scenario. Or he will use prewriting skills, such as identifying general references and using dictionary skills.

OPEN-ENDED QUESTIONS

In the testing world, open-ended questions include constructed response, short answer, and extended response questions. *Constructed response* questions ask students to respond with a sentence, phrase, or bulleted list to a variety of material—from identifying the main idea in a passage to responding to questions about spelling and grammar. *Short answer* questions ask students to respond with a written paragraph, while *extended response* questions may take your child up to 45 minutes to complete in essay form.

IMMEDIATE ACADEMIC ASSISTANCE

If your child does poorly on one or more sections of a standardized test, don't panic. A focused effort will be made to solve the problem relatively quickly. First, we'll work with you to identify the roots of your child's difficulties, which can often be attributed to two things: skill gaps and lack of confidence.

Once we assess the extent of the skill gaps, we'll be able to tailor your child's curriculum to her specific needs. Personalized instruction in reading, language arts, and math will restore your child's self-confidence as she learns at her own pace, excited about succeeding time and again in a previously weak subject area.

You can help your child prepare for these performance-based activities by asking the teacher to explain what types of items appear on the test. Once you know this, you can engage your child in activities that encourage problem solving and creativity.

How Do Schools Use Standardized Tests?

Schools (and related institutions and agencies) use standardized tests for a variety of purposes. Beyond measuring how well or poorly students perform, schools—or, more precisely, the agencies that govern them—use these tests to measure how well the school itself is performing. State assessment agencies use standardized tests to compare scores among towns, districts, and individual schools. Increasingly, as you've probably heard, poorly performing schools are feeling the heat to raise scores; administrators usually do this by changing their curriculum.

As a parent, you should be concerned not only with your child's scores, but also with her school's. How does the school rank in comparison with others in your district? In neighboring towns? With other states? Has the school's test scores improved or declined in recent years? How much of your child's curriculum is driven by standardized tests? Too much? Not enough? If you have concerns about these or other issues, talk to your school administrators. For detailed information, you may also want to contact your state's office of assessment.

Most important of all is how the school will use your child's individual scores. Increasingly, schools are using standardized tests as diagnostic tools to pinpoint students' strengths and weaknesses. Students needing extra help may receive tutoring both during the regular school day and after hours. Generally, this is a good thing, although there are instances when a child may feel burdened and/or stigmatized by participating in special after-school or even summer programs. Help of the same sort is available through private centers like *SCORE!* Educational Centers, an educational subsidiary of Kaplan.

Precisely because your teacher may use your child's test score diagnostically, it is vital that you be informed about the school's test score policies. Are their any specific consequences for your child's score? Make sure you discuss your child's strengths and weaknesses so that you can work with her not only in preparation for a specific test but throughout the school year.

How Long Do These Tests Take?

Perhaps the last test you took was the Scholastic Aptitude Test (SAT). All you can recall is sitting in a sea of strangers, wrestling with an endless stream of mind-numbing multiple choice items. Not exactly what you'd wish for your child, especially one who has barely graduated from the playground. You may have heard that your child will be tested for five days running. Not to worry—the test may run for up to a week (or longer), but the longest block is usually no more than about 50 minutes. While it's no picnic, most children are certainly able to cope with these blocks of time, especially if they're prepared. So be sure to find out how long each test segment will be and then discuss this with your child.

Classroom Preparation

Schools vary considerably in how they prepare students for standardized tests. The majority spend at least some time on them, alerting students to upcoming tests, discussing test formats, timing, and so forth. Some schools teach test readiness skills while others don't. Critics charge that certain school districts, especially those serving poorer children, come perilously close to "teaching to the test"—devoting virtually all class time to test-related drills.

Research confirms that test-taking skills improve performance, and that a lack of such skills prevents students from achieving valid test results. Certain students become easily confused under pressure and fail to understand directions during the test. The younger the child, the more likely this is to occur. But all children (and adults) who lack test-taking savvy are at a disadvantage. To ensure that your

WHAT IS CRITICAL THINKING?

Critical thinking is the ability to evaluate ideas on the basis of sound reasoning. Critical thinkers:

- Evaluate evidence
- Analyze assumptions and biases
- Identify faulty logic and contradictions in arguments
- Consider multiple perspectives
- Summarize and judge facts for themselves

You can spur your child's critical thinking by asking him questions such as these:

- Why do you think that?
- Explain your reasoning.
- Can you support your statement? How did the author support hers?
- What else could the author (problem, idea) mean?

child is adequately prepared to take tests—that he or she is "testwise"—be certain to ask the teacher the following:

- How will my child be prepared for the test? Does the school administer practice tests?
- Are the different question formats described and explained?
- Are specific directions, such as "all of the above," "as is," and so forth, explained?
- Does the teacher review time requirements and describe how students can pace themselves? (TIP: Some students spend too much time on the first part of the test or on the most difficult questions, leaving too little time for other items.)
- If there are separate answer sheets ("bubble sheets"), do the students receive practice filling these in?
- What can I do to help?

Sample Test Items

Look over the following test questions to get an idea of what your child may be asked to do on a standardized test. Notice how your child's skills will usually be assessed in context, stressing the functional use of language, mathematics, science, and social science.

These test items are similar to some of those found in the Stanford Achievement Test (Stanford 9), a norm-referenced test used in several states. Check out Kaplan's state-by-state listing of standardized test requirements at the end of this chapter to see which tests your child will be taking and which subjects she'll be tested in.

Reading Vocabulary Question

Be careful not to <u>fall</u> out of that treehouse!

In which sentence does the word <u>fall</u> mean the same thing as in the sentence above?

(a) Stock prices could <u>fall</u> drastically tomorrow.
(b) School doesn't start again until the <u>fall</u>.
(c) Christmas will <u>fall</u> on a Wednesday this year.
(d) I often <u>fall</u> off the balance beam in my gymnastics class.

YOUR LEGAL RIGHTS TO TEST TAKING

Several precedents and laws define legal rights related to taking tests in school:

- Under the Family Education Rights and Privacy Act of 1974, also known as the Buckley Amendment, you have a right to examine your child's academic records. If these records contain test scores, you have a right to see those scores.
- Your child has a right to due process. For example, your child must get adequate time to prepare for a test.
- Your child has a right to fair and equitable treatment. Schools cannot, for example, have different test score requirements based on gender or race.
- Schools are not, however, necessarily liable for tests and test results being misused. The best way you can protect your child from misuse of testing is to be knowledgeable about the appropriate uses of various types of tests.
  —"What Should Parents Know About Standardized Testing in Schools," by Carolyn B. Bagin and Lawrence M. Rudner. Published by ERIC. Accessed online at www.accesseric.org/resources/ parent/testing.html.

How Can I Help My Child Prepare for Standardized Tests?

Spelling Question

Read the sentences below. Decide if one of the underlined words is spelled wrong or if there is no mistake.

(a) He wants lots of <u>tomato</u> sauce on his pasta.
(b) I really didn't mean to take <u>advantage</u> of you.
(c) She received several <u>complements</u> on her new dress.
(d) No mistake

Language Question

Read the sentence below. If the underlined words contain a mistake in punctuation, capitalization, or word usage, choose the answer that is the best way to write the underlined section of the sentence. If there is no mistake, choose *Correct as is.*

<u>Whose the best soccer player</u> on the team?

(a) Who's the best soccer player
(b) Whos' the best soccer player
(c) Whose the most best soccer player
(d) Correct as is

Study Skills Question

If you need to find information on insects for a 12-page science report, where should you look?

(a) a dictionary
(b) a thesaurus
(c) an atlas
(d) an encyclopedia

Mathematics: Problem Solving Question

Lauren measured the length of her driveway and determined it was 480 inches. How many feet is 480 inches?

(a) 4 ft
(b) 10 ft
(c) 40 ft
(c) 48 ft

NUTRITION AND STRESS: THE DO'S AND DON'TS

Do eat:
- Fruits and vegetables
- Protein such as fish, poultry, beans, and legumes (like lentils)
- Whole grains such as whole wheat bread, pastas, and brown rice

Don't eat:
- Refined sugar and high-fat snacks (simple carbohydrates like sugar make stress worse and fatty foods lower your immunity)
- Salty foods (they can deplete potassium, which your child needs for nerve functions)

Mathematics: Procedures Question

Carlos spent a total of 50 hours raking leaves for all of his neighbors. He spent 20% of that time working with his twin brother. How many hours did Carlos spend working with his brother?

(a) 1.5 hours
(b) 10 hours
(c) 20 hours
(d) 30 hours

Science Question

Which of these is *not* a product of a living thing?

(a) milk
(b) butter
(c) sugar
(d) salt

Social Science Question

Which of these is *not* an ethnic group?

(a) Koreans
(b) Italians
(c) Germans
(d) Catholics

Managing Test Anxiety

Test anxiety is extremely common, for children and adults alike. In fact, feeling nervous before a test is perfectly normal. Your goal for your child should not be to rid him of nervousness entirely but to help him channel it constructively. Channeled properly, nervousness boosts performance.

In their concern about testing, some parents convey their own anxiety to their child. Try not to do this! As one industry expert puts it, "The more positive the approach to the test, the more accurate the data is." So if everyone involved—parents, teachers, and other administrators— conveys a positive attitude, your child stands a better chance of producing a score that truly reflects his knowledge and skills. Don't put so much emphasis on scoring well that he feels unduly pressured. Take a positive approach, one that emphasizes the fun and value of learning for learning's sake. Work with your child throughout the year, a little at a time. You can accelerate your efforts somewhat in the weeks before a test, but consistency throughout the school year will serve him better.

Like the rest of us, children fear most what they don't know and can't control. Children need to be prepared psychologically for standardized testing. The more you can prepare them for what will take place, the less anxious they will feel and the more they will be able to channel their nervousness constructively. Make sure they know what will take place. Ask the teacher to clarify each of the following questions, and then go over them with your child. Knowing the answers will cut down on confusion during the actual testing situation, allowing her to focus on the test itself:

- What kind of test is it?
- Where and when will the test be given?
- How is the test timed?
- Are questions permitted during testing?
- Can students go back and work on previous sections of the test if they finish a section early?
- Should students guess on questions they do not know?
- What should students do when they finish but others are still working?[1]

Generally speaking, it doesn't help to tell children who are anxious to "just relax" or "think about something else." If, however, you can help them to focus on the specific test-taking strategies outlined in this chapter, chances are that rather than feeling overwhelmed by such global thoughts as "I'm gonna fail," they will feel in control and empowered. As teaching experts Nell Ducke and Ron Richart put it, for maximum performance, your child's test-taking demeanor should be "serious, confident, and strategic."

KEEPING IT STRAIGHT

Some children have difficulty keeping their place on the test page or answer sheet. The results can be incorrectly marked answers. Teach your child to fold the test booklets and answer sheets so that only one page of each is showing. And remind him to check the page number of the test booklet every time he turns the page. This way, if two pages get stuck together when turning, the results won't be disastrous.

—*Teaching Test-Taking Skills: Helping Students Show What They Know,* by Thomas E. Scruggs and Margo A. Mastropieri. (Brookline Books, 1995)

---

[1]Phillips, Art, *Test Taking Skills for Primary Grades.* A SORD project. March 1983. Southern Oregon Research and Devlepment Committee (SORD).

DIVIDE AND CONQUER

At the beginning of a test, students should quickly compute how much time they have for each question. So if there are 60 items and one hour is allocated, test takers should answer, on average, no less than one question per minute. Of course, given that the questions will vary in difficulty, some questions will take less time and others more. And ideally, it's good to have time left over at the end of a test so that you can check your answers and return to those items that gave you the most difficulty. But using this method will help your child keep on track. To make it easier, she can divide the total time period into four equal periods. Thus after 15 minutes she can take note of how many items she has answered. If she's only checked off four, she'll know to adjust her speed accordingly.

—*Teaching Test-Taking Skills: Helping Students Show What They Know,* by Thomas E Scruggs and Margo A. Mastropieri (Brookline Books, 1995)

Test Taking Strategies

Standardized tests measure your child's knowledge in reading/language arts (reading comprehension, spelling and word usage, and written expression) math, and, sometimes, in the content areas taught in school, such as science and social studies. Understanding the curriculum and helping your child grasp important material is the single most important way you can help her score well on standardized tests.

Having said this, it is also true that a lack of test-taking skills can harm even the highest-achieving students. Here are some general strategies every test taker should know. Review these carefully with your child. They should become part of her background knowledge, as easily retrievable as the characters from her favorite novel.

Rule Number One: Answer the Questions You Know First.
The best test takers skip (temporarily) difficult material in search of the easier items. As they do, they mark the ones that require extra time and thought. This strategy buys time and builds confidence so they can handle the tough stuff later.

Your child should know that the test will include items that will be difficult even for the best students. He should also know that most tests do not get progressively harder. Many, though not all tests, are designed according to the "easy-hard-easy" model. So mulling over questions that are difficult at the expense of answering those you know is a poor strategy. Instead, the test-wise student builds his sense of mastery by tackling what he knows first.

This strategy will only work if your child correctly identifies those items to which he must return. Be sure to remind him to put a big circle around the number of any question he skips. When he goes back, these questions will be easy to locate.

Rule Number Two: Answer All of the Questions.
Nearly all of the tests your child is likely to take are designed to allow ample time to answer all questions. Since children

with the greatest number of right answers score highest, each question counts. So as a rule, it's a good idea to answer all of the questions.

There is the occasional "speeded test," designed to assess students on the basis of how many questions they can answer in the time allotted. In this case, of course, they should answer as many questions as possible, but not expect to answer them all.

Since most tests contain items designed to stymie all but the very best students, answering all the questions relies on two key test-taking strategies: *elimination* and *guessing*.

Rule Number Three: When in Doubt, Eliminate.

Oftentimes, children will have some knowledge of the information being tested. Savvy test takers use this information to eliminate less likely choices. Elimination helps narrow the possibilities, thereby increasing the odds that the test taker won't skip the question altogether or rely on random guessing.

If unsure of an answer, counsel your child to choose the one she thinks is best. Eliminate the most obvious poor choice(s) first, followed by those that are less obvious. She should then select among the remaining items, asking herself which one seems most reasonable.

Rule Number Four: Make Educated Guesses.

Closely allied to the elimination strategy is making educated guesses. This strategy recognizes that all test takers have their strengths and weaknesses, and that most tests include a certain percentage of items that most students will not be able to answer.

The test taker who makes educated guesses plows through with a "can do" attitude. Rather than reacting with an "I just don't know" and giving up, these students take things one step further, searching for what they might possibly know after all. This is especially effective with multiple choice items, since the answer does lie in front of them, and they have a one-in-four chance of getting it right even if they guess at random. But rather than rely on random guessing,

STANFORD ACHIEVEMENT TEST

The math portion of the Stanford Achievement Test includes test items assessing three content areas. These include:

Number Concepts
These questions ask students to demonstrate their knowledge of arithmetic procedures and properties of number systems.

Patterns and Relationships
These questions measure students' ability to recognize and extend patterns as well as demonstrate their understanding of the quantitative, geometric, or logical relationships between variables, data sets, or elements of sequence.

Concepts of Shape and Space
These questions ask students with to use and develop principles of measurement and geometric properties.

TIP: If two multiple-choice items are similar, except for one or two words, choose one of these answers.

your child should consider the following:

- What do I already know?
- What does my logical reasoning tell me?
- What key terms can I identify that might jar my thinking?
- What do I think the answer should be? Can I find an answer that most closely matches this?

Note that some tests, such as the Iowa Test of Basic Skills (ITBS) and the Illinois Goal Assessment Program (IGAP), actually penalize students for not guessing. Obviously, if taking these tests, your child should always guess.

Rule Number Five: Read the Entire Question.
Sometimes a child will decide he knows the answer to a question before he's through reading it. Students should read all questions through to the end, even if they think they know the answer. A better answer may occur to them if they carefully consider each option.

Rule Number Six: Manage Your Time.
Time is of the essence on standardized tests. Precisely because this is so, some test takers tend to get quite anxious about it. Merely knowing there are strict time limits can paralyze some kids, or at least considerably slow them down. Others may react by unnecessarily rushing through items, not giving themselves enough time to competently comprehend and respond to a question.

Obviously, the greater your child's anxiety about a test, the more likely he will be to fumble time-wise. This is just one more reason to stress the positive during the test-taking period.

Your child's teacher may or may not discuss time management with your child. Either way, a review never hurts. Ask the teacher how the test will be timed and discuss this with your child. As noted, most standardized tests are designed to allow students enough time to finish the test, but not to dawdle. A minority are "speeded tests," which measure how many items your child answers correctly in a given time period.

Regardless of the test type, keeping track of time and pacing yourself is key. And savvy test takers always use any remaining time to recheck the answers and review any hard questions they may be uncertain about.

Preparing for Reading/Language Arts Tests

The reading/language arts sections of most standardized tests assess your child in reading comprehension, spelling and word usage, and written expression. Many, if not most, also include listening and study skills subtests (assessing your child's familiarity with and ability to use reference works such as dictionaries, encyclopedias, almanacs, and so forth). All of these sections contain a mix of multiple-choice and open-ended items.

Reading Comprehension

The reading comprehension sections of nearly all standardized tests follow a similar format. Students are asked to read a passage and then respond to a series of questions, both multiple-choice and open-ended. The trend today is towards increasingly lengthy and more demanding passages—or "meaningful chunks," as described in one such test.

The new generation of standardized tests are looking for everything from simple recall of information to the more sophisticated skills of interpretation, critical evaluation, and personal reflection and response. Your child may be asked to explain why an event in a story occurred, for example, and how the story differed from something that occurred in his own experience. He may be asked to agree or disagree with the author's point of view, or to compare the article or story to another he has read.

Establish a Family Book Club. You can help your child to do well in reading comprehension by encouraging her to read a variety of materials, both fiction and nonfiction. Encourage her to practice reading at a higher level of difficulty, so she is prepared for the rigor of the test. Most

VERBS COMMONLY USED IN ESSAY QUESTIONS:

Analyze, compare, contrast, criticize, define, describe, discuss, enumerate, evaluate, examine, explain, illustrate, interpret, list, outline, prove, state, summarize.
—"Making the A: How to Test for Tests," ERIC/AE Digest, by Diane Lolou

important of all, schedule time to discuss what she's read. Ask her to identify the central idea, purpose, or theme of the work. Can she describe important characters, settings, relationships, events, and details? Can she summarize the work? What techniques does the author use? What's the author's point of view?

Students who perform well on this portion of the language arts test tend to be year-round readers. They are comfortable with sustained reading and take pleasure in it. They also can stand apart from the material they read and apply a critical stance. According to the National Center for Education Statistics' Reading Report Card for the Nation and States, students who have home discussions about their studies at least weekly have higher average reading scores than those who do so less frequently. So go for it!

Writing Assessments

As noted earlier, some tests now include direct assessments of writing. This timed subtest (usually 45 minutes) requires students to respond to a brief prompt by writing a story. Your child may also be asked to critique and revise a written passage for punctuation, capitalization, and correct word usage.

A prompt used on a recent Connecticut Mastery Test went as follows:

> Your local newspaper has printed several articles in favor of the idea of removing violence from television shows. Decide whether or not you agree with this point of view. Write to the newspaper editor to convince other readers to support your position either for or against violence on television.

Children who scored well on this assignment produced well organized essays that fully elaborated their reasons with specific detail.

Grab the Quill. As in reading, skillful writing is a matter of practice. Encourage your child to read the opinion page of the local newspaper. Discuss the piece in terms of its main

---

GET TO THE POINT

When you write, get to the point. Start off by including part of the question in your answer. For example, say a question asks, "Discuss the benefits and drawbacks of year-round schooling for children in children grades 3–12." Your first sentence might read, "There are some obvious benefits as well as many drawbacks to year-round schooling for children grades 3–12." Next, supply supporting material, such as well-known facts or your own opinions. If time allows, review your essay for grammatical errors, clarity, and legibility.
—"Making the A: How to Test for Tests," ERIC/AE Digest, by Diane Lolou

theme and supporting ideas. Encourage her to write and submit her own opinion piece.

During the actual testing situation, encourage your child to make a quick outline before she begins to write. By doing so, her thoughts will be more organized and she will be less likely to leave out important information.

Preparing for Math Tests

The math component of today's standardized tests reflect the growing belief that in addition to rote learning, test items should elicit critical thinking. And, as elsewhere, the all-multiple-choice format is no longer seen as adequate to fulfill this function. So in addition to straightforward questions that test computation skills and arithmetic procedures, your child is also likely to encounter test questions requiring him to actually demonstrate his reasoning and problem-solving ability. Some questions might ask him to draw a geometric figure, or perhaps construct a graph from information provided in a table. Others may require him to explain in writing how he arrived at the answer.

This shift from an emphasis on simply "getting the numbers right" to demonstrating conceptual understanding and problem solving in a real world context reflects the National Council of Teachers of Mathematics (NCTM) recommendations on curriculum and standards. The NCTM's recommendations, which, in a nutshell, strive to make mathematics meaningful, have been widely adopted nationwide, both in the classroom and on standardized tests.

Chances are high that your child will be tested on the following:

- Numeration (numbers and counting)
- Computation with whole numbers, fractions, decimals, and percents (including addition, subtraction, multiplication, and division)
- Ability to estimate and round numbers
- Ability to interpret (and sometimes construct) tables, graphs, and charts

STIMULATION

Many studies suggest that early stimulation of a child's brain and body can enhance general intelligence. When the child's natural curiosity is encouraged and fostered, and learning is made fun, intelligence is enhanced.
—*The Parent's Answer Book* by Gerald Deskin, Ph.D. and Greg Steckler, M.A. (Fairview Press, 1995)

KEEP A LOG

Have your child keep a "Web log" whenever he goes online. This will get him to analyze what he's seeing instead of just mindlessly surfing. Reporting his Web whereabouts will also discourage him from going to inappropriate sites.

- Probability and statistics
- Measurement and geometry (two- and three-dimensional shapes, area, volume, and units of measure)
- Problem solving (solving word problems, estimation, spatial reasoning, recognizing patterns)
- Algebra

For an overview of your child's math curriculum, we suggest you review chapters 8 and 9 in this book (7th and 8th grade math). To score well on the math test, he should be comfortable with this material. For further practice, engage in the learning adventures suggested in chapters 14 and 15.

Think Mathematically in Everyday Situations. Given the real-world application of many test items, encourage your child to think mathematically in every day situations. And don't forget to review the commonly used math terms, such as *sum, difference, product, quotient,* and *set.* A surprising number of students get stumped by these terms and don't progress beyond them. Review mathematical symbols, such as *greater than* (>) and *less than* (<).

Be Proactive. Given the variety of question types involved, it's important that, if at all possible, your child be exposed to practice items. This way, she won't be stumped by the novelty of the question types and will be able to focus instead on solving them. Ask the teacher if students will take practice tests. How much time will be spent practice items? If you are not satisfied with the answer you receive, you can always contact the test publisher (if a nationally administered norm-referenced test) or the state assessment office (if a state-administered, criterion-referenced test). In most cases you will be able to receive sample items from older tests, which you can then review with your child.

Finally, many tests require students to use a ruler and a calculator during certain portions of the test. To ensure that your child arrives prepared, be sure to find out well ahead of time whether he should bring these items with him.

The Basics of Body and Soul

You've heard the line about the "best laid plans." Too often we hear about kids who scramble in late on the day of the test. They may be harried because they went to the wrong room. Halfway through the test they're dizzy from hunger. The room is cold and they have no sweater, and so spend valuable time shivering instead of strategizing. Each of these scenarios is easily avoidable with a little planning.

Get Them to the Church On Time. Nothing will throw a child off more quickly than a poor start. Avoid this unnecessary pitfall by knowing when and where the test will be and by making certain your child gets there, and on time.

Burn off Steam. Encourage your child to exercise regularly before the test. A well-conditioned body lowers stress levels and increases performance. Beware, however, that she doesn't exert herself so much that she's fatigued on the day of the test.

Get Some Beauty Rest. Make sure that your child gets a good night's sleep before the test. The more rested she is, the more likely she will be to bring all her powers to bear on the test.

Dress comfortably. The best way to dress for a test is in loose layers, with sweater over shirt and so forth. This way, your child will be prepared no matter what the temperature of the room.

Eat a hearty breakfast. Your child should eat a nutritionally sound breakfast on the day of the test. He should also be well hydrated.

HELPING EACH OTHER

In the learning process, your child will eventually encounter some high-level processes that may be quite difficult. Acknowledge that you may have at one time done schoolwork like this, but you don't quite remember how it goes. Then ask your child to explain what she already knows—get her to teach you.

Making the Grade

STANDARDIZED TEST REQUIREMENTS BY STATE

In addition to those state-mandated tests listed below, many individual districts offer additional tests as needed. Contact your child's school administrators for more information.

STATE	TEST	GRADES	SUBJECTS	TIME OF YEAR GIVEN
Alabama	Stanford Achievement Test (Stanford 9)	3–11		Spring
Alaska	California Achievement Test	4, 7	English language arts, math	Spring
Arizona	Stanford Achievement Test (Stanford 9)	2–11		Spring
Arkansas	Stanford Achievement Test (Stanford 9)	5, 7, 10	math, reading/language arts, social studies, science	Fall
	Arkansas Criterion-Referenced Test	4, 8	math, English, reading, writing	Spring
California	Stanford Achievement Test (Stanford 9)	2–11	reading, language arts, math	Spring
	statewide standards-based assessment being developed			
Colorado	Colorado Student Assessment Program	3 4, 7 5, 8 10	reading reading, writing math, science math, reading, writing	Spring Spring Fall Spring 2001
Connecticut	Connecticut Mastery Test	4, 6, 8		Fall
	Connecticut Academic Performance Test	10		Spring
Delaware	Delaware Student Testing Program	3, 5, 8, 10 8, 11 4, 6	English language arts, math science, social studies	Spring Fall/Spring Spring 2000
District of Columbia	Stanford Achievement Test (Stanford 9)	1–11	math, reading	Fall/Spring
Florida	Florida Comprehensive Achievement Test (FCAT)	4, 8, 10 3, 5, 6, 7, 9 5, 8, 10 3, 4, 6, 7, 9 4, 8, 10	reading reading (multiple-choice) math math (multiple-choice only) writing	Spring
	Stanford Achievement Test (Stanford 9)	3–10	reading comprehension, math problem-solving (multiple-choice only)	

How Can I Help My Child Prepare for Standardized Tests?

STATE	TEST	GRADES	SUBJECTS	TIME OF YEAR GIVEN
Georgia	Georgia Kindergarten Assessment Program	kindergarten	reading, math	Spring
	Iowa Test of Basic Skills (ITBS)	3, 5, 8		
	criterion-referenced tests being developed	3, 5, 7	English language arts, reading	
	writing assessments	3, 5, 8		
Hawaii	Stanford Achievement Test (Stanford 9)	3, 5, 7, 9	math, reading	Spring
	Hawaii State Test of Essential Competencies (HSTEC)	10		
Idaho	Iowa Test of Basic Skills (ITBS)	3–11		Fall
Illinois	Illinois Standards Achievement Test (ISAT)	3, 5, 8, 10 4, 7, 11	reading, writing, math science, social science	Winter Winter
	Prairie State Achievement Test (in development)			Spring 2000
Indiana	Indiana Statewide Testing for Educational Progress (ISTEP)	3, 6, 8, 10	reading/language arts, math	Fall
Iowa	no statewide assessment program			
Kansas	Kansas Assessments (state-developed, standards-based)	3, 7, 10 5, 8, 10 4, 7, 10 5, 8, 11	reading writing, science math social studies	Fall/Spring
Kentucky	Commonwealth Accountability Testing System (CATS)	4, 5, 7, 8, 10, 11, 12	reading, writing, math, science, social studies, humanities, practical living/vocational	Spring
	TerraNova/Comprehensive Test of Basic Skills (CTBS)	3, 6, 9		

STATE	TEST	GRADES	SUBJECTS	TIME OF YEAR GIVEN
Louisiana	Louisiana Educational Assessment Program (LEAP)	4, 8	English, math, science, social studies	Spring
	Iowa Test of Basic Skills (ITBS)	3, 5, 6, 7, 9		
	Graduation Exit Exam	10, 11	English, math, science, social studies, writing	
Maine	Maine Educational Assessment	4, 8, 11	English language arts, math, science/technology, social studies, health/phys. ed., visual/performing arts, career preparation, languages	Spring
Maryland	Maryland School Performance Assessment Program (MSPAP)	3, 5, 8	reading, math, English language arts, science, social studies	Spring
	Maryland High School Assessments	9	English, algebra or geometry, government	
Massa-chusetts	Massachusetts Comprehensive Assessment System	4, 8, 10 3, 4, 7, 10 4, 6, 8, 10 5, 8, 10	writing reading math science/technology, history, social science	Spring
Michigan	Michigan Educational Assessment Program (MEAP)	4, 7 5, 8	math, reading science, writing, social studies	Winter
Minnesota	Minnesota Comprehensive Assessment Program	3 5 10 11	reading, math reading, writing, math reading, writing math	Spring
Mississippi	Iowa Test of Basic Skills (ITBS)	4–8	English language arts, math	Fall
	Tests of Achievement (TAP)	9	English language arts, math	
	Functional Literacy Exam	11	reading, math, written communication	
	Subject Area Tests	9–12	algebra, U.S. history, biology	
Missouri	Missouri Assessment Program (MAP)	4, 8, 10 3, 7, 11 3, 7, 10 4, 8, 11 5 5, 9	math communication arts science social studies fine arts health/phys. ed.	Spring Spring Spring Spring 2000 Spring 2001 Spring 2001

STATE	TEST	GRADES	SUBJECTS	TIME OF YEAR GIVEN
Montana	districts choose from among commercially prepared tests, i.e., Iowa Test of Basic Skills (ITBS), TerraNova/ Comprehensive Test of Basic Skills (CTBS), Stanford Achievement Test (Stanford 9)	4, 8, 11	reading, language arts, math, science, social studies	Spring
Nebraska	No statewide assessment program			
Nevada	TerraNova/Comprehensive Test of Basic Skills (CTBS)	4, 8, 10	reading, writing, math	Fall
New Hampshire	New Hampshire Educational Improvement and Assessment Program (NHEIAP)	3 6, 10	English language arts, math English language arts, math, science, social studies	Spring
New Jersey	Elementary School Proficiency Test (ESPA) Grade 8 Proficiency Test (GEPA) High School Proficiency Assessment (HSPA) being developed	4 8	math, language arts	Spring
New Mexico	New Mexico Achievement Assessment Reading Assessment Writing Assessment High School Competency Test	4, 6, 8 1, 2 4, 6 10–12	math, science, English language arts reading writing	Spring
New York	State Assessments Regents Exam	4, 8 5, 8 11 10	English language arts, math, science social studies English math global history/geography, U.S. history/government, science	Spring Spring 2000 Spring Spring being phased in for 2003

Making the Grade

STATE	TEST	GRADES	SUBJECTS	TIME OF YEAR GIVEN
North Carolina	End of Grade Tests	3–8	reading, math (multiple-choice only)	Spring
	Open-Ended Assessments	4, 8	reading, math (written out/problem solving)	
	Writing Assessment	4, 7	writing	
	Tests of Computer Skills	8	computer skills	
	Competency Tests	10	reading, math	
	High School Comprehensive Test	10	English language arts, math	
North Dakota	TerraNova/Comprehensive Test of Basic Skills (CTBS5) and Test of Cognitive Skills (TCS2)	4, 6, 8, 10	reading, vocabulary, language mechanics, math, spelling, science, social studies	Spring
Ohio	Ohio Proficiency Test	4, 6, 9, 12	reading, writing, math, science, citizenship	Spring
Oklahoma	Iowa Test of Basic Skills (ITBS)	3, 7		Spring
	Oklahoma Core Curriculum Tests	5, 8, 11	math, science, reading, history/government, writing, geography, arts	
Oregon	State-developed criterion-referenced tests	5, 8, 10 3, 5, 8, 10	science, social science reading and literature, writing, math	Spring
Pennsylvania	Pennsylvania System of School Assessment (PSSA)	5, 8, 11 6, 9 11 5, 8, 11	reading writing writing math	Spring Fall Spring Spring
Rhode Island	Metropolitan Achievement Test (MAT)	4, 8		
	Rhode Island Writing Test	3, 7, 10	writing	
	New Standards Reference Exams	4, 8, 10 4, 8	math English language arts	
	Health Education Assessment	5, 9		

How Can I Help My Child Prepare for Standardized Tests?

STATE	TEST	GRADES	SUBJECTS	TIME OF YEAR GIVEN
South Carolina	Cognitive Skills Assessment Battery	1, 2	general knowledge	Fall
	Palmetto Achievement Challenge Tests (PACT)	3–8	language arts, math science	Spring
	PACT Exit Exam	10	reading/English language arts, math, science, social studies	Spring
South Dakota	Stanford Achievement Test (Stanford 9)	2, 4, 8, 11	reading, math, science, language arts, social studies	Spring
	Open-Ended Writing Assessment	5, 9	writing	Fall
	Otis-Lennon School Ability Test (OLSAT)	4, 8		
Tennessee	TerraNova/Comprehensive Test of Basic Skills (CTBS), Complete Battery Plus	3–8 4, 7, 11	English language arts, math, science, social studies writing	Spring
	Tennessee Comprehensive Assessment Program (TCAP)	9	English language arts, math	
Texas	Texas Assessment of Academic Skills (TAAS)	3–8, 10 4, 8, 10 8	reading, math writing social studies, science	throughout year
	National Assessment of Educational Progress (NAEP)	4, 8	math, science	Spring 2000
Utah	Stanford Achievement Test (Stanford 9)	5, 8, 11		
Vermont	Vermont Development Reading Assessment	2	early reading	Spring
	New Standards Reference Exams	4, 8, 10	math, English language	
	Vermont Science Assessment	6, 11	arts	
	local districts choose a norm-referenced test (optional)	5, 9, 11	science	

Making the Grade

STATE	TEST	GRADES	SUBJECTS	TIME OF YEAR GIVEN
Virginia	Stanford Achievement Test (Stanford 9)	4, 6, 9	English language arts, math; science and social studies optional	
	Virginia Standards of Learning Test (SOL)	3	English, math, science, social studies	
		5, 8	English, math, science, social studies, computer technology	
Washington	Iowa Test of Basic Skills (ITBS)	3, 6	English language arts, math	Spring
	Iowa Test of Educational Development (ITED)	9	English language arts, math	Spring
	Washington Assessment of Student Learning (WASL)	4, 7, 10	English language arts, math	Spring
West Virginia	Metropolitan Readiness Test	kindergarten		Spring
	Stanford Achievement Test (Stanford 9)	311	English language arts, spelling, math, science, social sciences	
	West Virginia Writing Assessment	4, 7, 10	writing	
Wisconsin	TerraNova/Comprehensive Test of Basic Skills (CTBS)	4, 8, 10	math, science, English, language arts, social studies, writing	Spring
	Wisconsin Reading Comprehension Test	3	reading	
Wyoming	Wyoming Comprehensive Assessment System	4, 8, 11	math, language arts	Spring

CHAPTER 5

How Else Can I Affect My Child's Success?

Parents are the single most important factor in a child's educational success from the earliest months through the school years. Our shoes may be scuffed, our wallets thin, and our gasoline tanks running on empty,

GO BACK TO SCHOOL

When parents take the time to attend a school function—time off from an evening activity or time off from their own jobs—they send a strong message about how important school is to them, and, by extension, how important it should be to their child. When this sort of involvement occurs regularly, it reinforces the view in the child's mind that school and home are connected, and that school is an integral part of the whole family's life.
—from *Beyond the Classroom*, Laurence Steinberg, Ph.D. (Simon & Schuster, 1996)

but it is our effort, energy, and support that make the difference.

We all look back on that time when our toddler first held up a bug or a blade of grass and proudly named it for us. We cherish being a part of that moment of learning and hold on to the hope that every moment of learning in our children's lives will be as exciting and as important.

Children make those first discoveries both for themselves and for the loving adults around them. Your presence, your pride, your support, and your enthusiasm were an essential part of that moment and will continue to be a part of their learning moments for as long as they live with you. As children mature, enter school, and continue up through the higher grades, the intensity of their learning experiences changes and their public expectations of us change (try gurgling excitedly over your 13-year-old's mastery of the square root), but our basic role remains the same.

Spend Learning Time Together

We may do more supporting and less teaching once our children hit school, but there are many opportunities for support that have nothing to do with textbooks or classroom lessons. These are the times when you and your child can build a wonderful relationship around learning together.

BREAD AND BUTTER

Children who are physically and emotionally healthy perform better in school, have higher self-esteem, and enjoy positive relationships with their family and peers.

• Make preventive health care and education a priority for your family. Schedule routine checkups, health screenings, and immunizations to provide early detection and treatment of health problems.

• Serve a low-fat and high-fiber diet that includes five servings of fruits and vegetables each day. Choose nourishing snacks to round out a well-balanced diet.

• Encourage and participate in age-appropriate physical activity and exercise with your children.

• Promote your children's self-esteem and emotional health by understanding their needs, encouraging their independence, setting standards, and sharing your feelings and experiences with them.
—The National PTA®

One parent may discover a local garden club's edible-plant walk to take with his seven-year-old botanist. Another may share her skills with carving tools and linoleum blocks with her son. Others are willing to join a teenager under the car. All are engaged in learning with their children. These are the parents and children who are joined in a learning process that transcends the ordinary routines of living together.

Parents Can

We are sometimes intimidated by schools and schooling. This happens most frequently in later years when the more advanced mathematics, language, or science curriculum can leave us scrambling for reference books as we try to help our struggling young chemists or geographers. It can also happen in earlier years, particularly if our children have problems with specific skills like reading, and if the school is using teaching techniques different from the ones used when we were in school.

At such times, it's important to keep in mind that no one person and no single institution can possibly provide all of the care, support, and expertise that are required to educate a young human being. We, as parents, may not have the pedagogical skills or knowledge to teach a particular subject, but we are the primary support team, the cheerleaders, the enforcers, and, when necessary, the champions of our young students. As you read this book, you will also find that there are many ways to supplement and support your child's education that require only our energy and enthusiasm for learning (of course, knowing how hard parents already work, that is a big *only*).

Provide the Taste of Success

Good educators (good managers, successful politicians, and great generals as well) all know that success breeds success and that nobody thrives or learns in situations in which there is frequent failure. To learn well, we all need to build on successful experiences.

Learning should be tailored so that children can taste success. A fact, a skill, or a concept successfully acquired will stick—and contribute to *more* learning. This doesn't mean that learning won't be work. Learning, as we all know, often takes lots of work. Stumbles, guesses, and trials occur all along the way. These are part of the process and part of the learning. When something becomes too full of stumbles and sulks and tears, however, it's time to take a break.

A break is also a good idea when there are tears of frustration over a homework assignment. If your child is stumped and it's appropriate for you to help, lead him back to a simpler level. Try to break the present task into smaller steps. If the steps lead to small, recognizable successes, the original, frustrating task can be easily accomplished.

If you are working with your child and using the activities in this book, avoid situations in which defeat and disappointment seem likely. This is not always easy to do, but learning to read your child's reactions will help you know when to halt an unsuccessful attempt. While you pause, consider the child and the task, and then rethink the task. Can you break it into smaller units or subtasks? Can you try teaching in a different way? Or should you abandon it and try something totally different?

Providing tastes of success is like carefully laying a new course of bricks in a wall. If you have crumbly bricks and lumpy mortar, there'll be trouble higher up. When each brick is even and snug and the mortar satisfyingly set, you have laid the perfect foundation for a new course.

Learn to Listen

Good listening skills are necessary for learning, but they are equally (or perhaps even more) necessary for teaching.

The First Level of Listening. There's an old educational maxim, "He who does the talking, does the learning." Talking requires putting your thoughts together. The more your child talks about something that she's learning, the more putting together—learning—she does. This is a simple and extremely useful thought, but it's very easy to forget, even for the most experienced teachers.

MAKING IT FUN

Parents can show kids how learning basic skills applies to everyday life. Use the tools you have around the home, and have a lot of fun too. Do projects with your children. Focus on one child or all siblings. Turn measuring food ingredients into the lesson of the day. Split a recipe in half or double it. Whoa—there's a huge math lesson going on there! Do it. Use the measuring cups. Use the flour and the sugar. Break some things, make some mistakes along the way. Have fun. What do you have at the end of the "lesson"? Chocolate chip cookies, and the kids get to brag about how they got to make them. My mom's not the best cook in the world, but we really had fun cooking together.

PARENTS TEACH!

Parents are educators too. By the time your children enter school, you will have taught them more than they will learn during their entire school experience!

TEACHING LIFE

One mother told me that her daughter was really amazing at math and English, but she hadn't opened her mouth in school the whole year. This was a big issue for her and the teacher. I told her that at *SCORE!*, we interact with the children, and her mother said she didn't think that could really happen. I told the girl to raise her hand and say "I'm done," because when you do, you'll get a *SCORE!* incentive card, which children can use to redeem for prizes or gifts. The mom was surprised she even opened her mouth.

The mom called me a few nights later. Her teacher freaked out because the next day in class the girl raised her hand and said, "I have a question." The teacher thought, Oh my god, Lazarus has come out of the cave, because she never spoke up before. That's what's going on at *SCORE!*. We're teaching life things here, beyond what you learn in a textbook. We're teaching kids how to be people.

If *you* are quiet enough, you'll get the thrill of watching those miraculous moments when your child's learning takes place. The sound of the penny dropping can be the most important (and satisfying) sound in the world.

The Second Level of Listening. This level of listening is a bit harder. It requires you to be both quiet and as completely aware as possible of everything about your child. We use this skill unconsciously in conversations with our friends. We are sensitive to their facial expressions, read their body language, and monitor the tone of their voices. With your child, make this a more conscious process. Deliberately watch her face as an exercise is being written. Notice the enthusiastic posture (or discouraged or bored slump) as your child talks to herself during a hands-on activity. Pay attention to changes in behavior. These and many other subtle signals will help you determine how well, or how poorly, a particular educational activity is going.

Learn Something Yourself

We know a parent who began learning Hebrew at the same time as his child was learning to read. His child was having a struggle. Because this parent had to learn a new alphabet from scratch as well as how to read right to left, he was especially sympathetic with and supportive of his child's struggles.

Learning something new yourself has two other benefits (besides having a good time learning ballroom dancing or car maintenance or whatever). The first is that it makes you an observer of how your own learning process works, and that *always* makes you a better teacher. The second is that you are providing your child with an excellent model.

Remember Your Own Learning

Everyone who engages in teaching touches a lot of old hot buttons. There were subjects you loved, subjects you hated, teachers who helped you, and teachers you just couldn't please. These are useful memories, but they are primarily useful to you as an adult engaged in education. They can help you think about what works or doesn't work, but they can also bog you down while you're working with your child. As much as possible, keep your memories to yourself while you are working with your child at the homework table or using the activities in this book.

This is not an iron rule, though—nothing in education should be ironclad. If an old feeling or experience makes helpful sense at the moment, share it. All children are curious about their parents' lives as children, and you should share whatever you feel comfortable about sharing. Usually, however, it's better to do it at some other time.

Finding More Educational Resources

Beyond this book lies a whole world of educational opportunities. Like most parents, you are probably the phone book, resource manager, librarian, transportation officer, executive secretary, and personal assistant in your child's education right now. Here are a few ideas of resources to make your job more rewarding and easier.

Use the institutions around you. Almost all areas of our country are within range of a college, university, research field station, or county extension service. Such institutions often sponsor a variety of public educational events staffed by young, eager graduate students or professionals who are happy and proud to show and talk about what they do. Call them up and find out what they have to offer and get on their mailing lists.

Meet interesting neighbors. Ham radio operators, retired people with exotic hobbies, the guy who raises parakeets or poodles for sale, and many others like them live somewhere nearby. They are usually happy to share their stories and skills with interested families.

Plug into the Web. It can be confusing and it can be maddening, but the possibilities of finding facts, books, articles, connection resources, and you name it are so great that tuning into the hum of information on the World Wide Web is worth the effort. Having your own computer helps, but it isn't necessary. Libraries all over the country now offer

MANY INFLUENCES

If you are a good parent and you live in a neighborhood with other good parents, chances are that the lessons you have tried so hard to teach your child at home will be reinforced when your child comes into contact with other children, and other adults, in the community.
—from *Beyond the Classroom* by Laurence Steinberg, Ph.D. (Simon & Schuster, 1996)

LEARNING SITES

Factories, farms, greenhouses, fire stations—any place of business—can be a learning site for your child. Call these businesses up and see if they can handle family or small group tours.

OLDER AND WISER

Use your child's friends to help out with home learning projects, and keep everything fun and exciting. Sometimes older siblings can be great role models to younger children. I wanted my older sister to read to me all the time; have older brothers and sisters read to younger children. Parents need to encourage this kind of positive experience in the family.

BIG HEAD START

Teach your children how to use a dictionary, encyclopedia, or different kinds of software reference tools. Many kids don't know how to look up the meaning of a word because no one's helped them or shown them how. You don't learn some of these skills until late in school, so it's a big headstart if your children learn at home first.

access to the Internet as a resource and will be happy to help you search.

Make your own connections. Everyone seems to work harder and have less time these days. This is very isolating for parents who have the added responsibility of child rearing. You can be sure, however, that there are lots of people out there just like you. Use your PTA, visits to the park, church, or synagogue, membership in organizations, and contacts with other places where you meet adults with children to raise issues about children and education. This connecting can be as simple as finding enough interested families to organize a modern dance class or as complicated (and important) as galvanizing parents to take action against a program cutback in the local schools.

Contact home-schooling groups. Home schoolers have taken on the whole burden of their children's education and usually have done extensive research into the educational opportunities in the communities around them. Subscribe to any publications they produce, and talk with them about what they've found useful.

Check out professional and trade associations. Many of these groups have extensive educational and public relations resources that you can use to supplement hobbies or educational activities. Offerings range from posters and booklets to some quite sophisticated educational materials. Many libraries have indexed directories for professional and trade groups. You and your child could spend a pleasant time browsing through one of them looking for areas of interest together (and you'll be amazed at the variety).

Use the library with your child. Libraries not only offer special programs for families, they are increasingly defining themselves as community information and resource centers. Their bulletin boards reflect this and will guide you to unsuspected educational opportunities ranging from reading programs and book clubs, to arts and crafts classes, to author readings. And, of course, take advantage of the professional skills of the children's librarian.

Finally, don't forget your mother! Members of your extended family make wonderful resources. We often overlook the richness of wisdom and experience available in our own immediate circle. An aunt who crochets, a cousin who loves to do woodworking, or a grandparent who cooks some special food all have skills to share. Older relatives may have personal experiences like military service, life in another country, or skills in an occupation that no longer exists that they would be happy to share for oral history projects.

Making the Most of Small Moments

Teaching moments exist all around you. It's easier with younger children because their defenses aren't up and they ask great questions. But, in fact, older children are as curious and eager to explore if you open up situations. An example might be stopping by the road to read a notice board about an area of reclaimed prairie and then researching this at home. Budgeting for throwing a party is a natural. And minilessons don't have to be complicated. A game of "subway-stop bingo" (looking for all the letters of the alphabet on a subway station map) can change a tedious wait into a language arts lesson.

Remember—You Do Make a Difference

Whether you work on the Learning Adventure activities in this book, share your child's enthusiasm for all the right answers she got on The Kids' Home Learning Quizzes, zealously support your children's homework efforts, seek out exciting field trips, drive your child to an enrichment program, or do all of these, your support makes a big difference in your child's educational success. Everything you do, no matter how small a beginning, encourages and strengthens her learning. Thanks for making the effort.

MOVING FORWARD

One boy in our Center was not expected to walk or talk after a severe accident. He had a great recovery, but still has a bad vision problem and needs to sit very close to a computer screen. I told his mother that I had a good friend who also had poor vision and hearing problems, and he got accepted to a top college. He had to sit in the front row of class and tape lectures and use his laptop to record what he heard, but he adapted just fine to higher education. And I told this boy's mom that he could go to college—Berkeley, for instance, has an extension service for students who have challenging physical problems—and just to be aware of the opportunities out there. She started crying. "Nobody ever talked to me before about my son going to college. Nobody has ever made that a reality." If children under any conditions are given a taste of success, like moving forward in their skill levels, it's a good thing. Then it's not a matter or *if* the child is going to college, but which college to attend.

What's Being Covered in School?

CHAPTER 6

What's My Child Studying in Language Arts?

Students in language arts programs work within the same basic core areas from first grade on, with each year's work building on what has gone before. The emphasis on each core area changes with the grade level

THE RIGHT BOOKS

I loved to read while I was growing up, and there's nothing better a child can do than to read a lot. Sometimes your child may not have a natural interest in reading, but you just have to get the right books. Reading can greatly improve grammar and spelling. Does your child's natural interests involve motorcycles or trains or dinosaurs? Focus on these subjects and get materials on the subjects that your child will enjoy—any reading is productive.

as students master basic skills and add more complex ones. And, of course, programs vary greatly from city to city and from school to school.

In grades seven and eight, the language arts class sometimes grows up to a new name—English. In the areas of grammar and usage in particular, there is a great leap in sophistication of concepts that usually begins in fifth grade and strengthens through your child's middle school experience. Writing techniques build steadily throughout the school years. Skills are refined and developed at each level, as kids learn to write in different forms and genres. And while the earlier grades are devoted to developing basic reading skills, using a variety of methods, by middle school the emphasis shifts to recognizing, appreciating, and evaluating the various techniques that authors use in literature.

In short, literally hundreds of different skills are introduced and practiced in language arts. This overview presents major topics that continue in grades seven and eight, as well as specific skills introduced or emphasized in each of those grades.

Ten Core Areas in Language Arts. The following ten core areas form the basis of most language arts programs in these two grades:

Making the Grade

TEAMWORK

At a parent-teacher conference, find out the teacher's perception of your child's learning progress and get the teacher's recommendations for activities and projects that will help you reinforce classroom learning. Share your perceptions of your child's schoolwork at home and ask, "What do you see in school?" Ask "What can I do?" rather than "This is what you, the teacher, need to do."

Teachers deserve respect, and they probably know what they're doing. Parents won't get anywhere if they lecture teachers, say that the teacher is doing something wrong, or make accusations. "I just need more input from you. I've noticed this at home, and I want to keep the lines of communication open with you." The more a teacher knows about what parents are doing with their children at home—including whether children are feeling challenged or frustrated by a personal event—the better things will be to design a proactive approach to a child's learning challenges.

1. Language and Grammar: sentences (types and structure), phrases and clauses, parts of speech (noun, verb, pronoun, adjective, adverb, preposition, conjunction, interjection)
2. Usage: sentence fragments and run-ons, subject-verb agreement, noun and pronoun usage, pronouns and antecedents, problem words
3. Mechanics: capitalization, punctuation
4. Spelling
5. Composition: sentences, paragraphs, types of writing, writing across the curriculum, the writing process, composition skills (such as using dialogue, developing characters and setting), creative expression
6. Vocabulary
7. Reference and Study Strategies: using the dictionary and thesaurus, using the library, finding and organizing information
8. Thinking Skills and Strategies
9. Listening and Speaking Skills and Strategies
10. Literature and Reading: types of reading material, literary skills and terms, story elements, effective use of language, recognizing writing techniques, comprehension, responding to literature

Approaches to Language Arts Teaching. Approaches to teaching language arts, especially in the middle school (grades 6–8), vary greatly from place to place and even from classroom to classroom within a district. Different teachers, too, may emphasize certain core areas—literature, writing, mechanics—more than others.

The outlines that follow provide a general overview of skills that are likely to be introduced and taught in your child's 7th or 8th grade. But how much of each core and how it is handled is just as likely to vary widely. If your child's 7th grade teacher puts major emphasis on literature, for instance, there may be proportionally less emphasis on practicing grammar, mechanics, or spelling in isolation from reading activities.

Traditional Teaching While most schools have adopted the broader, more integrated program known as Language Arts, some still teach a traditional "English class." Here greater emphasis may be put on grammar, usage, and mechanics. Your child may more often be asked to write in a specific form, such as a personal essay or a descriptive paragraph, instead of informal writing forms such as journals. Literature may even be studied in a separate class or period from "English."

Interdisciplinary Team Teaching Teams of teachers working together are a feature of many middle schools. The goal of team teaching is to integrate and coordinate, through careful planning and timing, what kids learn in different disciplines and content areas. For instance, students may be reading a novel about pioneer life in Language Arts at the same time that they are studying the westward movement in social studies, landscapes of the West in art, and rocks and minerals in science.

Besides integrating ideas, this kind of sharing can also give your child the benefit of the knowledge and expertise of a group of teachers as well as exposure to different personalities and teaching styles. Some teaching teams have only two members, but four to five cooperating teachers is not considered unusual and often considered more effective.

In a school that emphasizes team teaching, your child may come home talking about his team's name and insignia and its goals and objectives. Teams may also take part in field trips and activities. One objective is to provide a feeling of "togetherness" for this group of kids who stay together and learn together. Their language arts learning is integrated with other subject matter.

Writing in Other Curriculum Areas Your student will often be asked to write reports for science or social studies or present creative writing projects (such as skits or scripts) in many classes—not just in English. Many language arts programs now feature specific units to help kids do this type of writing.

Also, in some schools, reading, writing, and projects in different subject areas are closely tied together in learning

PARTNERSHIP-2000 SCHOOLS

Educators and families agree that school-family-community partnerships are essential for children's success. Based on more than a decade of research and the work of many educators, parents, students, and others, we know that it is possible for elementary, middle, and high schools to develop and maintain strong programs of partnerships.

Ask your child's classroom teacher if your school and district is a member of the National Network of Partnership-2000 Schools. Set up by researchers at Johns Hopkins University in 1996, this group brings together schools, districts, and states committed to developing and maintaining strong programs for school-family-community partnerships. To receive more information and membership forms for schools, districts, or states, write to Dr. Joyce Epstein, Director, Partnership-2000 Schools, Center on School, Family, and Community Partnerships, 3505 North Charles Street, Baltimore, MD 21218; or contact Karen Clark Salinas at (410) 516-8818; fax at (410) 516-8890.

CAN WE TALK?

Many schools are going tech with automated phone systems that call home and leave messages for busy parents who work during school hours. One such system, U.S. Telecom International's PhoneMaster 2000 (call 800-835-7788), allows schools to notify parents of:
• Absentees and tradies
• Homework assignments
• School events
• Invitation to meetings
• Bond issues
• School cancellations
• Report card announcements
• Fines due reminders
Information hotlines also give students and parents instant access to an electronic bulletin board of important information for the home, including homework hotlines, attendance policies, sporting schedules, lunch menus, bus routes, and school policies.

TIME COMMITMENT

It's hard being a single parent and trying to find the time for learning activities and personal time with your child. I have to say, "What's more important: Eating dinner at 6:00, or spending some time doing homework together?"

units. This approach can be challenging, but it helps kids see how the things they learn in school are not just separate chunks of meaningless facts but are related to each other and to real life outside school.

What's Taught in Grade Seven?

By grade seven, your child knows a lot about how sentences and paragraphs are put together; she knows how to avoid fragments and run-on sentences. In grammar, emphasis continues on subject-verb agreement, irregular verbs, contractions, and types of pronouns and their agreement with antecedents. Your child has learned how to use and compare regular and irregular adjectives and adverbs.

Students at every level learn conventions and rules of punctuation and capitalization. By grade seven, most spelling issues are handled as review lessons, including the process of proofreading. Some new ideas, such as Greek and Latin roots, are introduced in this grade.

In a comprehensive language arts program, students have been writing stories, descriptions, letters, and other compositions since the early grades. New genres and skills are added in middle school. In composition, students learn the steps of the writing process and apply them throughout the succeeding grades.

Building vocabulary is another core area, with regular lessons to build vocabulary and use exact words. From the early grades, students learn to use a dictionary, thesaurus, and other library resources. In this grade, your child should be expected to put such resources to real use.

By grade seven, kids have encountered a variety of writing techniques and types of literature, both fiction and nonfiction. They are expected to comprehend what they read both literally and critically and to write their responses to the things they read. Sharing books and reading independently are both encouraged. Here is a typical 7th grade curriculum outline:

What's My Child Studying in Language Arts?

Core Area 1: Language and Grammar
- Recognize and analyze different types of sentences
- Work with dependent and independent clauses
- Use indirect objects in sentences
- Use interrogative, demonstrative, reflexive/intensive pronouns
- Understand the uses of coordinating, correlative, and subordinating conjunctions
- Recognize active and passive voice of verbs
- Recognize progressive forms of verbs

Core Area 2: Usage
- Use the correct tenses of verbs
- Use problem verbs correctly (e.g., *lend/loan*)
- Use reflexive and intensive pronouns
- Use indefinite and interrogative pronouns
- Choose correct forms of demonstrative pronouns (*this, that*) and pronoun homophones (*whose, who's*)
- Place adverbs, adjectives, and prepositional phrases in the right place in a sentence
- Use *between/among* correctly

Core Area 3: Mechanics
- Capitalize proper nouns and adjectives correctly
- Use correct capitalization in titles, letters, and outlines
- Punctuate sentences using commas, colons, and semicolons
- Use hyphens, dashes, and parentheses correctly

Core Area 4: Spelling
- Use Latin and Greek roots as aids to spelling and meaning
- Use prefixes and suffixes as aids to spelling and meaning

Core Area 5: Composition
- Write a persuasive essay or letter
- Write book reports
- Write a firsthand or research report
- Apply writing techniques to other curriculum areas

LIMIT TV TIME

Consumer Reports (August 1996) tested a new product called the TV Allowance by Mindmaster (call 800-231-4410 for ordering), a programmable timer that fits into the family TV set; they also make a companion product to control computer time. TV Allowance controls viewing time, but not the channels that can be watched, responding to commands a parent enters on a keypad. The magazine reported that the product worked reliably during their tests, and it was easy to use. Parents can set viewing time to the nearest minute, and it automatically shuts off when you turn off the set. The magazine concludes its review by saying, "A timer like the TV Allowance may help some parents whose kids have real trouble turning off the tube. But it's no substitute for parental guidance and rule setting. Whether you opt for the TV Allowance timer or not, start by talking with your kids to agree on rules for TV watching."

If learning is part of the everyday, it can be fun—kids like participating in real life.

BOOKISH CURIOSITY

Try to find books you and your child both can agree upon. Kids may not think they like to "read," but every kid wants to learn about his favorite place, his favorite animal, his favorite sport, and so on. Let books satisfy this curiosity.

IT'S A PRIORITY

Education is very important to my husband and me. We cannot depend solely on the public school system to provide it all, so we sit down with our son and we read a lot and do homework with him—things that we've made up or borrowed from outside education sources. We spend about an hour and a half of work a day on school subjects, and we do this together.

- Follow the steps of the writing process: prewriting, writing a first draft, revising/editing, proofreading, publishing
- Improve composition skills, including developing plot, setting, character, and point of view
- Develop skill in taking notes and making outlines
- Write effective introductions and conclusions to reports and essays
- Use exact words
- Compile bibliographies
- Practice creative writing and thinking activities (including drama and art)

Core Area 6: Vocabulary
- Understand unfamiliar words from context clues
- Recognize blended words
- Use and understand idioms
- Investigate etymology and language history

Core Area 7: Reference and Study Skills
- Use reference sources such as the dictionary, thesaurus, encyclopedia, maps, and graphs
- Understand skimming and scanning
- Recognize the parts of a book
- Find information, take notes, and outline research

Core Area 8: Thinking Skills
- Practice critical thinking skills
- Recognize propaganda, contradictions, and faulty conclusions
- Make analogies

Core Area 9: Listening, Viewing, and Speaking Skills
- Follow directions and predict outcomes
- Recognize bias, point of view, and persuasive language
- Recognize ways in which messages are given nonverbally
- Make spoken announcements

Core Area 10: Literature/Reading
- Read and appreciate different types of literature
- Recognize elements of plot
- Recognize and understand point of view

- Notice writing techniques such as repetition and foreshadowing
- Understand the use of setting, symbol, conflict, climax, and resolution
- Identify the theme of a work of literature
- Recognize the use of irony and satire
- Discuss or write about reactions to literature

What's Taught in Grade Eight?

Building on what he learned in seventh grade and earlier, your child will meet these new skills and concepts in 8th grade as his teachers prepare him to enter high school at the end of the year.

Core Area 1: Language and Grammar
- Recognize phrases and clauses using participles, gerunds, and infinitives
- Work with restrictive and nonrestrictive clauses
- Work with noun, adjective, and adverb clauses
- Use verbals (participles, gerunds, infinitives) correctly
- Recognize the active and passive voices of verbs and use them in sentences
- Work with demonstrative, reflexive, and intensive pronouns
- Use relative pronouns correctly
- Use adverbial phrases and clauses

Core Area 2: Usage
- Use possessive nouns and pronouns with gerunds
- Place adjectives and adverbs correctly in a sentence

Core Area 3: Mechanics
- Use commas, colons, and semicolons in sentences
- Know the correct use of the hyphen, dash, and parentheses

Core Area 4: Spelling
- Review spelling guidelines for regular and irregular verbs

STOCK UP

Many times parents can find great learning games at Toys R Us or other children's retail outlets . . . but also check out educational supply stores. Most cities have them, and that's where teachers go to add extra resources to their lesson plans. Look in your yellow pages under "Educational Supplies" for the nearest outlets.

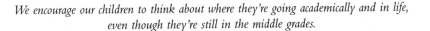

We encourage our children to think about where they're going academically and in life, even though they're still in the middle grades.

KEY CHOICE

When parents are choosing a school, they are not only choosing a principal, a school facility, and a faculty. They are also choosing classmates—and potential friends—for their child. Our study suggests that it may be this aspect of school choice—the choice of a peer group—that may be the most important, and that parents should keep this in mind when selecting a school for their child.
—from *Beyond the Classroom* by Laurence Steinberg, Ph.D. (Simon & Schuster, 1996)

Core Area 5: Composition
- Continue to develop writing skills in narrative, expository, and persuasive styles
- Develop skills in writing in other curriculum areas, such as science or history
- Write research reports, firsthand reports, and book reports
- Continue to develop skill in the writing process
- Write business and friendly letters and address envelopes correctly

Core Area 6: Vocabulary
- Write definitions of vocabulary words
- Continue work with roots, prefixes, and suffixes
- Investigate language history and etymology

Core Area 7: Reference and Study Skills
- Use library materials such as the card catalog, dictionaries, and encyclopedias
- Find and organize information for reports or test taking

Core Area 8: Thinking Skills
- Develop critical thinking skills such as sequencing, making analogies, and identifying cause and effect

Core Area 9: Listening, Viewing, and Speaking Skills
- Learn to listen and view critically and for information
- Deliver a speech with a purpose, such as giving instructions or telling a story
- Distinguish facts from opinions
- Make spoken announcements and introductions
- Follow parliamentary procedure in conducting a meeting

Core Area 10: Literature and Reading
- Recognize story elements such as setting, characters, plot, and theme
- Recognize the use of symbolic language
- Notice writing techniques such as foreshadowing, flashback, and rhythm

CHAPTER 7

What Language Arts Content Should I Review?

As you were reading the overview of what's taught in the Language Arts curriculum for grades seven and eight, most of it probably sounded familiar to you. The basic ingredients and structure of the English language don't change much, after all, even though they may be taught in different ways. But in the years since your own school days, the exact meanings of some terms and concepts have probably faded, leaving you a bit fuzzy on some of them. Here's a quick refresher in what those Language Arts terms and skills actually mean.

Core Area 1: Language and Grammar

This core area deals with some real basics of language—sentences, how they are constructed, and the words that make up sentences, called the "parts of speech." In 7th and 8th grade, the essential focuses are on reinforcing what kids already know about sentences and their structure, phrases and clauses, and parts of speech, especially verbs, pronouns, and conjunctions. Here we'll look at some grammar basics, just to review the concepts and the terminology.

Types of Sentences. Sentences are the basic building blocks of writing. Your young teen learns to recognize different kinds of sentences, which are named for what they do:

- *Declarative* sentences make a statement and end with a period.

HELPING KIDS LEARN

A huge thing *SCORE!* offers is our environment. It's not just our unique learning software system and the rewards of Score cards and basket shooting—it's the coaches too. We're the most important part of *SCORE!*. Fifty percent is academic and the rest is building kids' confidence and helping them learn from their mistakes and keep trying. We're there to help them every step along the way. Parents, too, can provide a positive "coaching" environment for their children and turn their home into a dynamic place for learning.

TIME FLIES

American youngsters spend far more time than students in other countries on nonacademic activities—such as part-time work, extracurricular activities, and socializing with friends—and far less time on school-related affairs, such as homework, studying, and reading. The ultimate source of our achievement problem may be how students spend their time out of school.
—from *Beyond the Classroom* by Laurence Steinberg, Ph.D. (Simon & Schuster, 1996)

TALK IT OVER

Parents always have to ask their children what they did in school, or their children just won't talk. They also just forget everything they did in school without being asked— they have too much on their minds. If you don't talk it over with them, then forget it!

- *Interrogative* sentences ask a question and end with a question mark.
- *Imperative* sentences give a command and end with a period or, sometimes, an exclamation point.
- *Exclamatory* sentences express strong emotion and end with an exclamation point.

Sentence Structure. Sentences are also classified on the basis of how they are put together:

- *Simple* sentences consist of one independent (main) clause and no other clauses.
- *Compound* sentences have two or more independent clauses, but no subordinate (dependent) clauses.
- *Complex* sentences have one independent clause and one or more subordinate (dependent) clauses.
- *Compound-complex* sentences have two or more independent clauses and at least one subordinate clause.

For more about independent and dependent clauses (main and subordinate clauses), see the section below on Clauses and Phrases.

Sentences have two basic parts: the *subject* and the *predicate.* The complete subject includes the word the sentence is about—a noun or pronoun—and all the words that accompany or modify it. The complete predicate includes all the words that say something about the subject's actions or state of being, whether that's running, thinking, or just existing in a certain time and place. Subjects and predicates can be as short as one word each, or they can be made up of many words. These two simple sentences have the same core subject and predicate: **Pavarotti** (subject) **sings** (predicate). OR Luciano **Pavarotti,** one of the world's most famous operatic tenors (subject), **sings** the title role in *Andrea Chenier,* an opera about the French Revolution, this season at the Metropolitan Opera in New York (predicate).

In the second simple sentence, all the words up through *tenors* are part of the complete subject. The rest are part of the complete predicate, telling where, when, and what the subject—Pavarotti—sings.

Parts of Speech. Within a sentence, individual words function as *parts of speech*, such as nouns and pronouns, verbs, adjectives, prepositions, and conjunctions. A quick review:

- *Nouns* name persons, places, things, and ideas. Pronouns (like *she, it, this, that*) replace nouns so that you don't have to repeat the noun.
- *Verbs* tell about an action or a state of being: *is, run, eat, seems, was talking, thought, will be coming.*

Modifiers are words and phrases that change, limit, or expand the meaning of other words. There are two kinds of modifiers:

- *Adjectives* modify nouns, offering descriptions of their color, size, mood, and other situations: *silver, happy, tall, angry, smooth, tree-lined, frightening, thoughtful.*
- *Adverbs* modify adjectives, verbs, or other adverbs. They give information such as how much or how many or simply how: *very, more, too, quickly, amazingly, slowly.* Many (but not all) adverbs end in *-ly.*

Prepositions and conjunctions are the glue and hooks that hold a sentence together. These small words are crucial in showing how the ideas within a sentence are related.

- *Prepositions* show how a noun or pronoun is related to other words in the sentence. Prepositions often refer to direction, or location, or time. They are always part of a phrase: *to* the lighthouse; *on* the counter in the store at the mall; *during* the winter of 1996.

- *Conjunctions* link words or groups of words together within the sentence (like the junction box where electrical wires come together): *When* the server came, I ordered cereal *and* skim milk, *although* I really wanted *either* waffles *and* maple syrup *or* bacon *and* eggs.

A final word of warning! In English, many words are versatile and can play different roles in a sentence. What part of speech any given word is often depends on how it is used in a sentence.

READ ALL ABOUT IT

Every parent would like to encourage her child to read more. Here are two books that fit the bill: *Hooked on Books!: Activities and Projects That Make Kids Love to Read* by Patricia Tyler Muncy and *Books on the Move: A Read-About It, Go-There Guide to America's Best Family Destinations* by Susan M. Knorr and Margaret Knorr. The first title has over 160 games, projects, and activities to help kids form a good reading habit. The second title helps parents and kids plan a weekend adventure, a quick day trip, or a long family vacation by taking an armchair tour of hundreds of great destinations across the United States (with hundreds of related children's books to read before, during, and after the trip). Contact Free Spirit Publishing at (800) 735-7323 or e-mail them at help4kids@freespirit.com

Making the Grade

Clauses and Phrases. Both clauses and phrases are groups of words that work as a single unit in a sentence. A *clause* is a group of words with a subject (noun or pronoun) and a predicate (a verb with its accompanying words). A *phrase* does not have a subject and predicate.

Let's look first at phrases. If you take apart any fairly long sentence, you're likely to find that it contains a number of phrases. Those phrases can be used as verbs, subjects, objects, or modifiers.

• *Prepositional phrases* begin with a preposition and usually end with a noun or pronoun. They're very common in sentences and most often used as adjectives or adverbs:

Look at that girl *with green hair!*
(prepositional phrase used as adjective, modifying *girl*)
Watch the sprinter come *around the curve.*
(prepositional phrase used as adverb, modifying *come*)

Other types of phrases are made with verb forms called *verbals.* They're a little less common in informal speech and writing and also slightly harder to use in sentences. Still, these kinds of phrases are very useful in good writing. Your youngster is likely to encounter them in 8th grade.

The three kinds of verbals are *participles, gerunds,* and *infinitives.* They are all forms of a verb. But while they do express action, they can't be used as the main verb in a sentence. Instead, verbals are used as nouns, adjectives, or adverbs, most often as part of a phrase.

Present participles are verb forms that end in *-ing*, while *past participles* commonly end in *-ed* or *-en.* Participles can be part of the verb in a sentence or clause: The band is *playing.* We *haven't eaten.*

Participles can also be used to make adverb or adjective phrases: *Sliding* into third base, the player was safe! *Nibbled* by the dog, the package of hamburger lay on the counter.

Participles can be used alone as adjectives, too: The *sliding* door tends to stick in hot weather. That restaurant is famous for its *singing* waiters.

A *gerund* looks just like a present participle—it's a verb form ending in *-ing*. However, a gerund is used only as a noun or as part of a noun phrase and follows some special rules.

> *Breaking up* is hard to do.
> *Meeting Superman* made Lois's dream come true. (gerund phrase)
> You can easily get there by *walking*.
> Jackson's *winning* the election was very controversial.
> (Notice that you use a possessive form with the gerund, as if it were any other kind of noun.)

The third kind of verbal is an *infinitive*, which usually starts with the word *to*. An infinitive is also usually used as a noun or part of a noun phrase, but it is sometimes an adjective or adverb.

> To *run* for the senate is Sara's ambition.
> Jeff is planning *to build* a new deck.

Dependent and Independent Clauses. Clauses, as we said earlier, have a subject and a verb. If the clause can be taken out of the sentence and stand alone as a separate sentence, it is an *independent* (or *main*) clause. If it can't, it is a *dependent* (or *subordinate*) clause. The following sentence is made up of two independent clauses joined by *but*, one of those vital little conjunctions: The pitcher threw a fast ball, *but* the batter swung and missed it.

Either of those clauses could stand alone as a sentence. But in the very similar sentence below, one clause is dependent and the other independent. Split the sentence at the comma, read the two halves aloud, and you'll see which is which: Although the pitcher threw an easy curve, the batter swung and missed.

Although the pitcher threw an easy curve . . . can't stand alone. It leaves the thought hanging in midair. You find yourself

YOUR RIGHTS AND RESPONSIBILITIES

Your involvement as a parent in a child's education takes many forms. From helping children with homework to attending school board meetings, your participation is important. One significant avenue for your involvement is through shared decision making, since this addresses the most basic elements of a child's school experience. As a parent, you should contribute to making decisions on issues affecting your childrens' education, health, and safety.

Parents have the *right* to
• Have a clear understanding of the processes to gain access to the appropriate school officials
• Participate in decisions that are made
• Appeal matters pertaining to your children

Parents have the *responsibility* to
• Know, help, and interact with your child's teachers and school administrators
• Communicate with and participate in the selection/election of school officials (e.g., school board members, superintendents, school councils)
—The National PTA®

Making the Grade

According to *Newsweek* magazine ("Standing Room Only," September 16, 1996), administrators and teachers are swamped trying to take care of a record 51.7 million elementary- and secondary-school students. These numbers top even the peak baby-boom years. The surging birth rates and immigration numbers are giving districts more students to cope with. Many voters are defeating school-construction bond issues, so students are learning in trailers, busing some kids to less crowded districts, and converting any available space into classrooms. In the West and Southeast United States, it's a problem finding enough teachers for the kids.

asking, "So? And then?" That makes it a dependent (subordinate) clause, something that needs another clause to support it and round out its meaning.

Within a sentence, dependent clauses can act as nouns, adjectives, or adverbs. In this next sample sentence, the italicized words are an *adverbial* clause telling *when*. Like an adverb, an adverbial clause can modify verbs, adjectives, or another adverb.

> The cruise ship will sail *when the tide turns*.

It's an adverbial clause that tells *when*. It modifies the verb *will sail*.

Restrictive and Nonrestrictive Clauses. There's another way of classifying clauses that your teen will learn about, probably in 8th grade. Some subordinate clauses are essential to the meaning of the sentence. They restrict the meaning. For instance: The book *that I lent you* is one of my favorites.

The clause *that I lent you* restricts the meaning to one specific book. Without that clause, the sentence doesn't mean the same thing. Therefore, that clause is essential or *restrictive*.

Other subordinate clauses add more information about the word they modify, but they don't really change or limit the meaning. For instance: The book, *which is by* Jane Austen, is one of my favorites.

Without that clause, the sentence still has basically the same meaning. The clause, though informative, is nonessential or *nonrestrictive*.

Pronouns. If it's been a while since you looked at English grammar, you may find it hard to believe that it's actually a lot simpler than the grammar of other languages. For instance, many world languages require you to change the endings of just about every noun, pronoun, and adjective depending on how they are used or where they occur in the sentence. Most English words, on the other hand, generally keep the same form everywhere. The meaning depends on word order within the sentence.

Pronouns, however, are the exception! Most of them do undergo some of those pesky grammatical changes, such as different forms for the subject—the "actor" in the sentence—and the object–the "acted on" in the sentence. Your 7th or 8th grader should be pretty clear about using subject and object pronouns (*I/me, we/us, who/whom*) correctly in writing. Still, she may come up with speech patterns that make you shudder, such as "Me and Julia are going to study together tonight." Students at this level learn about the various kinds of pronouns and their uses.

- *Relative pronouns* introduce subordinate (dependent) clauses. Relative pronouns are: *who, whom, which, that, whose.*
- *Demonstrative pronouns* point things out, making distinctions between things nearby and farther away. They also make distinctions in number: *this, that* (singular); *these, those* (plural).
- *Interrogative pronouns* are used in questions: *who, which, what, whom, whose.*
- *Reflexive/intensive pronouns*—the *-self* forms—either refer back to the subject or re-emphasize that the subject did the action:

> When Luca was shaving, he cut *himself*. (reflexive)
> Be sure the boss knows that I researched
> that report *myself*. (intensive)

Active and Passive Verbs. Verbs are words with a lot of different personalities. First, they have *tenses*—past, present, future, and some more complicated forms. But also, just like people, verbs have different *voices* and *moods*. Those are the aspects of verbs that your child is learning to recognize and use now.

A verb shows action, right? So how can a verb be *passive*? A *passive verb* (technically, a verb in "the passive voice") describes an action that happens to the subject, not an action that the subject does. A passive verb is constructed with a

MEGA DISTRICTS

The U.S. Department of Education, National Center of Education Statistics, lists the fastest-growing enrollments for school districts:

District	Increase	% Change
LA Unified (CA)	91,223	16.6%
NYC (NY)	87,163	9.5
Dade County (FL)	86,407	38.9
Broward Co. (FL)	64,118	51.0
Clark County (NV)	55,647	62.1
Palm Beach Co. (FL)	51,327	72.5
Gwinnett Co. (GA)	38,263	100.1
Orange Co. (FL)	34,893	44.3
Guilford Co. (NC)	30,214	124.7
Fresno Unified (CA)	27,127	55.1

SCHOOL OF LIFE

Education is really important, but the education life gives you is even more important. That's where my daughter will have to learn to communicate with people and to accept changes. I tell her to be somebody that can get along with others and strive hard in the areas of your choice.

FOR GOOD KIDS

Make sure to reward kids for being good. Good kids often receive no attention from their parents. If a child is acting up and you give him attention, that's a reward for negative behavior. Telling kids you think they're great and you're proud of them is so important. It's important to be recognized, and to take time out to do that.

VERBAGE

transitive verb: a verb that acts on an object; the action of the verb affects an object: The man *bit* the dog.

past participle and some form of *to be*. Compare these two sentences, the first active, the other passive.

> Thousands of protesters *stormed* the gates of the castle.
> (active voice)
> The castle gates *were stormed by* thousands of protesters.
> (passive voice)

The second sentence loses much of its liveliness, doesn't it? Sounds kind of stuffy. Any transitive verb can be passive, but why should it be? If you want your child to be a good writer, encourage him to avoid passive verbs.

The passive voice can sometimes be useful. Sometimes you don't know exactly who did an action or you don't care:

> The winners of Tuesday's elections *were announced* this morning.
> The road *was closed* for repairs.
> The town *was founded* in 1846.
> The manager of that department *has been promoted* often.

And sometimes you don't want to say who actually did something:

> It was *reported* that . . .
> Apparently a mistake *was made* in your order.

Progressive Form of Verbs. Your child has been working with various verb forms since the early grades. Something that may be new in grade seven or eight is the *progressive form*—a form that shows an ongoing or continuing action. It's made with the present participle—the *–ing* form of the verb—plus a form of the verb *to be*. There's a progressive form for every tense. (If you listen to yourself and others speak, you'll notice that Americans often use present progressive for many actions that occur in the present or the near future.) For example:

- I *am driving* to the store at 4:30 today. (present progressive)
- I *was driving* through that new subdivision yesterday when I saw a great house! (past progressive)

- I *have been driving* this make of car since I was a teenager. (present perfect progressive)

Conjunctions. Those useful little conjunctions are also divided according to the jobs they do in sentences. In grades seven and eight, students are expected to understand which kind to use in different sentence situations.

- *Coordinating conjunctions* such as *and, but, yet,* and *or/nor,* join elements—clauses, phrases, or words—that have equal weight or importance.
- Not surprisingly, *subordinating conjunctions* introduce elements that are of lesser weight—subordinate clauses, often adverbial. Common subordinating conjunctions include *although, since, until, unless, before,* and *while.*
- *Correlative conjunctions* come in pairs and link parallel elements: *either . . . or; neither . . . nor; both . . . and; not only . . . but also.*

Core Area 2: Usage

In the first core area, Language and Grammar, kids are concerned mainly with structure—how sentences are put together and the different elements that go into them. The core area of usage goes beyond that into the *right* ways to put sentences together and use language correctly. These skills are important in both speaking and writing.

Fragments and Run-on Sentences. Sentences are statements of a complete thought or action. Even a very short sentence can be a complete sentence if it has a subject (who or what is doing something) and a verb (a word telling the subject's action). *Chicago wins!* is about as short a sentence as you can have, but it is still a complete sentence.

In grades seven and eight, students are expected to recognize a statement that looks like a sentence but is actually a *fragment* or a *run-on* sentence.

- A *fragment* is just a piece of a sentence, often a stray phrase or a dependent clause (remember dependent clauses?), that starts a thought but doesn't complete it:

ALL IN THE FAMILY

Once people hear about such concepts as *family-like schools* or *school-like families,* they remember positive examples of schools, teachers, and places in the community that were "like a family" to them. They may remember how a teacher paid individual attention to them, recognized their uniqueness, or praised them for real progress, just as a parent might. Or they might recall things at home that were "just like school" and supported their work as a student, or they might remember community activities that made them feel smart or good about themselves and their families. They will recall that parents, siblings, and other family members engaged in and enjoyed educational activities and took pride in the good schoolwork or homework that they did, just as a teacher might.
—from "School/Family/Community Partnerships" by Joyce L. Epstein (*Phi Delta Kappan,* May 1995)

Making the Grade

USING THE TOOLS

Many newer reading and writing software programs give tools, but children have to figure out how to use them. Children are naturally active learners, and this is a plus when it comes to writing. Kids feel liberated at the computer. When they write a story by hand, much of their time and energy are spent on perfecting penmanship. Computers free them to concentrate more on the actual writing, according to Douglas H. Clements, a professor at the State University of New York at Buffalo, because pecking away at the keyboard can be less stressful than holding a pencil. The computer also allows kids to revise easily; they're less afraid to make mistakes and more likely to take some creative risks.
—from *Newsweek's Computers & the Family* newsmagazine (Fall/Winter 1996)

Whenever I see her.
Someone whom everyone liked and admired.

Other fragments are fragments because they use a verb form that isn't a main verb, such as a participle or an infinitive:

Traveling by train across the country (participle)
Jeff *to be* a good friend of all of us (infinitive)

• A *run-on sentence* is usually two sentences run together and separated by a comma rather than a period:

It's hard to decide about our vacation, there are
lots of places we'd like to visit.

Noticing and correcting fragments and run-ons is something your child ought to do as part of the process of editing papers and reports. Often the answer is to attach the fragment to a nearby sentence or to split the run-on or fix its punctuation. Here, for example, are some of the different ways that the sentence above can be corrected:

It's hard to decide about our vacation. There are
lots of places we'd like to visit.
It's hard to decide about our vacation; there are
lots of places we'd like to visit.
It's hard to decide about our vacation, because there are
lots of places we'd like to visit.

Using Correct Verb Tenses. The tenses of verbs indicate the time when the verb's action takes (or took) place. By now, kids know the six verb tenses and how they are formed (past, present, future; present perfect, past perfect, future perfect). In these grades, they need to become sensitive to making correct choices about which tenses to use in speaking and writing. Here's an example of the kind of exercise they may meet. A small shift in the tense of the verb gives these two sentences different meanings:

When the summer is over, Stan *will finish*
building the fence. (future tense)

When the summer is over, Stan *will have finished* building the fence. (future perfect tense)

Like all "perfect" tenses, the verb in the second sentence means that the action will be completed by the time mentioned. That is, Stan will do his building and get it done by the time the end of summer comes. In the first sentence, the action is still in the future. That is, Stan will do his finishing when the summer is over.

Here's another group of sentences with subtle verb tense changes:

I *worked* in Denver for four years. (past tense)
I *have worked* in Denver for four years. (present perfect tense)
I *had worked* in Denver for four years when I decided to move to California. (past perfect tense; another action or event has to be mentioned in order to complete the idea of this sentence)

Another idea that students meet at this level is that they should avoid unnecessary shifts in the tense of verbs within a sentence. In short, unless there's a real change in time, stick with one tense throughout a sentence.

Subject–Verb Agreement. Agreement between the subject of a sentence and its verb is another concern that continues from the earliest grades. Briefly, a singular subject takes a singular verb; a plural subject takes a plural verb. At these junior high grades, kids concentrate on some of the more difficult problems such as the following:

- Agreement when the word order in the sentence is interrupted or inverted
- Choosing the right verb for collective nouns such as *company* or *team* or *class*
- Choosing the right verb for indefinite pronouns such as *few, some, everybody,* and *someone*

Using Different Kinds of Pronouns. Pronouns, as you know, are sometimes tricky. As kids learn about different

WE'RE SORRY

My husband and I make mistakes sometimes, but we always apologize to our children and let them know that we're sorry. It's also part of being a good role model, acknowledging our errors. It allows them to understand that people are not always right and it's good to apologize.

CONTENT COUNTS

There are some great educational games and materials that you can load onto a home computer. Many of these can play the same way video games play, and they are so much more productive than *Mortal Kombat* or programs your child might be playing otherwise.

Making the Grade

TANGIBLE GOALS

We go to a Cal alumni camp, and all of the counselors are college students. They're great role models for my children. I take my son through the college campus where I went to school, I take him on the double-decker bus, show him the bowling alley, and all those fun things. It's motivating for him. He's also taking music lessons because he wants to be a local camp counselor; my son knows that they have to have a music background and be a university student. My husband and I helped set some goals with him that he's excited about.

STUDY BUDDIES

In *SCORE!*'s Study Skills class, we teach children general study skills, note taking, organization, report writing, and projects. We teach them right away how to go home and set up their desks. They need to have a dictionary and thesaurus on the desk and a writing resource book to help them in school projects.

kinds of pronouns—indefinite, interrogative, reflexive/intensive—they also learn to use them correctly. Two specific rules are useful:

- Pronouns must agree with their *antecedents*—the word that they replace and refer back to. They must agree both in number (singular or plural) and in gender (female or male).
- Demonstrative pronouns—those that point out something—must agree in number with the word to which they refer. *This* and *that* are singular. *These* and *those* are plural.

Choosing Pronoun Homophones. Some of the trickiest pronouns are those that sound alike—*homophones*—but have different spellings and meanings. Not only students, but also many adults mix these words up or spell them incorrectly. Here are some problem pairs:

- *whose* (possessive), *who's* (contraction of *who is*)
- *its* (possessive), *it's* (contraction of *it is*)
- *your* (possessive), *you're* (contraction of *you are*)
- *their* (possessive), *they're* (contraction of *they are*), *there* (adverb)
- *theirs* (possessive), *there's* (contraction of *there is*)

Using Problem Verbs. Certain verbs remain tricky even for the best educated people. Your child is no exception. In grades seven and eight, kids learn to make the distinction among problem verbs such as these:

- *lend/loan/borrow*
- *lie/lay*
- *sit/set*
- *accept/except*
- *rise/raise*
- *let/leave*
- *shall/will*
- *affect/effect*

Recognizing and Using Problem Words. Verbs are not the only tricky areas of word choice in speaking and writing. In grades seven and eight, kids learn about the differences and the correct usage for often mixed-up words such as these:

- *beside/besides*
- *good/well*
- *real/really*
- *many/much*
- *between/among*
- *less/fewer*
- *farther/further*

Correct Word Order. Stop and think for a minute about sentences in English—sentences that you say or write every day. How do you know what those sentences mean—who's doing the action, what the object of that action is? The answer is *word order*.

Many other languages depend, at least in part, on word endings that indicate whether a word is an object or a subject or what it modifies. But not English! English depends on word order—placing phrases and modifiers in the right place. This is a skill that becomes more important as children advance in school and begin to write more difficult papers and reports.

Word order generally is your best clue as to the subject, the verb, and the direct and indirect objects in a sentence. This comes quite naturally for native speakers of English. Here's the typical word order for some ordinary English sentences:

> Gloria hit the ball.
> The cat chased the mouse.
> I will read the paper.
> Madame Curie won the Nobel Prize.

All of those sentences follow a simple pattern: subject, verb, direct object—something receives the action of the verb. If there is an indirect object, it also has a place in normal word order:

> The coach handed *Jimmy* the towel.

Jimmy is the indirect object, while the towel is the direct object. You can usually check out an indirect object by trying the word *to* in front of it. That is, he handed the towel *to* Jimmy; he didn't hand Jimmy to the towel.

STRATEGIZE LEARNING

Make education fun and exciting, not "Oh, do I really have to study those words again?" Make your child excited about her teacher at school. You can be negative about the teacher, but you have to curb it in front of your child. When you're negative, your child becomes negative. And be open to hearing your child's complaints and negativity because she may have a valid problem that needs to be addressed. When your child shares with you what she's learning in school, tell her how exciting that is and how proud you are about what she's doing.

DIGGING DEEPER

The things that your child learns in school could send him to the library every day after school—he might be able to learn something new in school each day and have fun looking into it more. That's a great activity for you and your child to do together.

TIME TO READ

Read to your children and make the reading time together very enjoyable. We all sit together as a family and make the reading time fun and dramatic. We also make a big deal about new vocabulary words that we come across. We also provide workbooks for our children to use, and sometimes we share them with their teachers to show the children's progress.

GOOD JUDGMENT

Just as parents are best suited to selecting reading materials for their own children, they can exercise similar judgment as regards educational computer content. Remember: Focus on the content, not the technology. If you're the kind of parent who buys beautiful picture books and illustrated guides to wholesome educational activities for your child, there is some beautiful interactive content available for use on your computer. On the other hand, if you are the kind of parent who tolerates your child's reading comic books, watching lots of TV, and playing mindless, repetitive games, there is an astonishing variety of computer-based material to choose from.

Because we're used to how word order works in English, the meaning of those sentences is clear. Putting the words in a different order could reduce the sentence to nonsense.

Here's a slightly different word order pattern:

> The book is new.
> Fred is my brother.

The words following the verb in those examples are not objects, because they are not receiving any action. The first is an adjective describing the subject, the second a noun referring to (renaming) the subject. Because they're in the predicate, these words are called either a "predicate adjective" or a "predicate nominative" (noun). They are called *complements*. Complements occur only with verbs known as *linking verbs*, verbs such as *is* or *seems* or *appears*. Such verbs show a state of being, rather than action.

Word order for modifiers (adjectives, adverbs, and prepositional phrases and clauses) offer more flexibility. One good general rule to remember is: Keep the adverb, adjective, or phrase as close as possible to the word it modifies (describes). In this sentence, for example, moving the adverb *recently* can cause confusion.

> *Recently*, I heard that their house had been sold.
> I heard *recently* that their house had been sold.
> I heard that their house had *recently* been sold.
> I heard that their house had been sold *recently*.

So, what's the story? Did I hear this news recently? That's what the first two sentences say. Or did it happen recently? That's the meaning of the second two sentences, in which the adverb is closer to the verb *had been sold*. Only careful placement of the adverb can make that meaning clear.

Core Area 3: Mechanics

This core area, which focuses on capitalization and punctuation, becomes very important when your student is editing, proofreading, and correcting papers. By grades seven and eight, kids are doing quite a lot of writing, not only in English classes but also in other curriculum areas.

Capitalization. Kids learned about capitalizing the first words of sentences, quotations, and the like some years ago. They've been taught the rules for using capital letters for *proper nouns*—the names of specific people, places, or things—and for *proper adjectives*, the adjectives derived from proper nouns. (There are some variations, even among dictionaries and style experts, about capitalizing certain kinds of proper names, such as "the president" when referring to the president of the United States. Your child's teacher will probably have chosen a style guide or rule book to follow.)

Here are examples of capitalization for proper and common nouns and adjectives: *Common nouns* are general nouns that do not name a specific person, place, or thing. They are not capitalized: a country, the country of Italy, an Italian wine; a continent, Europe, a European vacation; the college, but Wheaton College; a river, but the Allegheny River; an army general, but General Colin Powell; the park, but Yellowstone National Park; a state, but the State of Arizona.

Correct capitalization for titles of books, movies, songs, TV shows, poems, etcetera; words of greeting and closing in letters; writing outlines; and writing bibliography references are also expected in 7th and 8th grade.

Punctuation. Learning correct punctuation also continues throughout the middle school or junior high language arts curriculum. Students will have gotten beyond the basics of end punctuation (period, question mark, exclamation point). They should be fairly adept at putting quotation marks in the right places and need to punctuate sentences using the comma (,), colon (:), and semicolon (;) and to use hyphens (-), dashes (—), and parentheses ( ) correctly.

Here are some of those uses, keeping in mind that the rules for commas, in particular, are quite complex:

IN A JAR

Why say *pale* when you can say *etiolated*? Is a cow a *grass-eating animal* or a *graminovorous beast*? *Wondrous Words in a Jar* by Deborah Stein is a plastic jar filled with 365 fortune-cookie slips of colored paper, each with unusual words and definitions. Pull out a new word each day with your child, and you'll liven your speech, build up a distinctive vocabulary, and have a terrific home-learning day-starter. Other *In a Jar* products include *Riddles in a Jar, Curiosity in a Jar, Attitude in a Jar,* and *Inventions in a Jar.* Contact Free Spirit Publishing at (800) 735-7323 or e-mail them at help4kids@freespirit.com

Making the Grade

YOU'RE INTERESTED

At *SCORE!*, we tell our children that we're really interested in what they're studying in school, and set up an expectation that what's going on in school *will* be talked about. Parents can set up that same situation at home. Make it clear that if they need any help, your child can always come to you—you will be involved in their learning process. The more you can reinforce and reiterate that, like scheduling a check-in each day, the better it will be.

Don't fall back on the attitude that your child's school will do everything, so you can fall back on them to get the job done. You can't know what's going on at school and not get involved in your children's learning at home—the two must go hand in hand. Get your child intrinsically motivated to communicate with you about school. Make talking about school part of your home culture.

- Use *commas* to set off words or phrases that interrupt the main sentence, such as words in direct address, appositives, and nonrestrictive phrases or clauses:

> Yes, Virginia, there is a Santa Claus. (*direct address*)
> Ms. Watters, the mayor of the city, spoke at the luncheon. (*appositive*, a noun or noun phrase that explains the words beside it—a common mistake is to forget the commas that close the appositive)
> Next weekend, which is the Fourth of July, is also the start of my vacation. (*nonrestrictive clause*)
> The Gothic mansion, standing on a hill, loomed over the small village. (*nonrestrictive phrase*)

- Use *commas* to separate clauses in a complex sentence and to set off longish introductory phrases.
- Use *commas* to separate dates and years (April 18, 1775); to separate words in a series (*lions, tigers, and bears*); and to separate city, state, and country (*Cleveland, Ohio; Nairobi, Kenya*).
- A *semicolon* provides a more emphatic break than a comma and less emphatic than a period. It may be needed to separate parts of a compound sentence or between independent clauses. A semicolon can also be used for clarity between items in a series if those items contain commas.
- Use a *colon* after the greeting in a business letter (*Dear Ms. Reed:*), to separate minutes and hours (*11:45 A.M.*), and to introduce lists (*. . . answer the following questions:*).
- A *hyphen* (-) is used with some prefixes (*ex-husband*) and in spelled-out compound numbers (*twenty-one*) and some compound adjectives (*rose-colored* glasses). Hyphens also divide a word at the end of a line.
- A *dash* (—) indicates a sharp break in thought. Teenagers usually overuse them!
- *Parentheses*, which always come in pairs, set off side remarks, examples, or other information that could be removed without changing the sentence structure or basic meaning.

Core Area 4: Spelling

While some people are naturally good spellers, others have trouble with this core area. For those who do have trouble with spelling, there are some helpful tricks and techniques. And in all cases, your child benefits from having a dictionary handy—and using it! Help your kid acquire the same habit of looking up words when necessary.

Roots Sometimes knowing a word's basic origins, or root, can help both in getting the letter patterns of the correct spelling and in remembering its meaning. For example, the Latin root *aud* relates to *hearing*. That spelling pattern occurs in words such as *audio, auditorium, inaudible*. The Greek roots *astro* and *aster* mean *star*. They give you the spelling patterns for *astronomy, asterisk, asteroid*, and even *disaster* (when the stars are really unfavorable).

Prefixes and Suffixes. Similarly, prefixes—word elements that precede a root—can help with both spelling and learning vocabulary. Recognizing prefixes helps in deciding when to double a consonant, as in *interrupt* (*inter,* "between" + *rupt,* "break") or *misspell* (*mis,* "wrong" + *spell*). If you know that the prefix *dis-* means "not," you can figure out that *disagree* (*dis + agree*) has only one *s*, while *dissatisfied* (*dis + satisfied*) has two.

Suffixes—elements that go at the end of a word—are equally useful in guiding spelling and helping to derive meaning. For instance, knowing that the suffix *-cy* means "state" or "condition" can help you spell *accuracy* with a *c*, not an *s*. Knowing the suffix *-ize,* which implies "causing to be," gives you the accurate spellings of words such as *mobilize, criticize,* and *sterilize*.

Core Area 5: Composition

Various kinds of compositions and creative writing are important at every stage of the language arts program. Kids study both the art and craft of writing, from sentence and paragraph structure to a wide variety of written forms. Here are some of the principal emphases in grades seven and eight.

MEDIA INFLUENCES

Monitor media influences on your children that are within your control. Forbid certain programming if necessary or "talk back" to your radio and television when media depict a lack of respect for life and property and use foul language. Do not give your children the impression you approve of or tolerate behavior that is inconsistent with your own family values and beliefs.
—The National PTA®

POCKET PAL

Ask at your bookstore for one of those great little, pocket-sized speller's books. American Heritage's version is called *Word Book II*. The whole family will be glad you did.

NET NECESSITIES

I think parents need to set limits, particularly with tools like the Internet. Children are naturally curious. We've sat down and talked about things we've read about regarding the Internet and how she needs to be careful. I've told her to let her mom know whom she's writing to. Parents have to let go of their children a little bit so they can learn, but children need to know they can't surf certain areas. I also won't leave her totally alone. I'll go in periodically and check up on her and see what she's doing. I also set up time limits with her too. "First you have to do your homework, then you have 20 minutes for going on the Internet."

Sentences and Paragraphs. Students learn to organize research papers and develop paragraphs from notes and outlines. They write topic sentences, choose details, and organize their presentation. They learn to vary sentence structure in writing.

Types of Writing. Even in early grades, kids write stories, poetry, reports, and in journals. By this level, they are working with a wide variety of writing forms:

- Personal narratives
- Expository writing using techniques of cause and effect, comparing/contrasting, giving instructions
- Persuasive essay or letter
- Book reports
- Firsthand or research reports
- Poetry
- Journal writing
- Writing about art and literature
- Write business and friendly letters
- Address envelopes correctly

Writing Across the Curriculum. Another area of language arts that gets increasing attention is that of students applying their writing abilities and techniques in other areas of study. Many crosscurricular programs pay specific attention to writing as it is used in social studies, math, science, music, health, geography, history, speech, economics, and a number of other areas.

Follow the Steps of the Writing Process. This process has become the main framework for teaching students to write. It follows these steps:

- *Prewriting*—These are the processes that precede putting words on paper, including brainstorming, making lists, choosing a topic, pinpointing the audience, doing research, and making an outline.
- *Writing a first draft*
- *Revising/editing*—In this important stage of the writing process, student writers have a chance to overhaul their manuscript. They may add details, change the introduction

and ending, revise sentences to give more variety, and refine the use of words and choose more exact words.

- *Proofreading*—At this stage, writers check spelling, punctuation and capitalization, and other mechanics. They do a final check of grammar and usage.
- *Publishing*—In this step, your child chooses how to present the material, whether in manuscript, on computer disk, as an audiovisual presentation, or in another form.

Improve Research and Composition Skills. Kids continue to work on writing skills, including developing plot, setting, character, and point of view. Here are other specific skills practiced in these years:

- Develop skill in taking notes and making outlines
- Write effective introductions and conclusions for reports and essays
- Use exact words
- Compile bibliographies
- Practice creative writing and thinking activities (including drama and art)
- Develop writing skills in narrative, expository, and persuasive styles

Core Area 6: Vocabulary

Expanding and building vocabulary continues from kids' earliest experiences with language. These are some of the techniques used in 7th and 8th grade language arts.

Context Clues. Probably the most common way of dealing with an unfamiliar word is to try to get its meaning from the words around it—from its context. Useful as this technique is, it can sometimes lead kids (and adults, too!) to go on misunderstanding a word's real meaning for years and years. Stopping to look up every unfamiliar word effectively kills any pleasure and enjoyment in reading. Still, at the end of a chapter or section, it's a good idea to check up on those word meanings you guessed at.

Etymology and Language History. Just as understanding base words, roots, prefixes, and suffixes can help with spelling, those aspects of a word can be even more

TOGETHERNESS

We've got a crazy lifestyle. I admit that my kids have done their homework in the car, en route to places. But my thing is, as long as we're together, it doesn't matter where we're at. I know there are certain areas and conditions where it would be better for them to do their homework, but right now, we have to do what we do, and we do it as a family. If I can't help one child with schoolwork, then my husband helps out while I'm with the other child. We do a lot of back and forth, and we let the girls interact with each other. Sometimes we throw out a topic, like one child has to write a creative writing story. So we brainstorm together. Our younger child can brainstorm right along with our older one. Once we were all looking together for pictures in magazines of objects that began with the letter V. Homework is important, it has to get done, and we do it together.

LOVE THE ATTENTION

When I was growing up, I used to ask my dad, "Dad, what does this word mean?" and he always replied, "Look it up! Look it up!" That wasn't fun. I wish it would have been something we could have done together: "Well let's go look that up together, son." It would have been a good learning experience for both of us. At *SCORE!*, I see that most children love adult attention. Raising kids takes so much time, and sometimes society is overly harsh with parents. It's a rough job—you work then you go home. Parenting takes a lot of time and patience. But developing this attitude of "let's do this together" with your child will make a big difference. "Let's explore this together" will set a good example with children.

useful in determining at least the approximate meaning of unfamiliar words. For instance, you know that the Latin root *culp* has something to do with fault or blame, as in culprit. In reading, you come across the term *culpable.* Putting together the root *culp* + the suffix *-able,* meaning "likely or able," you figure out that it means something like "at fault." (Then you can also use the word's context to see whether that meaning makes sense.)

Getting word meanings from their structure and etymology—their historical derivation—can be fun and challenging, but it has the same limitations as getting meanings from context. It's always a good idea to double-check with the dictionary for accuracy.

Blended Words. New ideas and developments sometimes demand new words to describe them. Advertising and public relations people are responsible for inventing some of these words; others spring out of popular culture to become part of the accepted language.

New words are often *blended words,* created by combining two words—and their meanings—and dropping some of the middle letters. Here are some common blended words:

* *brunch* = breakfast + lunch
* *motel* = motor + hotel
* *telethon* = television + marathon
* *splatter* = splash + spatter

Defining Vocabulary Words. Middle school students often are asked to write definitions of vocabulary words or key terms from other subject areas, such as science and social studies. They are encouraged both to write their own definitions and to use the words properly in the context of sentences. They are expected to know the meaning and use of each element in a dictionary definition (pronunciation, part of speech, multiple meaning, examples, and synonyms).

Core Area 7: Reference and Study Strategies

Throughout succeeding years of the Language Arts curriculum, students are exposed to an increasingly more sophisticated group of techniques and skills for gathering and using information. These skills are essential in the later school years as kids are expected to write research reports, evaluate information, summarize data, and learn techniques for taking tests.

Use Reference Sources. By middle school, your teenager should be able to use these four information-gathering techniques:

- Use alphabetical order and guide words to find entries in the dictionary, encyclopedia, and other resource volumes, and understand the meaning, etymology, syllabication, and pronunciation of words
- Use a thesaurus to locate and select appropriate and exact words, synonyms, and antonyms
- Use indexes and other aids to gather material from encyclopedias and other library resources
- Read and interpret information from maps, charts, and graphs

Use Library Resources. Kids should be familiar with school and public libraries and their resources. They learn to use card catalogs (whether printed or computerized) and to find a book on the shelves by using the call numbers given in the catalog.

Use Skimming and Scanning. Students learn to get information efficiently by skimming through the heads and subheads in a reference work to see whether it contains the desired information. They scan text quickly to see whether it is relevant to their subject, rather than spending time on irrelevant material.

Utilize the Parts of a Book. Most nonfiction and informational books, including textbooks, contain information beyond the main text. Students learn to use the

WRITING TOOL

Explore *Write Source 2000: A Guide to Writing, Thinking, and Learning.* This is a clever school and home resource for "writers and students of all ages," written and compiled by Patrick Sebranek, Verne Meyer, and Dave Kemper (D.C. Heath & Co.), available at bookstores or by calling (800) 235-3565 (then press 5). *Write Source 2000* covers everything from managing time, writing letters, spelling, and types of sentences to facts about the world, maps, atlas material, and other resources to use for writing. And it has tons of writing ideas and story starters.

STUDENT REFERENCE LIBRARY

Many students want to dig deeper and learn more for their creative writing and school research papers. For younger students, there's a need for a tool that parents and children can use together to explore any subject. Mindscape's *Student Reference Library* combines a lot of writing and research resources for students, plus other multimedia helps, into one CD-ROM: an encyclopedia, dictionary, thesaurus, manual of style, U.S. history guide, famous quotes, atlas, photos, maps, videos, animations, audio, and a Lycos search feature (hooking up with your Web browser) on the World Wide Web. Contact Mindscape at (800) 234-3088.

index and table of contents to locate information within the book. They also learn to find information on the title and copyright pages and in the appendix, bibliography, and glossary if a book has them.

Find and Organize Information. Students are expected not only to find and organize material for reports, but also to look at it critically. Some of the skills involved include these seven:

- Find and narrow a research report topic (Increasingly this includes the ability to seek information online.)
- Evaluate the material found, looking for bias or propaganda techniques
- Take notes from reference materials
- Organize notes and information into an outline
- Write a paragraph based on the outline
- Classify, compare, and contrast
- Apply research and reference material to test taking

Core Area 8: Thinking Skills and Strategies

Today's teaching techniques, in all subject areas, place great emphasis on developing thinking skills and strategies. These are some of the approaches to reading and analyzing material that middle school students are asked to use:

Ways of Thinking. The following six ways of working on problems and issues are learned about and practiced by youngsters in these years.

- Develop ideas through brainstorming
- Recognize cause-and-effect relationships
- Make generalizations backed by specific information
- Make analogies, look for ways in which different things have similar elements
- Use visualizing and creative thinking
- Study and appreciate works of art

Critical Thinking. Similarly, students hone six skills of analysis, skills that emphasize the importance of not being fooled by the language of others. They are expected to:

- Determine the accuracy and reliability of material
- Recognize contradictions within material
- Identify vague, overly general statements
- Recognize assumptions and identify questionable assumptions
- Identify fallacies in logic and faulty conclusions
- Recognize exaggerations

Core Area 9: Listening, Viewing, and Speaking Skills and Strategies

Many otherwise excellent students have trouble taking in spoken, rather than written, information. Modern communications, however, make skills in listening and speaking very important. From early grades, kids learn to listen to spoken material in order to get the main idea and details, to discover the speaker's purpose. They learn to listen for specific techniques used by a speaker. They also learn how to listen to stories and poetry for enjoyment. In 7th and 8th grade, these are some of the specific listening and speaking skills your kid may be asked to practice and master.

Listening and Viewing. These skills are key not only to your child's success in school (and in future work and interpersonal relations) but are recognized as necessary in preparing children for our media-dominated world. Skills they work on in reading are also important in the nonwritten aspects of language arts. For instance, listening and viewing are key to:

- Get instructions and follow directions
- Predict outcomes
- Distinguish fact from opinion
- Recognize persuasive language and images and ways speakers signal their ideas and intentions

In these grades, you can expect your child to need to take notes from a lecture or audio-visual presentation.

Speaking. These years also tend to offer increased opportunity for developing speaking skills. Here are some of the things your child may be expected to do.

ACTION!

There are parents who try to work with their kids at home, and they read to their kids and they make an effort to point out numbers, but we recommend that parents encourage kids to be more active—children can read to the parent, children can sound out the words themselves, and children can add the different prices at the store.

NEW LINGO

Parents should start kids young with learning a foreign language. Try to find programs in your community that don't just work out of textbooks, conjugating verbs and turning language into something bone dry. At *SCORE!*, we set up something like an acting class and Spanish comes alive with props, games, repetition, and singing. After only a week of this exposure, it's amazing the vocabulary words kids can pick up and the excitement they have for a new language.

REWARDS

Good behavior and good results, like an A in school, don't have to be rewarded with material things like ice cream cones. The positive talk from a parent is often a strong reinforcer, and children are hungry for the recognition. The memories that last are usually tied in to the nonmaterial rewards. "I remember when I tried really hard to learn something, and I did it, and my mom told me that she was really proud of me!"

- Make spoken announcements and introductions
- Deliver a speech with a purpose, such as giving instructions or telling a story
- Give a play reading
- Deliver an oral report or review
- Discuss writing and literature
- Conduct an interview
- Follow parliamentary procedure in participating in a meeting

Core Area 10: Literature and Reading

In the language arts curriculum, literature and reading have an importance far beyond simply comprehending and enjoying the written word. Many programs are now "literature based," meaning that literature serves as the launching place not only for reading but also for writing, listening, speaking, developing vocabulary, and other creative activities.

Read and Appreciate Different Types of Literature. From the early grades, kids have been reading different types of fiction and nonfiction. Recognition of specific genres (types of literature) and what makes them special becomes a part of 7th and 8th grade reading as they read and discuss:

- Fiction, including folklore, novels, excerpts from novels, and short stories
- Nonfiction, including biography, essay, informational articles, and expository writing (writing that instructs or explains)
- Letters and journals
- Plays and poetry

Recognize Techniques in Literature. Appreciating a work of literature (including film and plays) takes many different skills. In most language arts programs, students are asked to develop skills in recognizing and appreciating many elements of a work of literature, including the following:

- Recognize elements of *plot*, the work's story line.
- Tracing the plot also involves identifying the *conflict*—the

problem that drives the story. Students should be able to identify the *climax* of the plot—the turning point—and the *resolution*—the ending in which the author solves the conflict and ties up the loose ends.

- Recognize and understand *point of view*. In fiction, *point of view* represents the "eyes" and "voice" through which the story is told. It may be that of one person who sees and tells only his or her part of the story, or of several characters who give alternating points of view, or of an omniscient narrator who knows what is going on in all the characters' minds. In nonfiction, students learn to identify the perspective and intention that the writer has regarding his or her subject. This may relate to critical thinking skills such as recognizing bias.

- Recognize and identify the *characters* in a work of fiction or biography. Students should identify both major and minor characters and identify the part they play in advancing the narrative.

- Understand the use of *setting*. When and where a story takes place is not only necessary to understand the plot, it can affect the mood and the action; it can sometimes set the tone for an entire work.

- Identify the *theme* of a work of literature. Every work of literature has a theme, often several important themes. Common and familiar themes like "crime does not pay," "greed is ultimately self-destructive," and "love conquers all" can be treated in ways that are corny or sublime, depending on the quality of the literature.

- Recognize the use of *symbols* and symbolic language. Often a writer uses an object—say, a flower or bird or images of light and dark—to reinforce the themes of a work of literature. Understanding these can be crucial in understanding the work.

- Recognize ways authors use *imagery*—words that appeal to the senses of sight, hearing, taste, touch, and smell to make their work more effective.

- Recognize a writer's use of *figurative language,* such as vivid comparisons.

- Notice writing techniques such as *foreshadowing* and *flashback.* With these, an author plays games with time. In foreshadowing, the author gives subtle hints about plot developments that will come later. With flashbacks (a

WORTH NOTING

Most students don't learn how to use notecards in school for making book reports and research, and it's something that really kills them in school later on. Even though they're doing outlines in school, something's still not clicking mentally for them. Have your child plan ahead and help budget her time for making reports. Teach her to use notecards to jot down notes and quotes as she does her reading. Help her label notecards and show her how to lay them out on the floor and play around with them to organize the outline. Some students really get the hang of this skill in high school, but it's much better to start earlier!

CAST YOUR NETS

Parents can use other parents as models to help them bring effective learning into the home. Take examples from others. Use what you have on hand, and create a network of resources you can use. You might find some amazing tips that will help you.

CRITICAL VIEWING SKILLS

Set rules for TV viewing and adhere to those rules. Set a weekly limit for the amount of time children are permitted to watch television. At the start of each week, help your children select the programs or videotapes they want to watch. When the selected program is over, turn the television off and get involved in another activity.

Turn what you see on television into positive and educational family discussions and activities. Television can inspire creativity and educate and inform children and youth. When a topic on television sparks your child's interest, go to the library or museum and explore the subject further.
—The National PTA®

familiar technique in film), the writer gives brief scenes from the past that explain present developments.

- Notice writing techniques such as *repetition* and *rhythm*. Students are expected to be sensitive to the sounds of language, even in written works. Most writers, in addition to poets, use repeated words or sounds to achieve effects in mood, tone, and effect.
- Recognize techniques of *satire* and *irony*. In satire, the author uses humor and wit to make fun of an idea, behavior, or set of values. Irony is saying something, but meaning the opposite.

Understand and Respond to Literature. Seventh and eighth graders are asked to show their comprehension of literature in understanding its literal meanings, making inferences, and thinking critically. They apply the various types of thinking skills, particularly in dealing with nonfiction and informative writing. Kids are asked to respond to the works of literature they have read by discussing them, writing personal responses, and writing creatively about their reading. They are also asked to share books that they have enjoyed through book reports and to read on their own.

CHAPTER 8

What's My Child Studying in Math?

The elementary mathematics curriculum is designed around the essential math concepts and skills that are the foundation of all mathematics. Students in 7th and 8th grade learn from many of the same topic areas that they studied in earlier grades.

Eight Core Math Areas. The following eight core subject areas form the basis of most schools' elementary mathematics curriculum:

1. Numeration (numbers and counting)
2. Computation (addition, subtraction, multiplication, and division)
3. Geometry and Measurement (two- and three-dimensional shapes, area, volume, and units of measure)
4. Fractions, Decimals, and Percents
5. Graphing (bar graphs, pie charts)
6. Statistics and Probability
7. Problem Solving (solving word problems, estimation, spatial reasoning, recognizing patterns, experimenting and inventing new strategies, and other analytical skills)
8. Algebra

What's Taught in Grade Seven?

In grade seven, students typically see something new and many things that are old. Your child will extend his knowledge of our number system by studying rational numbers, numbers that can be represented by decimals and

NEW MATH

If parents are helping children with their math homework, they should have their kids articulate in their own words what the question is, and after they come up with the answer, to then explain how they figured it out. I did this with my dad when I was studying algebra in seventh grade. I was trying to figure it out, and when I finally did, it was a moment of elation for me—one of the best memories I had as a child.

FAMILY MATH

Family Math by Stenmark, Thompson, and Cossey (Creative Publications) has activities designed for special hands-on math sessions for parents and children grades K through 8. It includes material on counting, logic, measurement, probability, time and money, geometry, patterns, and much more. The Creative Publications catalog also contains a host of math games, manipulatives, books, colorful posters, and other math materials. Call (800) 357-MATH for a catalog.

fractions. (Oh, yes, he hasn't seen the last of those!) In addition, your 7th grader will learn about different kinds of exponents and will study scientific notation. He will solve inequalities, which are sort of like equations without the equal sign.

Most of your child's year will be spent strengthening what he already knows by using his skills in new settings. For example, he will use his equation-solving skills to solve more complicated equations. Your 7th grader also will study more involved functions, such as quadratic and nonlinear functions. Geometry and graphing typically are covered extensively in grade seven. Your child will use his knowledge of angles to construct and classify triangles, and he will learn more about polygons. He will also construct many kinds of graphs including graphs of inequalities and nonlinear equations, double-line graphs, histograms, box-and-whisker plots, and other graphs.

The following outline represents the content of the typical 7th grade math curriculum. Since each district designs its program of study to meet the needs of the local community, this summary may not describe your child's mathematics curriculum precisely. These topics are organized according to these eight core areas of the elementary mathematics curriculum. For descriptions of the topics and skills, refer to the next chapter.

Core Area 1: Numeration
• Identify and write rational numbers
• Compare and order rational numbers
• Read and write numbers with negative exponents
• Study zero exponents
• Use scientific notation
• Study absolute value

Core Area 2: Computation
• Add and subtract rational numbers
• Multiply and divide rational numbers

Core Area 3: Geometry and Measurement
- Construct triangles
- Identify and classify isosceles, equilateral, and scalene triangles
- Use the Pythagorean Theorem
- Find the area and perimeter of a polygon
- Identify corresponding, vertical, and adjacent angles
- Find the surface area of a pyramid
- Study and identify a tessellation

Core Area 4: Fractions, Decimals, and Percents
- Find a number when the percent is known

Core Area 5: Graphing
- Graph an inequality on a number line
- Read and graph double-line graphs
- Read and graph histograms
- Read and graph box-and-whisker plots
- Graph a nonlinear equation

Core Area 6: Statistics and Probability
- Learn about and use quartiles
- Study random numbers
- Explain independent, dependent, and complementary events
- Make frequency tables

Core Area 7: Problem Solving
- Solve problems involving rational numbers
- Solve problems involving scientific notation

Core Area 8: Algebra
- Solve equations using two steps
- Solve inequalities
- Study quadratic and other nonlinear functions
- Use functional notation
- Study other sequences, such as Fibonacci sequences

What's Taught in Grade Eight?

Grade eight mathematics introduces a number of new concepts, and it revisits and extends some old concepts

STUMPED?

A *SCORE!* Coach is a pretty special person. We've all done some amazing things with our lives. But to be expected to know everything, like the material our children learn in our centers—particularly some of the math!—is asking way too much of anybody. But we know the importance of saying to children whenever we're stumped, "Hey, let's try to figure this one out together."

I'm happy to tell that to parents too. Parents should tell their kids, "I don't know everything. That's what learning is all about. We learn every day." Parents can remind kids that learning happens every day, and it continues to happen once we leave school. You probably learn even more outside of school because you've got your basics down. Build your child's confidence *now* to prepare him for a lifetime of learning.

Making the Grade

HANDS-ON MATH

My son is quite challenged in math. He's not bad in math, actually—he got an A! He just lacks confidence. Hands-on experience is probably better than other forms of learning for him. When he was young, we counted out M&Ms, and we played with sticks that were different measurements. Now we work with geometry boards, tesselation kits and pattern blocks, and other manipulatives and math models to really drive the learning home.

LEARNING EVENTS

Learning moments between parents and children should become learning events. "We're going to work on solving algebra equations," and make it an event. Then when your child masters algebra equations, it's like it's up on a billboard for kids: "This is what I can do!" When a kid can say, "I can do Venn diagrams," that should become an event too. And so on and so on.

covered in grade seven. The goal at this grade is to consolidate all the knowledge students have gained in their previous school years in order to prepare them for introductory algebra in grade nine. The new concepts your child will probably encounter are irrational numbers, real numbers, inequalities in two variables, systems of equations, some new functions, and sets. Old concepts he will learn more about this year include exponents and graphing.

In grade eight, your child will extend his understanding of the number system to include both real numbers (the group of all the numbers he has learned up to now) and irrational numbers (such as square roots). In addition, your 8th grader will learn how to graph inequalities in two variables, and he will solve and graph systems of equations, that is, equations taken two at a time.

Your child will learn some new functions—the sine, cosine, and tangent functions—that are based on some ratios of the sides of a triangle. If these functions are unfamiliar to you, your reading of the next chapter will offer help in understanding them. Take heart, though—many parents possess rusty math skills!

Graphing plays an important role in this grade. Your child will twist and turn graphs in many different directions. He will translate, reflect, and rotate a given graph. In addition, he will shrink and stretch graphs (also called dilations). Finally, your 8th grader will learn about sets, that is, things taken as groups.

The following outline represents the content of the typical 8th grade mathematics curriculum. As noted earlier, each district designs its program of study to meet the needs of the local community, so this summary may not describe your child's mathematics curriculum precisely. The topics are organized here according to the eight core areas of the elementary mathematics curriculum. For descriptions of the topics and skills, refer to the next chapter.

What's My Child Studying in Mathematics?

Core Area 1: Numeration
- Identify and write irrational numbers
- Study real numbers
- Use the laws of exponents

Core Area 2: Computation
- Add and subtract irrational numbers
- Multiply and divide irrational numbers

Core Area 3: Geometry and Measurement
- Identify alternate interior and exterior angles
- Learn about inscribed angles
- Study dilations of figures
- Find the surface area of a sphere
- Study significant digits

Core Area 4: Fractions, Decimals, and Percents

Core Area 5: Graphing
- Graph an inequality in two variables
- Study the translation, reflection, and rotation of a graph
- Study the dilations of a graph
- Write the equation given a graph
- Graph systems of equations
- Draw scattergrams

Core Area 6: Statistics and Probability
- Calculate factorials
- Study correlation and dispersed points

Core Area 7: Problem Solving
- Solve word problems involving irrational numbers
- Solve word problems involving real numbers

Core Area 8: Algebra
- Solve systems of equations
- Study sine, cosine, and tangent functions
- Introduce sets and work with Venn diagrams

TAKING THE TIME

When I was growing up, I could do my homework by myself. Maybe it's just the way modern technology has gone crazy, but our oldest daughter needs some help with her homework, just to make sure she's on the right track. You have to be willing to sit down at the table with your child and spend some time. I can pay the bills before she goes to bed, but she needs to have somebody making sure that she gets the idea that homework needs to be done in a timely fashion before she can do other things. Help give kids the idea that you, the parent, are interested and know something about what they're studying, and help give kids something to share from their homework experience.

My son is the kind of child who won't let me teach him anything. He has to figure it out for himself, then he tells me.

CHAPTER 9

What Math Content Should I Review?

In this section, you can find descriptions of each concept and skill in the outlines of mathematics for grades seven and eight. The concepts and skills for both grades are organized together according to core area.

RELATE IT BETTER

In helping your teen with a math problem, you can explain something the same way over and over again, and sometimes your teen won't understand. You then need to step out of the situation and focus on, "How can I relate this better to my child? My child loves soccer, so maybe we'll try this math problem with soccer balls rather than cups of baking flour." Just drawing an analogy from something that means a lot to your teen may often be enough to really help.

For example, adding and subtracting rational numbers (a 7th grade skill), and adding and subtracting irrational numbers (an 8th grade skill) can be found under the head Core Area 2: Computation. You can use this section as a reference to review concepts and skills.

Core Area 1: Numeration

Numeration is a word for the system of numbers that we use. This core area is devoted to learning about numbers and comparing and rounding numbers.

Identify and write rational numbers. Why would anyone name some numbers rational numbers? The word *rational* is derived from the Latin word *ratus,* the past participle of the verb *reri,* which means to think, to reckon, or compute. Rational numbers are the ancients' computing numbers, that is, the ways that they used to record measurements.

Rational numbers are numbers that can be written as fractions. Since many decimals can be written as fractions, the rational numbers include many decimals. Some examples of rational numbers include

4 = 4/1, 1/2, −0.3 = −3/10, 0.9999999... = 9/10 and −5.090909... = −56/11

Are there numbers that are not rational numbers? Yes, two irrational numbers are pi, $\pi = 3.141592\ldots$, and $\sqrt{2} = 1.41421\ldots$. All decimals that do not have repeating digits are irrational numbers.

Compare and order rational numbers. To compare rational numbers, write them as decimals if they are not already in that form, and then compare the decimals place by place. For example, to compare 2/3 and 5/8, write each as decimals:

$$\frac{2}{3} = 0.66666\ldots \text{ and } \frac{5}{8} = 0.625$$

Since $0.66666\ldots > 0.625$, $2/3 > 5/8$.

Identify and write irrational numbers. Irrational numbers are numbers that cannot be written as fractions. These are numbers that do not have repeating decimals. Most square roots, such as $\sqrt{2}$, $\sqrt{3}$, and $\sqrt{5}$, are irrational numbers. Since $\sqrt{4} = 2$, it is not an irrational number.

Study real numbers. The set of real numbers include all the numbers that have been studied up to now. They include, the whole numbers (0, 1, 2, 3, etc.), the integers (the positive and negative whole numbers), the rational numbers, and the irrational numbers. What numbers are left, you may ask? Well, there are the numbers that are the square roots of negative numbers. For instance, $\sqrt{-1}$ is number that is not a real number. Such numbers, called complex numbers, are studied in the later grades.

Read and write numbers with negative exponents. In many schools, 6th graders study exponents, those little numbers that hover above and beside a number, such as 2^4. The exponent indicates the number of times the bottom number is multiplied. For example, the number 2^3 has an exponent of 3 and means multiply 2 three times. Thus, $2^3 = 2 \times 2 \times 2 = 8$.

In grade seven, students learn about negative exponents, that is, exponents that are negative numbers. Since a positive 3 means multiply the bottom number that many times, a negative 3^{-3} means the opposite, that is, you divide by the bottom number, called the base, that many times. Now, what number do you divide into? The short answer is 1. So,

$$2^{-3} = \frac{1}{2 \times 2 \times 2} = \frac{1}{8}$$

Since you are dividing, this definition of negative numbers works only for nonzero bases: 0 raised to any negative or positive exponent is 0.

Study zero exponents. Since there are positive exponents and negative exponents, then what about zero? Yes, Virginia, there is a zero exponent. Any nonzero number raised to the zero is always 1. That is, $1^0 = 1$, $(-2)^0 = 1$, $3.1555630 = 1$, $400^0 = 1$, etc. However, the expression 0^0 has no meaning—that is, it makes no mathematical sense.

Use the laws of exponents. Following are the laws of exponents for the following real numbers a, b, m, and n.

Law	Example
$b^m \times b^n = b^{m+n}$	$2^2 \times 2^4 = 2^{2+4} = 2^6 = 64$
$b^m \div b^n = b^{m-n}$	$2^4 \div 2^2 = 2^{4-2} = 2^2 = 4$
$(b^m)^n = b^{m \times n}$	$(2^2)^4 = 2^{2 \times 4} = 2^8 = 256$
$(ab)^n = a^n b^n$	$(3 \times 5)^2 = 3^2 \times 5^2 = 225$
$(a/b)^n = a^n/b^n$	$(2/3)^3 = 2^3/3^3 = 8/27$

Use scientific notation. Imagine having to write the number 794,000,000 miles—the distance between the earth and Saturn—on a regular basis. One zero more or less could mean losing $1.9 billion, the cost of sending the Galileo spacecraft to study the planet! Since scientists work with large numbers often, scientific notation is a way to make their lives easier.

- For numbers greater than 1, a number is in scientific notation if it is written in the form $a \times 10^n$ for some number a, a real number greater than 1 and less than 10, and whole integer n. For example,

MATH'S GREATEST HITS

According to *Newsweek's Computers & the Family* newsmagazine (Fall/Winter 1996), there were quite a few bestselling math computer software titles in 1996, including:

- *Math Blaster: In Search of Spot* (Davidson & Associates) for ages 6 to 12; (800) 545-7677
- *Math Blaster 2: The Secret of the Lost City* (Davidson & Associates) for ages 8 to 13
- *Mathematics* (boxed set by SofSource) for ages 10 to adult; (505) 523-6789
- *Math Heads* (Theatrix Interactive) for ages 10 to 14; (800) 955-TRIX
- *Major League Math* (Sanctuary Woods) for ages 9 to 13; (800) 943-3664

$$135,000,000,000,000 = 1.35 \times 10^{14}$$

because we move the decimal point to the left 14 times (see the figure) until you get 1.35 followed by a bunch of zeroes.

$$1.35 \times 10^{14}$$

- For the numbers between 0 and 1 (that is, decimals), a number is in scientific notation if it is written in the form $a \times 10n$. In this case, the only difference is that a negative integer n must be used. For example,

$$0.0000000000015 = 1.5 \times 10^{-12}$$

because we move the decimal point to the right 12 times until we get the number 1.5 preceded by a bunch of zeroes.

Study absolute value. We know that the value of the number −5 is the quantity having a measure of 5 negative units, such as −5°. The absolute value of −5, which is written $|-5|$, is the quantity 5 without the minus sign. Absolute value is just the amount without regard to sign.

- The absolute value of a positive number, such as 10, is just the number: $|10| = 10$.
- The absolute value of a negative number is the number without the negative sign: $|-10| = 10$.

Core Area 2: Computation

Computation refers to addition, subtraction, multiplication, and division. This core area also uses estimation to help perform the calculations and to check answers to calculations.

Add and subtract rational numbers. Write rational numbers as decimals before you add or subtract. You add and subtract decimals just as you add and subtract whole numbers. Just make sure that you keep track of the decimal point. Place one decimal below the other making sure the decimal points line up.

```
  14.647          14.647
+  7.196        −  7.196
  21.843           7.451
```

Multiply and divide rational numbers. To multiply and divide rational numbers, write the numbers as decimals or fractions and add or subtract. Multiply decimals as you multiply whole numbers. But, there's a wrinkle. The number of decimal places of the answer is equal to the sum of the decimal places of the two numbers you are multiplying.

$$
\begin{array}{r}
12.19 \\
\times\ 1.66 \\
\hline
7314 \\
73140 \\
\underline{121900} \\
20.2354
\end{array}
$$

Notice that the answer has 4 decimal places because 4 = 2 + 2 (the sum of the two decimal places in 12.19 and the two decimal places in 1.66).

To divide a decimal by a decimal, move the decimal point in the divisor to make it a whole number. (For example, you move the decimal point three places to the right to make 14.582 the whole number 14,582.) Then you move the decimal point in the dividend the same number of places to the right. Now, divide as you normally do.

Add and subtract irrational numbers. Well, the truth is that you *can't* add or subtract irrational numbers. They are decimals that go on forever, and you can't add or subtract forever. But, hooray for calculators! We can use them to estimate the values of the sums and differences of irrational numbers. For instance, $\pi - \sqrt{2}$ is approximately 3.14159 − 1.41421 = 2.72738. When you add or subtract, make sure you use estimates for the two irrational numbers having the same number of places. Rounding might be necessary before you add or subtract.

Multiply and divide irrational numbers. For the same reason, calculators save the day for this one, too. We estimate $\sqrt{3} - \sqrt{2}$ to be about 1.73205 − 1.41421 = 0.31784.

A CHICKEN IN EVERY POT

As the Internet becomes our new town square, a computer in every home—a teacher of all subjects, a connection to all cultures—this will no longer be a dream, but a necessity. And over the next decade, that must be our goal.
—from 1997 *State of the Union Address*, President Clinton

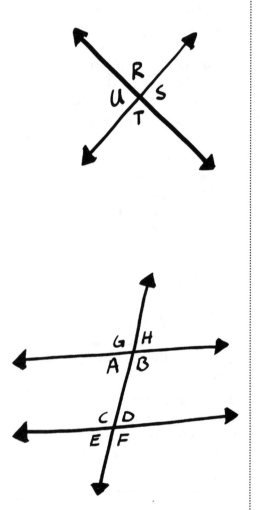

Core Area 3: Geometry and Measurement

Seventh and eighth graders learn more about angles and the special angles formed by intersecting lines. They also learn more about triangles. Also, they study special arrangements of figures as well as some changes to a figure.

Identify vertical and adjacent angles. When two lines meet in a plane, they form several types of angles.

- Two angles that do not have a side in common and are formed by the two lines are called vertical angles. For instance, angle *R* and angle *T* are *vertical angles*.
- Angles that have the same vertex and a side in common are called *adjacent angles*. Angle *U* and angle *R* are adjacent angles. These angles also are complementary because the sum of their measures is 180°.

Identify corresponding, alternate interior, and alternate exterior angles. A transversal is a line that cuts across two other lines and forms some angles.

- An interior angle and a nonadjacent exterior angle on the same side of the transversal are called *corresponding angles*. Angle *B* and angle *F* are corresponding angles.
- Alternate interior angles are angles that are on opposite sides of the transversal, are not adjacent angles, and are inside the region formed by the two horizontal lines. For example, angle *A* and angle *D* are alternate interior angles.
- Alternate exterior angles are angles that are on opposite sides of the transversal, are not adjacent angles, and are outside the region formed by the horizontal lines. For example, angle *E* and angle *H* are alternate exterior angles.

Learn about inscribed angles. An inscribed angle is an angle inside a circle that has the following properties.

- The vertex of the angle is on the circle.
- The ends of the rays forming the angle also are on the circle.

Angle *ABC* is an inscribed angle.

Construct triangles. Some schools continue to do constructions with a compass to show how the Greek mathematicians performed their mathematics.

Use these following four steps to construct an equilateral triangle:

1. Choose any two points *A* and *B*.
2. With the compass point on *A*, open the compass to the distance *AB*.
3. With the compass point on *A*, draw an arc. Repeat with the compass point on *B*.
4. The intersection of the arcs determines the point *C*, the third vertex of the equilateral triangle *ABC*.

Identify and classify isosceles, equilateral, and scalene triangles. Students in these grades study the following kinds of triangles:

- An isosceles triangle is a triangle with at least two sides of the same length.
- An equilateral triangle is a triangle with three sides whose measures are the same and three angles with the same measure.
- A scalene triangle is a triangle whose sides have different lengths.

Use the Pythagorean Theorem. The Pythagorean Theorem explains the relationship among the three sides of a right triangle. The longest side, labeled *c*, is called the hypotenuse; the other two legs are labeled *a* and *b*. The Pythagorean Theorem says the three sides of *a* right triangle—*a*, *b*, and *c*—are related by the equation:

$$c^2 = a^2 + b^2$$

The Pythagorean Theorem works only for right triangles.

Find the area and perimeter of a polygon. A closed figure formed by line segments is a polygon. Some common polygons include a triangle, rectangle, pentagon (five-sided polygon), hexagon (six-sided polygon), and octagon (eight-sided polygon). To find the area of a polygon, divide the

Inscribed Angle

Right Triangle

GOING FOR GOALS

One of my *SCORE!* moms is on a Nike® poster! She started training after her twenties, and she kept training until she made the Olympic track team. She's a great reminder to kids that we all have goals, adults as well as kids.

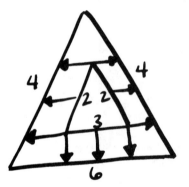

polygon into triangles, squares, and rectangles, and use the following formulas to calculate the area of each part.

- Area of a triangle $= (1/2)bh$ (b is the base and h is the height of the triangle)
- Area of a square $= s^2$ (s is the side of the square)
- Area of a rectangle $= l \times w$ (l is the length and w is the width)

Find the surface area of a pyramid. Surface area of a pyramid $= B + (1/2)Ps$ (B is the area of the base, P is the perimeter of the base, and s is the slant height of the face, that is, the length of the edge from the base to the tip of the pyramid).

Find the surface area of a spher. Surface area of a sphere $= 4\pi r^2$ (π is the irrational number called pi that is approximately 3.1415, and r is the radius of the sphere).

Study and identify a tessellation. A tessellation is a design made of repeated polygons or other shapes that covers the plane with no gaps or overlaps. A tessellation is like a tile floor that covers the entire room with no open spaces between the tiles and no overlap. Another example of a tessellation is a puzzle with interlocking pieces covering a table. The Dutch artist M. C. Escher used tessellations to create unusual worlds in which things are not as they seem.

Study dilations of figures. Think of how your eyes dilate after you've been in the dark for a few minutes. This is what we're talking about here. For example, if we double the length of each side of a triangle, we stretch it to get a similar triangle, that is, a triangle with the same shape but of a different size.

Study significant digits. Significant digits are related to the problem of the accuracy of measuring instruments. For example, suppose you used a stopwatch to measure the time it takes a speeding locomotive to barrel down a 100-foot stretch of track, and then you used that time to estimate its speed using distance = rate $\times$ time. You'd probably say the locomotive was traveling at about 100 miles per hour. Since $100 = 1 \times 10^2$, we say that there is 1 significant digit. Now, if you use a precision laser timepiece instead of your stopwatch, you might find the locomotive's speed was 138.7 miles per hour since $138.7 = 1.387 \times 10^2$. In this case, the number of significant digits is 4, the number of places in the decimal. You see, as the precision of the measurement increases, so does the number of significant digits.

To count significant digits, count all the nonzero digits in the number and include only zeroes that fall between two nonzero numbers. For example, 10101 has 5 significant digits, but 11100 has only 3 significant digits.

When you add, subtract, multiply, and divide measurements using significant digits, always round the numbers to the number of digits of the least accurate measurement. For example, if you multiply the two measurements 5.44 m and 0.5 m to get the area of some shelf space in a grocery store, then since 0.5 has only 1 significant digit, you must round 5.44 m to 5 m.

Core Area 4: Fractions, Decimals, and Percents

Understanding the concept of a whole and its division into equal parts is essential to understanding fractions, decimals, and percents. (Recall that percent is just a part of 100. For example, 80 percent of a 100 gallon drum means 80 out of the 100 gallons.) After reviewing fractions, decimals, and percents, 7th graders complete their study of percents by learning how to solve more percent problems.

Find a number when the percent is known. Suppose you know that 25 percent of a number is 8. What is the original number? If we let x be the original number and we use 25 percent = 0.25, then we have

$$25\% \text{ of } x = 0.25x = 8$$

The answer is $x = 8/0.25 = 32$.

Here's another example: Suppose you buy an automobile headlight on sale and save $12. If the discount is 10 percent, then what was the original price? Answer: Divide $12 \div 0.1$

WE ARE FAMILY

Set up a home culture where it's expected that "we are a family unit, we want to learn more about each other because we care about each other, and we will have certain ways we interact all the time." Practices like regular meals around a table with a common sharing time are key to establishing a home culture. It's hard in an age when adults work harder and longer, but we all need to make time for our children, and the other commitments to our children's lives will then flow from that.

ON SETTING GOALS . . .

Whenever I set goals with students, I say two things. I tell them that when I was their age, I wanted to be on the cross-country team in school, and to get good enough, I had to practice and practice. Then I ask them if there's anything like that going on for them, and I try to get them to talk about their goals and dreams. Share something cool from the "adult world" that shows you had to practice and practice to master or understand something. Kids love to see adults as people who make mistakes and aren't born perfect.

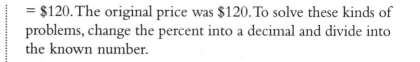

= \$120. The original price was \$120. To solve these kinds of problems, change the percent into a decimal and divide into the known number.

Core Area 5: Graphing

Graphs are an effective way to organize and display data. The shape of the graph and how it organizes data provides a great deal of information about the data.

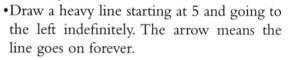

Graph an inequality on a number line. Suppose we have the inequality $x \leq 5$. To draw the graph of this inequality:

- Draw a number line.
  - Place a point on the line at 5.
  - Draw a heavy line starting at 5 and going to the left indefinitely. The arrow means the line goes on forever.

Things to remember about drawing the graph of an inequality.

Inequality Graph Components.

$\leq$ Solid dot and line pointing to the left.

$\geq$ Solid dot and line pointing to the right.

$<$ Open dot (o) and line pointing to the left.

$>$ Open dot (o) and line pointing to the right.

Read and graph double-line graphs. A double-line graph is just what the words say, a graph with two lines. Each line represents a separate set of data. For example, one line in the graph represents the ideal weights for adults under 35 and the other represents the ideal weights for adults 35 and over. Double-line graphs are useful to make comparisons about two sets of data.

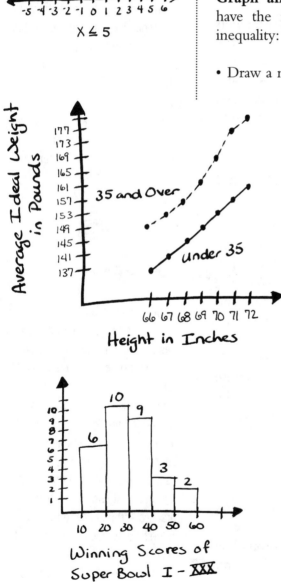

Read and graph histograms. A histogram is a special kind of bar graph that shows the number of times the data falls within certain assigned ranges of values. (The number of times the data falls within a range is also known as the frequency.) The given histogram, also called the frequency histogram, shows the number of times the winning score of the Super Bowl occurred within each range of scores.

- The title describes the data set.
- The horizontal axis gives the scores of the winning team.
- The vertical axis gives the number of times that the winning score fell within each range. For example, the winning team scored between 41 and 50 points three times.

Read and graph box-and-whisker plots. A box-and-whisker plot is another way to graph data. This type of graph shows how the data is spread out. It graphs the minimum, maximum, median, and two other values that determine the sides of the box.

Following are the steps for drawing a box-and-whisker plot for the winning scores of the first 30 Super Bowls.

1. Arrange the data in order from least to greatest.

14, 16, 16, 16, 20, 20, 21, 23, 24, 24, 26, 27, 27, 27, 27, 30, 31, 32, 33, 35, 35, 37, 38, 38, 39, 42, 46, 49, 52, 55

2. Find the median, the value that has as many values above it as it has below it. In this case, the median is the average of the fifteenth and sixth numbers:

$$\text{median} = \frac{27 + 30}{2} = \frac{57}{2} = 28.5$$

3. Now list the lowest 15 values and the median.

14, 16, 16, 16, 20, 20, 21, 23, 24, 24, 26, 27, 27, 27, 27, 28.5

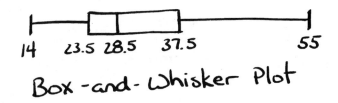

14   23.5 28.5   37.5   55

Box-and-Whisker Plot

Making the Grade

ASSISTIVE TECHNOLOGY

If your child has a disability, check into the possibility of assistive technology to help make learning easier. The Individuals with Disabilities Education Act (IDEA) says assistive technology is any device that helps a student with disabilities function better—like a talking laptop computer that "reads" papers and books to students through earphones. The law requires that schools make it available to students who need it to obtain the free, appropriate education IDEA guarantees. Some insurance companies will cover assistive technology devices, as will some community groups, corporations, foundations, and state governments. Check all possible resources to maximize your child's learning opportunities.

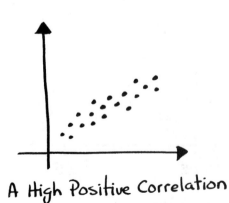

A High Positive Correlation

Find the median of these numbers.

$$\text{median} = \frac{23 + 24}{2} = 23.5$$

This marks the left-hand side of the box.

4. Now list the highest 15 values and the median.

28.5, 30, 31, 32, 33, 35, 35, 37, 38, 38, 39, 42, 46, 49, 52, 55

Find the median of these numbers.

$$\text{median} = \frac{37 + 38}{2} = 37.5$$

This marks the right-hand side of the box.

5. Draw the box-and-whisker plot by drawing a rectangle whose length goes from 23.5 to 37.5. Make the height of the rectangle any length you wish. Draw a vertical line through the box at 28.5 for the median.

6. Finally, draw horizontal lines to the left of the box to the minimum (14) and to the right of the box to the maximum (55).

The box in the middle shows the middle 15 values of the winning scores for the first 30 Super Bowls. Based on this data, you can say the chances of the winning Super Bowl team scoring anywhere from 24 and 37 points is about 50 percent. But, don't bet on it! The chance of not scoring within that range is also about 50 percent.

Draw scattergrams. A scattergram is a graph of points on a coordinate grid. You plot a scattergram to see if the points form some pattern. If a pattern exists, then you can say it is likely there is a relationship, called a correlation, between the two sets of data. For more information, see "Study correlation and dispersed points" in Core Area 6.

Graph a nonlinear equation. A nonlinear equation is an equation that has a variable with an exponent greater than

1. Some examples of nonlinear equations are

$$y = x^2 - 8x + 22 \text{ and } y = 12x^5 - x^4 + 17x + 108$$

You graph nonlinear equations by graphing some numbers that are solutions to the equation. (Solutions to an equation are numbers for x and y that produce an equality such as $9 = 9$.) Plot a point for each pair of numbers that are solutions. Draw a line through the points.

The graphs of nonlinear equations are not lines. Most of these graphs are curves that have one or more turns.

Graph an inequality in two variables. A graph of an inequality is some region in the coordinate plane. For example, the graph of the inequality $y > x + 1$ shown is the shaded region above the line. Every point in the region satisfies the inequality. You should try some to convince yourself and your child.

An inequality in two variables can be written in the form $y < ax + b$ or $y > ax + b$ for some real numbers a and b. To graph an inequality, follow these steps.

1. Graph the associated equality $y = ax + b$, and graph the line described by this equation.

2. Since this line divides the plane into two parts, test a point above the line and below the line.

3. You test a point by replacing y in the equation with the y-coordinate of the point, replacing the x in the equation with the x-coordinate, and then checking if you get a true statement. If you do, the region with that point is the solution to the inequality.

4. If the inequality is either $\leq$ or $\geq$, then the border of the region is part of the solution.

Study the translation, reflection, and rotation of a graph. Translations, reflections, and rotations of a graph preserve the shape of the graph; only its orientation changes.

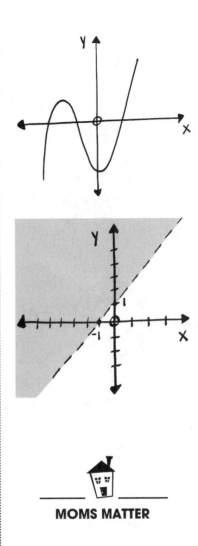

MOMS MATTER

Mothers at home are not being rewarded. They've never been financially rewarded, and they have not been rewarded in terms of respect. They're not considered professionals, but the skill levels for mothering are getting more challenging day by day. It's a challenge to keep up the family and kids and nurture our children's educational process.

Making the Grade

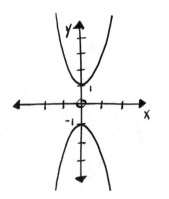

A reflection of a graph

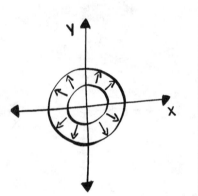

A rotation of a graph

It's like moving a chair in a room. The chair's position changes but its shape does not.

- A translation of a graph slides a graph up, down, to the left, or to the right as if it were a puck going across the ice.
- A reflection of a graph flips the graph from one side of a point, line, or plane to the other side so that it is the same distance from the point, line, or plane, and its orientation does not change. This is like flipping a pancake from one end of a griddle to the opposite end.
- A rotation (or turn) of a graph rotates the graph about a fixed point like spinning a pinwheel.

Study the dilations of a graph. A dilation of a graph stretches or shrinks a graph equally in all directions in such a way that its shape remains the same. Only its size changes.

Write the equation given a graph. To find the equation of a line given the graph, you need to write an equation in the form $y = mx + b$ and follow these four steps:

1. Find where the line meets the y-axis. The y-value of the point is b. If the line does not meet the y-axis, then $b = 0$ (see step 4).

2. Find the point where the line meets the x-axis, or choose any other point. Suppose the distance in the x-direction from where the line hits the y-axis and the second point is a. Suppose the distance in the y-direction between the two points is b. Then $m = b/a$.

3. Write the equation using the values for b and m that you found.

4. If the line does not hit the x-axis, then find the point where the line intersects the y-axis. If the y-value of this point is c, then the equation of the line is $y = c$.

Graph systems of equations. A system of equations is two or more equations taken together. To graph a system of equations, graph the equations on the same coordinate axis.

Core Area 6: Statistics and Probability

Statistics and probability are the tools used to analyze problems in our world. They are used for things like taking surveys of attitudes on smoking and finding the chances of winning the lottery. Frequently students choose the kinds of issues they wish to investigate. Since many topics for study are problems that students wish to learn about, they become involved and interested in learning the concepts.

Learn about and use quartiles. If you arrange some data in order, then the quartiles Q_1, Q_2, and Q_3 are the numbers that separate the data into four parts.

- About one quarter of the data is less than Q_1.
- Q_2 is the median: half the data is greater than Q_2, and half is less than Q_2.
- About three quarters of the data is less than Q_3.

Quartiles are used to locate a score in relation to other scores. For example, if your height is in the third quartile, then three quarters of the people are shorter than you.

Study random numbers. Since random means "without a pattern or purpose," random numbers are numbers whose digits have been chosen without any pattern or order. Random number tables are usually generated by computers and are used in simulations.

Explain independent, dependent, and complementary events.

- Two events are independent if one event does not influence the other event. Drawing two winning tickets in a raffle are independent events (unless perhaps the raffle is being run by the mob).
- Two events are dependent if one of the events influences the other. The event of rain today and the event that there are clouds in the sky are dependent events.
- Two events are complementary if one event consists of all outcomes that are not possible for the other event. For example, selecting a man as president and selecting a woman (that is, not a man) as president are complementary events.

COMPARISONS HAPPEN

Children deal with comparisons all their lives. That's part of the world. Everyone always compares themselves to others. Parents should downplay making negative comparisons, but you can't ignore that comparisons will always happen.

Parents often like to compare siblings. Kids can be so completely different—or the same—in terms of their levels of learning. Kids will already be comparing themselves to their brothers and sisters, but it's important for parents not to dwell on the comparisons. Even in school, kids get the sibling comparisons all the time, especially from teachers. I have an older brother, and I did really well in school but he didn't. My parents didn't make any comparisons beteween us, and we achieved things in different areas as a result.

Making the Grade

Make frequency tables. A frequency table is a table of the number of occurrences (that is, the frequencies) of each event, item, or piece of data. The frequency table shown on page 86 contains the frequencies for each winning score for the first thirty Super Bowls. The frequencies in a frequency table are graphed using a histogram (see Core Area 5).

Calculate factorials. A factorial, a number followed by the exclamation symbol (such as 6!), is the product of a decreasing sequence of numbers. Following are some common factorials.

$$6! = 6 \times 5 \times 4 \times 3 \times 2 \times 1 = 720$$
$$5! = 5 \times 4 \times 3 \times 2 \times 1 = 120$$
$$4! = 4 \times 3 \times 2 \times 1 = 24$$
$$3! = 3 \times 2 \times 1 = 6$$
$$2! = 2 \times 1 = 2$$
$$1! = 1$$

Factorials are used for counting the possible number of occurrences of events or number of arrangements of things. For example, factorials are used to count the number of possible arrangements of four players on the Spiders and Flies, two two-on-two basketball teams. Suppose the Spiders pick a player first from the pool of four players, and then the teams alternate picks. For each possible first pick by the Spiders, the Flies can choose from three possible remaining players. So, there are $4 \times 3 = 12$ possible arrangements of two players on the teams. After the Flies pick, the Spiders have two choices left; that is, the possible arrangements of three players is $4 \times 3 \times 2 = 24$. Finally, the Flies have one choice; that is, the possible arrangements of four players on the teams is $4 \times 3 \times 2 \times 1 = 4! = 24$.

Study correlation and dispersed points. A correlation is a relationship between two sets of data. For example, there is a positive correlation between a child's IQ and his success in school. Usually, the greater the IQ, the better his grades. If there is no correlation between the data, then the data points are said to be dispersed.

Frequently, correlation is studied by graphing the data in scattergrams (see Core Area 5). When the data points are scattered or dispersed all over the graph, then there is no correlation between the two sets of data.

Core Area 7: Problem Solving

Problem solving in math consists of a set of strategies for tackling word problems in an organized way and includes the following characteristics:

- Understanding and exploring the problem
- Thinking creatively and trying many approaches to the problem
- Persevering until the problem is solved or a new approach is discovered
- Answering the question and explaining how the problem was solved

Solving word problems is an art that requires patience and persistence. Use the following strategies to practice solving problems with your teen.

- Encourage her to think clearly and logically, and suggest that she ask many questions.
- Listen to your child to see if she understands the problem.
- Encourage her to explain her thinking.
- Ask "What if" questions to explore the problem and extend your teen's understanding.
- Encourage her to try different strategies to solve the problem.
- Praise her for being flexible, and congratulate her for taking risks and trying new approaches.

As your child solves problems successfully, she will gain confidence in her problem-solving abilities and will develop her thinking and reasoning skills. Problem solving is a key part of math that improves student achievement and contributes to self-confidence and a willingness to tackle math problems.

Solve problems involving rational numbers. Use many of the strategies listed above to solve these problems. Also

NEW-NEW MATH

In some schools now, we have the "new-new math," and the difference between that and what they've taught in the past is more of a problem-solving approach. Rather than focusing on memorizing math facts, like multiplication tables, they might take all the kids out to the playground and have them figure out the area of the soccer field or how much grass they'd need to purchase to lay sod down in a certain area. In many schools, there's more of a focus on the logical and problem-solving approach than ever before. I think, however, that critical math skills are still important for kids to have.

Making the Grade

use pieces of paper to represent fractions or strips of paper divided into 10 parts to represent decimals. Have your teen explore the problem using these items and ask "What if" questions to help her gain an appreciation for the problem.

Solve problems involving scientific notation. Scientific notation is used to work with very large and very small quantities (see Core Area 1). Before solving problems involving scientific notation, review the rules for exponents in Core Area 2. These are useful for multiplying numbers in scientific notation.

Solve word problems involving irrational numbers. The irrational number π is used in the area of a circle formula πr^2 as well as the volume and surface area of many three-dimensional figures. An irrational number that is the square root of some number usually crops up when you use the Pythagorean Theorem. When solving problems involving right triangles, review the Pythagorean Theorem (Core Area 3).

Calculators may be used to estimate irrational numbers. Some calculators have a square root key. Use the fraction 22/7 or the decimal 3.14159 as estimates for π.

Solve word problems involving real numbers. Since the real numbers comprise all the numbers students have learned, these problems make use of all the strategies they have acquired to solve problems. Some problems might involve different types of numbers, such as irrational numbers and whole numbers. Operations on these numbers may require calculators.

Core Area 8: Algebra

Algebra is the study of variables. It is an essential part of problem solving. To be a successful problem solver, your child should have a good understanding of algebra.

Practice working with variables with your child. Emphasize that working with variables is the same as working with numbers. All the rules for numbers also work with variables. Encourage her to see a variable as just another number; only for the present you don't know what quantity it represents.

Solve equations using two steps. Equations that are solved in two steps usually look like this:

$$2x - 7 = -11$$

Step 1. Add 7 to both sides of the equations.

$$2x - 7 + 7 = -11 + 7$$
$$2x = -4$$

Step 2. Divide both sides by 2.

$$\frac{2x}{2} = \frac{-4}{2}$$
$$x = -2$$

Solve inequalities. Solving inequalities is similar to solving equations. You can add a number to both sides of an inequality, and you can multiply both sides of an inequality by a number. Here are some examples.

• Add a number to both sides of an inequality:

$$x - 7 \leq 9$$
$$x - 7 + 7 \leq 9 + 7$$
$$x \leq 16$$

• Multiply both sides of an inequality:

$$2x > 6$$
$$\frac{1}{2} \times 2x > \frac{1}{2} \times 6$$
$$x > 3$$

But, there's one catch! Notice that both sides of the inequality were multiplied by 1/2. If both sides of an inequality are multiplied by a negative number, then the sign of the inequality must be reversed. That is,

$$-4x \leq 32$$

Making the Grade

TRY THIS AT HOME

There are many exciting innovations going on in mathematics right now! You should no longer tell children how to do math problems. Rather than say, "This is how you borrow" or "This is how you multiply," have your children articulate for themselves over and over again, "What is the question and how do I solve the problem?" It's exciting for kids to get together to work on a problem, explaining what the problem is and how they can tackle it. There will be many different ways that kids use to come up with the answer, and it's fascinating for them to see how everyone thought differently in the problem-solving process. It's also valuable to articulate the process—that's the real moment of learning, where it all starts to gel for them.

Math can be fun and creative!

MORE MATH, PLEASE

Improve your child's arithmetic skills. Learning to calculate will improve your child's concentration, as well as his reasoning skills.
—*The Parent's Answer Book,* Gerald Deskin and Greg Steckler (Fairview Press, 1995)

$$-\frac{1}{4} \times (-4x) \leq -\frac{1}{4} \times 32$$

$$x \geq -8$$

Study quadratic and other nonlinear functions. A nonlinear function is a function that is described by a nonlinear equation. Here are two examples of equations of nonlinear functions:

$$F(x) = x^2 - 8x + 22$$
$$G(x) = 12x^5 - x^4 + 17x + 108$$

Use functional notation. Recall that a function is a relationship between two sets of numbers. For example, the doubling function takes a number and doubles it. We usually write functions using letters. If we call the doubling function f, then $f(x)$ means we apply f to the number x and get the result $f(x)$ which is two times x.

- If f is the doubling function and $x = 3$, then $f(3) = 2 \times 3 = 6$.
- If f is the doubling function and $x = -5$, then $f(-5) = 2 \times (-5) = -10$.
- If g is the tripling function that multiplies a number by 3 and $x = 1/2$, then $g(1/2) = 3 \times 1/2 = 3/2$.

Study other sequences, such as Fibonacci sequences. A sequence is a list of numbers such as 1, 2, 4, 8, 16, etc. A geometric sequence is a sequence in which each term is the same multiple of the previous term.

Another sequence that your child might study is the Fibonacci sequence 1, 1, 2, 3, 5, 8, etc. In this sequence, after the first two 1s, the remaining numbers are the sum of the preceding two numbers. For example, $8 = 3 + 5$.

Another common sequence is 1, 4, 9, 16, 25, etc., which is the sequence of squares of the positive integers starting with 1, that is, $1^2, 2^2, 3^2, 4^2, 5^2$, etc.

Solve systems of equations. You can solve a system of equations in the variables x and y in either of two ways.

- Solve by graphing: Graph the equations. The solutions are the points where the graphs intersect.
- Solve with algebra: Solve one of the equations for a variable, say x. Suppose you get $x = 3y + 7$. In the other equation, in each place where x occurs, replace it with $3y + 7$. Now, solve for y.

Study sine, cosine, and tangent functions. The sine, cosine, and tangent functions are special functions because they are applied to angles in a right triangle.

Let's start with the sine function, which is abbreviated as *sin* and read "sine" (rhymes with *pine*). Since the sine function is applied to angles in a right triangle, consider the angle that measures 30° in the figure. Then

$$\sin 30° = \frac{\text{length of the opposite side}}{\text{length of the hypotenuse}}$$

The sine function always assigns a number from −1 to 1 to an angle.

The cosine function, written *cos,* is

$$\cos 30° = \frac{\text{length of the adjacent side}}{\text{length of the hypotenuse}}$$

The cosine function always assigns a number from −1 to 1 to an angle.

The tangent function, written *tan,* is

$$\tan 30° = \frac{\text{length of the opposite side}}{\text{length of the adjacent side}}$$

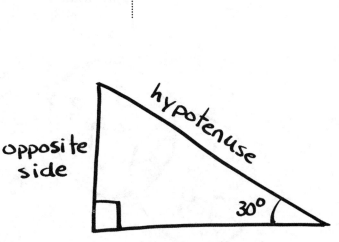

opposite side

hypotenuse

30°

adjacent side

FORMULA FOR SUCCESS

Having students believe that it is worth investing time and energy in school is a necessary condition for academic achievement, but it is not sufficient by itself. In order to succeed, students also must believe that they have some control over how well they do in school, that their performance is somehow related to their effort, and that trying harder will lead to an improvement in their grades and test scores. —from *Beyond the Classroom* by Laurence Steinberg, Ph.D. (Simon & Schuster, 1996)

Introduce sets and work with Venn diagrams A set is a group of objects. An element of a set is one of the objects in the set. A set is written as a list of elements inside braces. For example, the set of numbers of integers from 1 to 10 is written {1, 2, 3, 4, 5, 6, 7, 8, 9, 10}.

The union of two sets is the set that is the combination of elements from the two sets. The union of {1, 2, 3, 4} and {2, 5, 7, 9}, written {1, 2, 3, 4} ∪ {2, 5, 7, 9} is {1, 2, 3, 4, 5, 7, 9}.

The intersection of two sets is the set of elements that are common to both sets. The intersection of {1, 2, 3, 4} and {2, 5, 7, 9}, written {1, 2, 3, 4} ∩ {2, 5, 7, 9} is {2}.

Venn diagrams are used to show sets, their unions, and intersections. The Venn diagram shown displays {1, 2, 3, 4} ∩ {2, 5, 7, 9}. The shaded area shows the intersection.

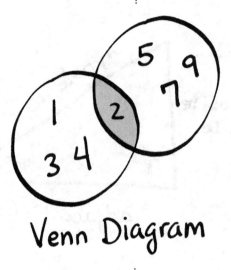

Venn Diagram

CHAPTER 10

What's My Child Studying in Science?

By seventh grade, science teaching becomes more systematic. Your child will begin to learn scientific models such as the molecular model of matter. Since children's mental abilities are maturing more

rapidly in these years, they are able to learn abstract ideas by generalizing from specific experiences. Generalizing from two or more abstract ideas, however, does not generally appear until later years.

The typical middle school science curriculum capitalizes on these newly developing abilities. Your child's science teacher will introduce scientific concepts as part of a living body of knowledge that is changing continually. Although students still do hands-on science, they will be encouraged to think about the scientific ideas that have remained the same over the centuries and about those that have changed.

Here are some of the goals of a quality middle school science program:

- Teaching the fundamental concepts in the biological, physical, earth and space, and chemical sciences, as well as technology
- Introducing the process of scientific inquiry through observing phenomena, measuring and recording data, and reporting findings
- Developing scientific attitudes such as curiosity, the respect for reliable information, critical thinking, and the importance of science in our lives
- Promoting analytical skills including doing experiments, measuring results, recording observations in tables, charts, and graphs, and making inferences

LIST YOUR QUESTIONS

Help your child realize what kinds of things she can investigate in science projects by having her list questions she has whenever the questions come up. Start with a poster or bulletin board on which you list any kinds of questions about the natural world (including humans), whether the questions come up over everyday things or during homework or lessons in science, math, art, or whatever.
—The Wild Goose Co.

Making the Grade

LET KIDS INVESTIGATE

• Nourishing positive attitudes about science as a worthy career choice

Science Is Fun. Good science education provides youngsters with enjoyable, thought-provoking activity. Encouraging an inquisitive attitude about doing science will strengthen your child's self-confidence in science. Many activities in this book are fun and easy. Doing them with your child will develop her curiosity about the world and promote her analytical skills. These activities are designed to supplement the experiments and other observations that she will do in school to develop her inquiry skills.

Middle school students typically plan and carry out more sophisticated tests than they did in earlier grades, and they use more complex measuring devices to gather data. Your child may use multiple lines of inquiry to study a question including experimentation, trial and error, survey, interview, and published sources. Many of these investigations combine fun and intellectual curiosity with instruction about scientific concepts and inquiry skills. The best programs also encourage problem solving and working cooperatively.

Seven Core Areas. The following seven core subject areas form the basis of most districts' middle school science curriculum:

1. Life Science
2. Physical Science
3. Earth and Space
4. Technology
5. Health Science
6. Inquiry Skills
7. Chemistry

The following outlines represent what educators consider the heart of middle school (or junior high) science. You will find that most topics and skills listed here are taught in your school. Some schools use an integrated approach to science that teaches the concepts in the context of a central theme or topic. For example, a unit focusing on a river may study the following concepts:

- Web of life within the river
- Energy obtained from the river
- How the river affects the land surrounding it
- Technology used to harness the river's energy
- Chemistry of the river

The integrated approach is usually thoroughly researched and contains many of the concepts and skills you'll find in these outlines.

What's Taught in Grade Seven?

Seventh graders begin to learn the *concepts* that underlie much of the science they did in earlier grades. For example, students begin to explore the concept of energy by looking at various kinds of energy transformations. They may investigate how heat and light can be generated by a chemical reaction. Students typically design and perform experiments in this grade. Seventh graders begin to explore the relationships between things, and they also learn about reproduction and genetic traits. By grade seven, health is frequently taught as a subject separate from science.

Core Area 1: Life Science
- Study interconnected global food webs from microscopic plants up to the largest animals
- Explore the relationships between organisms
- Understand genetic traits
- Learn about the process of sexual reproduction
- Recognize that new plants and animals result from selective breeding
- Learn that species are organisms that can mate and reproduce (for organisms that reproduce)

Core Area 2: Physical Science
- Learn about energy primarily through energy transformations
- Explore and describe the conservation of energy
- Explain that most of what goes on in the universe happens as a result of energy being transformed
- Begin to learn about inertia
- Study vibrations in ropes, strings, and in a water table and study the characteristics of the waves

TAKE A DEEP BREATH

Some parents are so scared and so invested in super academic success for their children. Many of my *SCORE!* students are expected to go to Stanford or another top school. But parents have to give their children the space to learn. If a child doesn't know certain skills, it's not an apocalyptic event. This is a chance for children to learn and for parents to lovingly encourage and reinforce. Take a deep breath if your child doesn't know the answer to a question, maybe something they're getting wrong in her homework. Then look at what your child doesn't know and use it as a goal to move towards.

HIGH-TECH SLEUTHS

In middle school, students begin to use computers just as scientists use them. They typically collect, store, and analyze data, they make tables and graphs, and they write reports with computers.

Making the Grade

Core Area 3: Earth and Space
• Recognize that the sun's gravity holds the earth and planets in their orbits
• Explain that the sun provides the light and heat for the earth
• Study the planets, their moons, and their rings
• Recognize that the tilt of the earth's axis causes the seasons
• Explain what causes the phases of the moon
• Explain the importance of the cycling of water in and out of the atmosphere to weather
• Understand the limited capacity of atmosphere and ocean to absorb wastes
• Learn how human activities change the land, ocean, and atmosphere

Core Area 4: Technology
• Make a technological device
• Use material tests to identify appropriate uses for materials
• Model ways in which resources are used to develop new technologies
• Explain a manufacturing process
• Describe how power systems work

Core Area 5: Health Science

Core Area 6: Inquiry Skills
• Design an experiment
• Use multiple lines of inquiry to analyze a problem
• Design a solution to a technological problem and describe its advantages and disadvantages
• Explain that some matters cannot be tested scientifically

Core Area 7: Chemistry
• Explain that all matter is made up of atoms and atoms form molecules
• Measure and predict changes in a gas sample
• Group elements with similar properties

What's Taught in Grade Eight?

Eighth graders usually study more sophisticated ideas such as process and change. For example, they learn the factors that cause climate change and they study evolution. Students gain a more complete understanding of experimentation. They learn how to vary the parameters of an experiment and how to identify the differences between experiments.

Core Area 1: Life Science

- Recognize how energy is transferred from one organism to another or between an organism and its environment
- Explain how energy can change within an animal
- Learn about breeding experiments that show the inheritability of traits
- Understand how small differences between parent and offspring can accumulate over generations
- Study how individual organisms with certain traits are more likely to survive
- Learn how layers of sedimentary rock can show the history of the earth

Core Area 2: Physical Science

- Explain how heat can be transferred through materials
- Develop an idea of electric and magnetic forces using magnets and electric currents
- Generalize gravity to all matter
- Learn that an unbalanced force acting on an object changes its speed or motion
- Learn that a force depends on the masses of the objects and how far they are apart

Core Area 3: Earth and Space

- Demonstrate that the sun is a medium-sized star
- Learn about comets, asteroids, and meteorites
- Learn about the universe and galaxies
- Identify and understand the factors that shape the earth
- Understand how sedimentary rock contains evidence of geologic history
- Understand how volcanic eruptions or meteors cause climate change
- Learn how small changes in the atmosphere or ocean cause climate change

**HOP ON
THE LEARNING CYCLE**

Use the Learning Cycle to help do fun science stuff at home! Here's a real-life example:

- **Explore**—Give your child a microscope and have her start looking at pond water, human skin, onion skin, or anything that can be called an organism and has a definite cell structure they can see under the microscope. Don't tell her about cells and then have them look for cells in the organisms. Just have them describe what she sees and compare one thing with another.

- **Explain**—Focus on the similarities between the organisms, and sooner or later, your child will latch on to the similarities in structure. Then you're ready to introduce the word *cells* and explain that all life forms contain these little chunks.

- **Apply**—Modify the "explore" phase of the activity. For example, instead of looking at a piece of onion skin under the microscope and describing what she sees, have your child look at a completely different organism and draw a picture of the cells in it.

YOUNG EXPLORERS

The more freedom we give children to explore, the more they learn—we've observed that in our *SCORE!* Learning Adventures program. One of our chemistry class Coaches, instead of providing a lab for kids, taught them the five steps of scientific thinking and then gave them the chemistry lesson plan. He said this end result is what you want to look for, he handed the lessons over to the kids, and they went for it! For about an hour and a half, they explored and worked super hard. Afterwards, the kids presented their findings. It was so much more creative than a controlled classroom environment would have been.

Core Area 4: Technology
- Learn about the impact of technological change in history
- Recognize the negative side effects of technology
- Explain how technology led the change from an agricultural to an information society
- Provide evidence that technology is developing faster than ever before
- Evaluate designs or devices
- Communicate the process of technological design

Core Area 5: Health Science

Core Area 6: Inquiry Skills
- Identify whether the differences between identical experiments are trivial
- Explain the importance of only changing one variable at a time in an experiment
- Reformulate ideas and technological solutions
- Understand that what people expect to observe often affects what they observe
- Explore the ethics of science

Core Area 7: Chemistry
- Recognize that atoms and molecules are in perpetual motion
- Learn that atoms in solids vibrate and atoms in liquids are more loosely connected
- Explain that temperature and acidity of a solution influence a reaction
- Study how substances in a closed system conserve the total weight in the system

CHAPTER 11

What Science Content Should I Review?

In this section, you can find descriptions of each concept and skill in the outlines of 7th and 8th grade science. The concepts and skills for both grades are organized together according to core area. For example, the planets, moons, and rings (a 7th grade topic) and the universe and galaxies (an 8th grade topic) can be found under the head "Core Area 3: Earth and Space." You can use this section as a reference to review concepts and skills.

FIRST IN THE WORLD

Secretary of Education Dick Riley and I visited northern Illinois, where 8th grade students from twenty school districts, in a project called "First in the World," took the Third International Math and Science Study, a test that reflects the world-class standards our children must meet for the new era. And those students in Illinois tied for first in the world in science, and came in second in math . . . . They prove that when we aim high and challenge our students, they will be the best in the world.
—from the 1997 State of the Union Address, President Clinton

Core Area 1: Life Science

It's mind-boggling that over one million species of creatures of all shapes, sizes, and colors inhabit the earth. From the earliest societies, people have been trying to learn about the living things in our environment. This core area studies the principles and processes that we have discovered to explain the diversity of life.

Study interconnected global food webs, from microscopic plants up to the largest animals. There are many environments in our world: forest, grassland, desert, mountain, and fresh and salt water. The plants and animals within them form great chains of life. Most living things rely on other living things for food. The growth and survival of each plant and animal is related to the plants, animals, and environment around them. For example, in the grasslands of Africa, animals such as giraffes, wildebeests, zebras, lions, and many species of birds and insects form a community. Students trace large food webs such as this on both land and water.

Making the Grade

PRESSURE COOKER

I think some parents put too much pressure on kids. Education is very important, but I see some of my daughter's classmates consumed by learning all the time. It's the only thing they're allowed to do. In our house we try to achieve a good balance for our children, including down time.

Explore the relationships between organisms. Living things are related in one of three ways.

- Plants and animals can cooperate—the fungi that grow on trees are an example. The fungi receive nutrients from the tree roots and, in turn, the fungi make fine webs that extend the tree's root system.
- A living thing can be a parasite living off another living thing, such as ticks that attach themselves to dogs. The parasite feeds off the dog, called the host, but the parasite does not kill the host. However, parasites can damage the host.
- Living things may prey on other creatures, such as lions that hunt and capture gazelles.

Recognize how energy is transferred from one organism to another or between an organism and its environment. Every living thing needs food to survive and reproduce. In the food chain, some organisms are producers and some are consumers. For example, plants are producers of food; animals are consumers.

Each time a plant or organism produces or consumes food, energy is transferred. Plants use light energy in the form of sunlight to produce food in the form of sugar. They either use the food or store it in their roots, leaves, and stems. Animals obtain the energy stored in plants when they consume them. When animals eat other animals, they obtain energy by digesting and breaking down the food. In this way, energy from the sun is distributed throughout the food chain.

Explain how energy can change within an animal. Energy changes form within an animal through the process of oxidation, which is the combining of matter with oxygen. Animals digest food by breaking it down mechanically and chemically. Then the food is oxidized, and some of the food is converted to heat energy.

Understand genetic traits. A funny-shaped nose or blue eyes are genetic traits you inherit from your parents. Traits are specific characteristics of a plant or animal that are handed down from parent to offspring. Some human traits include curly hair, dimples, and the shape of the fingernails. Traits are controlled by a part of a cell called the *gene*.

Learn about the process of sexual reproduction. To have offspring, many organisms produce sex cells. Sexual reproduction is the merging of a specialized female sex cell, called an *egg,* with a male sex cell, called a *sperm*. The fertilized egg carrying the genetic information from the female and male sex cells then multiplies to form the complete organism, all of whose cells contain the genetic information of the original female and male cells.

Learn about breeding experiments that show the inheritability of traits. The most famous breeding experiments were carried out in the mid-1800s by Gregor Mendel, an Austrian monk who loved nature and had an inborn curiosity. His famous studies examined how the traits of peas, such as the shape and color of the seeds, the color of the pods, plant height, and so on, can be inherited and can be controlled experimentally.

Recognize that new plants and animals result from selective breeding. New varieties of plants and animals have emerged by breeding for specific traits. For example, some varieties of dogs and horses are the result of selective breeding. Genetic engineering, the piecing together of genes of one species with the genes of another species, is a form of selective breeding.

Understand how small differences between parent and offspring can accumulate over generations. Since genetic traits are handed down from parent to offspring, over many generations traits that have helped organisms survive tend to predominate. Organisms having those traits have a better chance of surviving and passing them on to the next generation. That's why you will never see polar bears without heavy fur coats.

Learn that species are organisms that can mate and reproduce (or organisms that reproduce). Scientists classify organisms according to their traits. In this way,

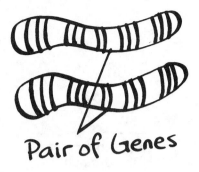

Pair of Genes

JUST A TOOL

A word to parents: Don't be overwhelmed by the hype. It's hard to pick up a newspaper or magazine these days without reading something about how technology is going to transform everything from shopping at the mall to performing brain surgery. While there's no question that computers are slowly becoming a valuable tool in the classroom, they are just a tool—like books or paper or pencils. And they're useless without good software and teachers who know how to make the most of the material.
—from *Newsweek's Computers & the Family* (Fall/Winter 1996)

Scientists are able to name the organism and learn how it is related to other organisms. Some traits that Scientists used to classify organisms include color, size, body structure, and methods of obtaining food.

The classification scheme we use today was developed by the Swedish scientist Carolus Linnaeus. A kingdom is the largest grouping, and a species is the smallest grouping. Organisms that mate and reproduce are considered as belonging to the same species.

Study how individual organisms with certain traits are more likely to survive. Imagine a tiger in the wild without claws or a flightless bird in the desert. Chances are those critters would be doomed to extinction mighty fast. Animals with certain traits, such as a white snowshoe rabbit, are more likely to survive because their white coat blends in with the snow fields and their big feet let them run faster.

Learn how layers of sedimentary rock can show the history of the earth. Over the long history of the earth, layers of rock, called sedimentary rock, have collected the remains of prehistoric plants and animals, called fossils. Fossils may be imprints of feet, petrified bone, plants, or animals frozen in ice or trapped in plant resin. Scientists study fossils to learn about the history of life and how species have changed.

Core Area 2: Physical Science

How do things work? How does a guitar make sound? What causes a rainbow? How do you make those ugly-looking, crunchy things that we call brownies? Physical science is the branch of science that explains the physical processes in our world and in the universe.

Learn about energy primarily through energy transformations. Every physical process involves the

THE SCIENTIFIC METHOD PART ONE

Here's the Scientific Method made fun and clear for parents to share with their children (the first three out of six points).

Think of an Idea: The first thing you need to do is think of an idea. It may be something you want to explain or do in an experiment or something you just want to study. The best way to get started is to adapt an existing experiment in a way that's unique to you. Ask a question that needs an experiment to get an answer.

Research Your Topic: Find out what's already known about the topic. See what you can add to the general body of knowledge. It's a good idea to take some notes.

Plan Your Experiment: This part of the Scientific Method is called the *procedure.* You make a game plan of when, where, how, what, and why you're going to do what it is that you're going to do and what you need to do it.
—The Wild Goose Company

transfer of energy or changing energy from one form to another. When a baseball hits a bat, an automobile cruises down a road, or a nuclear energy plant makes electricity, energy is transferred or transformed.

We usually think of energy in one of several forms:

- Kinetic energy, the energy of motion
- Potential energy, energy stored in an object
- Electrical energy, the kind that lights lamps
- Electromagnetic energy, the energy found in magnets
- Nuclear energy, the energy that powers nuclear plants

Although these energies look different, scientists currently think they are actually manifestations of two, more basic energies.

A baseball hitting a bat transfers energy from the player to the bat to the ball. An automobile takes the potential energy in gasoline and converts it into the kinetic energy of the motion of the car. A nuclear energy plant converts nuclear energy to electrical energy (electricity). In most physical processes, heat energy is an important byproduct of the energy transformation.

Explore and describe the conservation of energy. In every physical process, all the energy that causes the process is transformed or transferred. The energy needed to hit the baseball is transferred to the ball, which causes it to fly. However, energy is never lost. This means that the total amount of energy in the entire universe has not changed since time immemorial—not one iota. Students explore activities and perform experiments to demonstrate this concept.

AH HA!

THE SCIENTIFIC METHOD PART TWO

teacher

The Scientific Method continues.... After your child has (1) thought of an idea, (2) researched a topic, and (3) planned an experiment, then:

Do Your Experiment: Party time! This is where you get right down to the nitty-gritty of doing the experiment, collection of the data, rolling up the sleeves, and diving into the science fun. Remember to always follow safety rules!

Collect and Record Data: This is all the information that you're seeking. You'll include all your information in charts, data tables, lab notes, and records of observations.

Come to a Conclusion: Compile the data that you've collected, evaluate the results, answer the question you asked at the beginning, write a law describing what you observed, then ... collect your Nobel Prize!
—The Wild Goose Company

Making the Grade

BE LIKE MIKE

I tell students that Michael Jordan misses half of his basketball shots. If his first shot of the game doesn't go in, does he stop shooting? Nope. We have all these sports stars achieving great things, things in the Olympics nobody's ever done before, and yet somehow academically we don't continue with the "try until you succeed" mentality. Why in sports do we know you can fail so many times, but in school, you can't fail?

Explain that most of what goes on in the universe happens as a result of energy being transformed. Energy is what makes the sun shine, rockets fly, and rain fall. Every motion, biological process, and chemical reaction is the result of energy being transferred or transformed. It makes the world go round. Without it, the world would stop one day.

Explain how heat can be transferred through materials. Heat is transferred by the collision of atoms. (See Core Area 7 for information about atoms.) Heat is not the same as temperature. Heat is the energy transferred when something with a higher temperature meets something with a lower temperature—like your hand touching a cold window. The heat energy causes the atoms in the cooler object to vibrate faster and increase its temperature. Following are some conductors of heat:

- Silver conducts heat very well.
- Wood conducts heat at only 0.1 times the rate of silver.
- Water conducts heat at about 0.001 times the rate of silver.

Develop an idea of electric and magnetic forces using magnets and electric currents. Electrical energy is the energy in your home electrical outlets. This energy is produced by power plants using either oil, coal, natural gas, hydroelectric, or nuclear power. Electrical energy is delivered through transmission lines to transformers that control the strength of the electrical current and deliver it to your home in amounts that you can use.

A magnet is what makes a compass always point north. Those funny things you use to attach notices and other papers to the refrigerator are magnets. Magnets are used in televisions, telephones, and radios. Magnetic forces are used to store data on computer disks. Students explore magnets and learn about the forces around the magnets, called the *magnetic field*. Iron fillings around a magnet organize into the shape of the force field showing where the magnetic field is the weakest and strongest.

Study vibrations in ropes, strings, and in a water table and study the characteristics of the waves. A vibration, such as the strumming of a guitar string, is another motion that scientists study. These vibrations cause the air to move and create sound waves that carry the sound of the guitar. Students study the properties of waves formed by ropes, springs, and other materials. They learn that earthquakes create waves that disturb the layers of the earth's crust, damage property, and risk lives.

Generalize gravity to all matter. Every object exerts a force of attraction on every other object. Right now, the chair you are sitting in is exerting a very tiny force on you without you being aware of it! The force it exerts depends on its mass. Since its mass is not many thousands of times your mass, you will not feel the force. However, you do feel the force of the earth on you (gravity) because the mass of the earth is about 6.6 sextillion tons (that's 66 followed by 21 zeroes).

Begin to learn about inertia. Remember the magician's trick of pulling a table cloth out from under some plates without causing them to crash to the floor? That's an example of inertia at work. Inertia is the tendency of an object to resist changes in motion.

An object is like a conservative politician—it naturally resists change. Objects in motion prefer to stay in motion; objects at rest prefer to stay at rest (inertia). That's one of the fundamental laws of nature.

Learn that an unbalanced force acting on an object changes its speed or motion. Balanced forces are forces that are equal and opposite so that no motion occurs. It's like a tug of war that is stalemated. Each side is pulling with the same amount of force but in the opposite direction.

What happens if one side lets go? Well, this is an unbalanced force in action. The other side goes flying off in the opposite direction because there is no countervailing force. An unbalanced force causes a change in motion that is called an *acceleration*. An acceleration is a change in the motion of an object.

WHAT'S *MASS*?

Mass is the measure of the amount of matter in an object. Mass is different from weight (the measure of the force of gravity exerted on the object). The mass of an object never changes, but its weight does. For example, astronauts have to contend with the weightlessness of objects in space. An object in space does not have weight, but the amount of matter in it doesn't change.

Learn that a force depends on the masses of the objects and how far they are apart. We know that every object exerts a force of attraction on every other object. The size of the force depends on the mass of the object. The larger the mass, the greater the force. This explains why the sun holds the earth and planets in place, but you cannot hold your children in one place no matter how you try!

Core Area 3: Earth and Space

Humans have been studying the sky since the earliest times. The last years have seen many remarkable advances. Scientists have learned how the earth has developed and what the universe must have been like literally seconds after it was formed. This core area studies the processes that create the features of the earth as well as our solar system and the universe beyond.

Recognize that the Sun's gravity holds the earth and planets in their orbits. Just as the earth's gravity prevents us from flying off its surface, the Sun exerts a force, called *gravity*, on the earth and planets that keeps them in their orbits. Mercury, which is 36 million miles from the Sun, is the closest planet to the Sun and makes one complete revolution of the Sun in 88 days. Pluto, the planet that is over 3 billion miles from the Sun, is the farthest distance away. It makes one revolution every 248 years. You can really appreciate the ferocious power of the Sun when you consider that it exerts a gravitational force on a planet 3 billion miles away.

Explain that the Sun provides the light and heat for the earth. Without the Sun, life as we know it would not exist on our planet. The Sun provides the energy that plants use to produce the food that sustains life on the earth. The Sun sends its energy into space mostly in visible and infrared (invisible, short wave) light. Light from the Sun takes just a few minutes to reach the earth.

Demonstrate that the Sun is a medium-sized star. The Sun is a star near the edge of a galaxy of stars called the Milky Way. The Sun is the closest star to the earth. It would take thousands of years to travel to the next closest star, called Alpha Centauri.

The Sun is an average-sized star. The largest stars have diameters many thousands of times that of the Sun, and they have masses several hundred times greater. Because of this, the Sun is called a dwarf star.

The Sun is a huge, superheated ball of gas. Atomic reactions in its center generate the light and heat that the earth receives. Scientists estimate the temperature at the Sun's center is about 2,000,000° C (about 3,600,000° F). The Sun is about 865,400 miles in diameter and is about 1,000 times larger than the earth. Its fuel supply is expected to last another 5 billion years.

Study the planets, their moons, and their rings. A planet is a body of matter that travels around a star such as the Sun in a fixed orbit. At present, there are nine planets in our Solar System: Mercury, Venus, Earth, Mars, Jupiter, Saturn, Uranus, Neptune, and Pluto. While Mercury, Venus, and Earth are made mostly of solid matter, the planets beyond the earth are called gaseous planets because they are composed mainly of gases.

None of the other eight planets has an environment like Earth's. Planets closer to the Sun (Mercury and Venus) have a surface temperature much higher than Earth's; those planets farther from the Sun have a lower surface temperature. For example, Venus's surface temperature is about 470° C (878° F), and Uranus's surface temperature is about −209° C (−344° F). Although most of the other eight planets have atmospheres, none apparently has an atmosphere that could sustain life. Nevertheless, recent findings have scientists speculating that some forms of life could have existed on Mars thousands of years ago.

Although Mercury and Venus do not have moons—bodies that orbit planets—the earth has one moon, and the outer planets have anywhere from one to 18 moons. In addition, Saturn has a complex series of rings made up mostly of dust and chunks of rocks and ice.

THRILLER

My *SCORE!* experience has been wonderful. We were told there may be a low time when the academic work becomes harder and over daughter might not want to come, but we haven't found that yet. Every day she wants to come to *SCORE!*. I've gotten a lot of good ideas for home education from the program, too. I work more closely with my girl when she does homework, and we turn learning into quality, enjoyable time together. I was surprised how much I could contribute to her positive attitude about school! In just a few months, she's reading better, she's comprehending better, the math is so easy, she loves science—my daughter and I are just thrilled.

CHEW ON THIS

Try dinner conversations in which each family member needs to share or teach one fact with everyone. It can be silly or serious, significant or trivial!

Making the Grade

Learn about comets, asteroids, and meteorites. A comet is a large collection of ice, dust, and rock that travels together through space. Scientists believe comets are born in an icy cloud around the solar system beyond Pluto. The most famous comet, called Halley's comet, revolves around the Sun and completes one revolution every 75–78 years. Halley's comet last traveled near the earth in 1986.

An asteroid is a large chunk of ice and rock traveling in space. Most asteroids are found in an asteroid belt between Mars and Jupiter. Scientists theorize that these asteroids might have combined to form another planet if it were not for Jupiter's gravity. An estimated 30,000 asteroids are between Mars and Jupiter.

A meteor is a chunk of space rock that enters the earth's atmosphere. These chunks are drawn into the earth's gravitational field and are attracted to the surface. Although most meteors burn up before they reach the surface, the larger ones land on the surface. Meteors that hit the surface are called meteorites. The largest known meteorite weighing approximately 70 tons landed in southern Africa. In 1996, a meteor from Mars was found that seemed to contain evidence that some form of life may have existed on Mars hundreds of thousands of years ago.

Learn about the universe and galaxies. On a clear night in the country, far beyond city lights, you can see the twinkle of what seems like thousands of stars. Stars, the basic unit of the universe, are hot, glowing balls of gases that are huge celestial furnaces that burn the gases by atomic reactions under extremely high temperatures and pressures.

On a clear night, dozens of stars can be seen in the sky. The ancient Greeks organized the sky into constellations, groupings of stars that resemble common objects. For example, the Big Dipper looks like a giant ladle. Another constellation is Orion, the hunter. This group of stars shows the outline of a warrior holding a shield and club. Betelgeuse, one of the largest stars known, is on his left shoulder. The three bright stars in the middle indicate Orion's belt.

Constellations generally are not part of the same groups of stars; they are merely patterns in the sky made by stars at vastly different true distances from the earth. Constellations are a common method of using the sky to identify different directions—north, south, east, and west.

Stars are clustered in groupings called *galaxies* that usually contain billions of stars. Most stars that you see are part of the Milky Way galaxy, the system of about 200 billion stars, one part of which is the solar system. The Milky Way galaxy consists mainly of stars, gas, and dust. Stars in this galaxy vary in age from several hundred thousand years old to over ten billion years old.

The Andromeda galaxy is a bright galaxy of stars that is visible to the naked eye. It is 12 million trillion miles away.

Recognize that the tilt of Earth's axis causes the seasons. The earth revolves around the Sun at an angle like a spinning top that is not upright. Because of the way the earth moves around the Sun, sometimes the southern hemisphere is closer to the Sun than the northern hemisphere, and sometimes the northern hemisphere is closer to the Sun than the southern hemisphere. The half the globe that is closer to the Sun experiences summer and the other half has winter. If the earth were not tilted, then there would be no seasons. All the parts of the globe would receive the same amount of sunlight and heat every day.

Explain what causes the phases of the moon. As the moon revolves around the earth, the amount of sunlight that is reflected from the moon's surface towards the earth varies. The phenomenon produces what is called the *phases of the moon.* The following are four phases of the moon.

- New moon: In this phase, the moon is not visible in the sky. Since the earth is between the sun and the moon, little sunlight reaches the surface of the moon that we see, so little sunlight is reflected back to Earth.
- First quarter: The half of the moon that receives sunlight is visible.

PERSEVERE

It wasn't until my son was in the 4th grade that he was diagnosed with ADHD and also having a learning disability. I felt the school missed this and should have answered my earlier concerns. For two years I was told nothing was wrong with him. Parents need to demand answers sometimes, go with their gut feelings, and be involved. Our son is now in the 6th grade and although we still struggle with his attention, understanding how he is and how he learns has helped us. There are many different ways to help children learn, and parents just need to find the right way!

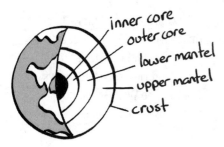

- Full moon: The entire surface of the moon that faces the Earth receives sunlight and is visible.
- Last quarter: The other half of the moon that we didn't see in the first quarter is now illuminated.

Explain the importance to weather of the cycling of water in and out of the atmosphere. Each man, woman, and child in the United States uses on average 140 gallons of water per day. Have you every wondered where the water comes from? The water cycle continually recycles water by the following process:

- Rain falls to Earth.
- Most of the water flows into lakes, rivers, ponds, and oceans as runoff.
- The water evaporates, forms water vapor (water in gaseous form), and drifts up into the atmosphere.
- In the atmosphere, the water vapor cools and condenses (turns back into liquid form), and then collects in clouds, which produce falling rain or snow.

Water is always recycling and replenishing the rivers, lakes, ponds, and ground water from which we get our water supplies. This cycle, called the *hydrologic cycle,* is one of the most important of the earth's systems. It causes much of our weather.

Understand the limited capacity of the atmosphere and ocean to absorb wastes. The atmosphere and oceans absorb wastes in the water and air; they are the earth's natural cleanup systems. However, there is a limit to the amount of pollution that the atmosphere and ocean can clean. For example, in many countries, the atmosphere cannot absorb all the pollution caused by automobiles and power plants. Some pollution falls back to the earth as acid rain, rain that is more acidic than usual. Acid rain damages the environment, kills animals, and destroys the earth's limited resources. Cleaning up air and water pollution and restoring the earth's resources is very difficult and expensive.

Complete most of an understanding of the factors that shape the earth. Earthquakes, floods, and volcanoes alter the surface of the earth, but there are many other processes operating underneath the surface. Scientists believe that underneath the surface are several layers of rock like the layers of an onion. The inner core of the earth is made of dense rock, mostly iron and nickel, about 100 miles thick. The next layer, the outer core, is made of the same rock in liquid form and is about 2,000 miles thick. The next layer, called the *mantle,* is about 1,800 miles thick and reaches almost to the surface. The final layer, the crust, is the one on which we live. It ranges from five to 25 miles thick.

Under the crust, the mantle has some unusual properties. Although it is solid, it is under tremendous heat and pressure that cause it to shift. In fact, because of this intense heat and pressure, the mantle is broken into sections called *plates.* As these plates move around, sometimes they crash into one another causing bulges or depressions in the surface crust (that is, mountains or ocean basins). The movement of these plates also cause volcanoes and earthquakes. While some changes in the earth's surface are abrupt, others occur more slowly. For example, movements of the mantle over thousands of years shifted continents and created mountains. Surface features can also be changed by wind and water.

Another geological formation that shapes the earth's surface is sedimentary rock, the rock formed by the gradual accumulation of sand and other rock particles. This rock forms layers that may build up and break through the crust, thereby creating mountains and other geographical features.

Understand how sedimentary rock contains evidence of geologic history. The thousands of layers of sedimentary rock gather evidence of geological processes, such as the forces operating on the rock as well as heating, melting, and recrystalization. The layers contain much information about the changing surface, and they usually contain fossils, the remains of plants and animals that lived in various periods of the earth's history. Scientists study the layers of sedimentary rock to learn about the processes that created the continents and the life forms that have inhabited the earth.

Understand how volcanic eruptions or meteors cause climate change. Climates can be altered abruptly by

GOOD SCIENCE DOUBTS

Here's some advice for parents when it comes to kids and science:

• Cut your kids some slack. Don't tell them they have to believe something like Newton's First Law just because it's the "right" way to look at things. There's no better way to turn kids off to learning.

• When you're talking about science concepts with kids, and the concepts don't jibe with everyday life, encourage kids to be skeptical. That's what scientists do. Tell them NOT to believe anything unless they're convinced. But make it clear that you don't have to believe in something to understand it. This amounts to an end run around those kids who will claim they don't have to get something right on a test if they don't believe it. Clever, but too sneaky!

• Use sentences like, "According to Newton's First Law, what should happen here?" That way, you make it clear that the purpose is to understand the concept and how it applies to a situation rather than to believe the concept.

• Show kids that even though it tends to contradict common sense, something like Newton's First Law helps predict a lot of things. In other words, it works. If it didn't work, we wouldn't use it.
—The Wild Goose Co.

Making the Grade

THE WHY FILES

The National Institute for Science Education has a nifty Web site with topics lifted from the headlines. Questions like "Is there life on Mars?" are addressed in fun, readable essays accompanied by charts and illustrations. Messaging boards and a great science image library make this a site worth exploring with your child: http://whyfiles.news.wisc.edu

volcanic eruptions or by meteors. Volcanic eruptions can spew volcanic dust into the atmosphere that travels thousands of miles and blankets the earth's surface, preventing the sun from penetrating the dust. These clouds of volcanic ash act as a layer of insulation that traps heat on the surface. If these eruptions continue long enough, the climate can be changed permanently.

Large meteors also can affect the atmosphere or ocean. The impact of a large meteor can generate millions of tons of dust and debris that can disrupt the climate.

Learn how small changes in atmosphere or ocean cause climate change. Small changes in the composition of the atmosphere or ocean can have dramatic effects on weather. For example, if the composition of gases in the air changes, heat that normally escapes might be trapped, and the surface temperature might rise.

If the direction of an ocean current changes, the water temperature of certain areas might change, thereby affecting the weather of the area. For instance, the Gulf Stream in the Atlantic Ocean carries warm water from the equator to Iceland where the warm water produces an unusually mild climate for a country that far from the equator. If that current ever changes, watch out, Iceland! They would be in for a major change in temperature and weather.

Learn how human activities change the land, ocean, and atmosphere. There are numerous examples of how human activities have affected the earth. Here are a few.

- Intensive agriculture and irrigation over the centuries has gradually destroyed large amounts of soil needed to grow crops.
- Widespread farming over the ages has reduced the acreage of forests on the earth.
- Scientists believe that human activities have gradually increased the average surface temperature of the earth. Human fires over thousands of years have increased the amount of sulfur dioxide and other gases in the

atmosphere. The gases trap heat and cause the surface to be warmer. This trend has accelerated in recent decades due to the air pollution generated by motorized vehicles and power plants.

Core Area 4: Technology

Technology includes the tools that have shaped our civilizations. When we think of technology, we usually think high tech: lasers, computers, fiber optics, the space shuttle, and CAT scan equipment. However, technology is also mundane things like the tools for building homes and the process of preparing food.

Technology has been largely ignored in most schools until recently. However, many educators now understand that they must prepare students to succeed in our technological society. In some leading schools, students are starting to design projects in the elementary grades. In middle school, the industrial arts curriculum is being revised to provide real technological education that informs students about the properties, powers, impact, and limitation of technology.

Make a technological device. To understand the process of technological development, students identify and study an actual problem, and then they design and build a device that solves the problem. As they analyze the problem, they use problem solving, critical thinking skills, ingenuity, decision-making skills, and research.

Use material tests to identify appropriate uses for materials. Material tests examine the hardness, tensile strength, and conductivity of a substance.

- Hardness is the ability of the material to withstand an intense blow. One common way to test for hardness is to strike the material with a heavy pendulum or other instrument.
- Tensile strength is the ability of the material to carry a heavy load. Tensile strength is measured in pounds (lbs) per square inch. For example, concrete can resist a load of 10,000 lbs per square inch; steel can resist a load of 50,000 lbs per square inch.

ACTIVE ROLE

Parents are often disappointed with their children's schools. Their expectations may be exaggerated. They expect a teacher to teach their kids everything. But when a kid is learning to read or add, there are many different stimuli in our environment that contribute to a children's learning—it doesn't all happen at school. Parents have a key role in their child's education. The more active role they take, the more their children will get out of school.

Making the Grade

WORKING IT OFF

At *SCORE!*, I see a lot of kids who have an extracurricular activity almost every day of the week—musical instruments, sports, gymnastics, martial arts. Part of these afterschool projects work out well. Many kids have extra energy, and it helps to work it off every day after school. Some kids can maintain that schedule and still have enough energy to go home and do well on their homework, and to interact well with their friends and family. But that's not every child!

• Electrical conductivity of a substance is the ability to conduct an electrical charge. Since copper is a good conductor of electricity, it is used in electrical wiring. Heat conductivity is the ability of a substance to conduct heat. Heat conductivity is important for the material that protects the space shuttle. Scientists chose a material that does not conduct the intense heat that the Space Shuttle is subject to.

You and your child can research why certain materials are used for certain purposes, such as, why silicon is used to make integrated circuits for computers.

Model ways in which resources are used to develop new technologies. Developing a new technology is a complex process that requires more than the creativity of a budding Edison in his workshop. Among the factors that must be considered are the following:

• Information
• Tools and machines
• Proper materials
• Energy to produce and, if necessary, drive the technology
• Capital, including both money and labor
• Vast amounts of time necessary to design and build the technology

Explain a manufacturing process. Students choose a manufactured item, such as a CD-ROM or running shoes, and research how it is made. If there is a manufacturing plant in your region, find out whether you can get a tour of the plant and talk with plant managers and workers. Learn what materials are used in the manufacturing process, what kinds of energy is required, how the raw materials are transformed into the finished product, and how the product is delivered to the user. If there is no manufacturing plant in your area, research a manufacturing process, starting at your local library. Newspapers, people in the community, videos, and the Internet are also useful resources. Some companies provide brochures and other informational packets about their manufacturing processes.

Describe how power systems work. Power systems convert energy into another form that our technologies can use. Systems have been developed to harness and transmit mechanical, electrical, fluid, heat, solar, and wind energy. The types of energy that are used include

- Nonrenewable fuels—such as oil, natural gas, and coal—that are used in power-generating plants
- Unlimited fuels such as solar energy that power solar panels and wind energy that powers windmills
- Renewable energy sources such as biomass, vegetation, or agricultural waste used as a fuel (for example, wood pellets or sugar cane waste), which are used to power generating plants

Understand the impact of technological change in history. One historic technological advance was the Industrial Revolution, a technological change based on waterpower, steam engines, and other motors, which had a profound effect on history. The new factories were magnets that drew people to the cities. These massive movements of people changed the face of the landscape. Industrialized countries gradually became urban countries in which most of the people lived in urban areas. As workers' standard of living rose, they became consumers who could purchase the latest technologies, such as the telephone and automobile in the twentieth century. Other examples of technologies that have had a profound impact on human society include the discovery of fire, the development of farming, the printing press, atomic weapons, and the Internet.

Recognize the negative side effects of technology. For ages, people have believed that technology was the answer to their problems. Even today, many people believe that the problems we face, such as war, pollution, and a declining standard of living, can be remedied with a technical "quick fix."

There is a price to pay, however, for some technologies. For example, the invention of the automobile has had a profound effect on American society. Our reliance on cars has spawned urban sprawl, the degeneration of the center cities, and serious air pollution.

SCIENCE HAS LIMITS

Scientists spend their lives asking why this or that happens. Most people assume that a good scientist will be able to answer a few why questions for them. Like, "Why do things fall to the earth?" Everyone knows it's because of gravity. Then you can ask, "Well, what is gravity?" Well, it's the thing that makes stuff fall to Earth. You see, the answer isn't really an answer at all, it just gives a name to something.

Now a physicist will give you a different answer. She will talk about a force that acts between all things, and she'll write down a formula that describes how the force behaves. But you can keep asking why questions, like "Why does this force exist?"

If you're looking for the "ultimate" answer to your why questions, science is the wrong place! Why do we bring all this up? Because we believe that if kids understood some of the limitations of science, they may not be so scared of it and may be willing to tackle those limitations head-on to find even more. —The Wild Goose Co.

Making the Grade

Explain how technology led the change from an agricultural to an information society. Many inventions led the evolution from an agricultural society to an information society. Here are some key innovations.

- Steam engine
- Cotton gin
- Electricity
- Telephone
- Radio and television
- Airplane
- Automobile
- Transistor
- Computer
- Fiber optics

Choose one invention and research its impact on society with your child. An encyclopedia and your local library are useful resources.

Provide evidence that technology is developing faster than ever before. The pace of technological change in the last 20 years has been breathtaking. Computers and other technical devices are used in almost every walk of life, from medical care to sports. One example of the pace of technological change is the rapid development of the Internet, the network of computers worldwide that allows anyone with a computer and a modem to communicate clear across the globe. Using this technology, you can acquire vast amounts of information at the touch of a button.

Evaluate designs or devices. Technology changes to meet the needs of a problem or when new devices are invented. For example, the devices for recording and playing music have evolved over the last 100 years. Though music was originally stored on metal cylinders, technology evolved to plastic long-playing albums, then to tapes, and now to compact discs. Each design should be evaluated and analyzed for the materials it uses, its efficiency and effectiveness, and the quality of the output.

Study with your child how devices have changed or been improved. For example, you and your child might research how and why the rotary telephone has been replaced by the touchtone telephone.

Communicate the process of technological design. Students give examples of how the information related to technological design is communicated. Technological designs may be represented in drawings and plans. In addition to written reports, other methods that may be used to present a design include photographs, videos, and graphs showing the results of tests.

Core Area 6: Inquiry Skills

Students have a natural curiosity about how things work. Performing their own investigations leads them to a deeper appreciation of science. Students develop the skills to design their own experiments and test technological solutions. Frequently, these investigations involve extended projects in which students perform multiple trials and progressively refine their tests.

Identify whether the differences between identical experiments are trivial. In an experiment, it is crucial to recognize relevant and irrelevant information. For example, if you are testing if various areas of your skin are more sensitive to hot and cold than other areas, then the relevant information might include various parts of your skin, the temperature of the substance, and the length of time your skin is exposed to the substance. Irrelevant information might include the shape, color, or texture of the substance.

Explain the importance of changing only one variable at a time in an experiment. As part of an experiment, it is important to vary only one part of the experiment at a time. Changing more than one variable prevents you from recognizing which one is responsible for a new result. Sometimes, it is not possible to control outside variables, such as the wind direction or speed when testing a new kite design.

BORN THAT WAY

Some kids don't get a lot of parental pressure about school performance, but they put a tremendous amount of internal pressure on themselves to succeed. It's important for parents to recognize this and come up with a plan to combat it. Some students start crying when they don't get consistently perfect or high marks on a test or assignment. When these kids get into high school, they're going to have nervous breakdowns. When they get into college, forget it! If these kids are in a class with other bright students, and they're perhaps not in the top of the class, they are going to freak out. Parents often feel self-conscious about their stressed-out child—they wonder if it's something they did. Kids have personalities from the day they're born, and some kids are simply like this.

A PLACE TO SUCCEED

Not only does *SCORE!* give kids a place to make mistakes, we also give them a place to succeed. Many children don't care about school. They'll go through school as if it's a social thing, and doing well isn't a priority. If they do well in school, they might not get recognized to the extent they are when they're at *SCORE!*. So we're a place where kids can do well and be recognized for their achievements. When they make three months of progress, they get a big bronze ribbon and their name up on a mountain on the wall, and the whole center knows that they've finished their goal. It's a really positive place and everyone congratulates them. A child can never get enough positive feedback like that.

Reformulate ideas and technological solutions. Improving experiments and technological solutions requires some trial and error—and ingenuity. For example, suppose you want to make a kite and you find a pattern. After making the kite from paper and testing it, you may need to alter the design of the kite to make it a larger or a different shape. Also, you can try a different material, such as cloth or plastic.

Design an experiment. Suppose you want to find out whether there are differences between skin sensitivity to hot and cold. You could test different areas of your hand for sensitivity to hot and cold water by dipping each area into pans of hot and cold water.

To design an experiment, you need to follow these steps:

1. Write a clear statement of what you want to investigate. Explain what you will be studying and the data you will collect.
2. Identify the equipment and measuring devices you will need to gather your data.
4. Write a clear plan of your experiment explaining each step carefully.
5. Perform the experiment and collect the data.
6. Write a report and explain your observations.

Design a solution to a technological problem and describe its advantages and disadvantages. Part of the design of technology is an understanding of its advantages and disadvantages. For example, suppose you need to move a piece of heavy furniture into your house and you make a ramp to roll the furniture on some rollers. The advantages are that you don't have to lift the furniture and that the ramp covers and protects the stairs. One disadvantage is that this solution does not solve problems of maneuvering the furniture through doorways and around corners.

Use multiple lines of inquiry to analyze a problem. To analyze a question, it is frequently necessary to use several different methods including experimentation, trial and error, taking a survey, doing some interviews, or researching the problem. For example, researchers have used many strategies to discover possible cures for the AIDS virus. Many scientists have studied how the virus works to try to find a cure. Others have used trial and error; they have tried using existing drugs and different drug combinations to fight the virus. Still others have done surveys and interviews to learn if social factors may play a part in the disease.

Understand that what people expect to observe often affects what they do observe. Sometimes an individual's beliefs about what should happen prevent the discovery of unexpected results. Scientists are aware of this problem and arrange ways for avoiding it. One check is to have several researchers conduct the research independently.

Learn about the ethics of science. When research involves humans, potential subjects should be informed of the risks and benefits of the research, and they should be given the opportunity to refuse to participate. Since animals cannot make such choices, special care should be taken when using them as subjects.

Explain that some matters cannot be tested scientifically. Although science can study natural processes, there are many phenomena that science cannot explain. Many human behaviors, including a person's likes and dislikes or a person's religious beliefs, cannot be studied scientifically.

Core Area 7: Chemistry

The word *chemistry* conjures up images of mad scientists fanatically experimenting in their labs, or acres of petrochemical plants and their maze of pipelines and smokestacks. But nature is our largest chemistry lab. Chemists study the processes that substances use to create the matter in our world. Chemistry is the study of how substances are made and how their parts react with other substances.

Explain that all matter is made up of atoms and that atoms form molecules. Most matter that we see is made up of combinations of basic substances, called elements. The smallest unit of an element that still has all the properties of

CYBERSCHOOL

Go to this site and you'll be hit with a variety of educational information. The articles here are fun and different and slightly disorganized, but the real prize is the Surfin' Librarian page, with loads of links to museums, libraries, maps, and education sites on the Web. Check out this cool tool at: http://www.infoshare.ca/csm/index. htm

LOG-ON LEARNING

There's a classroom service for your child that doesn't require field trips, school bus rides, lunchboxes, or teacher conferences. It's a cyberservice that goes right into your home via the Internet. A group called OnlineClass has offered some fascinating courses taken by thousands of kids. Class samplings: Blue Ice (all about Antarctica, including actual links for students directly to scientists and explorers in Antarctica), U.S. politics (specially timed to coincide with the presidential elections), and Student Ocean Challenge (kids follow sailing fleets around the world). To register and obtain more information, reach OnlineClass at: http://www.usinternet.com/onlineclass

the element is called an atom. Anything smaller is just a part within the element, such as a proton or a neutron in an atom of oxygen. The length of an average atom measures about 0.000000004 inches, and it takes about 6×10^{22} atoms to make up a cubic inch of solid matter.

There are over 100 elements. At normal temperatures, most elements are solids. Only two elements are liquids, and eleven are gases. Oxygen in the air we breathe is an element. Other common elements include aluminum, chlorine, and copper.

Elements combine to form compounds. Atoms combine to form molecules, the basic unit of a compound. Water is the compound of one oxygen atom and two atoms of the element hydrogen (as in hydrogen peroxide). Other common compounds are carbon dioxide, sodium chloride (table salt), and vinegar.

Recognize that atoms and molecules are in perpetual motion. A substance occurs in one of three states: solid, liquid, or gas. The way that matter changes form is explained by the movement of atoms and molecules. At absolute zero (−273° C, which is about −459° F), these particles are at rest. At warmer temperatures, atoms and molecules move faster. The degree of activity of the atoms or molecules determines the state of the matter.

Learn that atoms in solids vibrate and that atoms in liquids are more loosely connected In a solid, the atoms (for elements) or molecules (for compounds) are so close together that they vibrate. Very small forces keep the atoms or molecules in their places. This gives the solid its hard quality. In liquids, the atoms or molecules have more room to roam. This ability to move about allows liquids to flow. In a gas, the atoms or molecules separate and are free to move in any direction that gives a gas the freedom to float into any space that is available.

Measure and predict changes in a gas sample. Changing the volume of a gas changes its pressure and temperature. The pressure comes from the free-flowing molecules in the gas hitting a surface and causing a force. The temperature comes from the rate at which the molecules are moving. The higher the rate, the higher the temperature.

Think of blowing up a balloon. As you blow air into the balloon, huge numbers of molecules of air are sent into the balloon. As the number of molecules increase with the balloon, more of them hit the surface, the balloon inflates, and the pressure rises. And what happens to the temperature? Since you are increasing the number of molecules in a confined space, they are more liable to hit one another, and go speeding off faster and faster, causing the temperature to rise.

Explain that the temperature and acidity of a solution influence a reaction. An acid is a substance that tastes sour. The citric acid in a lemon is what makes your lips pucker. The acids in your stomach are among the strongest acids. Strong acids combine together more readily than weak acids.

In all reactions, the bonds between molecules are made and broken. With each event, heat is either absorbed or released. In many reactions, as bonds are formed, heat is released. The higher the temperature of a solution, the faster the reaction. If some reactions produce energy faster than it can be released into the surroundings, an explosion will occur.

Study how substances in a closed system conserve the total weight in the system. In a reaction occurring in a closed system—such as a tightly capped beaker, no atoms are created or lost. The total number of atoms does not change after a reaction. Thus, if there are 75 grams of hydrogen and oxygen before a reaction, then combining these elements will produce 75 grams of water and oxygen after the reaction.

HOW YOU SAY IT

When communicating, the way you are received is affected by many elements:

• **Your body** (Are you tensed up, turned away, slouching, pointing a finger, shaking a fist?)

• **Your timing** (Are you speaking fast? Slowly? What moment did you choose for your communication? How do you pause, space your words?)

• **Your facial expression** (Are you smiling? Squinting? Raising eyebrows? Gritting teeth?)

• **Your tone of voice** (Are you shouting? Whispering? Sneering? Whining?)

• **Your choice of words** (Are they biting? Accusative? Pretentious? Emotionally laden? Ambiguous?)

Often it's not *what* you say, it's *how* you say it!
—from *Bringing Up Parents: The Teenager's Handbook* by Alex J. Packer (Free Spirit Publishing, 1992)

Making the Grade

Group elements with similar properties. The elements are grouped according to the following classifications:

- Metals—These elements are highly conductive, have a bright luster, and are soft and easily molded. Of the first 103 elements, 75 are considered metals.
- Nonmetals—Seventeen elements are considered nonmetals because they do not exhibit any characteristics of metals. Nonmetals easily combine with metals to form compounds.
- Semimetals (metalloids)—Between the metals and nonmetals are elements called *semimetals* that have some characteristics of metals.
- Inert gases—These elements usually occur as gases and do not combine with other elements to form compounds.

What Can We Do at Home?

CHAPTER 12

Learning Adventures— 7th Grade Language Arts

PICTURING GOALS

Kids need constant positive feedback. Try making a picture or drawing with your child that helps her color in her goals, like drawing a mountain with a chapter of a book at each level. Just the little coloring when she works on her goals will help her see how many study steps she's getting done.

SOME HOMOPHONES

fair/fare, hair/hare, coarse/course, hoarse/horse, plain/plane, paced/paste, pitcher/picture, cents/sense, sum/some

❯ A Bare Bear

Homophones—words that sound alike but have different spellings and meanings—pose problems for spellers. But they can also be a lot of fun.

In this word game, you, your child, and other family members work to invent the funniest—and hardest to guess—pairs of homophones.

At a Glance

Grade/Subject: 7th/Language Arts—Spelling, Vocabulary
Skills: recognizing, distinguishing, and spelling homophone pairs
Materials: dictionary
Time: 20–30 minutes whenever you have an opportunity

Getting Ready

Do a quick review of what homophones are: pairs (and some triplets) of words that *sound* alike but are spelled differently and have different meanings.

After dinner, or in the car, or at similar times, are good opportunities to introduce this "sounds alike" game. Most kids will catch on quickly. The challenge is to expand their vocabulary to include the often less-common word in the pair. Keep the game informal and fun.

Making the Grade

WHAT'S MORE

Sketch or draw your clues instead of giving a spoken definition—for instance, a scowling face (a *mean mien*).

———

See what puzzles you can make from homophone triplets such as: *two/too/to; they're/there/their; I/eye/aye.*

———

Look in the library or bookstore for books of word games and puzzles.

———

Get acquainted with the entertaining wordplay poems of Ogden Nash, starting with his poem *one "one-l" lamas and "two-l" llamas.*

———

Write poems based on the funny mental pictures created by homophone pairs.

Step One

Start by giving a definition that your child can answer with a homophone pair. Here are some samples:

Q: What do you call a large animal that loses its fur coat?
A: A bare bear.

Q: What do you call a tired-out root vegetable?
A: A beat beet.

Q: What's an underage coal worker called?
A: A minor miner.

Take turns offering challenges and definitions. Be sure to stick to the rules—two meanings for the same word don't count. The two have to be spelled differently.

Step Two

Have your child create a little wordplay book in which he writes all the questions in one section and then writes the answers upside down in the back.

Step Three

Here's another way to play. Not all homophone pairs form neat phrases, but many of them can be used to fill the blanks in amusing, offbeat sentences. Take turns making up sentences for this version of the game. Here's how: One person makes up a sentence that uses homophones but substitutes a blank for each homophone. The trick is to make the sentence include enough information for the other person then to guess what words will fit the blanks. For example:

I _____ the _____ of buffalo stampeding past the tent. (*heard/herd*)

Jim's _____ was expanding, so he decided to let the chocolate cake go to _____. (*waist/waste*)

Step Four

Have your child add all the examples you both create of this kind of homophone puzzle to his wordplay book. As before, he should write the answers upside down in the back.

▶ BOOKS ON TAPE

Commuters, travelers, and millions of other people now enjoy listening to popular books on tape in their cars, on the subway, or as they travel. These tapes are recorded by actors or the book's own author. Imagine how much fun it would be to have favorite books recorded on tape by your own child, either by herself, or perhaps with you or other family members taking different roles as characters or the narrator.

You and your child can choose and record favorite books or stories, using your own choices as well as favorites of other family members. If you travel on business, you might enjoy listening to your child's voice reading a story. From another perspective, a kid who gets homesick while away from home at camp or visiting grandparents may enjoy listening to a family tape of a familiar book.

This activity can help build facility both in reading aloud and in developing a variety of speaking skills.

At a Glance

Grade/Subject: 7th/Language Arts—Literature, Listening and Speaking Skills
Skills: reading aloud, speaking expressively
Materials: cassette tape recorder with microphone
blank cassette tapes
favorite books or stories
Time: 1/2 hour to an hour recording sessions, two or three times a week while recording a book (Recording additional books will take similar amounts of time. Probably one hour is the maximum productive time for any single recording session.)

Getting Ready

The most important preliminary decision is, of course, what book or story to put on tape. Will it be a kids' classic, like one of the Dr. Seuss books? A shortened version of an old favorite like *Little House on the Prairie* or *The Incredible Journey?* Or a more modern classic? Science fiction? Mystery?

If you have made a practice of reading (and enjoying) children's and young adult books with your kid, you'll probably have a number of ideas and suggestions. So will your kid. Remember that this is a joint project. Decisions take compromise.

READING PROBLEMS?

Does your child have a reading problem? As your child reads aloud with you, watch for these things:
• **Mispronunciation**—This covers saying the word incorrectly or adding or omitting words in sentences. Your child should be able to read eight out of ten words accurately. If your child stumbles over more than half the words, he or she might have a reading problem.
• **Fluency**—This is the smoothness with which your child reads. Does your child read with emphasis in the proper places so that you can easily understand what she is reading? Does your child read in a halting, choppy manner? If your child struggles with too many words, her fluency will be poor, and this may indicate some underlying reading difficulties.
• **Skipping lines/losing one's place**—While your child reads, ask him to look up at you, then ask your child a question, especially in the middle of a longer paragraph. Then ask your child to continue reading. Count how long it takes your child to find his place again. If the child takes longer than five seconds, he may have a reading problem.
• **Comprehension**—This is probably the most important area of reading. As your child reads, write down at least seven questions to ask her when she is finished. Your child should get at least five right. If your child has a score of three or less, she most likely has a problem with comprehension.
For more information on how to work with your child and improve reading, check out *The Parent's Answer Book* by Gerald Deskin and Greg Steckler (Fairview Press, 1995); contact Fairview at (800) 544-8207.

As your teenager develops facility in reading aloud, it can be turned to good community use. Suggest that she volunteer to be part of the local library's story hour or as a volunteer to read to students or to older people with vision problems.

Imagine the thrill for a small kid when his baby-sitter—your child—turns up with a cassette tape of one of his favorite books or stories, as read by his own sitter! Not only does making the tape give your child practice in reading and speaking, but it also encourages the younger child's love for reading.

Suggest to your teenager that she record a story as a birthday or holiday gift for a younger sibling or relative.

Step One

Length is one consideration in choosing a book. Make your first project a short book—even a classic folk tale or fairy story. For later projects, work together to choose certain chapters or even prepare an abridged version of the book.

After choosing a book to record, decide who will take part. Perhaps you can read the part of the narrator while your child reads the dialogue. Work together to assign reading parts.

Be sure you both know how to operate the tape recorder!

Step Two

Find a quiet place for your recording sessions. Before you begin the actual recording, you and your child and all other participants should read a few rehearsal paragraphs into the tape recorder.

Listen to these rehearsal tapes and notice your mistakes. If there aren't many, you might just keep going. Otherwise, erase and you're ready to start fresh.

Step Three

Read and record the parts you assigned. Don't try to record more than a few pages at a time. At the beginning, stop frequently to listen to the results. Don't be overcritical. Relax and enjoy the story.

Share the reading duties as equally as possible. Take turns reading and being "sound engineer" in charge of recording.

When your recording is done, share it with friends and family members. Then start thinking about the next book you want to record on tape.

▶ GET THE POINT (OF VIEW)

"Hey, whose story is this anyway?" No doubt you've heard someone begin telling about an experience only to have the story taken over and finished by someone else. What difference does it make who tells the story? Well, a lot actually. And one big part of that difference depends on whether it is told from the first- or third-person point of view. Each has its unique advantages and purposes. In doing this activity, you and your child explore the concept of literary point of view and what these advantages and purposes are.

At a Glance

Grade/Subject: 7th/Language Arts—Reading and Literature, Composition, Thinking Skills
Skills: analyzing point of view, critical thinking, narrative paragraph writing
Materials: four or five brief narrative selections from books, magazines, and newspapers
paper and pencil
Time: 45 minutes to an hour

Getting Ready

Review the concept of point of view in literature—the vantage point from which the author presents the action of a story (See Core Area 10 in the chapter on Language Arts content). Remember that material written in the first-person (or limited) point of view presents action, emotions, and opinions known only to that character. The third-person (or omniscient) point of view enables writers to present the inner thoughts and feelings of all the characters and is not limited to reporting action known only to one character.

In gathering reading selections for this activity, keep them brief and include examples of both first-person and third-person points of view. They can range from the latest news to excerpts from novels, biographies, autobiographies, and history books. (The variety of narratives found in any issue of the *Reader's Digest* usually includes both omniscient and limited point of view.)

Step One

Read the first selection together and ask your child which point of view the author has used in writing it.

- How did she decide which point of view it is?
- Why does she think the writer chose that point of view?
- What effect does the point of view have on the telling of the story?
- Does she think it was a good choice? Why?
- What difference does she think it would make if the story were told from a different point of view?

COMPUTER WISDOM

How much time should children spend on a computer? The phrase "on a computer" misses the point. It all depends on what they're using a computer to do. If kids are using a computer to write creatively, to analyze biological data for a school project, compose a symphony, or to improve reading and math skills, never fear. As with reading and writing, it's pretty safe to let children set their own limits. There's little danger of their reading and writing too much.

On the other hand, your children should not sacrifice a single hour of outdoor play or cozy fireside conversation to play mind-numbing video games. The sad fact is that this is what most kids do most of the time when they're "on the computer."

MAKE IT CLEAR

We must make it clear in the minds of young people and parents that the primary activity of childhood and adolescence is schooling. — from *Beyond the Classroom* by Laurence Steinberg, Ph.D. (Simon & Schuster, 1996)

Making the Grade

Go through the rest of the selections. You probably will not need to read each entirely; the point is to read enough to get a good sense of the point of view and how it works in the narrative. Discuss each selection in the same way. Look for any patterns of usage. For instance, is omniscient (third-person) point of view more effective for certain purposes, while limited (first-person) is more effective for others?

Step Two

Then suggest a brief writing activity that is fun to do together. Each of you should pick an event in your life and write a short narrative paragraph about it autobiographically (which requires using the first-person point of view), telling only what you personally could know about it.

When you have finished, put it aside and then retell the same narrative from a biographical standpoint—that is, write about it in the third person. Remember, in the third-person point of view, you are omniscient; you can include the thoughts and feelings of others.

When you are done, compare your two versions. Read them aloud to one another. Talk about the differences between them, which versions each of you prefer, and why.

- Did you have to think about the events and the people involved differently in order to tell your story in the third person?
- Is the event you wrote about more effectively written about from the first-person or third-person point of view?
- Which way do you think makes the better story—first-person or third-person point of view? Why?

Step Three

Here's another thing that is fun to do to explore point of view. Take turns describing an experience first from an omniscient point of view and then from the first-person point of view of an everyday object involved in it. Here are some ideas:

- Frying an egg for breakfast. (In addition to the third-person view, there could be three first-person versions: the frying pan's, the egg's, and the person who fries and eats.)

"Things are really heating up around here."

- Riding a bike to school. (Give an account of the ride written in the third-person point of view, then write accounts given by the rider and by the bike.)

▶ IT'S THE APOSTROPHE'S PROBLEM

The apostrophe is one of those little things in punctuation (or is it spelling, or both?) that can bedevil students. Because this punctuation mark has several uses, mistakes are common. Practice in using the apostrophe helps build the awareness that it is necessary for good proofreading skills. Help your child tame this versatile little demon before its (not *it's*) antics mess up his writing!

At a Glance

Grade/Subject: 7th/Language Arts—Mechanics, Spelling
Skills: uses of the apostrophe
Materials: pencil and paper
red pencil for corrections
timer
Time: 1 hour

Getting Ready

Here's a quick review of the uses of the apostrophe. Read it over with your child, or have her read it to you, giving additional examples of her own.

- An apostrophe is used to indicate that a letter has been left out in the spelling of a word: don't.
- An apostrophe with the letter *s* is used to make the possessive form of nouns: cat's nose, cats' noses.

Step One

Have your child compile a list of as many contractions as she can think of. If she runs out of steam, the two of you can look through some books or magazines for passages with dialogue. Because contractions are characteristic of most people's everyday speech, you will frequently find them wherever writers present people talking.

Step Two

Next, have your child set up two columns on a sheet of paper.

WATCH LANGUAGE CHANGE

Nothing changes as fast as everyday speech. And contractions (needing their apostrophes, of course) are right up there being born and dying off. A common contraction in earlier times was *shan't*—as in "We *shan't* be needing candles in the Edison household."

THE WHOSITS TEST

The simplest proofreading trick is to train your child to read every use of *who's/whose* and *its/it's* and substitute either *who is* or *it is*. This test quickly reveals whether it's correct.

Making the Grade

IT'S CONFUSING, IT IS!

Who's confused by *whose*
pronoun?

its/it's
whose/who's

its and *whose* = possessive
pronouns, cousins of *his* and *hers*

it's and *who's* = the contractions of
it is and *who is*

GET AROUND IT

Some people call English flexible,
others call it sneaky. Either way,
you can get around the *'s* after a
word ending in *s* (like Moses'
words) by rewriting the sentence
(*the words of Moses* or *the words
belonging to Moses* or *the words
that Moses spoke*). Rewrite the two
sentences in Step Four to eliminate
the *'s* as much as possible.

The left column should be titled *Folks I Know* and the right column *What I'll Remember Them By*. Brainstorm a list of names under the left-hand column; make some names plural—like the *Smiths*. Then, in the right column, write something characteristic about the people you've listed. Then edit the people's names to the correct form of the possessive. For example, *Jesse's skis, Sarah's sense of humor, the Polanskis' truck*.

Step Three

Now see how many sentences you and your child can write using words from the *its/it's* and *who's/whose* pairs. Here are two bad examples. Have your child practice proofreading by seeing how fast she can find the mistakes in them.

- Whose standing up for the students who's punctuation is wrong?
- Its clearly heard when the arrow hits it's mark.

Set a timer for five or ten minutes and make this a "It's Whose?" race. Players earn 2 points for each sentence with two of these pronouns in it, 6 points if a sentence has three of them, 12 points when all four pronouns are in one sentence. *However*, you both must write (and proofread) carefully because 2 points are deducted for every mistake. The two sentences illustrated above would penalize the writer 8 points (4 pronouns)!

Step Four

Of course, it wouldn't be English if there weren't a few complications. Go over the following three special cases together. Think up more examples for each.

1. The possessive form of plural nouns ends in *s* and has the apostrophe stuck at the end.

   They replaced all the teachers' desks.

2. Here is another possessive exception: The possessive forms of *Moses* and *Jesus* and names that end with the sound *eez* are all traditionally written without the extra *s*.

   You won't find references to Jesus' life in Euripides' plays.

3. Here's a case of tricky plurals. To form the plural form of abbreviations and of letters used as nouns, an apostrophe in front of *s* is used: SOS's, Ph.D.'s, x's.

Step Five

Have your child write the answers to these questions using the correct form for the use of apostrophes.

- What lower case letters do you dot and cross?
- How many of what letters are in the word *tic-tac-toe?*
- What popular candy has letters for its name?
- Well behaved and careful people mind what letters?
- If I have a TV and you have a TV, how many do we have?
- What degrees are granted to new doctors upon graduation?

▶ LIBRARY LEARNING

Your local public library holds a treasure of information and entertainment—if your child knows how to dig it up. Maybe the two of you already established a library habit when he was small—making regular visits to take out children's classics and new books. Or maybe he doesn't yet have the Library Habit.

Even if you're a regular visitor for new novels or mysteries or thrillers, you may not have used the library's many other resources. Finding information in the library is a skill that your child will need increasingly as he goes through middle school and on to high school and college. This activity can help him develop a skill that's easy, efficient, and natural.

At a Glance

Grade/Subject: 7th/Language Arts—Reference/Study Skills
Skills: using the dictionary, finding information in the library
Materials: list of topics to look up
index cards or notebook and pencil
Time: 1/2 hour two or three times a week at home; several visits to a local library

Getting Ready

If you're not a regular library user, make your get-acquainted visit to your local library or branch. Find out what system your library uses to identify books: the traditional Dewey Decimal System or Library of Congress numbering. Is the card catalog on computer? (Most city libraries now have computerized catalogs, while those in smaller towns may still be on index cards in drawers.) Many offer both.

WHAT'S MORE

Have your child go through one front-page story and one editorial column of your local newspaper with an editor's eye. Circle any and all contractions. Are there any mistakes? Rewrite the sentences and restore the contracted words. Does it change either the meaning or the tone of the piece to do this?

Do a Contraction Search through the spoken words of characters in a book by Charles Dickens or Mark Twain. What unusual contractions can you find?

Contractions often come into our language as a way of approximating the spoken word. Think about some of the speech forms that you or your child (or people you hear) use in everyday speech. "Touch down and four t' go," for example. Have your teen make her own private list of made-up contractions.

SPORTS AND STUDIES

Girls and boys both get a lot of support from success in sports, and it's not just a "boy thing." This winter at Lake Tahoe, I went down a black diamond ski run and nearly killed myself, but there were all these 14-year-old girls and younger who were handling it in style and having a great time. Parents should encourage their kids to take up sports because it gives them so much confidence. Some sports offer opportunities for kids to succeed and be strong in something that can eventually give them confidence in academics.

Parents should identify the strengths in their children, and it may not be in sports. If academics or sports isn't their strength, then find out what is and tie that back in to the academics. You can't start out in gymnastics walking back and forth on the floor. Of course not. You worked on it and got better in it. You can do the same thing with reading and math. It takes the practice and perseverance to move forward.

While you're there, pick up information on other services the library offers, such as newspapers, videos and recordings, Internet access, films and lectures, story hours, and guest speakers and performers. Don't hesitate to ask a librarian for information. And be sure that both you and your child have library cards!

Step One

Sit down with your child and brainstorm a list of topics, people, or ideas of interest to look up in the library on your first visit.

From the list, pick a topic that interests you both—a person or place or event in the news, a sport or hobby, a skill or craft to learn, a project to consider for home. Have him write the topics on index cards on separate pages in the notebook. If he has a research paper or a report to write for any class, you can use this activity as an opportunity to help him get started on the research. (Beware of being maneuvered into actually doing his research, though!)

Step Two

With the index cards or notebook, visit the library together. Discuss the options you have for finding information.

For example, for current events especially, you may want to use the periodicals index (magazines and journals) or look up recent newspapers. The periodical index can be rich in information on the past as well as the present, since magazines and journals include articles of all kinds. *The National Geographic* alone, for instance, has an index to all its articles.

For quick information on, say, a person or place or invention, you can turn to a multivolume encyclopedia and *Who's Who*. For in-depth information, choose a key word for the topic and look up the books listed in the card catalog under that word. Each book in the library has a call number that indicates its place on the library shelves.

Step Three

Now, plunge in together on your search for information. Use all your library resources that seem appropriate.

Whenever your child finds a reference—the name and issue dates for a magazine or the call numbers for a book—remind him to write these down on the index card for that topic or list them beside it in the notebook.

Step Four

The final step in your library quest is to help your child find the book he wants. You may need to ask the librarian for magazines or newspapers and for videos and recordings. Use the call numbers (and a map of the library if necessary) to find books on the shelves.

▶ PROPAGANDA ALERT!

In this information-rich society, it is more important than ever for kids to be able to evaluate the impact of media messages. You can enjoy spending time with your child encouraging him to think about what he is reading and viewing. Explore that old question, "Can you believe everything you read (and view)?" by analyzing material in newspapers and magazines to identify examples of successful and unsuccessful, direct and subtle propaganda.

At a Glance

Grade/Subject: 7th/Language Arts—Thinking Skills, Composition
Skills: recognizing propaganda, making comparisons, critical thinking and writing
Materials: newspapers, magazines
paper and pencil
TV programs
Time: 20–30 minute sessions; perhaps weekly sessions over a number of months if your child has the interest

Getting Ready

Select some newspaper or magazine sections (both articles and advertisements) to use for your discussions.

Step One

Start by brainstorming some of the ways that the attempts are made to influence you through the media. Some techniques you may come up with include:

- Exaggeration—taking something too far; an overstatement such as an ad for a computer: "Everything you'll ever want in a computer."

WHAT'S MORE

Make a colorful poster about some of the features of your local library that will encourage others to use its services.

Use the card catalog or other library resources to find books to read to a younger sibling or when baby-sitting.

Invent a system to arrange and catalog the books in your own home library.

CRITICAL VIEWING SKILLS

Set rules for TV viewing and adhere to those rules. Set a weekly limit for the amount of time children are permitted to watch television. At the start of each week, help your children select the programs or videotapes they want to watch. When the selected program is over, turn the television off and get involved in another activity. Turn what you see on television into positive and educational family discussions and activities. Television can inspire creativity and educate and inform children. When a topic on television sparks your child's interest, go to the library or museum and explore the subject further. —The National PTA®

OUR HANGOUT

Around my house, it's important for our children to see their parents reading a lot. We live close to a library, so that's our neighborhood hangout. Sometimes I feel that my kids' school homework and assignments prevent them from reading as much as they should.

WHAT'S MORE

Select different TV time slots in which to watch together. Identify the propaganda techniques used during the time slot and accompanying different kinds of programs such as sports events, children's programs, family entertainment, soap operas, talk shows, etc.

- Testimony—an endorsement by someone that people recognize such as Bill Cosby's commercials for Jell-O™.
- Card Stacking—creating a false impression by omitting facts; what it doesn't say is as important as what it does say). For example, an ad that says: "Our candy bar costs the same as it did five years ago" does not say that the candy bar is now two ounces smaller than it was five years ago.
- Selective Vocabulary—using words that qualify statements in such as way as to create a certain level of expectation but really promise or guarantee nothing. For example, a product which claims to "help fight acne" is actually also saying that since it only helps, other remedies are necessary and you are left on your own to figure that out!

See what other ideas the two of you can come up with. Think of examples for each and list more examples for the techniques listed here.

Discuss how your child feels about the use of the media for promoting opinions and products.

- How does he think people learn about these techniques? Or do they ever learn? Or should they?
- Who uses these techniques? Why?

Step Two

Next spend some time reading through the materials you've collected for the activity. As either of you comes across an example of a persuasion technique, read it aloud and talk together about it. If it is possible to mark the paper you are using, have your child highlight the phrases and places he sees propaganda at work.

- What technique or techniques are being used and why?

Look for examples of both subtle and direct uses of propaganda.

Step Three

After reading, highlighting, and sharing what each of you found, go back and talk about examples.

- Which seem most effective?
- Do any provide useful information?
- Do any have entertainment value along with their effort to persuade?

Talk about other ways that the same message could be given without the use of propaganda.

Step Four

Have a weekly "propaganda review" session like this together, sometimes using television viewing instead of printed materials.

Step Five

After several weeks of your explorations and discussions, start to explore these issues:

- Is propaganda always bad?
- Is propaganda necessary?
- What are some ways that readers can deal with it effectively?

When your child has explored these questions for a while, ask him to choose one and write his own analysis that gives his answer to the question and reasons for his views. He can draw upon the rich store of experiences you and he have shared in your weekly sessions.

▶ PICTURE THIS

One of the time-honored techniques for studying sentence structure is diagraming. In effect, a sentence diagram is a picture of the sentence and all its components. All those components are arranged in a pattern that makes their functions in the sentence clear.

Diagraming can be a real breakthrough for kids who have visual or kinesthetic styles of learning. A diagram seems very real. It can make the relationships among sentence parts much clearer than abstract descriptions or labels. Doing sentence diagrams can be fun since they have much of the appeal of solving puzzles.

At a Glance

Grade/Subject: 7th/Language Arts—Language and Grammar
Skills: diagraming the sentence structure of simple sentences
Materials: notebook and pencils
Time: about 1/2 to 3/4 hour twice or three times a week

WHAT'S MORE

Pose the question "Is propaganda more effective on TV or in print?" Have your teen cite examples from each medium and tell whether he thinks moving pictures with sound or photographs with text deliver messages in a more powerful way—or which is more effective for which purposes and which audiences.

Collaborate on writing or making storyboards for a commercial about some product or service, and use various propaganda techniques.

READING MONSTER

When kids see their accomplishment, no matter how small the goal, they get such a kick out of it. At *SCORE!*, I set a goal in reading with one boy who hated to read. After working with him a few times and tracking his reading progress, he gained more confidence. His dad now has to remind him to do his math homework because he takes up so much time reading. I helped to create a little reading monster!

Making the Grade

AFTER HOMEWORK!

Television is more like a reward we use with our children. If they get done with their homework or chores, we respect their feelings and personalities and let them pick their own programs to watch. We watch TV with our children, too— and a lot of their shows are funny. We all laugh at them together and even imitate the commercials.

WHAT'S MORE

Hang a small blackboard or chalkboard on the kitchen wall. Use it to diagram sentences from family conversations.

Once you've diagramed a sentence, play with it by adding more adjectives or other modifiers to the diagram.

Make a Diagram Mobile out of a cool simple sentence. The body of the mobile can be a wire coat hanger, and use thread or string, construction paper or cardboard, colored markers, pipe cleaners, or other craft materials to design a "moving sentence sculpture."

Getting Ready

For your own security, here's a quick review of the basic diagram for a couple kinds of simple sentences.

The first pattern is Subject/Verb/Direct Object.

Jack bought a red bike.

Jack | bought | bike
           \a \red

On the main line, the subject comes first. A vertical line crossing the main line separates it from the verb. A shorter straight vertical line separates the verb from the direct object. Modifiers are placed on slanted lines leading down from the words they modify.

The second pattern is Subject/Verb/Indirect Object/Direct Object.

Toby sent Sally a letter.

Toby | sent | letter
      \Sally \a

For the indirect object, add a lower horizontal line connected to the verb by a slanted line.

A third basic pattern is Subject/Verb/Predicate Adjective (or Predicate Nominative). Remember, these are words after the verb that refer to the subject, either to describe it or rename it. Usually, but not always, the verb is a form of *to be*.

Samantha's hair is very curly.

hair | is \ curly
   \Samantha's \very

It can also be a verb like *seems*:

Winnie seems sad today.

Winnie | seems \ sad
                \today

The pattern is rather like the first except that a slanted line separates the predicate adjective (or nominative) from the verb.

Step One

Sit down with your child, think of two or three simple sentences, and write them down. Or skim the evening paper for such sentences.

For this activity, try to choose only simple sentences: with one subject and one verb. (For an activity in diagraming more complicated sentences, see the Language Arts activities for 8th Grade.)

Step Two

Draw the basic simple sentence diagram. If your child has studied diagraming in Language Arts, ask her to start the diagram with the basic subject and verb. If not, go over the basic diagram and show how it gives a graphic picture of any sentence.

Fill in the subject and the verb. Then work together to add other elements such as direct objects, indirect objects, adjectives, or adverbs.

Step Three

Next, try to think of sentences spontaneously that will challenge the other person. Pick simple sentences that you can do quickly to reinforce this diagraming pattern.

Step Four

How long you continue work on diagraming depends in part on whether you can see that this approach is involving your child's interest and making abstract concepts seem more real. It will also depend on the amount of emphasis placed on diagraming by your child's teachers.

UP A FAMILY TREE

Last year we did a family tree writing project. We got to call the kids' grandmas and find out where Great-Great So-and-So was from. We found out there were many similarities between my background and my husband's, and we were able to get out the atlas and see that these people were from Scotland and these people were from England . . . . The stories were so interesting coming from the grandparents. "Well, your great grandmother had 15 kids!" We both come from large extended families, and finding out about them was something the kids will always remember.

WATCH CLOSELY!

Parents are lucky if they're focused on education in the home as an everyday, fun aspect of their lives. Most of the "teachable moments," those special times when things really click for teens and they finally understand something, won't usually happen in a formal setting with 38 other school children sitting around. Parents will get to observe those exciting moments in the more informal home setting.

VERB FAMILIES

Present	Past	Past Participle
begin	began	begun
drink	drank	drunk
ring	rang	rung
shrink	shrank	shrunk
sing	sang	sung
spring	sprang	sprung
swim	swam	swum
draw	drew	drawn
fly	flew	flown
grow	grew	grown
know	knew	known
throw	threw	thrown
bite	bit	bitten
choose	chose	chosen
fall	fell	fallen
eat	ate	eaten
give	gave	given
see	saw	seen
take	took	taken
write	wrote	written
tear	tore	torn
wear	wore	worn
go	went	gone
is	was	been
do	did	done

▶ SNAP!

Verbs are not always easy to get right—some are tricky and seem to follow their own rules! Here's a way to practice quick recognition of irregular verb forms with a little competitive twist.

At a Glance

Grade/Subject: 7th/Language Arts—Usage, Language and Grammar, Spelling
Skills: recognizing and using irregular verbs
Materials: index cards cut in half
paper and pencil
Time: 20 minutes

Getting Ready

Since you'll be using present, past, and past participle verb forms, here's a quick reminder of what those verb forms are about:

- A verb changes its form to show tense and to agree with its subject. The tense of a verb tells when an action takes place.
- The present tense of a verb names an action that happens regularly: *I go to the gym every day.* It can also express a general truth: *Gym workouts benefit my health.*
- The past tense of a verb names an action that already happened. For example: *I went to the gym every day last week.*
- The past participle is a form of the verb that describes past action and requires a helping verb such as *be* or *have.* For example: *I have gone to the gym for two years.*

Use this knowledge to make a set of cards. Have your teen help you make them.

Step One

Start with a quickie review of verb forms before dealing the cards. You might write down the three example sentences provided under "Getting Ready," above, and ask your child to identify the verb in each one and tell how and why it is different in each case. Make sure you use the words *present, past,* and past *participle.* Give more examples if you feel your teen needs them. Then propose playing a card game that involves quick recognition of irregular verb forms.

Listed here are 20 verb families that you and your child can use for making the game's deck of cards. You can make up sets of cards for all or just some of them, as long as you select an even number.

Say you decide to go with sixteen of the verb families; that means you will have three verbs times 16 sets for a total of 48 cards. Have your child help choose which verbs to include in your set. Write one word on each card. The more cards in the deck, the more fun; but you can begin with a smaller deck.

When you have made your deck of cards, check them over together to be sure that you have all three forms correctly spelled for each verb. Then shuffle the deck and get ready to play!

Step Two

Deal out all the cards evenly and place each pile neatly face-down in a stack in front of each player. The players' job is to turn his cards over one by one, looking quickly to find verbs that match by tense: present, past, or past participle.

To start play, you each take your top card and turn it face up at the same time. If the cards are both the same verb tense, either of you may say, "Snap!" Whoever says "Snap!" first gets all the cards in the other's face-up stack. Captured cards go face-down at the bottom of the face-down stack of the person who said "Snap" first. The game then continues. (If disagreement arises, use the chart above to check for matching forms.)

If the cards do not match verb tense, they stay face-up and you both turn over your next card, again attempting to flip right at the same time. You may have to turn several over in this way until you see matching ones. The object of the game is to capture all the cards from your opponent.

Step Three

Sometimes, especially if the deck of cards is not very large, the game can go on quite a while as players stacks of cards grow and shrink, but both of you should hang in there. When that happens, you can agree to stop at a certain time if no one has captured all the cards. If you stop, the player with the most cards in both face-up and face-down piles wins.

Step Four

Have your teen dig up more irregular verbs and make more cards to add to the deck. Put the deck wherever you keep family games and play again from time to time. Encourage other family members to play.

WHAT'S MORE

Make the activity a little more difficult by requiring the person who says "Snap!" to also use the word correctly in a sentence before collecting the matching verb cards.

Make the game into a Rummy format. Deal each player nine cards. The rest go face down in a stack. On your turn, you ask your opponent for a verb form (present, past, or past participle using the correct form of the verb) that you need to complete a family in your hand. If your opponent doesn't have it, you draw. When you get all three verbs in a family, you put them down. The goal is to be the first player to put all your cards down.

Look up the etymology of verbs in a dictionary. How do they differ from most regular verbs?

Play with more than two people so that you have to look for matches quickly on more than one other verb card.

Making the Grade

▶ STOP, LOOK, AND LISTEN!

The world around us is full of mistakes in grammar and usage—from signs in grocery stores to announcers on the radio. Help your child practice his own skills in grammar and usage by applying them to the signs and speech of everyday life.

Psychologically, this can be great for your kid's self-confidence. Finding mistakes made in the adult world can give him an appreciation for what he's learning in language arts. He can think, "Well, I'll sure never make a mistake like that. I know better!"

At a Glance

Grade/Subject: 7th/Language Arts—Grammar and Usage
Skills: usage of problem verbs and irregular adjectives and adverbs
Materials: notebooks and pencils for each participant
Time: make this activity a part of other errands and activities, such as shopping, listening to the radio, and listening to other people (Review the results twice or more a week.)

Getting Ready

The only thing needed for this activity is awareness. Stop to look at signs and listen critically to ordinary people, to radio and TV announcers, to politicians, etc.

Step One

With your teen, pinpoint some areas of usage that you'll look for specifically, in writing and in speech. Keep a running log in your notebooks of mistakes that either of you hears or reads. Be sure to include the context of each usage blooper.

Here are some tricky areas to watch and listen for:

• borrow, lend, loan
• let, leave
• bring, take
• more, less, fewer
• good, bad, well, badly
• teach, learn
• double negatives

Step Two

Add a touch of challenge to finding these common grammar mistakes by making a review of them a twice-weekly event. Encourage your child to share any really good finds as soon as he's discovered them.

Step Three

The final step in recognizing common grammar mistakes is being able to correct them. As you and your child share your findings, be sure that he knows how to correct them and use the troublesome words correctly.

FREE STUFF

Check out the classic kids' activity book *Free Stuff for Kids* (published annually by Meadowbrook Press/Simon & Schuster) for a great collection of places your child can write to for free or inexpensive items from a variety of clubs, organizations, sports teams, and manufacturers. For a Meadowbrook Press catalog, call (800) 338-2232.

CHAPTER 13

Learning Adventures— 8th Grade Language Arts

OPEN FOR DISCUSSION

We have a lot of discussions at home, in very impromptu ways. We talk during long drives and commutes, at the dinner table— everywhere. Anything that happens to any of us, we just talk about it.

We try to get together every evening as a family for dinner. Sometimes my husband is there, and sometimes he's working late, but we carry on discussions at the table. My oldest son has a debate coming up in school about "Are we better off now than we were 1,000 years ago?" and that became a dinnertime conversation.

▶ A GIFT OF WORDS

The popularity of books on tape shows that reading aloud is not a lost art but something that many people of all ages can still enjoy. While your teenager probably no longer wants to be read to, she can now pass on that pleasure—by reading to a younger child, to an older relative whose eyesight may be less than perfect, or to someone else outside the family.

Here's how you and your teenager can give someone a "Gift-of-Reading certificate," a gift not just of words but of her time and thoughtfulness. At the same time, she'll gain valuable practice in reading aloud and exploring the literature that other people enjoy.

At a Glance

Grade/Subject: 8th/Language Arts—Literature, Speaking Skills
Skills: reading aloud, appreciating different types of literature
Materials: light-colored construction paper
colored marking pens
scissors
stapler

Word-a-day calendars build vocabularies and keep a daily focus on strengthening language skills.
Give a gift of words to your teenager.

Time: about 3/4 hour to prepare each gift; then 20–40 minutes of reading time

Getting Ready

You can look for opportunities to suggest the "Gift-of-Reading" idea to your teenager. Perhaps, as the holidays are coming, she's said, "I'd really like to give a present to so-and-so—the kids I baby-sit, Grandma, Uncle Felix" (you'll know the list)—"but I don't have any money." Or maybe you have a neighbor whose health is poor. "You know, I'd really like to do something nice for Ms. Jackson—she's home alone a lot of the time, but I don't know what to do for her."

Giving any of those people a gift of 20 or 30 or 40 minutes of reading from their favorite story, novel, or poem can solve the gift problem. In return, your teenager can not only feel good, but also expand her reading skills and horizons!

Step One

Discuss with your child the likes and reading tastes of the person (or people) she's chosen for a gift certificate. If it's an older person, she can try to find out what some of that person's favorites are. Does he like the works of a certain poet or essayist? Or does she enjoy a romantic novel or a tale of adventure?

If it's a neighboring child, someone for whom your child baby-sits, or perhaps a younger sibling, that child probably has favorite books and stories, too. Or she can introduce the child to her own childhood favorites.

What your child is giving, really, is her time and attention. Still, it's useful to be able to suggest something if when she asks her intended recipient what he likes, he says, "Oh, I don't know. You choose." Or it's great to introduce a child—not to mention adult—to some new reading experience that the person will enjoy.

Step Two

Use the construction paper and markers to cut out, make, and decorate a "gift certificate" form or coupon. The wording can be specific or general:

"This certificate entitles [name] to one-half hour of reading aloud each week during the month of January. With love from Jennifer."

"Dear Timmy—As your birthday present, I'll read you all of *Charlotte's Web* during your birthday week. From Jake."

"This certificate entitles my Grandpa to 1/2 hour of reading from the Aubrey-Maturin sea novels (any one he chooses) twice a week during July. Love, Mary."

Step Three

Once the gift certificates are given, keep your interest in the project high and obvious to your teen. Although it's your child who is doing the actual reading, check with her to see how it is going, what book she is reading, and whether she'd like to expand the idea to other people. Read the book yourself and talk with her about it.

▶ BACK TO FRONT

For kids who are having trouble with spelling, practicing and memorizing spelling words probably seems like a real drag. Here's an activity that doesn't at first look like spelling practice but in fact is a really entertaining way to think about the spelling and structure of words.

Palindromes are words, sentences, or phrases that read the same backwards and forwards. The sentences can be read either letter by letter or word by word. Here are some examples.

• Words: noon, toot, wow, sees, madam

• Phrases (letter by letter):
A man, a plan, a canal—Panama!

• Sentences (letter by letter):
Madam, I'm Adam.
Able was I ere I saw Elba. (supposedly said by Napoleon, of course)

• Sentences (word by word)
One for all and all for one.
Writing her about mum kept mum about her writing.
Dressing in style brings style in dressing.

BUMPY ROAD AHEAD

Older students may hit a place where they don't think it's cool to be learning any more and school's not cool. Parents of older students need to start looking for very positive role models, people who are cool and have accomplished things. This will help students work through the tough spots. Some parents complain that their children don't listen to them any more, so those good role models will help reinforce a parent's positive goals.

GETTING BETTER

I had a girl at my center call me over to her desk one day. "The last two years, I really wasn't good in anything. But at *SCORE!*, there's lots of things that I'm good at and I'm getting better. Now I'm excited to go back to school." In *SCORE!*, kids have a chance to succeed, no matter what their academic level.

I'm glad that parents are also trying to give their children chances to succeed in academics while learning at home. Some kids aren't getting recognized in school and aren't able to see that they're getting better. Parents can help them get the confidence to see that they can get better no matter where they're at—and that feels good to them. The kids who are doing well have the confidence to know that they can still get A's, but also the kids who are at B and C level can move up too.

Writing a palindrome that actually makes sense can be challenging, but trying to do so can bring some entertaining results. Meantime, your child is unconsciously practicing—and becoming very aware of—his spelling!

At a Glance

Grade/Subject: 8th/Language Arts—Spelling
Skills: spelling, using vocabulary
Materials: 20–50 blank index cards
scratch paper and pens or pencils
dictionary
Time: up to one hour to make your first bank of palindrome words
3/4 hour to 1 hour once a week or so, fooling around with these words, as long as you're both interested

Getting Ready

If you're a fan of crossword puzzles or anagrams, you may have a headstart in this activity. Otherwise, be sure you have your dictionary handy.

Step One

Together with your child, brainstorm (and use the dictionary) to create a bank of good palindrome words. Make index cards for two different kinds:

• Words that read the same backwards and forwards: noon, mum, did, level, refer

• Word pairs, words that read backwards to form another real word: doom/mood, on/no, won/now, ban/nab, edit/tide, star/rats

Just leafing through the dictionary will help you find many surprising word pairs like these. Encourage your kid to browse the dictionary and try out different words backwards to see whether they work out as other, different words. You're probably both in for some surprises.

You might also make some cards for "linking" palindromes. These are short words and phrases that read the same backwards and forwards and can be useful in holding your phrases or sentences together in letter-by-letter palindromes. Here are some: was/saw, not/on, at/a, as/a.

Step Two

Now try thinking out loud together about those backwards-and-forwards words and how you can put them together in phrases or sentences. Remember that in letter-by-letter palindromes, the letters from several different words can run together to make the backward version.

For instance, when you read the well-known palindrome about "a man a plan a canal . . . " backwards, the final word "Panama" is made up of the *p* from *plan*, plus "a man a"—reading backwards, of course.

Step Three

So, plunge in and get started, using the words from your cards. Fool around on the scratch paper with words and combinations, reading your efforts aloud to each other.

At first, don't even try to make palindromes that make sense. Make nonsense phrases, then try to think of situations or make up stories in which you could use them.

Here's a palindrome story: A traveler in western England's moor country arrived at his inn one night, but was disappointed in his accommodations. Glumly, he wired his travel agent: "Room not on moor!"

Step Four

Some people find word-by-word palindromes a little easier to start with. Try some variations on the pattern of "one for all and all for one." Then ease back into the challenging, but satisfying, letter-by-letter versions.

❯ DEAR CRABBY

Advice columns have been a staple of our newspapers and magazines for several generations. Sometimes the answers to readers' questions are right on the mark, and sometimes they are, as one teen we know put it, icky sweet. Not all children enjoy satire and sarcasm, but for those who do (and who might also have trouble going back over their written work), this is a perfect activity. Writing bad-tempered advice letters is an opportunity to let off steam, think about it, and then rewrite to polish it up.

WHAT'S MORE

More palindromic word pairs:
stun/nuts, grub/burg, plug/gulp, evil/live, speed/deeps, spot/tops, deer/reed, as an/NASA

Try making up a story leading up to these palindromes:
Tops as a spot! (ad for a resort?)
Mood won, now doom. (pessimistic fortune cookie?)

TIME—THE BEST EDITOR

Ideas can tumble out onto paper, but taking active thoughts from the idea stage to the communication stage often requires taking time to provide some careful work. And taking time off between first draft and revision gives a writer a fresh perspective on what has been written. Young writers, especially, tend to be reluctant to go back over their material. This is even more true today when the instant and unedited gratification of e-mail, fax, and telephone all tend to reinforce bad habits.

Making the Grade

SPORTING DAD

My husband coaches all our children's basketball and baseball teams. He does a newsletter on the computer for the kids' teams, and they all love writing and desktopping it together: Play of the Week, Kids Who Made their First Baskets of the Season . . . . He's big on motivation.

WHAT'S MORE

Write or dictate a letter of protest. Sometimes letters written in the heat of indignation come out sounding a little too strong. If they rest for a couple of days, and are rewritten in the light of cool reflection, they often produce a more thoughtful (and more easily accepted) letter.

Your child can try his hand at a more serious advice letter. If you have any family issues, sibling or otherwise, that aren't too loaded, they can be used— "Dear Crabby (or whoever), I have a brother who always leaves my books lying around on the floor. How can I get him to put them away?"

At a Glance

Grade/Subject: 8th/Language Arts—Composition
Skills: writing and editing short pieces
Materials: appropriate clippings from advice columns such as Ask Beth, Dear Abby, or others from syndicated or local papers or magazines
paper and pencils (including a red one!)
Time: 1/2 –1 hour on two separate occasions

Getting Ready

Read and discuss the examples of the columns you have found. Talk about the tone and length. Do the columns use a familiar first person (I think you should...) or a more official third-person point of view? Is the tone friendly or bossy? Which letters do you prefer? What makes them better?

Step One

Have your child invent the personality of an imaginary, bad-tempered advice giver. He should then write a short paragraph describing this unpleasant person. Discuss the paragraph and decide on a name for the person (and therefore the advice column).

Step Two

Together, dream up several different questions that might be addressed to this grumpy advice giver. Read them through and decide together on a couple of questions that it would be fun to write responses to.

Have him write answers to each of the questions for his column. He should keep in mind the personality and point of view of his crabby persona as he writes. When done, set the letters aside for a while.

Step Three

After a few days, come back to the letters, and have your child read them out loud. Encourage him to talk about what he thinks works well in his letters and what needs changing.

- Do the letters make clear sense?
- Has he kept a consistent tone for the voice of this crabby advice giver?

• Are the spelling, grammar, and punctuation all correct for publication?

Then have him edit the letters, making improvements and correcting any writing errors.

Step Four

Post the Dear... column for family enjoyment and invite more questions for the crabby advisor to respond to!

▶ HEY, CALL OFF YOUR DOGGEREL!

All languages have a rhythmic, musical quality. This quality, along with careful thought and the right mix of emotion and vocabulary, is at the heart of poetry. There are many serious kinds of poetry, romantic, elegiac, heroic; and then there is doggerel. Doggerel is a rude, rhythmic, bumping-along, make-fun-of-it-all form of poetry. *Mad* magazine and the books of Dr. Seuss are full of examples of this kind of fun-loving verse. Doggerel is easy to write and, once you get started, hard to stop. It's a great way to play with words, thoughts, and rhymes, and fun for two people to do together.

At a Glance

Grade/Subject: 8th/Language Arts—Composition, Language, Mechanics
Skills: writing short verse, practicing hearing and use of rhythm and rhyme
Materials: pencil and paper (rhyming dictionary, optional)
Time: 1/2 hour whenever inspiration or inclination strikes

Getting Ready

Here are the two tricks for writing doggerel:

1. Find a good beat. English sentences almost always have a rhythmic quality to them. Take the phrase like "When writing directions..." Say it over a few times and the rhythm pops out at you, "When writing directions..."
2. End your lines in words that are easy to rhyme, like *feet, ate, nice,* or words ending in *-ing.*

DOGGONE

doggerel n.—trivial or poorly constructed verse, characterized by monotony of rhyme and rhythm and trivial content.

WHAT'S MORE

Read some Mother Goose rhymes out loud. Many of these qualify as doggerel and they have different beat and rhyme patterns that you might want to imitate.

Folk songs such as "My Darling Clementine" and "Sweet Betsy from Pike" have doggerel lyrics. Their tunes are ideally suited to accompanying this verse form. Make up your own words to one of these songs.

Or, to put it in doggerel:

> When writing directions or giving advice,
> Don't squeeze your poor readers in a too-wordy vise.
> Keep it quite simple; the beat's the main thing,
> And then with some rhyme, you'll get them to sing.

Step One

Introduce the idea of doggerel to your teen. Chances are he'll quickly realize he knows more about it than you do since, basically, that is what rap "music" is all about.

Spend some time playing with short, rhythmic phrases. Read the back of a cereal box, a movie review, or just about anything at all, and pick out the short sentences or segments of sentences that have a beat. Write down some that the two of you think have possibilities for turning into doggerel of your own.

Step Two

Brainstorm a list of words, and think of as many rhymes for each of them as you can. Make a list of rhyming words.

Step Three

Now you're ready to compose some doggerel. One of you should pick out a phrase and extend it so that it has enough words to have a line with a strongly repeated beat. End the line with an easily rhymed word. The next person has to write a line that follows along with the same beat and idea and that ends with a rhyme for the word at the end of the first line. Keep going back and forth for as long as you can. You can keep the same rhyme going or change it every two lines.

Then choose another first line and take turns again supplying a line. This time, however, try another rhyme pattern by making the odd and even lines end in rhymes.

Keep fooling around with ideas for doggerels and make up as many as you want, as long or short as you want! Write them down. Punctuate them correctly.

**AN ELEGY ON THE DEATH
OF A MAD DOG**
by Oliver Goldsmith

Good people all, of every sort,
    Give ear unto my song;
And if you find it wondrous short,
    It cannot keep you long.
In Islington there lived a man,
    Of whom the world might say,
That still a godly race he ran,
    Whene'er he went to pray.
A kind and gentle heart he had,
    To comfort friends and foes;
The naked every day he clad;
    When he put on his clothes.
And in that town a dog was found:
    As many dogs there be—
Both mongrel, puppy, whelp, and hound
    And curs of low degree.
This dog and man at first were friends;
    But, when a pique began,
The dog to gain some private ends,
    Went mad, and bit the man.
Around from all the neighboring streets
    The wondering neighbors ran;
And swore the dog had lost its wits,
    To bite so good a man.
The wound it seem'd both sore and sad
    To every Christian eye;
And while they swore the dog was mad,
    They swore the man would die.
But soon a wonder came to light,
    That showed the rogues they lied—
The man recover'd of the bite;
    The dog it was that died.

Step Four

Once your writing team has the basics down, you're ready for larger tasks. Pick a subject such as the mishaps on a family vacation or the heroic efforts needed to clean the refrigerator, and turn it into a doggerel epic.

▶ IN YOUR CARDS

Junior high students often do a lot of serious report writing in preparation for high school. It can be scary. A lot of kids feel like they just can't get started. Here is an activity that shows your child a good way to prepare for report writing. It gives her a way to practice the first steps in the writing process in a more light-hearted way by reading and thinking about a publication she enjoys reading, and then writing up a report to recommend it to a friend.

At a Glance

Grade/Subject: 8th/Language Arts—Reference and Study Skills
Skills: preparing to write a report
Materials: pencil and paper
3" × 5" cards, white, yellow, and green (or any other two colors in addition to white)
teen-selected magazine
Time: 1/2 hour for each step—Spread the steps out over several days.

Getting Ready

Have your child choose a magazine that she enjoys or would enjoy reading such as *Mad*, *Seventeen*, or any fan, sports, fashion, hobby, or news magazine, and get her a copy. Tell her that you'd like her to write up a report on the magazine and that in doing so, she'll learn a great way for writing reports that she'll have to do for school in the future!

Step One

Ask your child to browse her magazine cover to cover. As she does, have her make notes on the green cards of anything that strikes her either positively or negatively. For instance, besides articles or ads, which graphics or photographs are worth mentioning (good, bad, hip, boring)? The notes don't have to be

WHAT'S MORE

When your writing team has produced one or two doggerels that you think are fun, use a tape recorder to make you own rap numbers.

SOURCE IT

Every time your child makes a note, she should write down the page where she found the information or got the idea. Why bother? As any writer will tell you, no matter how sure you are that you'll be able to remember it a day or two later, you won't. In the more thoroughly prepared reports required in high school and college, there is a formal and standardized way of recording this information. Right now it's just a question of getting into a valuable, good habit.

WHAT'S MORE

This process can be adapted to write a report about a favorite book. Your child can substitute descriptions of chapters, settings, and characters for the feature headings.

INTUITION WORKS

Intuition is a very handy tool for writers of all kinds. It's not a precise ability, it's just paying attention to the thoughts that flicker in the corner of your mind. Sometimes the feelings you have when you first encounter something will provide topics or observations that you can use later when you're writing down your impressions. They are always worth collecting. Have your child jot them down, but they are just notes and don't have to be systematic.

JUST THE FACTS, MA'AM

Good expository report writing is ten percent inspired writing and 90 percent gathering and organizing facts—and saving them in a way that you can easily use. This latter part of the task can seem like a lot of work, but, when approached systematically, it's more fun than expected.

carefully written, just notes to herself. This is the impression-gathering stage of the work. Have her jot down on the card the page numbers of anything she refers to.

Step Two

Have your child read through the magazine again, this time paying closer attention to the details of the magazine. This is the fact-gathering stage. She should figure out, and record on white cards, the total pages in the magazine as well as the total pages in each of the following categories: stories, regular features, advertisements, letters from readers, and any other features or columns that are particular to this magazine.

She can work out the percentages of the total for each section, if she wants (divide the total pages into the number of feature pages and convert the decimal fraction into a percentage).

Step Three

Tell her next to pick what she thinks is the best part of the magazine and the worst part. She should use separate white cards for each, making notes on the cards (using more if she needs them) on details about what is appealing or unappealing about each.

Have her also write up a white card (or set of cards) for one other noteworthy feature of the magazine. If there is something that sets this magazine apart from all others, set up a card for that as well.

Step Four

Your child will find the detailed publication information about her magazine on the cover and in the publication box printed inside somewhere near the front. This includes the publication date, where the magazine is published, and what volume and number this issue is. (This is the information you would give to someone who might want to look up the magazine in a library.) This information should also be written out on a white card.

Step Five

Have your child use the yellow cards to write down the headings for her report on the magazine. She'll need one card for the introduction, several for the features and hard facts about the magazine, one each for worst and best, one for the final recommendation, and others for anything else she thinks she might want to write about in her report.

Step Six

Lay all the cards out on a flat surface. Place the white cards below the appropriate yellow headings cards and the blue cards next to any white cards that they relate to. Now she can begin writing paragraphs to go with each of the white cards and assembling the whole report.

▶ IT'S GREEK TO ME

Because of its history as a language, English has many words based on Greek and Latin roots and base words. Prefixes or suffixes or both are attached to these root words to form many, many familiar words.

If your child knows the meanings of some often-used Latin and Greek root words, she'll have a jump start on learning the meanings of a great many unfamiliar words. Combined with a knowledge of common prefixes and suffixes, this skill will do a lot to broaden her working vocabulary. But best of all, by exploring word roots, you both will find new fascination in the language you hear, see, and use every day.

At a Glance

Grade/Subject: 8th/Language Arts—Vocabulary, Reference Skills
Skills: recognizing Greek and Latin root words, understanding word history and etymology
Materials: 10 to 20 blank index cards
colored markers
notebook and pencil
dictionary (to check words)
Time: 1/2 hour once or twice a week

Getting Ready

You don't have to study ancient Latin or Greek, but you may want to look up a comprehensive list of common Latin and Greek roots and their meanings in English. You can find such a list in most grammar handbooks. You can also find them in the etymology portion of dictionary entries.

Step One

Together, cut the index cards in half to make twice as many smaller cards. Then collaborate to make a small deck of Root

---

WHAT'S MORE

Television shows generally move at too quick a pace for good note taking, but if you have a VCR and a favorite recorded program of your child's, she can adapt the quick-note-on-the-card technique to writing a detailed review about the show.

ETYMOLOGY?

Etymology is the history of a word tracing back to its origins. Its own etymology is that it comes from the Greek words *etymos*, meaning "true", and *logos*, meaning "word."

WHAT'S MORE

Read about etymology in the explanatory section of your dictionary.

Use your dictionary to seek out roots of words and create your own personal list of what you find.

Track down the meaning of these roots: *neo, zo, eco, biblio, jud, fect, fac, cogn.*

Inventing words based on Greek or Latin roots is great fun and a great test for seeing whether your child has really grasped the idea. Be sure she can define her new word.

Write a science fiction story in which you use Greek and Latin roots to invent words describing new ideas, machines, and beings.

In a book of names, look up the derivation of your own name and those of friends and family.

Cards using the marking pen and index cards. Here's a list of sixteen common Greek and Latin roots for making your first "deck":

script, scribe (Latin) = write	*phone* (Greek) = sound
port (Latin) = carry	*ast[e]r* (Greek) = star
rupt (Latin) = break	*demo* (Greek) = people
vid, vis (Latin) = see	*morph* (Greek) = form
crypt (Latin) = hidden, secret	*geo* (Greek) = earth
cred (Latin) = trust, belief	*tele* (Greek) = distant
sent, sens (Latin) = feel	*graph* (Greek) = write
vita (Latin) = life	*bio* (Greek) = life

Find enough more from exploring the etymology entries in a dictionary to complete your set of cards.

Step Two

Turn the pile of cards face down on the table between you and your child. Throw dice or toss a coin to see who goes first.

Step Three

The first player draws a Root Card and must supply or invent a word based on that root word. If either of you invents a word—accidentally or intentionally—it must meet the criteria explained in Step Four.

To get a turn, the other player must supply (or invent) another word based on the same Greek or Latin root. The first player must then supply a third word using the same root. If she can supply a third word, she keeps the card in her pile. If she cannot, the second player keeps the card and takes the next turn.

If the second player cannot supply a word based on that root, the first player keeps the card, draws again, and the process starts over.

Step Four

There are two ways to judge the word that a player suggests. First, is it a real word? You can both agree that it is or check it in the dictionary. As you do, be sure your kid notices that the meaning of the root word may sometimes shift slightly, making it harder to apply the meaning.

For instance, it's easy to see the root *script* ("write") in a word like *scripture* or *manuscript*. But it's a little harder in the word *conscript*—

a draftee—whose name was "written" on a list of people called into the army. That's where the dictionary and its explanation of a word's derivation can come in handy.

Step Five

The second test, for invented words, is more challenging and creative: If it's not yet a real word, is it a useful coinage? For example, science fiction writers invented the word *teleport* to describe a way of traveling through space—in short, "Beam me up, Scotty."

Though not yet a standard word, *teleport* was a clearly useful invention. Similarly, in this game the inventor of a word based on one of these roots must define and defend it well enough to convince the other player that it's a useful word.

Step Six

When all the Root Cards have been drawn, the winner is the person who has kept the most cards. To expand and replay the game, you may want to create more cards.

▶ Language on the Line

Diagraming a sentence means essentially drawing a picture of the structure of the sentence. All the components of a sentence— subject, verb, phrases or clauses, modifiers—are arranged into a pattern or diagram that shows how they all relate to one another. The diagram makes the relationships among sentence parts much more concrete than an abstract description can. For this reason, diagramming can be really helpful for kids who have visual or kinesthetic styles of learning.

The activity "Picture This," suggested for seventh graders, sets up the basic pattern for diagraming a simple sentence. In this activity, you and your child tackle more complicated sentences and wrestle them into wonderful pictures of English at work!

At a Glance

Grade/Subject: 8th/Language Arts—Language and Grammar
Skills: diagramming the sentence structure of compound and complex sentences
Materials: notebook and pencils
Time: about 3/4 to 1 hour two or three times a week

INNATE CURIOSITY

Computers are useless without good software and teachers who know how to make the most of the material. Children still need to explore their world with all their senses. Schools have one mission—to develop children's innate curiosity and desire to learn. Parents can help by lobbying to make sure schools and teachers have the resources they need.
—from *Newsweek's Computers & the Family* newsmagazine (Fall/Winter 1996)

BRITANNICA ONLINE

One of the world's most comprehensive reference source, *Encyclopedia Britannica,* weighs in at 44 million words! There are nifty search and retrieval capabilities and linking via the Web to make this a powerful way for your children to research anything under the sun. Browse and search through *Britannica,* plus *Merriam-Webster's Collegiate Dictionary,* the *Britannica Book of the Year,* and more. Try the site for a free visit, but regular searches require a subscriber's fee. Go to http://www.eb.com

Getting Ready

To begin, you may want to look back at the 7th grade activity on sentences with just one independent clause. Decide whether you and your child should do that activity before going on to this one. Review the three basic patterns for simple sentences that it introduces:

- The first is Subject/Verb/Direct Object.
- The second is Subject/Verb/Indirect Object/Direct Object.
- A third basic pattern is Subject/Verb/Predicate Adjective [or Predicate Nominative], in which a noun or adjective referring to the subject follows a linking verb.

Step One

A compound sentence has two (or more) independent clauses of equal weight, commonly joined by a conjunction such as *and, but, for,* and *or/nor.* It's probably easiest to start by thinking of the two clauses as two simple sentences.

Ask your child to think of two simple sentences that could go together, and write them down. Then think of a conjunction that will join them to make sense.

Here are two examples:

Mom bought Jody a purple sweater
but
the color was too bright.

Kilimanjaro is the highest mountain in Africa
and
snow usually covers its peaks.

Step Two

Working together, have your child diagram the two clauses of the compound sentence as if they were two simple sentences. Start by having him draw two basic simple-sentence diagrams, one above the other, leaving space below each for lines that will contain other elements.

He can then place the subject and verb for each clause on the main line of each diagram. Remember that a vertical line crossing the main line separates the subject from the verb. A short, slanted line separates the verb from a predicate nominative or adjective.

A short, straight vertical line separates the verb from the direct object.

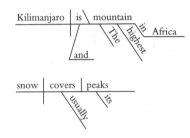

Step Three

Have your kid add a steplike line, holding the conjunction, between the verbs of the clauses. Then work together to add other elements such as direct objects, indirect objects, adjectives, or adverbs to both clauses of the sentence. Modifiers go on lines slanting down from whatever they modify.

Together, dream up more compound sentences, and diagram them.

Step Four

Once you feel your child has a good grasp of the structure of compound (and simple) sentences, go on to complex sentences. These have an independent clause and one or more subordinate (dependent) clauses.

For now, stick with sentences that have just one independent clause and one subordinate clause. Remember, though, that a subordinate clause can go in any number of different spots in the sentence. To draw the diagram correctly, your child must be able to identify the word that the clause modifies.

In the following complex sentence, the dependent clause (underlined) modifies the subject.

Tony's car, <u>which he bought last week</u>, is a vintage Mustang.

Step Five

When your child diagrams this sentence, he has to reapply the things he has just been doing. Since all clauses—dependent or

HELP FOR THE HOME

You are never alone. Here are just a few of the places you or your child can contact for caring assistance:

Attention-Deficit Information Network
475 Hillside Avenue
Needham, MA 02194
(617) 455-9895

National Organization of Adolescent Pregnancy and Parenting and Prevention
1319 F Street NW, Suite 401
Washington, DC 20004
(202) 783-5770

National Mental Health Association
1021 Prince Street
Alexandria, VA 22314
(800) 969-NMHA

National Family Violence Helpline National Council on Child Abuse and Family Violence
1155 Connecticut Avenue NW, Suite 300
Washington, DC 20036
(800) 222-2000

Alcoholics Anonymous General Service
PO Box 459
Grand Central Station
New York, NY 10163

AIDS Hotlines, Suicide Prevention, and Rape Hotlines
Every city has them—check your phone book under "Community Services."

SO, HOW WAS IT?

Parents should do more than just ask, "How was school today?" That might just elicit the response, "It was okay." Ask instead, "What did you do in school today?"

independent—have subjects and verbs, he will diagram each clause separately, much like a simple sentence. First, have him pick out the dependent clause and identify the word it modifies in the sentence. Next he should diagram the two clauses much as he did the two independent clauses above.

The difference lies in where he attaches the dependent clause to the main clause. The clause in the sample modifies the subject *car*. So a dotted line connects *car* with *which*, the pronoun that starts the dependent clause. (In diagraming the clause, be sure your child notices that *which* is the object of the verb *bought*.)

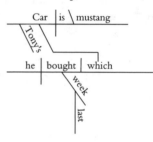

Step Six

Dream up more sentences. It can be fun to make the sentences pretty complicated and challenge one another to diagram them. When you run into difficulties, just consult your child's textbook or have him take your tough ones to his teacher for advice.

Although diagraming sentences can be fun, it isn't an end in itself. Rather, it is just a technique for making sentence structure clearer. How much you play with it will depend partly on whether you feel it's an effective way for helping your kid increase his mastery of language. It could also depend on the amount of emphasis that your kid's teacher places on diagraming.

▶ LET'S GO THERE!

"We have to research for school! Boring!" your kid complains. How did research get such a bad rap? How about helping your child to enjoy the process of looking for information? Doing some research together tied in with taking a trip or traveling to a vacation spot will strengthen her researching muscles and put researching where it belongs—in a positive light.

Before going on a family trip, whether for a day, a weekend, or longer, get together with your kid to make plans, get information, and research the history and background of where you're going. Although researching for a real trip has great immediacy, researching a fantasy trip is wonderful too.

Going anywhere is more fun when you know what you're seeing and what there is to see. In the end, your kid's research gives her practice in valuable language skills and makes a family vacation more fun for everyone.

At a Glance

Grade/Subject: 8th/Language Arts—Composition Skills, Speaking Skills, Reference Skills
Skills: writing different kinds of letters, finding and organizing information, skimming and scanning
Materials: road atlas or highway maps
notebook and pen
file folder for clippings and photocopies
stationery and stamps
typewriter or word processor
Time: 3–4 hours a week for several weeks in advance of the planned vacation or trip (The amount of time depends in part on the length and itinerary of the planned trip.)

Getting Ready

Start with a family meeting to decide where you will be going, or at least what kind of place you're looking for—a quiet lake cottage, a tropical beach, an American or European city, a family nature trip. Or decide on a fantasy trip that you want to make.

You and your child also need to discuss how you will be going to work together to make the vacation plan. Read over the steps and think about who will do what.

Finally, set up a Travel File to bring together all the information and notes that you find.

Step One

Start out at your local library. Together, consult the card catalog. With some new, computerized library catalogs, books you may be able to find will include not only regular travel guides about your destination but also novels, essays, and histories about that place and its people. Nowadays it may even include videos.

Make notes of the call numbers of the resources that look as if they may have something to suit your needs. Then divide the list with your child and collect the materials you've chosen.

WHAT'S MORE

Don't overlook fiction and biographies as a great source for background information about many destinations. Check out some of the excellent historical novels written for young people and share them with your child.

If your child has helped plan a vacation by car, let her be the navigator when you go. Work with her to transfer an itinerary to a road map. As you travel, she will read the map and give directions to the driver.

Everyone can learn in the course of traveling, too. If you avoid interstates and travel other highways, you'll see historical markers and monuments in hundreds of small towns. Stop to read them. Who were those people? What was that event? Have your child make notes for looking them up when you get home.

MAP IT OUT

If you belong to AAA, contact your local office and ask for information and maps about the place you are researching.

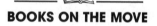

BOOKS ON THE MOVE

Whether you're planning a weekend adventure, a quick day trip, or a long family vacation, start with an armchair tour of *Books on the Move: A Read-About-It, Go-There Guide to America's Best Family Destinations* by Susan Knorr and Margaret Knorr. It describes hundreds of destinations across the United States and hundreds of related children's books to read before, during, and after the trek. Created by librarians, this book combines travel and learning to make family trips more fun and meaningful. Contact Free Spirit Publishing at (800) 735-7323 or e-mail them at help4kids@freespirit.com

Step Two

Most libraries and many magazine stands can offer another good source of travel information. Travel magazines and the travel sections of newspapers can give you up-to-date insights and inside information. And don't forget the *National Geographic*; your librarian can probably supply the magazine's special index of places.

You can find articles through the *Periodicals Digest* at your library and sometimes in the card catalog, too. As you and your child find articles, skim through the contents and decide whether they belong in your Travel File. Make photocopies of articles at the library that you want to keep.

Step Three

Another place to find information about a place is from a tourist office. Encourage your child to practice two kinds of information gathering: writing letters and making phone calls to request information.

Even though children her age spend a lot of time on the phone, this kind of adult telephone call takes a very different kind of speaking-listening skill. Remind your child to have her questions ready and to keep a notebook and pencil handy to take down information.

Also encourage her not to be disheartened if the person at the other end "treats her like a kid." On the other hand, congratulate her if she succeeds in getting useful information without being patronized or talked down to.

Step Four

When you've all done your research, check out what you have. Do you know enough about where you're going, when, and for how long? Do you know what reservations are necessary?

Gather the family to plan an itinerary, with your child acting as recorder to take notes of details like the following:

- Where will you be each day?
- How long will you travel and by what means?
- Where will you stay each night?
- What will you see and do there?

All that information should be in your file folder. You and your child have planned well. Have a great vacation—real or pretend!

▶ NEGATIVE ADVERTISING FOR FUN

Political advertising in recent elections has aimed at making the opposing candidate look as bad as possible. What if you applied this technique to other kinds of advertising—say, those for perfumes or clothing or restaurants?

The whole family—or just you and your child—can join in this mudslinging activity. It's a challenge to writing skills and vocabulary, for players must supply antonyms or other negative words that fit the subject of the ad. It's also good practice in recognizing the techniques of propaganda and persuasion. And the results can be a lot of fun.

At a Glance

Grade/Subject: 8th/Language Arts—Critical Thinking, Vocabulary, Composition
Skills: recognizing exaggeration and persuasive techniques, supplying antonyms, creative writing
Materials: newspaper or magazine advertisements
notebooks or writing tablets for each player
thesaurus (optional)
Time: 20–30 minutes for each ad, repeated once or twice a week for as long as interest continues

Getting Ready

With your teen, skim through magazines and newspapers (those that you're willing to cut up) to find advertisements with fairly long blocks of text. Good possibilities are ads for cars, resorts or hotels, electronic or exercise equipment, phone services, and airlines.

Each of you choose one or two to rewrite as negative ads—ads that make you want to do just the opposite of what the copywriter wanted!

Step One

Read through the ads you've chosen. Briefly discuss what the ad

IN A RUSH

I think a lot of students are overbooked—the so-called "hurried child" complex. Some parents say their children have homework all evening, while others say their kids never have homework and they have no idea what they're learning in school. Overall, kids these days are really busy, and many parents work out of the home or there's only one parent in the household, and everyone tends to be overscheduled.

Making the Grade

WHAT'S MORE

Another place to try this activity is when you're in a restaurant with a menu that gushes about each dish. Verbally, revise each of the menu descriptions as a negative description.

Think of something in your own life to write a negative ad about—health class, the soccer league, a school dance, your family pet.

As an antidote, you might want to write a positive ad as a companion piece for each of those negative ads.

wants the reader or consumer to do. Have your child circle or highlight the adjectives, verbs, and other words that give a favorable image or try to influence the consumer's attitude and promote interest in obtaining whatever is advertised.

Step Two

Now get to work to get rid of those "good" words and replace them with negative words. For example, here's a typical sentence from an ad for a vacation cruise:

"Throughout every day of your cruise, exciting optional excursions on shore are available to enhance your enjoyment of each fascinating destination."

How much fun can you have totally destroying this ad's intent? Here's one shot at it:

"Once in a while, when the guide feels like it, boring and expensive excursions on shore are available to intensify your boredom with these tedious places."

Brainstorm together to think of really awful descriptions. Turn to the thesaurus to find more devastating or unusual synonyms and antonyms.

Step Three

When your first negative ad is finished, read it aloud to share with other family members. Have fun wreaking havoc with the other ads you have collected.

Step Four

As a variation—especially after you've done this activity several times—you and your child can try rewriting the same ad separately, from scratch. Then compare your "negative" results.

▶ TOM SWIFTIES

"Did anyone say punctuating quotations would be easy?" questioned Tom markedly.

Tom Swift was the hero of innumerable books several generations ago. They were formula techno-adventure stories with titles like

Tom Swift and the Electric Airplane or Tom Swift and the Invincible Toothbrush. The quality of writing wasn't too high and Tom himself was given to proclaiming things in a standard way. Whatever he said was usually followed by an adverb describing how he said it. A group of jokes called Tom Swifties grew up around this writing style. The joke involves choosing an adverb that has something to do with what Tom said. Since Tom Swifties are easy and fun to create, they're a great way to practice using quotation marks as well as adverbs.

At a Glance

Grade/Subject: 8th/Language Arts—Mechanics, Grammar, Vocabulary
Skills: punctuating quotations, choosing adverbs
Materials: pencil and paper
tape recorder (optional)
Time: 1/2 hour, and whenever inspiration strikes thereafter

Getting Ready

Here are some sample Tom Swifties. Read them over with your child, and talk about how the adverb plays on the idea in what Tom says. Check out the one at the top of the activity too.

- "Who set fire to my chair?" asked Tom heatedly.
- "I've lost my voice," said Tom absently.
- "The vampires have drained me," said Tom emptily.

Step One

Together dream up at least five Tom Swifties and have your child write them out, punctuating them correctly.

Go over the punctuation together and talk also about how the adverb plays on the meaning of what Tom says.

(From now on, You can do this step any time, any day, anywhere just for the nonsense fun of it, whenever either of you thinks up a Tom Swifty.)

Step Two

Try turning your Tom Swifties into a little story. Together, figure out a situation in which Tom might say any of them and then weave all the quotations into a story (as silly as you like). You can

QUOTATION PUNCTUATION

Have your child write down some dialogue from a favorite television program and then rewrite it with correct punctuation. (If you have a tape recorder handy, tape the audio dialogue and play it back to make things easier.)

EXAMPLES

Here are some examples of the standard forms of punctuation for quotations:

"If you're late for dinner, you'll eat alone," said Rose.
Rose said, "If you're late for dinner, you'll eat alone."
"I heard you the first time," said Sybella.
"I'm late!" exclaimed Sybella.
"Did you want to eat alone?" asked Rose.

Notice where the question mark and exclamation point come in the last two examples.

add other characters who also say things always with adverbs describing how they said it). For example,

> "Who set fire to my chair?" asked Tom heatedly.
> "I did with this match," said Igor strikingly.
> "Well," said Tom blackly, "I'm completely scorched!"
> "You look nice in dark colors" said Igor fashionably.

Remember that in dialogue, you must begin a new paragraph each time the speaker changes.

Step Three

Since a lot of jokes involve people saying things (dialogue), writing jokes also provides an enjoyable opportunity to practice the use of quotation marks. Have your child dictate a favorite joke to you and write it down without punctuation. (If he has trouble thinking of one, suggest he tell you a Knock, Knock joke. Then have him punctuate it correctly.

Dictate a joke to your child and have him write it down using correct punctuation.

CHAPTER 14

Learning Adventures— 7th Grade Math

WHAT'S MORE

Who was Pythagoras? Use library resources and/or search on the Internet for *Pythagoras.* Check out this site: http://windows.engin.umich. edu/people/ancient_epoch/ pythagoras.html)

Use toothpicks (or blocks or dots on a grid) and build as many square numbers as you can. (Ignore the square number 1: it's not very interesting.)

▶ BREAKFAST WITH PYTHAGORAS

The Pythagorean theorem is one of the oldest and most famous theorems in all of mathematics. (Danny Kaye even sings a song about it in a delightful Technicolor movie based on the life of Hans Christian Anderson!) In algebra, it's usually written as $a^2 + b^2 = c^2$, where c is the longest side of a right triangle (the hypotenuse). But algebra is a "recent" mathematical invention. First came geometry.

So, slip into your togas to get in the spirit of the ages and get ready to recreate how Pythagoras might have come up with this theorem more than 2,000 years ago.

At a Glance

Grade/Subject: 7th/Math—Geometry, Algebra, Measurement
Skills: problem solving, squaring numbers, measuring lines and angles
Materials: 25 square chips—square cereal pieces will do fine
graph paper
pencil
scissors
ruler
protractor
clear tape
calculator (optional)
Time: 30 minutes

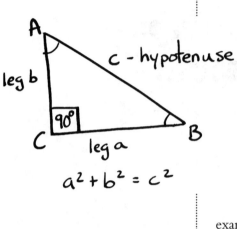

$$leg\ b$$

$$c - hypotenuse$$

$$90°$$

$$C \qquad leg\ a \qquad B$$

$$a^2 + b^2 = c^2$$

WHAT'S UP?

An *exponent* is a number written above and to the right of another number called a *base*. An exponent tells you how many times a base is used as a *factor* (part of a multiplication). For example, 2^3 means 2 x 2 x 2.

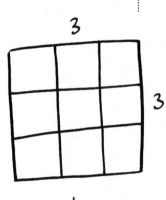

9-unit square

Getting Ready

Before getting started, you might want to review the basics of a right triangle and the squaring of numbers. For more information about sides and angles of right triangles, check out the activities "Off on a Tangent" and "Is This TV Right?"

"Square numbers" are numbers that are the product of two smaller, identical whole numbers. The smallest square number is 1, because $1 \times 1 = 1$, which is often called "the unit square." The next square number is 4, because $4 = 2 \times 2$.

An exponent of 2 is used as a shorthand way to represent a square number. So, 3×3 can be written as 3^2 and read as "3 squared." Most calculators have an automatic "squaring" key. When you enter a number and then press the this key, you see its square.

A square number also represents the area of a square. For example, 3^2 represents the area of a square whose sides are each three units. The area is 9 because the interior of this square contains 9 unit-squares.

Step One

Dump 25 cereal squares on a table. Check to select ones that are square or very nearly so.

Have your child arrange the pieces so that they form a square, and discuss its properties.

• What are the lengths of the sides of the square?
• What is the area of the square?

Have your child write the expression that relates the length of the sides of the square to its area, that is, how the sides are used to calculate the area. The ask him to write an expression using an exponent and read the expression back to you. ($5^2 = 25$, read "five squared equals 25.")

Step Two

Now, from the 25-unit square above, have your child remove some of the squares to create a 16-square. Write and read its expression back to you, $16 = 4^2$.

Have him rearrange the nine tiles he removed into a 9-unit

square; then write and read the expression for that square, $3^2 = 9$.

Finally, challenge him to use exponents in writing an arithmetic expression for the connection between the 25-square he started with and the 16-and 9-squares. (Hint: The desired expression involves a sum.) If it eludes you for now, do the rest of the steps and come back to this challenge afterwards.

> # Here are the first ten square numbers:
> # 1, 4, 9, 16, 25, 36, 49, 64, 81, 100

Step Three

Now move on from breakfast cereal to paper. Using a sheet of graph paper, have your child draw and then cut out a 25-unit square, a 16-unit square, and a 9-unit square.

Arrange the cut-out squares so that one corner of the 9-square and one corner of the 16-square touch adjacent corners of the 25-square. Then position the two smaller squares so that two of their corners just touch. The opening between the six corners should look like a triangle, with one side of each square forming a side of the triangle.

Hold down the three squares, while your child uses a pencil to carefully trace along the sides of the squares that form the triangle. Remove the squares and next to each side of the triangle, have him record its length.

Step Four

While you point to the longest side of the triangle, have your child locate the angle opposite that side and line up a protractor so that he can measure the number of degrees in that angle. The angle opposite the 5-side should be about 90°. What kind of triangle is this?

Tape the three squares along their corresponding sides of the triangle. Write the area of each square inside its square.

Step Five

Now, become Pythagoras. Together, analyze what the areas of the squares and the sides of the triangle have to do with one another. Talk about the relationships among the type of triangle formed by the three squares, the areas of the squares on the sides of the triangle, and the lengths of the sides. Ask your child to come up

WHAT'S MORE

On graph paper draw squares whose areas are 64, 225, and 289. Cut them out and show how they can be put back together to demonstrate that in a right triangle $a^2 + b^2 = c^2$.

___

Use the grid lines on a sheet of graph paper to draw a right triangle whose two shorter sides are 5 and 12. Draw the hypotenuse and measure it. Then, draw the squares on each side. Show that the areas of the squares satisfy $a^2 + b^2 = c^2$.

QUOTH PYTHAGORAS

In a right triangle, the square of the hypotenuse is equal to the sum of the squares of the other two sides.

his own informal statement of the Pythagorean theorem based on what he sees.

▶ CODES AND CIPHERS

Ever since time began, people have used ciphers or codes to transmit secret information. The Roman general Gaius Julius Caesar (B.C. 100–44) was one of the first people to use a coding technique known as an additive cipher.

In this activity, you and your child will learn how to create additive ciphers and use algebra to describe them. All you will need is some graph paper, some construction tools, and your imagination.

At a Glance

Grade/Subject: 7th/Math—Algebra
Skills: creating and writing expressions to represent algebraic transformations, using number sequences
Materials: graph paper
pencil
2 sheets of poster board or construction paper
compass
ruler
scissors
thumbtack or brass fastener
Time: 30–45 minutes

Getting Ready

Find a quiet corner where you and your child can recreate Caesar's code and other additive ciphers to amuse and baffle friends.

Step One

Use lower-case letters—a, b . . . z—and write out the 26 letters of the alphabet inside a square of the graph paper. This alphabet is called the *cleartext*. Leave a space between each letter so that the letters will be easy to read.

Under each letter of the cleartext, rewrite the alphabet shifted three units to the right. To distinguish the shifted alphabet from the cleartext, use upper-case letters. That is, under *d*, write *A*, the

WHAT'S MORE

How many possible additive ciphers are there? Under the cleartext alphabet, write all possible ciphertext alphabets that result from progressive shifts to the right. Write the corresponding algebraic expressions for each row.

___

What happens when you create an additive cipher using (x + 26) as the key? Use it to decode this message: "This is a silly cipher."

___

Good ciphers should be all but impossible to decode—except by the receiver. Discuss with your child the most "secret" aspect of an additive cipher.

___

Research secret codes and ciphers. Make a list with your child of favorite codes and send messages back and forth that only the two of you can read!

fourth letter after a in the alphabet; under e, write B, and so on. Continue until you have matched all 26 letters. The new alphabet is called the ciphertext.

Step Two

Now that you've created a ciphertext like Caesar's, decode this message:

KL LKB BSBO HBBMP X PBZOBQ PL TBII XP X ZEFIA

Step Three

Algebra gives us an easy way to describe the shift used to create this cipher. Caesar's ciphertext shifts the alphabet 3 spaces to the right, so that a corresponds to D. Since algebra often uses x as a variable, let x represent a, the first letter of cleartext. Therefore, the expression for the ciphertext is $x + 3$. This is the key to Caesar's code.

Suppose the key to another code is $x + 7$. On the same sheet of graph paper, create the ciphertext that corresponds to this key. What letter in the ciphertext corresponds to a (see sidebar for answers)?

Step Four

Now encode a message to send someone. First, write out the message on the graph paper, leaving a space between each word of the message. Then, under each letter of the message, substitute the corresponding letter of the ciphertext.

Give the message to an intended receiver along with the key. See if she can translate your message.

Step Five

Writing out a ciphertext starting from the alphabet and using an algebraic expression as a key takes time. It's also easy to make a mistake. Fortunately, in 1470, an Italian, Leone Battista Alberti, invented a circular device that makes it easy to decode such ciphers.

Use two sheets of sturdy poster board or construction paper, and on each sheet, use a compass to draw a circle. The

CIPHER ANSWERS

"No one ever keeps a secret so well as a child." Victor Hugo (1802–1885)

$(x + 7)$
A corresponds to T.

Cipher's Table

	a	b	c	d	e	..
x + 1	Z	A	B	C	D	...
x + 2	Y	Z	A	B	C	...
x + 3	X	Y	Z	A	B	...

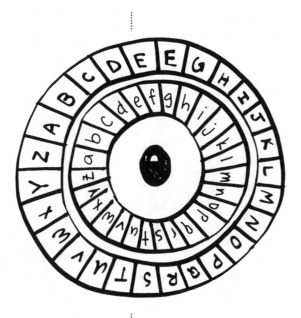

inner circle should be smaller than the outer circle. Cut out the circles and mount the smaller one inside the larger one so that they have the same center. Put a thumbtack or brass fastener through the center so that you can rotate the circles separately.

Use a rule to divide the circles into 26 regions (sectors) and label the inner circle with lowercase letters to represent the cleartext. Label the outer circle with uppercase letters to represent the ciphertext. Your final device should then be ready to go.

▶ EVERYDAY NUMBER SEARCH

Numbers are essential to daily life, but few of us think about how many numbers of different magnitudes (numbers in the hundreds, thousands, millions, etc.) we see and use in our daily life. Although scientific notation is usually used by scientists, you and your child can use it to look for everyday numbers of different magnitudes. As the two of you brainstorm and search for numbers of different magnitudes, you'll be amazed at the variety of numbers that you use or hear about everyday.

At a Glance

Grade/Subject: 7th/Math—Numeration, Computation
Skills: working with scientific notation
Materials: newspapers, magazines
paper and pencil
Time: 30 minutes

Getting Ready

Since you and your child will use scientific notation to find types of everyday numbers, review writing numbers in scientific notation with her. Remind her that any number, whether it's just $10 or $.01 or something more impressive, like 5 million people, can be written in scientific notation. Turning numbers into scientific notation is a bit like the fun of turning words into a

---

WHAT'S MORE

Try the same process with numbers having negative exponents on 10 when written in scientific notation (that is, numbers between 0 and 1). You may need to rewrite a number as a part of a larger quantity, such as 1 day = 1/365 yr. = 0.0027 yr. = 2.7×10^{-3} yr. Minutely small numbers may be obtained from scientific references.

handy code or shorthand. Also, review the metric and standard U.S. measurement systems with her. They can be found in any almanac of encyclopedia.

Step One

Start by asking your child to name some one-digit numbers that are a part of her daily life. For instance, the number of rooms in your home or the number of subjects in which she has homework. Have her write these everyday numbers in scientific notation. (They should be written with the exponent 0 on the 10, since 10^0 equals 1.) For example, if you have six rooms in your home, she should write 6×10^0 rooms.

Step Two

Now her "code" or "number shorthand" writing gets a bit less simple. Have her name an everyday number that gives an exponent of 1 on the number 10 when written in scientific notation. (Remember, 10^1 equals 10.) Brainstorm together examples from your daily life for as many exponents of 10 as you can. It might be the number of kids in her class, the price of running shoes, the number of ounces in a package of cookies, etc.

How about the price of TV set, the number of people in your town, or the capacity of a sport's stadium? What exponent of 10 do you need to express those numbers? (Think about what 10^2 equals, for instance.)

Rewrite the information on Metric/U.S. Measures using scientific notation.

Step Three

Expand your search for everyday numbers further by looking for ever larger numbers in a newspaper or magazine. Discuss possible strategies to use (such as making a chart) for looking for the numbers that can be expressed using scientific notation 10^3, 10^4, 10^5, 10^6, etc.

Find at least one example for as many exponents of 10 as you can find. See how many different varieties of numbers you can find. You can use more than just financial and population data. In addition to the news and business sections, look in the sports, health and science, and even lifestyle sections.

CHOOSE YOUR MEASURE

Metric/U.S. Linear Measure
(1 meter = 3.28 feet)
10 millimeters = 1 centimeter
100 centimeters = 1 meter
1,000 meters = 1 kilometer
12 inches = 1 foot
3 feet = 1 yard
5,280 feet = 1 mile

Metric/U.S. Weight
(31 grams = 1 ounce)
1,000 milligrams = 1 gram
1,000 grams = 1 kilogram
16 ounces = 1 pound
2,000 pounds = 1 ton

Metric/U.S. Fluid Measure
(1 liter = 1.057 quarts)
1,000 milliliters = 1 liter
1,000 liters = 1 kiloliter
16 fluid ounces = 1 pint
2 pints = 1 quart
4 quarts = 1 gallon

WHAT'S MORE

Research some units that are used to measure "extreme" things, that is, things that are incredibly large or small—for instance, light years and nanoseconds. Give the value of each "extreme" unit in terms of a standard unit. For example, write the value 1 light-year in terms of miles. Write each value using scientific notation.

Making the Grade

Step Four

Have you exhausted your search? Not quite. Now look for examples of even larger numbers in such publications as almanacs, encyclopedias, and other reference books. Try to use only numbers that have some relation to everyday life, such as the U.S. or U.N. budget, advances in technology, or information on world population. You'll be amazed at how large a number you can find.

▶ FIRST TO 5

Get ready for a fast, lively game that uses basic math facts. First to 5 is a card game in which you make rational numbers and add them to try to reach the total 5. Although this game seems deceptively simple, players need to know how to estimate the values of rational numbers to progressively add them in order to get to 5 without going over it.

The instructions in steps one and two give you the rules for the basic game to get you started. Once you have played it for awhile, you might want to make up your own variation. This is the kind of game that can evolve as your child's mathematical skills develop.

At a Glance

Grade/Subject: 7th/Math—Computation
Skills: adding rational numbers, estimating rational numbers
Materials: deck of cards
calculator
paper and pencil
Time: 30 minutes

Getting Ready

Explain to your child that this game involves adding rational numbers. Make sure she knows that a rational number is a number that can be written as a fraction. Since you can use your calculator to add fractions, she will not need that skill for this activity. However, estimating the values of fractions is important for plotting strategy. Practice with your child how to estimate the value of fractions.

From a deck of cards, take out all the jokers and face cards (jack, queen, and king) and put them aside. You will not need them for this game.

Step One

Shuffle the cards and deal 12 to your child and 12 to yourself. Tell her to look at her cards and place one on the table face up so that you can both see it. Then you choose a card from your hand and play it face up next to the first card. From these two cards a fraction is made, using the lower value as the numerator and greater number as the denominator. (An ace has a value of 1). For example, if your child plays a 9 of any suit and you play a 2 of any suit, the fraction 2/9 is formed. Record the fraction. This value is the start of the running total that is kept for the game.

Step Two

Now it's your child's turn to play a card to make a fraction by combining it with the card you played. Tell her to choose a card from her hand and form a fraction using the values of her card and the card you played in the same manner (the lower card is the numerator and the greater card is the denominator). Add this fraction to the running total, and record the result. (Doing the addition for the running tally is where the calculator comes in handy.)

Step Three

You probably get the idea now. Continue taking turns playing a card and forming fractions using the values of the last two cards. The winner of the hand is the first player who makes the running total as close to 5 without going over it. The first player who wins three hands is the winner of the game.

▶ LAST ONE WINS

Mathematical problem solving can happen in many different areas, but few are more intriguing than strategy games. Two-person strategy games have been around throughout human history, and there are literally thousands of them. They range from simple and short games like Tic Tac Toe to more complex classics like Go and chess.

Here are three easy-to-learn games that not only offer hours of interesting game playing, but will also enable the players to learn how to take a game apart to find the optimum playing strategies. All three are "take away" games—that is, they require two players to alternately remove pieces according to specific rules. In each game, the person who takes away the last piece wins!

TEENS AND CALCULATORS

Should your teen use a calculator to do her math homework? If the focus is on getting to the answer and thinking how to solve a problem, don't discourage her from making needed calculations with a calculator. If the lesson focuses on calculating numeric answers to specific math problems, however, encourage your teen to set aside the calculator and use the old noggin! Nothing substitutes for knowing your math facts.

Making the Grade

HERE'S A HINT

At the end of the game, if you leave one, two, three, four, or five pieces, your opponent will certainly win. That means that 1, 2, 3, 4, and 5 are all losing "leaves." If, however, you leave six pieces, can you see that no matter what your opponent does, you will be able to take the last piece on his next turn? And in fact, whatever he takes, you will be able to win on your next turn. That means that 6 is a winning "leave," since you will certainly win whenever you leave 6 pieces for your opponent.

WHAT'S MORE

Try the games with three or more players. You may want to change a rule in some cases to make the game work better with more than two players. Can you still figure out an optimum strategy when you have more than one opponent?

At a Glance

Grade/Subject: 7th/Math—Problem Solving
Skills: making charts, analyzing patterns
Materials: 40 pieces—such as poker chips, dried beans, toothpicks, pennies, etc.
paper and pencils
Time: 3/4 to 1 hour for each of the games

Getting Ready

In each game players have a number of pieces (anything small can be used, or you can draw circles on paper and remove them by crossing them out). Even if you are using pieces, have pencil and paper available to keep track of winning moves and how many times each player wins and loses.

Step One

First you need to learn the rules of the three games.

High Five: Start with 32 pieces in one pile. Players alternate taking from one to five pieces away. The person who takes the last piece is the winner.

By Row: Start with four rows of three, five, seven, and nine pieces respectively. Players may take as few as one or as many as the entire row, but may not take pieces from more than one row on each turn. The person who takes the last piece is the winner.

Up Three: Start with 40 pieces in one pile. The first player may take one, two, or three pieces. After that, each player may take up to three pieces more than the opponent's previous move. The person who takes the last piece wins. For example, if your opponent just took five pieces, you could take up to eight pieces. If, however, you decide to take only one piece, your opponent could take no more than four pieces.

Step Two

You and your child can play each game at least half a dozen times and see if you can get any ideas for how to play it more effectively. Unlike chess, all three of these games are simple enough to allow you to figure out some, or possibly all, of the winning strategies. That doesn't mean that you are likely to figure them out completely without many hours of work. But even without coming up with a perfect winning strategy, you and your child can still figure out enough to be better players.

Step Three

Discuss your strategies. Your child might like to make a steadily growing chart of good and bad moves. But how do you determine what is a good or bad move? You might make a really good move in the beginning of the game, but because of a bad move later on, you might not win.

Step Four

Your child can make charts of winning and losing "leaves" for each of the three games. As these charts get longer, you can start looking for patterns of winning and losing moves. The larger your chart and the more patterns you discover, the better you will get at playing these games.

❯ MEN AND MEANS

How would you like to be president of the United States? Would your child like to become president? Given the intellectual, emotional, physical, and financial resources, can anyone run for president?

Age is one requirement for becoming elected president. The Constitution requires a person to be at least 35 years old. Can you or your child name the average age of the people who have become presidents of the United States? How close to 35 were they? How "close" is close? Is there a trend toward electing younger presidents? Examining the ages of the most recent ten presidents provides interesting answers, as well as a good reason to compute!

At a Glance

Grade/Subject: 7th/Math—Numeration, Computation, Graphing, Statistics
Skills: arithmetic computations, working with negative numbers, graphing, and interpreting data
Materials: pencil and paper
graph paper and colored pencils
ruler
calculator (optional)
Time: 45 minutes

WHAT'S MORE

Change a single rule for one of the games and see how much it changes the strategy for the game. For example, change the rule to say that the person who takes the last piece is the loser. Or change the number of pieces you start with, or the number you can take on each turn.

Invent a completely new two-person "take-away" game with any rules you like, and then try to figure out a winning strategy for playing it.

REFRESH AND REPEAT

Neuropsychologists, scientists who study the physiological functioning of the brain, have discovered that there are measurable physical differences in the brain when long-term learning occurs. These changes take place only when short-term memory events are refreshed and repeated. What is learned is the result of repeated use. So, parents, make sure your children are practicing what they learn. Reinforce the learning in as many different ways as possible!

Making the Grade

NUMBERS GAME

Statistics is the science of collecting, organizing, and interpreting numerical information called *data*.

DO I QUALIFY?

Check out the other Constitutional requirements for a person to be elected president of the United States. Do you or your child qualify?

GOVERNING AGE

Name	Age at Inauguration
Clinton	46
Bush	64
Reagan	69
Carter	52
Ford	60
Nixon	55
Johnson	54
Kennedy	43
Eisenhower	62
Truman	60

Getting Going

Statistics are just numbers. The statistics used in this activity are the mean and the standard deviation.

Averages refers usually to the arithmetic mean of a set of observations (data). The mean is calculated by finding the sum of a set of observations and then dividing that sum by the number of observations. The data in this activity are the ages of the last ten U.S. Presidents.

The standard deviation is a number that tells you how spread out the data are from the mean. The standard deviation (usually abbreviated *s*) is calculated in a way that is similar to calculating the mean—that is, you add up some numbers and divide the total by the number of numbers that you added. The major difference is that you must also do some subtractions, calculate some squares, and finish by finding a square root. Learning to calculate a standard deviation provides a great way to practice basic arithmetic computations and a real-life answer to the old question, "Why do I have to learn arithmetic?"

Step One

Using a history text, encyclopedia, almanac, or other resource, locate a copy of the U.S. Constitution. Together, look for the section that deals with the criteria for being elected president. Ask your child when she would meet the qualifications. Discuss, too, your ideas about why the founding fathers picked that requirement along with your ideas about it.

Step Two

Have your child use the information about the ages of the last ten presidents to make a four-column table with each name in column 1 and each age at first inauguration in column 2.

Together, look at the data, and decide what you each think the average age of the presidents at inauguration appears to be, based on this data. Write down each guess. Then, share your guesses, write them down, and talk about your reasons for choosing that number.

Step Three

Now work together to compute the mean of these ten presidents at inauguration.

- Have your child add the numbers in Column 2.
- Divide the sum by the number of items in Column 2.
- Round the result to the nearest tenth. This number is the mean.

Compare this number to the predicted average you each made in step two. How close was your predicted mean to the actual mean? Compare this value to the minimum age required by the Constitution. What seems to be true about how old most of these men were when inaugurated? Who were exceptions?

Step Four

To examine the spread of the data, have her draw a horizontal and vertical axis on a sheet of graph paper, with the horizontal about two inches from the bottom of the page and the vertical axis about 1.5 inches from the left edge. Along the horizontal axis, make ten marks, one for each president. Skip a few spaces between each mark. Label the horizontal axis "presidents" and under each mark, identify the President by writing his name or initials.

Begin the vertical scale at 30 (rather than 0—Why?) and divide the vertical scale into intervals of 5 years up to the maximum number necessary to plot the oldest president's age. Label this axis "Age at Inauguration (years)."

Read out the inaugural age of each president, as your child plots the corresponding point on the graph. When she has plotted all the points, have her use a ruler and a colored pencil to connect the points. Since the points do not lie on one straight line, the graph is called a "broken line" graph. Talk about what you see.

- Are the points spread out a lot or are they pretty close to the mean?
- Who is closest to the mean? Farthest?
- On average, how close to 35 was the age of the "most average" president?

Step Five

Does your graph suggest that, on average, most presidents were about the same age at inauguration? This is where the concept of standard deviation comes into play. Your child should locate on the vertical axis the value of the mean (that you calculated in step three) and use a different colored pencil to draw a horizontal line from this point across the graph, through the broken-line graph. This line makes more visually graphic "how spread out" the data

MEAN FORMULA

$x\text{mean} = \frac{1}{n}(x1 + x2 + \ldots + xn)$,

where n is the number of observations, and x represents each observation. For these data,

$x\text{mean} = \frac{1}{10}(47 + 65 + 70 + 53 + 61 + 56 + 55 + 44 + 63 + 61)$

WHAT'S MORE

Who was the oldest person ever inaugurated as president of the United States? The youngest? Calculate the standard deviation of all 41 and see how close each of them was to it.

Find other data that you can graph and calculate the means and standard deviations. An almanac is full of intriguing possibilities—the population or area of states or nations, the size of national parks, the size of the Great Lakes, immigration data, sports statistics, and more.

STANDARD DEVIATION FORMULA

The formula for standard deviation looks pretty scary. But, except for the square root sign, it's sort of like calculating an average.

$$s = \sqrt{\frac{[(age1-mean)^2+(age2-mean)^2 + \ldots +(age10-mean)^2])}{10}}$$

WHAT'S MORE

Look up the ages of the rest of the presidents at inauguration and determine the mean age at inauguration based on all of them. Compare this mean to the average age of the most recent ten. The information on their ages is easy to find in any almanac. (Count Grover Cleveland only once.)

Do the same for Canadian prime ministers and compare your results.

ANSWER

The standard deviation of these ten ages should be 7.67.

are from the mean. Now, work together to calculate the spread of the data, or the standard deviation. Here is how to carry out the calculations represented in the formula for finding the standard deviation of a set of numbers.

- Write the label "(age – mean)" above the third column of the table you created in step two.
- Subtract the age of each president (the number in column 2) from the mean of all ten presidents' ages and record each difference in column 3. Be careful: some numbers will be negative.
- Write the label "(age – mean)²" above the fourth column of the table.
- Now square each number in column 3 and record the square in column 4. (All numbers will now be positive.)
- Add the ten numbers in column 4.
- Divide that sum by 10.
- Finally, find the square root of the result of the division to the nearest whole number. You can use a calculator, a table of squares (often found in a math book), or trial and error.

Step Six

Have your child use the graph to measure the distance on the graph from each point to the horizontal, mean line (below or above it) drawn to represent the mean of the ages. Ignore whether the distance is in a negative or positive direction because you are interested only in how far away the point is from the mean. Write down each distance as she calls it out. When she has measured all ten distances, discuss how each distance compares to the standard deviation. Some distances will be less than the standard deviation and some will be greater.

- Which of these presidents was closest to the standard deviation?
- Which is furthest?

Use the formula for calculating means to now find the average of these lengths. The number you get should match the number you got for the standard deviation because the standard deviation (that is talked about all the time in statistics) is the average of all the amounts that data differ from their mean. (Don't worry if your calculation is slightly off; it is probably because of rounding.)

❱ THE PERCENT DETECTIVES

How many times have you seen something that is proclaimed to be "25 percent less," or "30 percent off," or "down 10 percent"? Maybe it's a cracker that has "25 percent less fat," clothing on a rack marked "30 percent off," or a report that the crime rate is down 10 percent. But, what are they talking about? 25 percent of what? 30 percent off what? down 10 percent from what? To become an informed consumer and citizen, your child needs to learn how to search for a key piece of information—always to ask, " percent of what number?"

As Percent Detectives, you and your child look into the details talk of percentages. By intelligently examining claims involving percentages, he'll come to understand exactly what they are saying and might even find some that just don't stand up to the mathematical facts!

At a Glance

Grade/Subject: 7th/Math—Fractions, Decimals and Percents
Skills: find a number given the percent, estimating percents
Materials: newspaper or magazine
paper and pencil
calculator
Time: 30 minutes

Getting Ready

With your child, practice how to find the percent of a number. Remind him that a percent (that is, a part of a hundred) must be a percent of some number. For example, 25 percent must be 25 percent of some number, such as 25 percent of 80. In this case, 80 is the number of which we take 25 percent. Let's call this number the "percent of" number.

Ask your child how to find 25 percent of 80. Remind him that 25 percent is the same as $0.25 = 25/100 = 1/4$. Then explain that you multiply 1/4 times 80 (which can also be done by multiplying 0.25 times 80). For practice, make up a few more percent problems, and ask your child to identify the "percent of" number for each problem and then solve the problem. (You could use the cracker-clothing-crime examples given at the start of this activity.)

WHAT'S MORE

Calculating the ratios of fat (in grams) to total weight (in grams) of low-fat and higher fat products is a more accurate comparison. Have your child calculate the ratio of fat to total weight for the two products. Ask him to divide the ratio of the low-fat product by the ratio for the regular product to get the percent.

Your child can calculate the recommended daily requirements of fat, cholesterol, sodium, protein, and other nutrients by using the nutrition facts listed on the package of some product. Divide each amount per serving by the percent of the daily amount. Now compare these daily totals with the recommended daily requirements you find from another source. Your local public librarian can help you find another source.

Making the Grade

PESKY PERCENT

Caution! Remember how pesky percent problems can be? When you're told that a $40 shirt is on sale for 10 percent off the regular price, then 40 x .10 = 4 gives the discount from the regular price. (To find the sale price, subtract the discount from the regular price: sale price = $40 − $4 = 36.) On the other hand, if you know that the shirt is 10 percent less, you need to divide the discount ($4) by the percent (10 percent) to find the "percent of" number ($40). This rule applies to any percent increase or decrease.

Step One

Using a newspaper or magazine, search with your child for articles and advertisements that use a percent. Of the percents you found, how many tell the "percent of" number? For example, if a store is having a sale of 25 percent off all winter clothing, does it say what price the percent is taken off of? Are the "percent of" prices ones suggested by the manufacturer, or are they the store's "everyday low price"?

Step Two

Have your child choose one case in which the "percent of" number is not given. It could be an advertisement of a sale or a news report about a decline or rise of 25 percent. You both may be surprised to discover that it may take time to find one that gives the price saving or the actual decline or rise as well as the percent.

Now the task is to find the "percent of" number. Remind him that since you multiply the percent by the "percent of" number to get the final result (the saving or decline or rise), you need to do the opposite to find the "percent of" number. (You find the "percent of" number by dividing the saving, decline, or rise by the percent.) Have him find the "percent of" number.

For instance, suppose a news article reported that in April you got 4 inches more rain than you received in April last year, an increase of 40 percent. Then, to find the "percent of" number, divide 4 by 40 percent = 0.4 to get 4/0.4 = 10 inches.

Step Three

Now help him choose a case in which the final price or actual rise or decline is not given. Call the store or other source and ask for the "percent of" number as well as the actual price reduction of the item or the decline or rise. Have your child divide the actual increase or decrease by the "percent of" number to find the percent increase or decrease. How does his result compare with the published percent?

Step Four

Try your investigative powers on a claim of a food product. Many foods claim to have as much as 50 percent less sodium or fat. Have you ever wondered what this means? Help your child find a low-fat or low-sodium product in a grocery store that boasts the percentage less fat or sodium. Does it also give the "percent of" number? If not, have him look for the amount of fat or sodium per serving (in grams) in the nutrition facts on the package. Using this information, ask him to find the "percent of" number by dividing the amount of sodium or fat in grams by the percent. This "percent of" number is the amount of fat per serving that the manufacturer claims has been taken out of the original, higher-fat product. Adding the "percent of" number to the amount of fat per serving of the low-fat product should be roughly equal to the amount per serving in the higher fat product.

▶ ROLL UP YOUR SLEEVE AND ROLL 'EM

People have been playing games of chance since the beginning of recorded history. And mathematicians have been studying the probability of various outcomes in these games to understand what is really going on with these numbers. Here's a way for you and your child to join them in rolling dice to answer some questions about probability.

At a Glance

Grade/Subject: 7th/Math—Probability, Fractions
Skills: finding probabilities, record keeping, fraction practice
Materials: at least 4 dice
lined paper and pencil
Time: 3/4–1 hour

Getting Ready

Because a die has six sides, when you roll a single die, there are six equally likely possibilities of what number will come up. The probability of any particular number (5, for example) coming up on a single die is 1/6, one in six possibilities. Probabilities are often expressed in the form of a fraction: the numerator is the number of ways the desired outcome can happen (in this case there is only one way that a 5 can come up on a single die) and the denominator is the total number of possible outcomes (6, because there are six sides). This doesn't mean that if you throw a

LEARNING ADVENTURES

In *SCORE!*'s Learning Adventures, we provide children with hands-on learning to introduce key concepts in academic subjects. These are one-week seminars, and in that short time we inspire kids and spark their curiosity and desire to study subjects further. That is good advice for parents too. You can provide little learning experiences for your children at home, just to spark their intellectual curiosity. There are so many opportunities at home to learn.

Making the Grade

TIPS FOR TEENS

For attitude problems with your parents:
- Avoid put-downs and threats.
- Put your thoughts and feelings in forms that don't come across as disrespect or "bad attitude."
- Use I-messages. Actively listen.
- Stay away from your parents when you're in a bad mood.
- Be sure you know specifically what it is in your attitude they don't like. Deal with those issues directly.
- Rebuild trust.
- Make your folks feel better (e.g., apologize, do a good deed, etc.).
- Gather intelligence. Seek out hidden agendas.
- Identify your parents' feelings. Do they feel neglected? Unloved?
- Identify what "good attitude" would be to your folks. Then go for it!
—from *Bringing Up Parents* by Alex J. Packer, Ph.D. (Free Spirit Publishing, 1992)

LISTEN UP

Listen to your teens. If they're doing homework, find out what they do know, then help to build on that. Sometimes a teen will ask a question and an adult will start to explain each and every step, when it might be just the last step they needed help with.

die six times (or throw six dice all at once), you will always get one 5. Probability is a mathematical concept that helps us understand what is likely to happen if we do something many times, but it doesn't guarantee any individual outcome.

This activity involves exploring the concept of probability with your child by seeking answers to the following three interesting probability questions.

Questions
- If you roll three dice, are you more likely to have at least two of a kind ("doubles") showing or not?
- If you roll two dice, what is the probability of getting a total of seven?
- If you roll two dice, are you more likely to get an odd total (3, 5, 7, 9, 11) or an even total (2, 4, 6, 8, 10, 12)?

Step One

To figure out the first question, you need to roll three dice 100 times. Although that is a lot of rolling, it goes quickly when you share the work. On the paper, make two columns for recording the results of every roll. The chart should have two columns, one for success (two matching numbers) and one for failure (no two of a kind).

Each of you predicts how many times out of 100 rolls you think at least two of a kind (two of any number) will be rolled. Write your predictions down. Then take turns, each rolling the three dice ten times until you have made 100 rolls altogether. As one of you rolls, the other records the results of each roll.

Step Two

After 100 rolls, count up the number of successes and failures. Express the results in the form of a fraction, decimal, or percentage. For example, if doubles came up 29 times, you would have been successful 29/100 (or .29, or 29 percent) of the time and unsuccessful 71/100 (.71 or 71 percent) of the time. Write your results under your predictions. How close were your predictions?

How do you know whether these rolling results were a fluke? Try it doing it again one or more times to see whether the probability remains constant.

Step Three

Now for the other two questions. Begin by each of you predicting the probability for each of these questions about rolling two dice:

• Probability of rolling a total of 7 with two dice
• Probability of rolling an even total with two dice

Then, just as you did with the first question, check your predictions by throwing the dice one hundred times and keeping track of the results. Your columns for the 7-total test could be headed "7" and "not 7"; for the other test they could be "even" and "odd."

Repeating the process several times for each question will give you a good idea of whether your results are unusual or not. If you tested the same question three times and got 12, 98, and 47 successes respectively, that would be very surprising!

Step Four

As you've discovered (as you shake out your tired rolling arm), working out probabilities empirically—that is, by physically doing it—is tiring and time consuming. Math to the rescue. You can work it out theoretically, using fractions.

Finding out the theoretical probability of something happening, in the form of a fraction, requires counting the number of possible ways that something could happen, using that as the numerator of the fraction, and then putting that number over the number of total possible outcomes. Go over this process with your collaborating dice roller.

For example if you were throwing one die and wanted to know the probability of rolling an even number you would count the number of even numbers that could come up, which is three (2, 4, and 6), and therefore put 3 on the top of your fraction. On the bottom of the fraction, you would put the number of total possible outcomes you could roll, which is six (1, 2, 3, 4, 5, and 6). The resulting fraction 3/6 is, then, the probability of rolling an even number with one die. Of course, 3/6 can be reduced to 1/2, so the probability of rolling an even number with one die is 1 in 2 tries. You can also convert the fraction to a decimal (.5) or to percent (50 percent). This means that the likelihood would be 50 percent in favor of rolling an even number with one die.

SHORT CUT

To save time and counting, count up the number of lines on a sheet of paper (most have about 28). Then fold the paper in half lengthwise twice to make four columns. Cross off all but 25 lines. Now divide each of your four folded columns into columns, one headed "matched" and the other "mismatch."

WHAT'S MORE

Make up your own probability questions with dice, playing cards, or coins. Make your gut predictions; then express the theoretical probability using fractions as described in step four. Then test your predictions with a large number of trials.

Make predictions about the real life probabilities. For example, if you watch the people passing by your house on a particular day, what are the chances that they will be wearing glasses? After making predictions, test your guess by keeping track of 100 people.

Making the Grade

ANYTHING BUT TV

My husband and I don't encourage a lot of TV watching at our house, but we will encourage our teenager to do anything creative with us— cooking, woodworking, building clubhouses, tiling our bathroom.

Express your test results as fractions, reducing them to their lowest possible terms, and converting them to decimals and percents. Check out how close your empirical trials came to the theoretical probabilities by creating fractions for each of the original three questions, using the process described in this step.

CHAPTER 15

Learning Adventures—
8th Grade Math

IT CLICKS!

Parents shouldn't be giving teens all the answers when they do schoolwork together. Your teen won't understand what's going on if this well-intentioned spoonfeeding happens on a regular basis. Focus on providing "teachable moments" for your child, rather than forcing the information down. Teachable moments are times when you can tell that something new has really clicked for your teen. Maybe she's struggling with Roman numerals, then all of a sudden, you know she gets it!

▶ BABY, HOW COLD IS IT OUTSIDE?

Chances are the thermometers you have at home measure temperatures in degrees Fahrenheit. However, people in most other parts of the world use the Celsius scale. Because of that difference, travelers often are puzzled about what to wear when they travel outside the United States. For example, if you hear that the temperature in Toronto, Canada, is 20°C, should you take a sweater or winter coat?

At a Glance

Grade/Subject: 8th/Math—Algebra, Graphing
Skills: plotting points and graphing lines, using graphs to convert temperature scales, representing lines with equations
Materials: Fahrenheit (inside/outside) thermometers
Celsius thermometer (optional)
graph paper
pencil
ruler
fever thermometer
Time: 30–45 minutes

Getting Ready

Here is some background for you and your teen to consider. The Celsius and Fahrenheit thermometers are based on the freezing and boiling points of water. Using centigrades, the Celsius

Making the Grade

WHAT'S MORE

Use the library to learn who Fahrenheit, Celsius, and Kelvin were.

Which scale do you think is easiest to use and why? Write up your idea about whether the U.S. should change to the Celsius system.

Do some hot and cold research: look up a few common substances and plot their freezing and boiling points on the graph drawn in Step One. Find out why your tongue sticks to an icy cold metal surface.

Dry ice forms at –78°C. What is its chemical name? What happens when it melts?

The equation to change from degrees Fahrenheit to degrees Celsius is $C° = \frac{5}{9} F° - 32$. Make a table and calculate values of C for values of F. Draw this graph.

---

thermometer shows that water freezes at 0° and boils at 100°. This creates a scale divided into 100 degrees.

In the Fahrenheit system of measurement, however, water freezes at 32°F and boils at 212°F. Do the simple subtraction to arrive at the fact that the Fahrenheit scale is therefore divided into 180° between those two extremes.

The difference between the two scales means that a unit on the Celsius scale is $\frac{9}{5}$ times larger than a unit on the Fahrenheit scale.

In other words, $\frac{(212 - 32)}{(100 - 0)} = \frac{180}{100} = \frac{9}{5}$. You'll need this number, $\frac{9}{5}$, to convert temperatures in degrees Celsius to temperatures in degrees Fahrenheit using this formula:
$$F° = \frac{9}{5}C° + 32°.$$

Step One

Review with your teen the design and purpose of thermometers. Look one over carefully and talk about what thermometers measure. When and why people use them? Brainstorm several familiar types and uses in your lives, e.g., weather, cooking, medical, refrigeration, home thermostats, transportation, industry.

Review together the information in Getting Ready. Tell your child that together you are going to create a graph that will make it easy to change from one scale to the other—just in case you're planning a trip outside the United States.

Step Two

Draw a large x- and y-axis on a sheet of graph paper. Create a horizontal scale ranging from about –50 to 100 and a vertical scale from –50 to 220. Divide each axis into appropriate units. Label the horizontal axis "degrees C" and the vertical axis "degrees F."

Plot the corresponding freezing and boiling points of water: (0°C, 32°F) and (100°C, 212°F). Label each point with its coordinates. Then, use a ruler and draw a line through the two points. Extend the line so that it intersects the x-axis. Write the coordinates of this point of intersection on the graph.

Use the graph to talk about figuring out temperature. For example, have your teen imagine being a weather person responsible for reporting temperatures around the world. Make up questions for each other like these:

- If it's 20°C in Toronto, what will you report to Americans, who need to hear Fahrenheit degrees?
- When it's 80°F in Florida, what temperature will you report to the Canadians?
- When it's 10° in Chicago, what will you tell folks in Mexico City?

Step Three

Take each other's temperature using a fever thermometer. If only one scale is given, use the graph to find out what its equivalent is in the other scale, and then plot the point. If both scales are given on the thermometer, graph the point on the line. In either case, label the point.

Step Four

It's not always cool to carry graph paper around when you travel, nor can you always make a graph large enough to read extreme temperatures. So the conversion equation comes in handy.

It's much simpler to remember the Fahrenheit-Celsius relationship as an equation: $F° = \dfrac{9}{5} C° + 32°$. Together, look at the graph again to figure out where the numbers in the equation appear to come from. For example, why is there a 32 in the equation? Substitute some values for C in the equation and check the corresponding values for F. Mark them on the graph.

Here is a simple rule that will help you change Celsius temperatures to Fahrenheit temperatures: "Double a Celsius temperature and then add 32." Examine the equation again and see who can explain why this approximation works pretty well. (Hint: What whole number is $\dfrac{9}{5}$ approximately equal to?)

BODY TEMPERATURE

Normal body temperature is 36.9°C or 98.6°F.

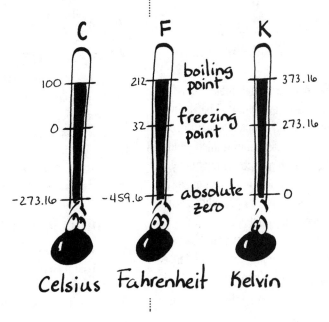

HOW ZERO IS ZERO?

Temperature is a measure of molecular motion. The greater the molecular motion, the hotter a substance is. The less motion, the colder it is. *Absolute zero* (0°K) is the temperature at which all molecular motion stops. Scientists have been able to freeze certain materials and get very close to this temperature, but it's impossible to achieve, even in a laboratory under very controlled circumstances.

You may want to borrow a chemistry book or simple handbook of chemistry to look up the freezing and boiling points of some common substances, such as carbon dioxide (dry ice), nitrogen, mercury, alcohol, etc.

BE PREPARED

Parents should tell their teens, "I don't know everything. That's what learning is all about. We learn every day." Parents should remind childs that learning happens every day, and it continues to happen once we leave school. You probably learn even more outside of school because you've got your basics down. Build your teen's confidence now to prepare him for a lifetime of learning.

Step Five

Scientists everywhere use a third temperature scale called the Kelvin scale. It is closely related to the Celsius scale: that is, 0°C equals 273°K, and 0°K equals −273°C. 0°K is called *absolute zero*. Nothing gets colder than that.

Make a new set of x- and y-axes and let the horizontal axis represent the Celsius scale and the vertical axis represent the Kelvin scale. Write "degrees C" along the horizontal axis and "degrees K" along the vertical axis. Plot the two reference points between the Celsius and Kelvin scales and draw the line that represents the relationship between the scales.

Look at the coordinates of some points on the line. Write an equation in terms of C° and K° that represents the relationship between the two scales. (Here's one: $K° = C° + 273°$.)

▶ FOUR 4s

Here's an intriguing brainteaser: How many numbers can be calculated using only 4s, and always four of them? For instance, 44/44 is an arithmetic expression that equals 1. You can express the number 2 using four 4s like this: $4/4 + 4/4 = 2$. Okay, you're ready to keep going. How about expressing 3?

This activity challenges you to help your child to use four 4s, and any arithmetic signs you want, to make arithmetic expressions that equal each of the numbers between 1 and 100.

At a Glance

Grade/Subject: 8th/Math—Computation, Problem Solving
Skills: problem solving, computation practice, using a calculator
Materials: paper and pencils
large chart paper
colored marker
calculator (optional)
Time: 1–3 hours spread out over a number of weeks

Getting Ready

With your child, review the following mathematical concepts: the four basic arithmetic operations +, −, ×, and / (addition, subtraction, multiplication, and division), as well as parenthesis, fraction lines, exponentiation, decimal points, square roots, and factorials. If necessary, review these in the Mathematics Content section of this book.

Any of these operations are available for carrying out the challenge of the activity. For example since the factorial $4! = 1 \times 2 \times 3 \times 4 = 24$, and since 4 divided by $4 = 1$, the expression $4! + 4 + 4/4$ equals 29. So now you've got four 4s for the numbers 1, 2, and 29. Review with your child how the rule of the Four 4s challenge was used to make those three numbers.

The Rule: Four 4s must be used for each equation, and no other numbers can be used. As many arithmetic signs as you need can be used.

Step One

Have your teen lay out his four 4s challenge on chart paper, by writing the numbers from 1 to 100, arranged in two or three columns, leaving enough room to the right of each number for the equation.

Fill in the equations you already have for the numbers 1, 2, and 29 (or different equations if you can come up with any better).

Step Two

Work together to find equations that equal each of the numbers on the list, then fill them in on the chart paper next to the number. Doing all the numbers in one sitting is unlikely to be possible. Some equations will come very easily and others will be real stumpers!

Decide together how you want to proceed. You may choose to start at 1 and work up without moving on to the next number until you have solved the one before it. Or you may prefer to just play around with the four 4s and when you come up with a number that you haven't solved yet, fill it in on the chart.

Step Three

As you play around with the numbers, you'll find lots of two- and three-number expressions that you can use as building blocks for other mathematical expressions. For example, $4!/.4 = 60$. Knowing that, you can solve many of the numbers over 50 in the second half of the list.

WHAT'S MORE

Try picking one specific number (or more) and see how many different ways you can form equations that equal the chosen number.

Try the challenge with a new chart, using a different number instead of 4. For instance, use four 5s or perhaps five 7s or any other combination you like.

Another great challenge would be to use all of the numerals from 1 to 9 exactly once and any arithmetic signs (or perhaps only certain ones) to make equations. You could add any other restrictions that might make it more interesting (like keeping the numbers from 1 to 9 in order for each equation!).

Post the chart somewhere handy. Any numbers that you don't get yet will be there offering a challenge for you anytime your child feels like tackling one—until the entire chart is completed.

▶ GROWING INTERESTED

"A penny saved is a penny earned" is good advice, and that is worth more if the money is saved in a savings account rather than under a mattress. Money that earns money is certainly worth our "interest."

Alas, interest is also what is paid for the privilege of borrowing money or using credit—a lesson students often learn too late. One important thing for your young consumer to learn, whether she's saving or borrowing, is to always shop for the best deal on interest rates. Here's a chance for her to explore what compound interest is and how it affects what she saves and/or borrows.

At a Glance

Grade/Subject: 8th/Math—Numeration, Money, Calculation, Graphing
Skills: using decimals and percents to calculate compound interest, graphing data and predicting values by extending a graph
Materials: paper and pencil
graph paper
ruler
calculator
Time: 30–45 minutes

Getting Ready

Check that your teen is familiar with the terms used in calculating interest. Money deposited in a savings account is called the *principal.* The interest earned on most savings accounts is called *compound interest* and is calculated multiple times during the life of the deposit. Simple interest, on the other hand, is calculated only once.

Interest can be compounded at different intervals: once a year (annually), twice a year (semiannually), four times a year (quarterly), or even every day (daily). Rates of interest vary depending on factors too complicated to worry about here.

INTEREST, INTERESTER, INTERESTEST

Interest is the price a borrower pays for the use of credit or money.

Simple interest is calculated by multiplying the principal by the interest rate (expressed as a decimal) and by the time (in years) that the principal is held. The formula is $i = Prt$.

Compound interest is interest paid on the principal as well as on previous interest left on deposit.

Step One

Discuss the difference between borrowing and lending. Ask your child if she knows what usually happens when someone borrows or lends money, particularly through a bank. If she has a bank account, review it together, paying attention to banking words, such as *deposit, interest,* and *withdrawal* as they occur. You might also want to review a charge-account statement. In its case, look at statement balances and interest rates and talk about what they mean.

Step Two

When investing or saving money, it pays (literally) to take a long view. Have your teen pretend that on the day she was born, a stranger secretly deposited $1.00 in a savings account in his name. This deposit has been earning interest at a rate of 8 percent compounded annually.

Have her guess how much the account would be worth today if there were never any additional deposits or withdrawals.

Step Three

On a sheet of paper, have her make a table with three columns as shown. Calculate the amount of interest on that $1.00 for the first year at an annual rate of 8 percent. Round the interest to the nearest cent and write the amount in column 2. Then, add the interest to the initial deposit (the principal) and record the total value of the deposit in column 3.

Have her repeat this calculation for each of the rows in the table, up to her current age.

- How close was the guess in step two?
- Any surprises?

Step Four

Next she should use a sheet of graph paper and a ruler to draw a horizontal scale that extends from 1 to at least 20 and label that line "Time (yrs.)." Then have her draw a vertical scale so that the data in column 3 of your table will fit easily. Label this axis "Amount ($)."

WHAT'S MORE

Find out what interest rates are being offered by various banks in your area. Calculate the earnings possible on a $100 (or some other constant number) deposit at the various rates over a fixed period of time.

Research where the word *bank* comes from. Research what banks do with the money people deposit.

Calculate how much interest you would pay until the debt was paid off if you paid off a $250 loan in monthly payments of $50 at an interest of 2 percent of the unpaid balance each month. Figure out also how many months would you have to pay.

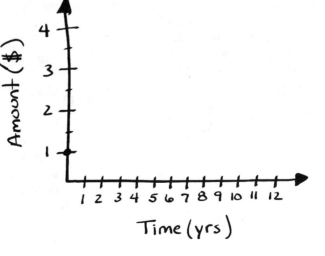

BEST FIT

A *best-fit curve* is a smooth line that can be drawn through a set of points on a graph.

WHAT'S MORE

Why do you suppose that TV manufacturers use the length of a diagonal to indicate the size of a TV set?

What is the area of your TV screen?

Do all 13" TVs have the same dimensions? How about a 25" set? Go to a store that sells TVs and check their sets to find out.

To plot the points in columns 1 and 3 of the table, help your child find the year along the horizontal axis and the accumulated dollar amount along the vertical axis. The point where a vertical line drawn from the year and a horizontal line drawn from the dollar amount cross each other is where she should plot the point.

When she has plotted all the points, she should examine how they lie on the graph and draw a "best-fit" curve through the points, starting at point (0, 1).

When all the money up to your child's present age has been plotted on the graph, extend both the horizontal and the vertical axes and the curve. Use the curve to predict how much that $1.00 deposit will be worth in 25 years, in 35 years, etc.

Step Four

Ask your child whether she would like to begin a savings account now (if she doesn't already have one), and discuss her reasons why or why not.

▶ Is This TV Right?

Newspaper ads and flyers boast of televisions that are getting ever bigger and ever smaller too! How is the size of a television screen measured anyway? What does a 7" difference between a 13" TV and a 20" TV mean in terms of size, not cost and picture quality (although they are all related)? If you have more than one TV in your home, are they the same size? In fact, what size is your TV? What size did the store say it was?

By the way, if you don't have a TV set handy, you could also try this activity on a computer screen.

At a Glance

Grade/Subject: 8th/Math—Geometry, Measurement, Fraction and Decimals, Computation
Skills: measuring, evaluating expressions, verifying properties of right triangle, computing squares
Materials: television set(s)
tape measure, ruler (inches), or yardstick
paper

pencil
calculator (optional)
Time: 30 minutes

Getting Ready

The mathematical idea behind this activity is an application of the Pythagorean Theorem: $a^2 + b^2 = c^2$, where c is the hypotenuse of a right triangle. What Pythagoras discovered was that in a right triangle, the square of the hypotenuse is equal to the sum of the squares of the other two sides. (For more about that try the activity "Off on a Tangent.")

In this activity, you work with this theorem from the other end. That is, when the sum of the squares of two smaller sides of a triangle equals the square of the largest side, then the triangle is a right triangle. With your child, check this out. Draw a triangle with sides that measure 3, 4, and 5 and then show that it is a right triangle by squaring each of the sides.

Step One

What size is the TV set you watch most often? What does that number mean?

With a tape measure, ruler, or yardstick, each of you measures the length and width of the screen, with the other watching and recording the measurements in inches. Be sure to measure the dimensions of the screen only, not the cabinet. Compare your measurements.

Chances are the numbers won't be "nice" neat whole numbers, so try to be as accurate as you can. Use fractions or decimals as necessary, since accuracy is important. In working out decimals or fractions, remember that the smallest measurement on most rulers is 1/16.

Repeat any measurement if there's a significant difference between what you and your child found. If you can't agree, ask another member of the family to help.

SQUARE TALK

To square a number, multiply it by itself. That is, the square of 8 is 64, because $8 \times 8 = 64$.

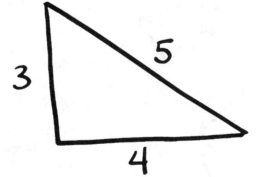

POLYGONS HAVE DIAGONALS

A *diagonal* is a line that connects nonadjacent corners of a polygon. A *polygon* is a many-sided figure. For example, a *triangle* is the smallest polygon and has no diagonals, since every corner is adjacent to the other two. A four-sided figure is a *quadrilateral* and has two diagonals. A *pentagon* has five sides and five diagonals. A *hexagon* has six sides and nine diagonals.

Step Two

This time, take turns measuring the two diagonals of the screen. Again, compare your measurements and repeat this step until you agree on the lengths. (They should be equal.)

So, what size is your TV? What does it mean when someone says that she just bought a 40" TV? (Other than she spent a lot of money!)

Step Three

A diagonal divides your TV screen into two triangles whose sides consist of a length, a width, and a diagonal of the screen.

Using multiplication, have your child calculate the relationship among the measurements of the length, width, and diagonal in each half of the TV screen. Follow these steps to see:

- Square each number.
- Add the two smaller square numbers.
- Compare the sum of the two smaller squares numbers to the square of the diagonal.

Describe what you have learned about the TV screen. (Be sure you have measured accurately.)

Step Four

Measure the length, width, and diagonal of a larger or smaller TV than the one you measured in the previous steps. See if what you discovered in step three is true for a different size TV.

Step Five

Now here is the TV shopper's $64,000 (or maybe $640 or $1,640) question: Suppose that there is only a 2" difference between the advertised sizes of two TV sets—for instance, for sets advertised as 25" and 27", how much bigger is the screen area of the larger set?

▶ Magic Squares

What do a sacred Chinese turtle, Albrecht Dürer, and Benjamin Franklin have in common? Magic squares! (Of course?)

Magic squares are arrangements of numbers that have fascinated people around the world for centuries and centuries. Legend has it that during the 4th century B.C., a magic square known as the Lo Shu appeared on the back of a sacred turtle as it crawled out of the Lo River. Centuries later, in the German artist Albrecht Dürer in the 1600s incorporated a magic square in his engraving called "Melancholia." Benjamin Franklin, in the 1700s, created his own version of a magic square. Exactly what is so magic about a magic square?

At a Glance

Grade/Subject: 8th/Math—Problem Solving, Numeration, Computation,
Skills: using patterns, logic, and computations to solve number problems
Materials: paper
pencil and eraser
Time: 30–45 minutes

Getting Ready

A magic square is a square table made up of equal numbers of rows and columns. The number of rows and columns is the "order" of the square. For example, a 4 × 4 magic square has order 4.

The properties of a magic square are fairly simple. The sums of the numbers in any row, column, and the two main diagonals are equal. This sum is called the "magic constant" of the square.

Step One

Look at the diagram of the 4 × 4 magic square in Dürer's engraving with your teen and have her figure out where the magic lies. Tell her that every magic square also has a "magic constant." Can she discover what it is? (Give her hints like "Try making computations" as needed to help her find how the rows, columns, and diagonals add up.)

WHAT'S MORE

Create a 3 x 3 magic square using the digits from 1 to 9.

Show why there is no 2 x 2 magic square.

Make some more unique 4 x 4 magic squares and challenge other members of your family and your friends to create other 4 x 4 magic squares.

Can you use the numbers from 1 to 25 to make a 5 x 5 magic square? (There are 68,826,306 of them!!)

Step Two

Albrecht Dürer made that 4 × 4 magic square famous by including it in his engraving. In 1693, Frenchman Bernard Frénicle de Bessy determined that there are actually 880 different 4 × 4 magic squares! Here's another one.

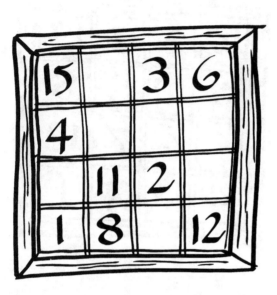

Each of you should copy the square on a piece of paper and work independently to complete it. Remember, the numbers in the square go from 1 to 16. The rule is that the sum of every row, every column, and both diagonals must be the same (the magic constant). Which of you can solve the puzzle first?

Compare your solutions when you finish. They should be the same. Talk together about how you went about solving the puzzle.

Step Three

Now that you have seen two of the 880 unique 4 × 4 magic squares, you can try to arrange the numbers from 1 to 16 and create two more that are completely different from the two you've now seen.

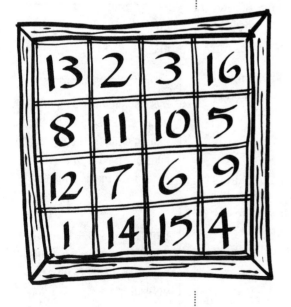

Your goal is to make your magic squares unique, that means "one of a kind." Compare the Dürer square and the one completed in step two. Notice how the numbers are in very different positions with respect to one another. Simply rotating or reflecting a solved magic square does not create a unique magic square. Here's why:

- Rotating a magic square, such as Dürer's, around its center keeps the numbers in the same relative position to one another. Rows become columns, and columns become rows.
- Reflecting (or flipping) Dürer's square over an edge is like holding up a mirror to it. The columns

remain the same, and only the order of the numbers in each row is changed.

To make your unique magic squares, each of you should draw a 4 × 4 square table on a sheet of paper, and when you're both ready, begin! (Set up a timer to see who comes up with the solution first!) When you think you've found a unique square, examine it carefully to be sure that it's magic and that it's unique. Compare your solutions when you're both done and talk about the strategies you used for solving the square puzzles. Then, congratulate yourselves on a job well done. Only 876 unique 4 × 4 more magic squares to go!

▶ More Magic Squares

Magic squares have intrigued people for centuries. Although there is exactly one unique 3 × 3 magic square, there are 880 unique 4 × 4 magic squares and an unimaginable 68,826,306 unique 5 × 5 magic squares!

But there's more to magic squares than just arranging numbers in square patterns. Applying the arithmetic of a square to geometry produces colorful designs. And playing with the rules makes solving magic square puzzles even more intriguing.

At a Glance

Grade/Subject: 8th/Math—Numeration, Computation, Logic, Problem Solving
Skills: using patterns, logic, and computation to solve number problems and create unique designs
Materials: paper, pencil, and pen
graph paper
eraser
straight edge
variety of colored pencils or markers
calculator (optional)
Time: 30 and up—depending on luck/skill with the challenge puzzles (can be spread over a number of sessions)

LEARN FROM TV?

Just sitting and watching TV won't help your child learn anything—at least not much of any value. TV watching is a passive activity. A group of kids watching TV will be quiet, with nothing busy or active going on. If you could squint inside their heads, you wouldn't see a lot of learning taking place.

Learning occurs when information is used. This comes from the simple rote repetition of factual material, or when new materials are used for analysis, discussion, or creation and problem solving. If the material isn't thought over, refreshed, and processed, it simply sits briefly in our short-term memory and then is gone.

WHAT'S MORE

Construct a 3 x 3 "prime" magic square using the number 1 and the prime numbers 7, 13, 31, 37, 43, 61, 67, and 73. (Adapted from *Amusement in Mathematics* by H. E. Dudeney (Dover Publications, 1970), page 125.

A magic constant can be calculated by evaluating the expression $\left(\dfrac{n^3 + n}{2}\right)$, where n is the order of the square. What is the magic constant of a 5 x 5 square? Try creating a 5 x 5 square.

Getting Ready

Review the Learning Adventure activity "Magic Squares" to see what's magic about a magic square and the rules for making them.

Step One

This is an opportunity for you and your child to create some interesting designs based on magic squares. On a sheet of graph paper, each of you should draw 16 dots arranged in a 4 × 4 square pattern. (Leave a couple of squares between each row and column so that the dots are evenly spaced but not too close together.) Each dot marks the place for a number in a magic square.

Each of you should now choose a 4 × 4 magic square. (You could use the square from Dürer's engraving in Magic Squares or ones you created in that activity. For each dot on your graph paper, write in the number that lies in the same position within the magic square you chose. For example, next to the dot in row 1, column 2, write the number in row 1, column 2 of the magic square you chose. Write these numbers lightly in pencil to erase later.

Step Two

With a straight edge and a pen, connect the dots in numerical order. That is, draw a line from dot 1 to dot 2, from dot 2 to dot 3, and so on. The line segments will overlap as you create a line design. Complete the design by connecting the last to the first dot (dots numbered 16 and 1). Then use the straight edge and pen to connect the dots around the outside of the square to create a frame around the design. Erase the numbers.

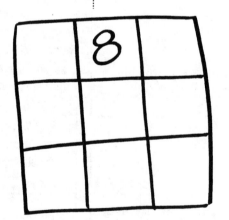

Dudeney's Challenge

Step Three

Color the regions formed by the lines very carefully to make sure that no two adjacent regions have the same color. Use as few colors as possible. When each of you has completed your design, compare the results. Is there magic in your patterns?

Repeat these steps with several unique magic squares and see what results you get and what you like best.

Step Four

These last two steps in this activity each pose a famous magic square puzzle for you and your child to collaborate on solving.

The numbers in a magic square are usually consecutive, whole numbers: 1, 2, 3, …. But they don't have to be. In 1917, Henry E. Dudeney, an Englishman who loved puzzles, created one called "The Troublesome Eight." He put the number 8 in the center of the top row of a 3 × 3 square and challenged the world to create a magic square.

Take him up on his challenge. Remember that each row, column, and diagonal must add up to the same sum. There's no rule, however, that says that all the numbers in the square have to be whole numbers; you might try a few halves.

Step Five

Here is the other challenge for the two of you to try. Traditionally, the magic constant in a magic square is a sum. But Martin Gardner, another lover of puzzles, created a magic multiplication matrix centered around the year 1964. The magic constant in this case is a product. Can you complete the matrix?

▶ Midpoint Mania

Can you get your hands on some string, thumbtacks, and a ruler? With these ordinary materials you and your child can discover surprising relationships among midpoints, lengths, and perimeters of triangles.

You and your young geometer will start with a triangle and trace its sides with string to "see" its perimeter. Along the way, you'll measure lengths, locate midpoints, and discover a pattern that is basic to the study of triangles. In the end, your child should have a much clearer understanding of the concept of perimeter and the meaning of its corresponding formulas (and you will too).

At a Glance

Grade/Subject: 8th/Math—Geometry
Skills: measuring side lengths of triangles, finding their midpoints, determining perimeters, and drawing conclusions about the relationships among points and lines in triangles

MATH MAGIC

Check out these two books for more fun with math puzzles and challenges: *Amusements in Mathematics* by H. E. Dudeney (Dover Publications, 1970) and *The Magic Numbers of Dr. Matrix* by Martin Gardner (Prometheus Books, 1985).

WHAT'S MORE

On graph paper, draw a right triangle *ABC* so that the two sides that form the right angle (*AC* and *CB*) have the same length. Use the graph paper or a ruler to find the midpoints of the three sides. Then, connect the midpoint of *AC* to the midpoint of *AB,* and connect the midpoint of *CB* to *AB*. What kind of figure is formed?

Making the Grade

Materials: graph paper
pencil
ruler (inches or centimeters)
string (about 3')
push pins, thumb tacks, or staples
scissors
Time: 30 minutes

Getting Ready

You might want to do a little advance reading if you haven't spent much time lately thinking about midpoints, perimeters, or triangles. You can use a dictionary or check the glossary in a math textbook to reacquaint yourself with these terms and look at the Core 4: Geometry in the Mathematics Content section of *Making the Grade.*

Step One

With your child, draw a large triangle on a sheet of graph paper. Make its sides large enough to measure with a ruler, especially if it's a 12" ruler. Label the triangle at its vertices (corners) using the letters *A, B,* and *C* (all uppercase). On the same sheet of paper, create a table such as the one shown here in which measurements can be recorded.

Put one end of a long string on top of vertex *A*, and use a thumb tack to anchor the string there. Pull the string along side *AB* so that it overlaps the side. At vertex *B*, use a second thumb tack to anchor the string. Do not cut the string.

Lay the string along side *BC,* anchoring it with a tack at vertex *C*. Pull the string along side *CA* and when you reach the vertex where you began, cut the string. Remove the thumb tacks and stretch out the string. Voilà! This is the perimeter of the triangle. Lay the string along a ruler and measure its length. In the table, record this perimeter value to the nearest tenth, for instance 25 and 3/8th inches would be recorded 25.4 inches.

Step Two

Use the ruler and measure the lengths of each side of the triangle—*AB, BC,* and *AC.* In the table, record the lengths

AB	BC	CA	Perimeter
1.5	2	3	6.5

$$PD = side\ 1 + side\ 2 + side\ 3$$

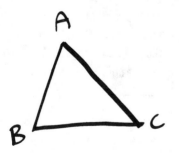

to the nearest tenth. Use the formula to calculate the perimeter of ΔABC and record the value in the table. (Your child should know that the formula for the perimeter is PΔ= side1 + side2 + side3.)

Now, compare the value of the perimeter you got in this step with its string perimeter. Are they equal? They should be very close (depending on how carefully you measured). If not, repeat the steps.

Step Three

Next, you'll find the midpoint of each side of ΔABC. Divide the length of AB by 2, and use the ruler to mark off the length from either A or B. Label the point M. For example, if AB = 3 inches, then M lies $\dfrac{1}{2"}$ inches from A and $\dfrac{1}{2"}$ inches from B.

Repeat this step and find the midpoint of BC. Label it M. Find the midpoint of AC and label it O. Use the ruler and connect the three midpoints to draw ΔMNO.

Step Four

Use the method in step one and measure the perimeter of ΔMNO using a piece of string. Record this perimeter value in the table. Compare this new value to the string perimeter of ΔABC. Write an expression that compares the two values.

Step Five

Measure the sides MN, NO, and MO with the ruler. Add these lengths to the table rounded to the nearest tenth.

Compare the lengths of the sides of this triangle with the lengths of the sides of the original triangle. What relationship do you see? (They should be $MN = \dfrac{1}{2} AC$, $NO = \dfrac{1}{2}AB$, $MO = \dfrac{1}{2}BC$.)

Use the perimeter formula and calculate the perimeter of ΔMNO. Compare this result to the string perimeter of ΔMNO (see answer sidebar).

- How do they compare? (The perimeters should be approximately equal.)
- What mathematical conclusion can you draw from these trials?
- How can you test your conclusion?

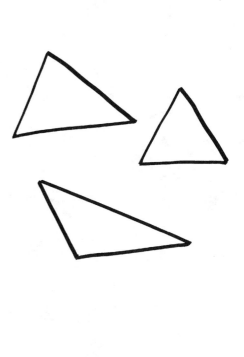

▶ OFF ON A TANGENT

Adults have all kinds of rules and advice for children—like "Avoid spending time in the direct sun." But what child listens when having a tan is "in" and dry and wrinkled skin seems eons away? Obviously, we can't avoid going out in the direct sun. But when is it safe to stay outside on a sunny day? A good rule of thumb is that if a person's shadow is longer than a person's height, a nasty burn might be in store.

At a Glance

Grade/Subject: 8th/Math—Geometry
Skills: drawing right triangles, measuring sides and angles in right triangles, calculating tangent ratios

$$\left(\frac{\text{opposite leg}}{\text{adjacent leg}} \right)$$

Materials: graph paper
protractor
yardstick or measuring tape and 12" ruler
Time: 30–45 minutes the first time
15 minutes each time you check the sun's height thereafter

TRIGGY STUFF

The word *trigonometry* comes from two Greek words: one that means "triangle," and the other that means "measurement."

Getting Ready

How how long anyone's shadow is depends on how high the sun is in the sky. With your teen, imagine a ray of sunlight stretching out through space towards Earth. When you, your child, your dog, your corner tree, etc., come between the ray and Earth, shadows—and invisible right triangles—are created. It's these triangles that are the bases of using trigonometry (trig, for short) to figure out how high the sun is and whether it's time to go undercover.

Step One

Help your child get started by drawing and discussing a right triangle, such as this one. First, there's a right angle, here labeled *C*.

The other two angles are acute (less than 90° each). Here, they are labeled *A* and *B*. The side opposite *C*, the right angle, is labeled *c* and is the "hypotenuse." The other two sides are called "legs." Their labels are *a* and *b*, depending on which angle they lie opposite.

The tangent (tan) is a trig ratio between the legs of a right triangle. Have your child use the labels for the legs and write the two ratios.

Each of the two ratios represents the tangent of one of the acute angles. Have your child choose −A. Then, help her find the leg that is opposite ∠A. (That's little *a*). This is the numerator of the tangent ratio. The other leg (*b*) is its denominator. The tangent of ∠A is $\frac{a}{b}$ which we write as tan $A = \frac{a}{b}$. (What is tan *B*?)

Step Two

Now tackle this problem together. Suppose you and your child are both standing outside on a sunny day when each of you casts a shadow half as long as your height.

* Is the tangent ratio between her height and shadow the same as the tangent ratio between your height and shadow?
* How high is the sun in the sky?

Supply Height Leg Use the yardstick or tape-measure and measure each other's height in inches. On two sheets of graph paper—one for each of you—draw vertical line that represent each of your heights. Use the squares of the graph paper to create a scale that makes sense. (Each square might equal 6 inches.) Label the top of the line (your head) *B* and the bottom of the line (your feet) *C*. Write your height next to that vertical line.

Supply Shadow Leg Remember that your shadows are half as long as your heights. Using the same scale as before, each of you should draw a horizontal line on your graph paper to represents your shadow. Start from your "feet" (point *C*) and draw a line that's half as long as the line representing your height. Label the head of the shadow *A*. Write the lengths of the shadow underneath the line.

Supply Hypotenuse Each of you should now draw the third side of your triangle (the hypotenuse) by connecting the two heads: points *B* and *A*. The angle at *C*, where your "real" feet meet the feet of your shadow, is the right angle of the two triangles. Now you each have a right triangle to work with.

TANGENT TABLE

Some calculators have buttons that display the tangent of an angle. If you don't have a calculator, here are some tangent values. These are reported as decimals because you can divide the two numbers in a tangent ratio and get a decimal. Here's an example: If tan $A = \frac{36}{52}$, the corresponding decimal is 0.692 ≈ 0.700. Find 0.700 in the table, across from 35°. Therefore, ∠A would be about 35°, because the tan 35° = 0.700.

angle	tangent
5°	.087
10°	.176
15°	.268
20°	.364
25°	.466
30°	.577
35°	.700
40°	.839
45°	1.000
50°	1.192
55°	1.428
60°	1.732
65°	2.145
70°	2.747
75°	3.732
80°	5.671
85°	11.430

Making the Grade

WHAT'S MORE

Suppose you're standing and waiting for a bus around noontime. Explain why your shadow moves if you don't.

___

Now suppose your shadows are twice as long as your heights? Repeat the steps to figure out how high would the sun be in the sky when you cast a shadow twice your height.

___

Figure out whether it is safe to stay outside in the direct sun if the tangent of the angle at the head of your shadow is 1?

___

Is it before 10 A.M. or after 10 P.M. when the tangent of the angle at the head of your shadow is 0? Why?

Step Three

So, how high is the sun in the sky? How does the tangent ratio of a taller person compare to the tangent ratio of a smaller person?

Work separately on your sheets of graph paper and set up the tangent ratios for the acute angles at A. Write the fractions as decimals by dividing the two numbers. Compare your results.

Step Four

Look at the table of tangent values. Find the angle that has a tangent value closest to the one you each calculated. How high is the sun in the sky when your shadow is half your height?

Use a protractor and measure $\angle A$. Does it match what you calculated using the tangent table?

Step Five

Now take your measuring tape outside and measure your shadows, and figure out just how high the sun is on a sunny day. Try in the morning. Try it at noon. Try it in the afternoon.

Try it again at the same three times three months from now!

CHAPTER 16

Learning Adventures—
7th Grade Science

IT REALLY WORKS

We help a lot of parents at *SCORE!* with their teen's educational problems. Many parents tell me that they have a hard time with their kids conceptualizing things. All I tell them is that conceptualization begins with imagination. Have your teen imagine something—that's where learning starts. Whether it's taking a break and thinking about how something might be or drawing a diagram on paper with your teen, using the imagination to conceptualize a difficult learning task really works.

▶ ABOUT SCIENCE TOOLS

Doing science requires tools, materials, and a place for record keeping. Since we've written the activities in this book for you to do with your child at home, there are no elaborate requirements for either tools or materials. To get off to a good start thinking about science activities with your child, read through this page together and work out a general list of the items you'll be likely to use in doing science at home.

None of the activities in this book involve direct hazards. Some, however, do require the use of simple hand tools, and some involve household materials that should be used carefully. Safety notes have been included in individual activities, but, even if you skip the rest of this activity, read the note here on personal safety.

At a Glance

Grade/Subject: 7th and 8th/Science—all activities
Skills: preparation
Materials: Most of the tools and materials you'll use can probably be found around your house; a few you may need to buy or borrow. To save you the trouble of rounding up everything you need each time, this activity lists some of the general equipment and materials you and your child could have on hand already for experiments and record keeping.

DOING SCIENCE SAFELY

Everybody makes mistakes and everybody has minor accidents. You can make sure that these stay minor by observing two basic rules:

• **Use Safety Glasses:** Any activity that requires hand tools or where there is the chance of materials breaking or shattering (whether it's science or a hobby project) should be done only while wearing safety glasses. They are inexpensive and available in hardware stores and most arts and crafts stores.

• **Thorough Washing:** Although none of the materials needed for the activities in this book use strongly toxic materials, hand washing after using any chemicals or solutions is an important habit to learn. All tools, utensils, and materials should also be kept clean. This is a safe practice and also makes good scientific sense, the results of otherwise excellent experiments can be thrown completely off by cross-contamination from previous trials. That is a first principle that all scientists must learn

Time: Allow part of an evening to talk over what you may need and to round up tools and materials. You may also want to plan a trip to a hardware store.

Step One

Science activities do take up space and sometimes create a bit of clutter. Talk about where in your home would be the best place to do science activities and where you might set aside space for storing equipment, books, and materials. A closet shelf or some storage boxes should provide ample room.

Step Two—Tools of Science

Science for 7th and 8th graders involves lots of doing and the list of useful tools for doing suggested here is certainly not all inclusive. You may already have other useful items in your home and you may think of more as you go along.

Hand Tools—a small drafting compass, triangle, small hammer, an assortment of nails and screws, screw driver, hand drill (an electric drill is optional), a sharp model making knife, wire cutters, pair of pliers, tape measure.

Observation Aids—a magnifying glass, a small and accurate magnetic compass. A low powered microscope is fun (and revealing!) to have, but not essential.

Measuring Instruments—rulers, yardstick or meterstick, thermometers (outdoor and body), stop watch or digital watch with timer function, a kitchen scale (0-5 lbs., if it has metric readings as well, so much the better).

Recording Materials—small spiral notebook for note taking, reminders, and doodling (a very handy tool, but not necessary if you make your own Science Notebook as described below.), pencil and pen, set of colored pencils, pocket calculator, calendar with spaces big enough to make reminder notes for observation schedules and for recording events (preferably one that shows the phases of the moon).

Miscellaneous Matter—rolls of 1/4" or 1/2" masking tape, 3/4" clear tape, small role of duct tape, ball of twine, scissors, a few plastic vegetable bags, small earring-sized boxes, plastic model cement, white glue, a variety of rubber bands, pocket knife (or equivalent), assortment of batteries, roll of bell wire from a hardware store, and assorted jars and boxes for keeping things.

Step Three—Scientific Record Keeping

A large, loose leaf, ring binder notebook is a valuable tool for recording data, information, illustrations and diagrams, and longer reports on science observations. A number of the activities require one. Your child can create the science notebook from the materials listed below.

Notebook—a sturdy standard school sized three-ring notebook at least 1" thick will serve your needs. If there are inside pockets, and you add extra pocketed dividers, and a pouch for a calculator, so much the better.

Paper—gather as wide a variety of papers as you like, lined, plain, and graph papers are all useful. To include have colored paper or oak tag just punch out the holes to fit.

Miscellaneous—a small calculator and paper punch come in handy, and a calendar small enough to fit into the notebook is useful. After a while, your child may want to decorate the cover with materials of her own choosing—a collage of images cut from magazines or some other treatment consistent with her experiences with the activities.

▶ BASIC CABBAGE

We're still quite a way from having the hand-held devices of science fiction to help us assess the physical environment, but one handy test device is sitting, waiting for you in the supermarket! If you've ever made a salad with red cabbage and used a vinegar or lemon juice dressing, you've probably noticed that the purplish cabbage leaves turn a reddish color. Some chemicals in the cabbage change color when exposed to the acids in the dressing. When they are exposed to basic materials like salt, they turn to blue-green.

Testing the acid and base characteristic of materials is a useful test in chemistry (as well as in fish tank and garden!). With a little cabbage juice, you can set up your own field testing station.

At a Glance

Grade/Subject: 7th/Science—Chemistry, Inquiry Skills
Skills: testing for chemical properties
Materials: red cabbage (it usually looks purple, in spite of the name), fist size or larger

BIG CITY SCIENCE

Living in an apartment or in a big city doesn't rule out experiences with nature that encourage your teen's interest in science. Even small flats have room for plants and some kinds of pets. Plant a windowsill garden. Try planting the seeds from grapefruit, avocado, or green or red bell peppers (let the seeds dry before planting). Outside your home, visit parks, zoos, science museums, aquariums, arboretums, or public gardens. Look into hikes run by park rangers or groups like the local Nature Conservancy or Audubon Society.

CHEM-GOURMET

While you're boiling cabbage for this activity, you and your teen can slice a carrot into ovals and boil them in a separate pot for about the same amount of time. After you've saved the purple liquid, drain the cabbage and carrots. Lightly sauté a small, finely chopped onion in olive oil; then add the cabbage and carrot ovals and sauté them until done to your taste. Season with salt and, if you like, a sprinkling of caraway seeds. Yum!

Making the Grade

WHAT'S MORE

Grind up raw vegetables and mix them with water to make testable solutions. If some register as acid or base, cook them to see whether cooking alters the quality. Try to cook them with an acidic material like vinegar or a base like salt. What happens if you cook them in a soft drink?

Pick a test container from one end of your tested solutions and a test container from the opposite end and note the solution that produced each. Take some of the second substance and slowly add it to the first container. What happens? Can you get the same results if you reverse things at the other end of the acid-base line?

Expand your search beyond ordinary kitchen items. Collect rain or snow from outside, mix some dirt from a park or garden with enough water to get an almost transparent solution. Try some laundry detergent, saliva, and maybe some saliva mixed with mouth wash. If you find a lot of things to test, you may want to start a another bigger chart!

at least 6 small glasses (or clear plastic containers of similar size and shape), such as test tubes, baby food jars, pill bottles, or spice jars
tape for labeling containers
acidic materials such as vinegar or lemon juice
basic materials such as common salt or baking soda
teaspoon and tablespoon measures
medicine dropper
colored pencils
science notebook
piece of white oak tag or cardboard at least 18 inches long.
Time: 1–2 hours

Getting Ready

Have your child chop or coarsely grate a fist-sized chunk of red cabbage (about 1/2 pound). Place it in a pot and add enough water to cover it. (If you live in an area with very hard water, use filtered or distilled water.) Bring it to a boil and then cook for 5 to 10 minutes. Usually you toss the cooking water and save the cabbage. But this time it's the deep blue-purple liquid that you want to keep. (You can save the cabbage for supper.)

Step One

You and your child can begin by doing some crude tests just to see how the cabbage juice indicates whether a solution is base or acid. Fill three of your transparent containers about half-full with the cabbage juice. Set them in a row somewhere in good light.

Take a substance that you know to be acid, like vinegar, and add it to the first container—one teaspoon or tablespoon at a time until the liquid changes color. Make a label that says "acid" (you can add the name of what you added also) and attach it to the container.

Then take a substance that you know to be a base such as baking soda and mix it into water by stirring it until no more will dissolve to make it a saturated solution. Add this saturated solution to the third cabbage juice container on the other side of your middle control container. Make a label that says "base" (and the name of what you added if you wish) and attach it to the third container. Label the center container "pure cabbage juice."

Step Two

Have your child note the hues of the three solutions and experiment with colored pencils to approximate the colors so that she can begin to record her test results in her science notebook. Set up two columns on a note book page; the first is for the name of the test substance and the second for the color that the cabbage juice becomes. Under her illustration of the results, she should describe what she did to get those results.

Step Three

The blue-purple cabbage juice and the acid and base solutions will serve as the reference indicators. Your child will be judging other solutions by their colors , so set these three up in a row. Putting them in a sunny window or placing a white sheet of paper behind them will make the colors easier to see.

Step Four

Now you and your child are ready to investigate—to begin finding out just what's basic (and what's acidic) around your house. Have her begin by gathering some of the many solutions and materials available in your kitchen.

Some will need some preparation for testing. Salt, sugar, flour, baking powder, and other dry materials, for instance, will need to be mixed in water first to make a testable solution. Some liquid materials can be tested right away, but others, those that are too dense or too dark to show colors, will need to be thinned with water.

Have her fill some of the empty containers half-full with the cabbage juice and slowly begin adding your test materials, a little bit at a time. If and when the solution turns a different color, place this container where you think it should fit among your reference containers, label it and describe it on your data sheet. If it doesn't change color, the solution you're testing is roughly neutral, neither acid or base. Note this as well.

Step Five

The final step is to have your child take the data she's collected and develop a chart. Use a piece of oak tag or cardboard to set up a long chart (how long will depend on the number of test solutions she's tried). Use the three original samples as the center and the two end points for the chart. She should indicate which end is for the acid solutions and which is for the base solutions. Then use the colors from the list to lay out the test samples from strongly acid to neutral to strongly basic. She can indicate the

BEING PRECISE

If you are working with very small containers, use a medicine dropper to add your solutions a drop at a time. Cabbage juice works, and it's fun, but it isn't particularly precise. Variables such as the age of the cabbage and the quality of your water will affect it in different ways. Try comparing the results that you get with a more accurate indicator by using the aquarium test litmus papers or solutions that are available in pet stores.

CAREFUL!

Explore the chemistry of household materials enthusiastically, but some are potentially dangerous either by themselves or when mixed with other substances. Have your teen read cautions and warnings on the labels of even common household materials. Avoid working with drain cleaners and any cleansers with strong solvents or chlorine. Clean all containers and utensils thoroughly after each test and when you're finished with the experiment. And don't forget to wash your hands!

PETS AND SCIENCE

Getting to know and care for animals—from goldfish to gerbils to golden retrievers—is a great kind of hands-on biology lesson for preteens and teens. They can learn firsthand about a pet's life cycle, intelligence and behavior, feeding and grooming habits, adaptation, and reproduction.

Before choosing a pet, have your teen read about different animals, birds, fish, and other creatures and the care each requires. Be clear about who will be responsible for feeding, exercising (regular walking, if necessary), and clean up (the aquarium, cage, litter box . . .). Having a pet is a great science learning experience, but parents just might end up with much of the responsibility. Be prepared for a mixture of rewarding learning experiences, some heartwarming times, and a lot of work.

color of each sample on the chart or color in a strip running along the entire bottom of the chart showing the colors slowly shifting from one extreme to the other. She could even take photographs of the containers and arrange the pictures to illustrate the chart.

▶ COOKIES OF CLAY

Engineers are constantly looking for and testing new materials. Some materials replace older ones in traditional uses, while others make new technology—such as space flight and advanced medical procedures—possible.

Testing a material can show both its advantages and disadvantages, as you and your kid will discover in this activity. While the activity is focused on an ancient material—clay—you can expand the process to apply to many other materials.

At a Glance

Grade/Subject: 7th/Science—Technology, Inquiry Skills
Skills: testing materials for characteristics and appropriate uses
Materials: clay (real modeling clay, not plastic)
cookie sheet and aluminum foil
oven (Don't try this in a microwave!)
science notebook
Time: about 2 hours

Getting Ready

Baked clay and other minerals are among the very oldest materials used by humans, but you'll find these materials—ceramics—used in many areas of a modern home, too.

Step One

To start this activity, take a tour with your kid to identify some of the ceramics in your house: bathroom sinks, floor and wall tiles (though some are plastic), enamel-coated cookware, dinnerware and pottery, perhaps tiles for hot dishes. Even bricks are a kind of ceramic. Talk about what uses the items have and what they have in common.

Step Two

Now together you'll test some of the properties of ceramics. As you do, have your kid list the qualities you find and note how they make this material useful (or not) for certain purposes.

First, have your kid mix clay with enough water to make it manageable and then shape five or six small thin clay disks about the size of cookies. He should measure the diameter of several of the disks and note it directly on the soft clay.

Put a layer of aluminum foil on a cookie sheet. Place the clay cookies on the pan. Put them in a hot oven—400°—for about an hour.

Have your child write up the experiment in his science notebook, describing the process and preparing to report the testing and results.

Step Three

After the hour, take the pan from the oven and let the clay cool. Discuss how you have now already tested one property of a ceramic: how it responds to high heat.

- Does it break?
- Does it evaporate?
- Does it shrink in size or expand?
- How does it taste? (Just kidding!)

Set a hot dish or pan on one of the ceramic disks to test this property further. Put another of the disks in the freezer to test the effects of cold.

Then have your kid test for flexibility by trying to bend one of the clay pieces.

Next, test for brittleness. Strike another piece with a hammer. (Wearing safety glasses is a good idea for this step.)

Be sure that each test and its results are reported in the science notebook.

Step Four

Encourage your kid to think of other tests for the ceramic material. For instance, you might scratch it with a nail file or pour water over it. Have him note each test and what it shows.

WHAT'S MORE

Look around your house and take an inventory of the many different materials in a specific area. For instance, just on your dinner table you may have ceramic dishes, glass goblets, stainless steel utensils, wooden salad bowls, and cloth or paper napkins. What kinds of tests would be appropriate to try on each?

Research how and why ceramic tiles are used in spacecraft such as the Space Shuttle.

Expand your experiments with clay to making pottery vases or sculpting animal figures.

Look into the work of materials testing companies and laboratories such as Underwriters' Labs.

Making the Grade

Lightness in weight is important for some uses of materials. Challenge your kid to think of a way to determine simply whether a ceramic is lighter in weight than the same amount of another material—say, iron, steel, wood, or aluminum.

Step Five

Now apply your findings. What advantages and disadvantages of ceramics did you find in your testing? Talk about how the ceramics in your house are used. What qualities are important in those uses? (For instance: durability, ease of cleaning.) How did your tests reveal these qualities?

Step Six

Testing other materials can be fun and challenging for your kid. You have to keep in mind what each material's properties are and what it might be used for. For instance, if you test a fabric, you'd want to know how it reacted to fire and to water, to staining and stretching, etc. (Keep basic safety precautions in mind.)

▶ EGG DROP

Mechanical engineers tackle challenging and intriguing problems every day. This activity is a good chance to let your child experience a challenging mechanical engineering problem.

We all know that if we dropped an ordinary egg from ten or twenty feet high onto a hard floor it would break. Even if it was placed inside of its own egg carton, it would probably break if it were dropped from a high height. Using items found around your house, your child will be challenged to construct a container that will protect the egg from a fall.

At a Glance

Grade/Subject: 7th/Science—Physical Science, Inquiry Skills, Technology
Skills: learning about velocity impact force air pressure
Materials: eggs
plastic sheeting
shoe box

miscellaneous items found around the house

Time: 1-2 hours

Getting Ready

Explain the challenge to your child. You'll need a place to drop the egg container he creates. It should be at least a ten-foot drop—the higher the better. You'll put the plastic sheeting on the surface just in case the egg does not survive. Your child should see the drop site before beginning so that he can estimate the force of impact.

Step One

To help him understands the challenge, you child should make a few test drops of other items. Dropping items such as a ping-pong ball, a baseball, an empty shoe box, a cake of soap, a ball of clay, a rolled up sock etc. will help in understanding how impact can effect different items.

Step Two

Encourage your child look around the house for items that he could try using to construct his egg drop container. A shoe box is a likely candidate for the outside of the container, though there are many other possibilities. Tape, string, and rubber bands are likely to be helpful in constructing. Let your child do the choosing. Discuss with him his ideas about how the various items he collects might be used.

Step Three

Once your child has brought together the chosen items, construction can begin. Encourage him to put some items through initial drop testing to see how they will hold up to impact. Not only is it not important that the entire container be completely finished before the drop, but by pre-testing his materials, he is likely to develop his design more successfully.

Building, testing, refining, re-testing, tinkering, testing, and final adjustments, before ultimately dropping the container with an egg inside, is a likely sequence that will allow your child to experiment with different possibilities.

WHAT'S MORE

Adding one or more arbitrary guidelines can change the challenge greatly or lead to fresh challenges. Allowing or disallowing parachutes is one possibility. Requiring that the entire construction be made from natural materials found outdoors is a difficult challenge that might be used to follow up the first egg drop.

Consider requiring that the container be as light as possible. This will greatly change the materials that are likely to be picked by your teen.

What would happen if the egg drop container were dropped from a higher point? A ten story building? An airplane? Studying the acceleration due to gravity and terminal velocity might help your child understand what the forces might be like as the drop point gets higher.

Making the Grade

Step Four

When all adjustments have been made to the container it is time to schedule the actual egg drop. Discuss the upcoming event with your child. Point out all scientists recognize that before testing anything, they must be ready to pick up and go forward if their work fails. It is a good idea to realize that failure is a likely option and to be ready to learn from whatever happens. Frequently, more can be learned from something that does not work the way it was intended, than from something that succeeds.

Step Five

Make an occasion of the container's big test. Assemble a small audience; introduce your young inventor; have him explain the problem he has (he hopes) solved and the process he used to create his technological solution. (If you have a video camera you might consider filming the occasion.)

When the container lands, have him ceremoniously open it and find out whether it worked. Interview him about the results and what he plans to do next.

▶ GETTING VIBES!

Can't stand the music blasting from your teenagers' boom box? Here's a graphic way to explore together the actual physical effects of those vibrating sound waves and what happens when sound waves strike your eardrums.

Seeing how sound energy creates visible movement—vibrations—can help your kid understand the principles underlying other kinds of vibrations and wave motions, from ocean waves to the traveling shock waves produced by earthquakes.

At a Glance

Grade/Subject: 7th/Science—Physical Science
Skills: studying vibrations, transfer of energy
Materials: round plastic container (margarine tub or the like)
large sturdy rubber bands
thin plastic bag or plastic wrap
1 teaspoon each, rice and sugar
portable radio or boom box
Time: 45 minutes–1 hour

Getting Ready

Have your kid stretch the plastic bag or wrap it tightly across the mouth of the container, using the rubber bands to anchor it. The plastic should be pulled smooth and tight, as if it were the membrane of a drum.

Step One

He should then turn on the boom box and select a favorite rock station. Lay the rice grains on the plastic and put the container near the speaker. Experiment with changing the volume of sound and with turn it on and off.

Discuss how changes in the volume of sound affect the rice grains as the sound waves tickle, strike, or bombard the plastic membrane (and everything else in the room). Talk about the connection between the amplitude (size) of the sound waves and the increase or decrease in the dancing motion (vibrations) of the rice grains.

Step Two

Brush the rice grains off (saving some) and sprinkle the sugar on the plastic drum. Experiment with the radio again, noting again any differences in the behavior of the sugar.

Brush off most of the sugar and put a few grains of rice on the drum mixed in with the sugar and watch the dances you can create with sound.

Talk about how the membrane of the eardrum is like and not like the membrane you have created on the plastic carton.

Step Three

Once you have the basic idea established, look at some more subtle variations.
- When the volume remains the same, are the reactions to high notes different from reactions to low notes?
- Try classical or "easy listening" music instead of rock and notice any changes.

Make notes about each of your experiments.

WHAT'S MORE

The classic Slinky toy, actually a large spring, is another good tool for demonstrating wave motion and how sound travels through matter.

Repeat this activity using colored sugar (the kind sold for decorating Christmas cookies). Notice the patterns formed in the sugar crystals by the vibrations.

If your teen has a guitar or other stringed instrument, experiment with plucking a string near the container, using either rice or sugar. Notice that the string itself visibly vibrates, as does the plastic cover.

▶ MOONING AROUND

Our nearest neighbor in space, the moon, presents a constantly changing face, not only at night but often during the day as well. The moon's phases are a dramatic demonstration of the relative positions of the moon itself, the Earth, and the sun.

Understanding clearly the changing phases of the moon can help your kid get a solid grasp of how these three bodies are moving in space relative to each other. It can also make night-sky viewing more than just romantic.

At a Glance

Grade/Subject: 7th/Science—Earth and Space
Skills: observing phases of the moon and understanding their causes
Materials: calendar showing phases of the moon (in words or icons)
science notebook or sketch pad and pencils
globe (or large ball) and an orange (or smaller ball)
flashlight
Time: 15 minutes a night, two to three times a week (every 2-3 days) for a full moon cycle of 30 days.

Getting Ready

The moon notations on a calendar will show the four major moon phases: new, first quarter, full, third quarter. Plan your observation periods to start with a new moon—actually the dark of the moon, when the moon is between the sun and Earth, and the sun's light falls on the side we cannot see because it is turned away from us.

Plan to observe not only the four major phases but also the in-between stages. There are four waxing (increasing) phases between new moon and full moon, when we see more and more of the lighted side. And there are also four waning (decreasing) phases between full moon and the final crescent, as we see less and less of the lighted side of the moon.

Step One

Observe the moon together as frequently as the weather and your schedules will allow during a lunar month. Note that the first observation—the new moon—may show only a faint reflection

---

WHAT'S MORE

As an alternative demonstration, use a globe (or large ball) for the Earth, a smaller ball (or orange) for the moon, and a flashlight or lamp for the sun. (Don't worry about relative size.)

The moon has inspired countless songs and poems. Write one of your own.

Together, develop a "Dance of the Moon" based on your simulation. Choose music. The person playing Moon might hold a large white or silver circle of paper in front of her chest. Or Sun, Moon, and Earth can all make original costumes.

or rim, because the moon's lighted side is facing the sun. You will see a thin slice about one day after the new moon, then a real crescent.

To get a true picture of the moon's movements, make your observations at the same time each night. Each time, have your teen write down the date and then make a sketch of what you both observe, showing the lighted area (as well as reflected light outlining the full sphere). Have her add observations and notes based on your conversation as you watch the moon.

There's a crescent moon both before and after a new moon. Note that the "horns" of the crescent face different directions, depending on whether the moon is waxing or waning. The sketches will make that clear. The phase between crescent and full moon is called gibbous (GIB us).

Step Two

As you observe the different phases and positions of the moon in the sky, discuss with your kid just what you're seeing and what it means about the relative positions of Earth and the moon.

Next to the sketch of each phase as you see it from your vantage point, have her make a second sketch showing the moon's position relative to Earth in that phase. Shade the dark and light sides. (Be sure she understands that though people refer to the "dark side" of the moon, the side turned away from us is not always dark. It's really just the "far side.")

Step Three

After several observations, check to see that your kid has a solid understanding of both the phases of the moon and the moon–Earth–sun movements that cause those phases. We always see the same side of the moon—not because the moon stands still in the sky but because it rotates (turns) once on its axis during the same amount of time that it takes to revolve around the Earth.

To demonstrate this, you and your kid can play the parts of Earth and Moon to simulate a "fast forward" viewing of a month. "Earth" stands still while "Moon" walks in a circle counterclockwise around "Earth" to simulate the passage of a month. At she moves, Moon turns slowly (also counterclockwise) so that she makes a full turn in the same amount of time—that is, about one-quarter turn at each quarter of the circle. Surprise! Moon is always facing toward Earth!

HUMPTY DUMPTY

The term "gibbous," used for the middle phases of the moon, comes from a Latin term meaning "humpbacked."

DIZZY SPIN

Of course, Earth really turns around every day of a month, but since you are simulating 28 days in probably about 4 minutes, 28 spins would leave you too dizzy to see the moon at all!

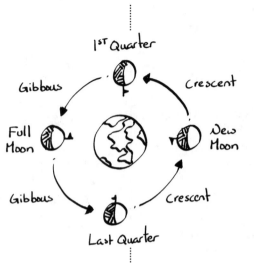

RED ROVER, RED ROVER

The NASA Mars Pathfinder spacecraft will land on Mars around July 4, 1997, controlled by scientists and engineers 35 million miles away. Mars studies will heat up in your child's science classroom for years to come! See if your child's teacher knows about the "Red Rover, Red Rover" project. Students from classrooms all over the world will build their own Mars-scapes and LEGO space rovers operated via computer software that mimics NASA's control programs. For detailed information you can pass on to your child's teacher, call LEGO Dacta at (800) 362-4308, or visit their Web site at http://www.lego.com/learn

Step Four

To demonstrate the phases of the moon, repeat your role playing simulation, but this time, position a flashlight to one side or have a third person take the part of "Sun," holding a lamp steady. Dim the room lights somewhat so that the lighted areas of "Moon" are visible. After this demonstration, have your kid revise her sketches if necessary.

Step Five

With the diagram and your demonstration in mind, go outdoors again to make several more observations of the moon. What's happening in the sky will now be a lot more understandable.

▶ MYSTERY BOXES

Here's a great hands-on project that can help a teen develop intuition about the basic physics concepts of inertia, momentum, and collisions. After building several mystery boxes, your child will be challenged to figure out what each one contains. Each box will contain one or more balls as well as any number of obstacles, barriers, obstructions, or attachments to affect the movement of the balls. These boxes will not only be challenging puzzles for you both to solve, but they will also lead toward fundamental discoveries about the physical world.

At a Glance

Grade/Subject: 7th/Science—Physical Science, Inquiry Skills
Skills: inertia, momentum, changing variables, problem solving
Materials: several medium sized boxes (shoe boxes or other similar boxes)
balls (various sizes, weights, and compositions)
masking or duct tape
cardboard tubes
cardboard
string
miscellaneous materials of your choice to use in the boxes
paper and pencil
Time: 1 hour

Getting Ready

You will want to construct the mystery boxes without your child around. Gather all the materials together. It is not really important how large the boxes are or what kind of balls you use. Marbles, steel ball bearings, Styrofoam balls, clay balls, round beads, ping pong balls, and golf balls are just a few of the possibilities. The greater the variety, the more interesting the activity.

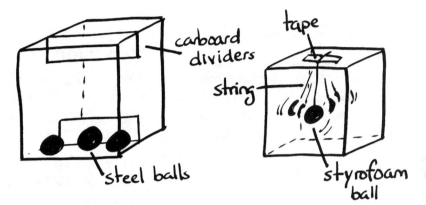

How to prepare your boxes Using the duct tape and other materials construct obstacles, barriers, and attachments inside the box. Think about how you want to alter the movement of the balls. Here are three examples of simple boxes:

You can make each box as simple or complex as you want. It could include a maze on the bottom, balls swinging from strings, balls inside tubes, several round beads strung on a string attached to two opposite sides, several balls connected together, a ball attached to a spring, a ball inside a balloon, balls attached to the sides with a rubber band, a piece of material attached to four sides as a barrier, heavy balls taped securely to one side, etc. Each box could have just a single "concept" or you could put several obstacles or attachments in one box for a more difficult puzzle.

Attach the top securely with tape, string, or large rubber bands.

Step One

Present your boxes and have your child handle each box one at a time—pick up the box, shake it, rock it side to side, whatever, as long as she doesn't open it.

Step Two

With paper and pencil, your child should draw what she thinks is inside the box. Questions like the following can help her exploration:

• How many balls does it sound like are inside?

EARTH SCI ON COMPUTER

Look into Pacific Interactive's software title *Bill Nye the Science Guy: Stop the Rock!* (ages 9 and up). Your child will perform experiments in order to save our planet from an off-course comet. This title, and other science greats on today's retail shelves, turn learning into an exciting game. Another Earth Science title to check into: 7th Level's funny and learning-filled primer, *The Universe According to Virgil Reality* (ages 8 and up).

- Are they all the same weight?
- What changes in weight and balance are felt as the box is moved in various ways?
- Are the balls moving freely or are they attached in some way?
- Do they collide with each of the six sides of the box?
- Are there any barriers or other restraints to the movement of the balls?
- If so, what is the configuration of the barriers?

Step Three

After she has guessed what is in a box and drawn what she thinks its inside looks like, have her open the box and examine its interior. Have her compare her drawing to what she finds. Encourage her to talk about her experience with each box.

- How would she change the drawing?
- How does she think the sounds and feelings of changing weight and balance communicated the interior reality to her?
- What parts of the interior affect inertia? How?
- What parts affect momentum? How?

Step Four

Invite her to create some boxes for you and other members of the family and friends to try guessing about.

YEAST BEASTS

Yeasts—the spores of small fungi, bacteria, and viruses—can all be found in our atmosphere. On a microscopic level, it can seem mighty crowded. Our lives and our food supply depend to a certain extent on the presence of the beneficial members of this crowd. Fortunately, our bodies have evolved defenses against the less friendly ones. Sanitary water supplies and good personal hygiene are an added protection.

▶ HEY, SOMETHING'S ON THE BREAD!

If you eat sourdough bread, use vinegar, or drink a glass of wine or beer, you're tasting firsthand evidence of the work of airborne microorganisms. If you discover a lump of blackened and slimy lettuce at the back of the vegetable cooler in your refrigerator, you've encountered more of them.

We share our atmosphere with an abundant variety of life forms so small that we can't see them. We depend on them not only for our bread and wine, but also for the very soil that wheat and grapes grow in.

The yukky stuff that sprouts on leftovers may be unwelcome in your refrigerator, but it contributes to the process of decomposition that reduces complex organic materials to simpler forms, which in turn become the substance that feeds new life. It's fun to observe and manipulate this process.

At a Glance

Grade/Subject: 7th/Science—Inquiry Skills, Health
Skills: observation, record keeping
Materials: 4 or more clear plastic containers (1 cup) with lids, or similar sized glass jars with lids
several slices of bread
set of measuring spoons
1 teaspoonful of salt
1 teaspoonful of sugar
magnifying glass
science notebook or booklet for record keeping
Time: 1 hour to prepare, with an overnight wait
observations of 5–10 minutes every day or every other day for two weeks to a month

Getting Ready

No advanced preparation is required other than assembling the materials. There is a health caution for this activity: Not all of the organisms that float around us are beneficial and there can be some contamination from handling. Don't taste any of your creations and avoid inhaling them too closely. Thorough hand washing is recommended.

Step One

Have your child wash out four of the containers with very hot water and set them aside to dry upside down. While they drain, she should cut the bread into 1" squares. Plan to use four or five cubes for each container—there should be enough so that each container gets the same amount.

Step Two

Next, turn the containers over and pour two tablespoons of water into each of three of them. Use a clean paper towel to thoroughly dry the fourth. Add the sugar to the water in one container and stir. Add the salt to the water in a second and stir. Drop an equal amount of bread cubes into all four of the containers.

Set the four containers on a table overnight with their covers off. Cover them the next morning and put them aside in a warm location, but not in direct sunlight.

Step Three

Have your child check the containers every day. Look closely and

---

WHAT'S MORE

If your family debates the quality of different kinds of bread, you might want to let the microorganisms be the judge! Set up an experiment using four equal containers and four different varieties of bread.

To test the effects of other ingredients on your bread cubes, you can repeat the basic investigation and substitute other common substances for the salt and sugar. What happens if you use milk, rubbing alcohol, baking powder, cocoa, or liquid soap? Keep records of each trial. What promotes growth? What prevents growth? What else might you try?

For the artistically inclined: Make a small bread sculpture using toothpicks to hold the cubes together. Seal up your masterpiece after moistening the bread (a light spraying with a spray bottle works well). You'll probably want a larger container for it. Let it stand for a long time and watch and record all the changes.

MORPHING

As in other cultures, the preparation of certain traditional Japanese foods relies on the action of airborne yeasts. A special glutinous rice is cooked in water for a long time to make a sweet drink (or porridge) called *amasake* (babies love it!). If this is exposed to the air and then allowed to ferment, an alcohol is formed which can be distilled into *sake*. If the fermentation is allowed to continue, *rice vinegar* will form.

WE'RE NUMBER ONE!

Parents have the number one role in their children's education. Everyone and everything else is just secondary. Hopefully you make the right choice who your child's second most important educational partner is, but you're the number one.

note when colonies of different colored microorganisms begin to appear. Continue observations on a regular basis for as long as you want and write down any and all changes.

- How quickly is the bread covered with mold?
- What colors predominate?
- Do colonies seem to come and go or do some just get bigger?

Have your child fish out some interesting-looking bread cubes with tweezers, kitchen tongs, or a spoon and examine them under a magnifying glass. (Cubes can be placed on a clean plate or paper towel.) Have her make a picture in her science notebook of what she sees.

Step Four

You and your child can run a small experiment to check the idea that the organisms that colonize and decompose food are airborne. Thoroughly wash out two containers and set them upside down to dry. Put some bread cubes into an oven and toast them. While they are toasting, finish drying the containers and lids with a paper towel. Then wipe each clean container and lid with a tissue soaked with alcohol.

When the alcohol has evaporated, place half of the cubes on an upside down lid, sprinkle them with water, and place the container (upside down) over them. Drop the other cubes into the other container (leaving it right-side up) and sprinkle with water. Do not put the lid on the second container. Put the two containers aside and make regular observations to see what happens. Have your child note changes and draw sketches of them in her notebook. You'll probably have to sprinkle water on the exposed cubes to keep them moist. Discuss what you discover.

- Which container grows more little colonies?
- If things grow on each, are they different in texture or color?

▶ THE WEB OF LIFE

One important concept studied in seventh-grade science is that of the web of life—the relationships and connections among living things. Kids learn that plants are producers of food, while animals are consumers—of plants and other animals. The pattern by which an organism eats something else to get energy and may, in turn, be eaten by another organism creates a food chain.

In this activity, you and your kid explore different food chains leading to food webs—the complicated patterns that tie together food chains within an ecosystem or habitat. You can look at these connections both locally and globally.

At a Glance

Grade/Subject: 7th/Science—Life Science
Skills: tracing the interconnections of food webs that link organisms, from tiny plants to gigantic blue whales
Materials: posterboard or large sheets of drawing paper
nature/wildlife magazines and flyers (that can be cut up)
marking pens (two colors) for labeling
guides to local plants and animals (optional)
library resources (optional)
Time: about 1 hour, twice a week if possible

Getting Ready

For a supply of pictures of plants and animals, collect back issues of nature and wildlife magazines, as well as advertising flyers or brochures for books, trips, and the like. Issues of National Geographic are great too.

Step One

To start, have your kid make a simple drawing of the different foods on your table for a single meal. Begin with a separate list of all the plant foods, such as carrots or beans or lettuce. Discuss why plants are producers, where they are located on the food chain, and where the energy in plant foods comes from.

Step Two

Then for each of the other foods, discuss the food chain that produced each of the other foods such as milk, cheese, chicken, beef, or fish. For example, since cheese is a dairy product, the cow that produced the milk from which it was made got its food from eating grains and grasses. The food chain for cheese therefore has one step or link: grains and grasses. Have your kid write down the different organisms in each food chain. Then list the foods—plant or animal—that each one of those organisms ate to get energy.

SCIENCE THAT COMPUTES

Many programs for your home PC will give teens good science experiences. Here are a few you can start to investigate:

• *Ozzie's World*, Deluxe Edition—Lots of animation, video, and games ranging from simple sorting and matching with Ozzie the sea otter to more involved science experiments, all with tons of replay value. Contact Digital Impact at (800) 775–4232.

• *Simpark*—Part of the popular "Sim" software series, this is another engaging, creative way for kids to develop a complete environment/ecosystem, complete with choices for regions and animal and plant species (with great games to help you "Identa-Species"). Contact MAXIS at (800) 33–MAXIS.

• *Devils Canyon*—Be a "Time Blazer," and travel back to the age of the dinos to learn all about fossils and massive reptiles while playing a challenging rescue game. Contact TeraMedia at (800) 818–3990.

• *Wide World of Animals*—Here's a complete animal encyclopedia, with pictures, articles, audio and video, and mini-documentaries on 700 critters. Contact Creative Wonders at (800) KID–XPRT.

Remember that most domestic animals eat mainly plant foods. But don't forget that domestic and wild birds eat not only seeds and but insects, too. Some birds—but not those that people usually eat—also hunt and eat small animals, fish, and other birds. Fish eat a variety of foods.

Encourage your child to use library resources to track down what might be in various food chains.

Step Three

Now move on to the more complex picture—a food web, which is made up of all the overlapping and interlocking food chains in a specific location. Decide on the area you and your kid will map. You might choose a local habitat, such as a nearby park or wetlands. Or you can choose somewhere exotic—a jungle or desert or ocean that you can research. Then make a list of the plants and animals from that habitat that you want to put in your food web.

Naturally it would be impossible to include all the organisms even in small area, such as a backyard. Discuss what plants and animals you want to choose—about twelve to twenty organisms is a manageable number. Remember to include several plants, as food producers, as well as interim organisms such as bacteria and insects. (Don't forget that most plants need to be pollinated and depend upon busy insects for that job.)

Step Four

In your source materials, find and cut out pictures of the organisms you've listed. Paste them on your posterboard or drawing paper. If you can't find a picture, make a quick sketch and label it.

Now have your kid use colored markers to draw the different food chains that link all these organisms. Use one color to link plants with plant eaters, another to link meat eaters with their meals. When she's drawn the food chains, their interlocking and crisscrossing lines will create the food web for that locale.

WHAT'S MORE

Design a poster showing a food chain or a food web in another specific habitat, such as a desert or a river.

If you have a family pet, draw the food chain of which it is a part. In the wild, would it be prey for other animals?

Visit the zoo to see some of the animals you included in your food web. Are the foods they eat in the zoo the same as they would eat in the wild?

CHAPTER 17

Learning Adventures— 8th Grade Science

THE WRIGHT STUFF

The Wright brothers are often presented in school as examples of perseverance. They provide an even more valuable example of how good science can be done. Wilbur and Orville were much more than just two guys with an idea and a bicycle shop. They thoroughly researched all that was known about flight at the time; and when information was inadequate, they conducted their own experimental research. They kept meticulous notes of all their work, developed testing equipment to gather information, and endlessly experimented with models and prototypes.

▶ It's All Wright

Even the most inspired guesses in a scientific investigation are backed up by hard experimental work. Sometimes theories and conjectures don't stand up to the rigors of practical trial and error, and sometimes such experimentation opens new and unexpected doors. Paper airplanes are a simple, entertaining, and inexpensive way to put the basic concepts of experiment building to work.

At a Glance

Grade/Subject: 8/Science—Inquiry Skills, Physical Science, Technology
Skills: building and testing experimental models, record keeping
Materials: several sheets of 8-1/2 by 11 paper
a larger sheet of paper
roll of masking tape
paper clips
corrugated card board (from a carton or pizza box) or oak tag
Time: 1 hour

Getting Ready

Steps one and two provide two very different kinds of flying model. Plan to have your child practice building and testing the flight characteristics of each.

Step One

This style of paper airplane is probably the most familiar kind of paper airplane and it's quite possible your child can already make one without using the directions illustrated here.

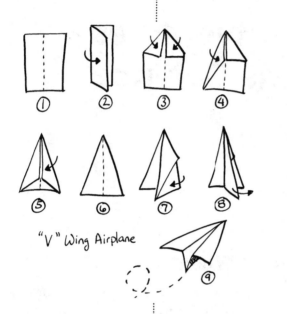

"V" Wing Airplane

Start by using standard-letter sized paper to make the first model. Then, make one larger version and one smaller version. Fly all three versions a number of times. Talk about and make a record of their flight characteristics (such as distances flown, speed, tendency to loop or turn, etc.) in your science notebook.

Step Two

Next make another type of paper airplane. The soaring tube is a more unusual design and has its own interesting flight characteristics. Make it in different sizes and experiment with them. Then fly your versions; discuss what happens; and record your observations in your science notebook.

- What is the best way to launch it? (Hint: Try holding it at the V and flipping it up and out.)
- Can you throw it so that it flies straight? Which size works best?
- Does a small tube work better than a large one?

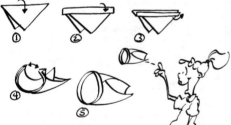

The Flying Tube

Step Three

Paper airplane flight depends on two sources of energy. The first is the forward velocity imparted by the thrower, and the second is the pull of the earth's gravity. The throw gives the plane height and, as it falls back, the pull of gravity is balanced by the push of the wings against the air. Have your child draw a simplified diagram of a flight path and indicate where and how these forces are operating. Test out and discuss various forces.

- Is throwing harder a better strategy?
- What if you throw straight up?
- What if you were to drop it straight down from a high location without throwing it at all?

Step Four

You and your child have built and experimented with two types of paper fliers. You have explored their characteristics and speculated about the forces involved in flight. Now it's time to try combining the flier elements to see what happens.

Have your teen build some duplicates of the tube flying shape in different sizes and attach them to different parts of a successful V flier. Small strips of masking tape can be used. (Masking tape can be reused several times and won't tear paper if it's carefully removed.) Here are some possibilities to experiment with:

- Will a tube attached to the upper surface of a V flier help? Try different locations from front to back.
- What about two smaller ones attached under the wings?
- What happens if you attach two V fliers side by side?
- What about two tubes side by side? (A thin strip of oak tag or tightly folded paper can be used to lay a support across the upper surfaces.)
- Does adding weight anywhere help or hinder flight?

Step Five

It often becomes hard to keep good records once you get rolling with an experimental project. Enthusiasm and the rush of new ideas tend to get in the way of keeping track of things. Your job as parent can be to help your child behave as a real scientist by remembering to record what is going on. (Sometimes you can take turns testing flight as the other person takes notes.)

If your child has a lot of ideas and a lot of trial models, it's helpful to make notes about what works and what doesn't and what he'd like to try next. You can be a supportive partner by offering to be the record keeper. Later, when he's worked out a flier that he'd like to remember, have him use the notes both of you have made to write up a report that includes data about the trials, the dimensions and details of the flier, and instructions on how to build it.

▶ ATOMIC KITCHEN

Eighth grade science often focuses on studying properties of matter and the behavior of atoms and molecules. Your kitchen counter and stove can become a home chemistry lab, where you

FLYING TIP

Selectively increase the weight of the paper flier. Use paper clips to add weight and alter balance. (Adding weight will also increase the energy of the fall.)

WHAT'S MORE

Research the books and kits available for paper airplane enthusiasts. Have your child pick a particular characteristic such as distance or direction that he would like to explore and select plans that emphasize that.

It's only a short step from paper fliers to kites—another fertile area for experimentation. Would either of the two fliers in this activity function well as kites? What provides the energy that keeps kites aloft and how can you control it? Give it a try! Books about how to build kites are also found in libraries and on the Internet.

If you have any small balsa wood or plastic gliders around your home, try modifying them with flying tubes, weights, and V-flier shapes.

MAKE A CHANGE

SCORE!'s major impact on teens is the difference in self-confidence that you can very visibly observe. Kids come into the program thinking they're horrible in something, they can't do well in it in school—and it's great to watch them develop confidence and conviction in a subject. They see that they can do the schoolwork and they might even be really good at it. Just having that self-confidence can carry into all areas of a teen's life. Any time parents can make a change like that in a child, it's the most productive thing they can do!

REAL-LIFE LEARNING

We do a lot of cooking together with our kids. We measure food coloring and other ingredients together. Parents need to make education practical for kids, and if learning is part of the everyday, it can be fun because kids like participating in real life.

and your child can investigate some of those principles.

Here's a way you can both demonstrate the effects of molecular motion as well as the ways that heat affects the motion of molecules. You also look at some ways to plan a good experiment.

At a Glance

Grade/Subject: 8th/Science—Chemistry, Inquiry Skills
Skills: demonstrating molecular motion, understanding importance of changing only one variable in an experiment
Materials: 2 clear, heat-proof glass mugs or tumblers
liquid food coloring (the kind that dispenses drop by drop)
finely ground spice such as cinnamon or paprika (with enough color to be easily visible)
cologne or aftershave lotion
other sources of scent (optional—such as cut and/or cooking onion, incense, ammonia, etc.)
cotton ball
stopwatch (or watch or clock with a second hand or digital seconds)
science notebook
Time: 45 minutes–1 hour

Getting Ready

Plan to work on this activity in the kitchen, where you have both water and heat available (stove, oven, or electric kettle). Have your child assemble all the materials before you start.

Step One

Your child should begin by filling one glass mug with cold water and then squeezing a drop or two of food coloring into the water. Discuss why the food coloring spreads out through the surface of the water. (It has to do with the movement of the water molecules.) Have him record this first step in the notebook.

Step Two

Next, he should empty out the mug, wipe it clean, and then refill it with clear cold water. Fill the other mug with very hot water, and set the two containers side by side. Each of you now holds a food coloring dispenser and adds two drops of food coloring to the containers at the same time. Watch while the food coloring spreads through the water. Discuss what you see, and have your teen describe in the science notebook the differences between the action in the two containers.

Ask your child to explain his ideas for why the food coloring disperses faster in the hot water than in the cold water. (He should explain that heat makes the water molecules move more quickly than the molecules of the cold water, spreading out the coloring faster.)

Discuss how whether moving water disperses food coloring faster that still water could be tested another way.

- What materials and preparations would be needed?
- What procedure would he follow?
- What would he do to make sure that water movement was the only variable that differed in his test?

Step Three

For another molecular demonstration, drain, wipe dry, and fill one of the mugs again with cool water. Have him sprinkle a fine layer of the spice over the water's surface. Now watch what happens, noticing how the flecks of spice move through the water.

Let the mug stand for a while, then look at the spice again. Have your child describe and record the behavior of the particles, along with his explanation for the behavior.

Step Four

Now place the mug near (but not on) a source of heat, such as a stove burner or the spout of a kettle. Watch how the spice flecks begin to move through the water more rapidly. Have your child compare their behavior with what happened with the food coloring. What does he think would happen if the water boiled?

Then discuss why you didn't begin this experiment by putting the spice into hot water. Be sure your child understands that it's important to change only one variable of an experiment at a time—or else you won't know which factor caused any changes you might observe.

Step Five

Finally, test by smelling at how molecules travel in air, too. To demonstrate this, one of you should stand in a far corner of the room with closed eyes. Note the time to the second (or use a

MENTION THEIR PROGRESS

We constantly brainstorm at home about how important the future is for our children, and it's all tied in with how well they're doing. We constantly mention their progress, and they like to hear how well they're doing.

WHAT'S MORE

Research water molecules and draw a picture of the pattern of a water molecule. Use it as the basis for a stencil or other design.

Visit the library to obtain materials to read about some of the scientists who discovered and studied atoms and molecules.

Why does the handle of a spoon get hot when the other end of the spoon is placed in hot tea? Ask your teen to explain this phenomenon using the same principles you explored together in this activity.

room with closed eyes. Note the time to the second (or use a stopwatch) as the other of you puts a few drops of heavily scented cologne or aftershave on a piece of cotton, and then waves the cotton in the air. The person closing his eyes should announce the moment he smells the scent, and the cotton waver should record the time it took for the smelly molecules to travel across the room!

Think of other variables to experiment with such as:

- Changing the scent used
- Changing the distance between "blind smeller" and "scent waver"
- Putting an obstacle between smell and smeller

Step Six

Encourage your teen to write up all the experiments you try together (and to think up additional ones to try as well as record). Have him review the write ups and write a paragraph or two about the activity of air and water molecules.

PLUS AND MINUS COLOR

We experience color in two different forms. These are usually described as *additive color* and *subtractive color*. It might be easier to think of these as *radiant* color (additive color), which is light as radiation, and *reflective* color (subtractive color), which is light reflected from a surface.

Radiated colors combine to form white light which is why they are called additive. Reflected colors combine to form black and that is why they are called subtractive. When you see a color that is being emitted or radiated, you are seeing the pure hue of a portion of the spectrum. When you see a reflected color, it is the only hue that is not absorbed by the surface you are looking at.

▶ COLOR WHEELIES

Color is a property of the small portion of the electromagnetic spectrum that we sense directly. It is so much a part of our everyday lives that we almost take it for granted. The study of color and our ability to perceive it is an area in which physical science wonderfully overlaps biology and psychology. Because of overlap, and since studying and thinking about color often raises unexpected questions, it's a perfect subject for 8th graders to explore.

At a Glance

Grade/Subject: 8th/Science—Inquiry Skills, Physical Science
Skills: experimental procedures, changing variables in an experiment
Materials: several pencils with erasers
compass or drafting square
oak tag or other thin cardboard (white is preferable)
colored pencils, markers, oil crayons, or paint
common pins
magnifying lens
graph paper (optional)

3/4", round, solid color labeling stickers (small circles traced around a penny or nickel and colored in can also be used)
low power microscope (optional)
variable speed electric drill (optional)
Time: 3/4–1 hour

Getting Ready

Use the magnifying glass to give yourself and your child an up-close-and-personal look at the illustrations in comic books or a color comic strip and the photographs in a magazine (check out the TV screen as well). Notice the use of patterns of dots in both cases and how the dots differ from place to place depending on the color.

If your child has had lots of experiences with color in art classes and understands the differences between primary and secondary colors, you can skip reviewing it. If not, use red, yellow, and blue (the primaries) to mix new colors. Combine them in pairs and describe the results (these are the secondary colors). What happens when you mix all three?

Step One

As the two of you saw when you looked very closely at a printed illustration, groupings of colored dots look like a different color when viewed from a distance. The same is true if different colors are viewed in motion. Your child can test this by making a color wheel.

Draw several circles 4–5 inches in diameter with a compass. If you don't have a compass, use the soup can method shown at the left.

Punch a hole through the center of each of your circles with a pin. Next you'll need to add colors to the wheel.

Step Two

Your child can begin with a simple experiment. Make a circular row of colored dots around the outer edge of the wheel. She can use round

Making the Grade

WHAT'S MORE

This activity deals primarily with reflective or subtractive colors. With a little effort, you can adapt the color wheel to explore additive color. Use a large hole puncher (like that used for making grommet holes) to make circular holes around the rim of a larger color wheel. Cover the holes with colored tissue paper, theatrical gelatin strips, or pieces of colored cellophane. Hold a small, but intense, flashlight behind the wheel, and spin the wheel rapidly. This needs two people, a spinner and an observer.

Find a color photographic portrait with a prominent eye. Study the eye under a strong magnifying glass or low power microscope. With a piece of graph paper and colored pencils reproduce the dots in the picture on a larger scale. How far away do you have to stand from your dot version for it to look like the eye in the picture?

Look up Georges Seurat, Claude Monet, Camille Pissarro, and other Impressionist artists to see how they experimented with color.

colored label dots from a stationary store, or she can make her own dots by tracing a penny or a nickel (don't worry about having the dots come out exactly even). Pick any pair of primary colors for your label dots or color in the circles alternating two primary colors as you work around the rim.

Then mount the wheel with a pin pushed through the center of the wheel and into the eraser of a pencil. Spin it. (Holding it up against a white or neutral background makes the visual result easier to observe.) Discuss what you see.

- What happens as it spins?
- Does the speed of rotation make any difference?
- What do you observe?

Encourage your teen try the other two possible combinations of pairs of primary colors. What colors appear?

Step Three

Now the two of you can explore variations to see what happens.

- What if you don't alternate colors but place all the dots of each color along one half of the outer rim?
- What if you do alternate colors by twos?
- What happens if you make the circle of dots closer to the center of the wheel?
- What difference does it make how close together the colors are placed?

Brainstorm other ways of arranging dots to see what color effects can be obtained.

Step Four

Different patterns on the color wheel can produce surprising results. Use the yin and yang symbol as a pattern for two primary colors by drawing it on a color wheel and then filling the two sides with two primary colors. Then see what happens when you spin it.

- What is it?
- What are the characteristics of the new color that appears?
- Is the new color a primary color or could you mix it from other primary colors?

Try other patterns that use two colors, spirals, squares, or just plain blobs.

Step Five

Have your child make a color chart based on her observations of her color wheel experimentation.

▶ Dog Designer Genes

We are only beginning to unravel the underlying mechanisms of genetic inheritance, but human beings have employed practical techniques for manipulating inherited traits for thousands of years as a quick comparison between almost any domestic animal and what we know about its wild ancestors makes obvious.

Today, as folks develop transgenic pigs to create medications and genetically altered cotton plants that produce plastic polymers, it's useful to pause and gain some perspective on the genetic revolution by examining more familiar cases of what breeders have already accomplished. How, for instance, have 300 internationally recognized breeds of dog come into being? In this activity, you will examine the alterations made in one domestic animal, and think a little about the implications.

At a Glance

Grade/Subject: 8th/Science—Life Science
Skills: see breeding depends upon inheritability of traits and how small differences between parent and offspring can accumulate over generations, explore the ethics of science
Materials: reference books on dogs and dog breeds
pen, pencil, colored pencils, and paper
magazines—those for dog owners and breeders as well as others that contain material about or pictures of dogs—(optional)
science notebook
Time: 1 hour to many hours—depending upon interest

Getting Ready

Make a visit together to a library to borrow a few books on dogs and dog breeding to use for reference. Look for books with clear pictures; detailed physical descriptions of each breed; and information about the origins, advantages, and drawbacks of each breed.

DOG HISTORY

Dogs have been associated with humans about 10,000 years and are probably our oldest domesticated animal. Whether humans first sought them out as hunting companions because of their sense of smell and tracking skills, or dogs began the association by attaching themselves to bands of humans as scavengers is unknown. Historically, dogs have worked as hunters, haulers, herders, and guards; and the tasks and responsibilities they have taken on continue to grow. They have adapted to live in the entire geographical range of human habitation, from the Arctic wilderness to warm and densely populated cities of the tropics.

FOR CAT LOVERS

Cats have also been associated with humans far back into history. Although they have not been bred for work in the way that dogs have, certain mutations have been favored, distinct breeds have been developed, and their presence offers fascinating sidelights on human migration. The double front paw mutation was established in New England during colonial times and, when the Tories fled north during the American Revolution, they took their double-pawed cats with them into the Canadian maritime provinces. White cats were special to the Norse and, until recent times, they tended to be found most frequently in areas settled by immigrants from old Scandinavia.

WHAT'S MORE

Have your child research another domestic animal such as the horse, cow, sheep, goat, or pig. What were the ancestors like? Where did some of the breeds arise? Are certain breeds better adapted to certain environments? Write your state's agricultural extension service for information. If you have access to a 4-H club, you will find valuable materials there too.

Step One

Either during the library visit or later at home, have your child decide on three very different breeds of dog to research. The advantage of doing this step at the library is that once the breeds are selected, more specialized books may be chosen to borrow.

Brainstorm together the variety of roles that domestic dogs have played with humans. Make as long a list as the two of you can think of. Then, in choosing breeds to study, your child can consider whether she wants to study very different breeds that have been developed to meet similar human needs or breeds that each play a different role.

Step Two

Have your child set up a page in the science notebook for each breed and make notes there about the general characteristics for each. Here are some things to look for and note:

- Ear: size relative to head, drooping, erect, or bent
- Coat: solid or mixed colors, color range within the breed, fur texture and length
- Size: average height at shoulder and average weight
- Head: broad or narrow; characteristics of face
- Legs: long or short in relationship to the length of the dog's body; sturdy or slender
- Temperament: high-strung, mellow, or low key, kinds of activities preferred, etc.

Step Three

Have your child research each of her chosen breeds from the standpoint of practical breeding. What jobs were (and are) these dogs bred for? What characteristics (both physical and behavioral) do they have that make them suitable for this work? Write notes for each breed that lists this information.

If possible, she could interview one or more owner of each breed of dog and then write up what she learns from each interview in her notes on that breed.

Step Five

Have your child create a chart that will summarize what she has learned about physical characteristics in relation to the breeding of these dogs. List each breed and its job on the left-hand side and the characteristics across the top, then fill in the specific information.

Encourage her to make a booklet containing her information about each breed by writing up her information neatly. She might also cut out illustrations from old magazines or photocopy from books to illustrate each section.

Step Six

Together imagine your ideal dog. Talk over what the two of you like and dislike about the dogs that you have studied so far. What would be an ideal dog for your family? What appearance and what other characteristics would you want it to have and why? Would it be just a pet? Would it have any specific job(s)? What breeds would you involve as parents in attempting to breed such a dog and why?

Invite your child to write up a description of her ideal dog, to give the new breed a name, and even draw a picture of it.

Step Seven

Many specialized dogs have physical problems related to their bred-in characteristics. Pugs and bulldogs, for instance, have respiratory problems. golden retrievers and German shepherds have a tendency for hip problems, and greyhounds are likely to be particularly sensitive to cold weather. These specific problems can be used to raise the general issue of the ethics of breeding to influence characteristics. Have a discussion with your child about what she thinks is good and bad about breeding animals for specific traits. Is it fair to the dogs? What about other animals? Who should make these decisions?

▶ FOSSIL FINDERS

A prime source of information for detectives of Earth's geologic history is stored in layers of sedimentary rock. These rocks, such as sandstone or limestone, were formed as sediments piled up on lake beds and the floors of shallow seas. Leaves, stems, and parts of ancient invertebrate animals were buried in the layers of sediments. As the sediments became rocks, the plants and animals were preserved as fossils. What does study of such fossils reveal about Earth's history?

DOGGY DOPE

Many kennel clubs publish magazines. As the principle agency in the United States for maintaining a registry of dog breeds, the American Kennel Club registers over a million purebred dogs a year. It offers a great deal of information about dog breeds and breeding, both online and by mail.

Making the Grade

┌─ **WHAT'S MORE** ─┐

Get books and articles about fossils from your library (and use the Internet if it's available) to learn more about what you might have seen.

From your information, make up a local guide to "Fossils in the Floor," naming the buildings where fossils are in the stone and describing what you found.

Depending on where you live, plan a field trip to look for fossils in nature. Choose a place where sedimentary rock—limestone or sandstone—has been exposed by a road cut or construction area.

Do research to find out what your state or local area was like in a past geologic era—such as the Mesozoic (the age of the dinosaurs). The location of ancient lakes or oceans is a good clue to finding fossils.

You might think that a natural history museum or rock shop would be the only place to find fossils. But in fact, you and your child have a good chance of discovering fossils yourselves as you make field trips to local buildings and as you sharpen your ability to "see" into rocks.

At a Glance

Grade/Subject: 8th/Science—Earth and Space, Life Science
Skills: examining sedimentary rocks for evidence about Earth's history and past life forms
Materials: hand magnifying glass
sketchbook and drawing pencils
tourist guide or guide to local architecture (optional)
Time: variable, depending on the number and extent of your field trips

Getting Ready

Your is likely to have studied certain kinds of common fossils in her science class. To assure that you both have an idea of what you're looking for, look through some source books that illustrate commonly found fossils. These may be seen in her textbook and in an encyclopedia and books available at your local library.

Step One

Make a list of buildings in your area that have entrance halls, floors, stairways, or walls made of marble or polished limestone (which can look like marble). A large percentage of those types of stone will contain fossils of primitive plants and animals.

Public buildings such as a town hall, library, courthouse, and post offices—perhaps even your child's school—are all likely possibilities. Many new office buildings also have used marble or polished stone to achieve elegance in lobbies and hallways.

From your list, choose one or two buildings for the first fossil-hunting field trip that you will make together.

Step Two

Go on your fossil-finding expedition. Don't forget the magnifying glass and science notebook or materials for recording what you find. Success in fossil hunting depends on a keen eye and careful observation.

Look down and around at the marble walls, floor, or columns. Look especially for any oddly shaped smudges, unusual shapes, differences in color. Have your child look more closely. Could that circular shape be the fossil remains of a plant stem or the plant-like crinoid, seen crossways? Can you detect a part of a leaf? Perhaps a spiral shell?

Step Three

Have your child make sketches of the shapes found in the marble or limestone. Talk about each one and have her make a few notes about it along with note on both the building and exact location where it as found.

You may feel sure that some markings in the stone are fossils, and less sure about others. With the sketches, your child can check them out later in a reference book.

Step Three

Meanwhile, back at your home, between trips, here are two activities you can do together that sharpen your powers of looking for fossils. They each reveal the number of different angles from which you might see a piece of fossil plant or animal in a slab of rock.

Jurassic Jell-O™ Cook a variety of a few different shapes of pasta: shell, spiral, hollow ziti, rotini. Mix the cooked shapes into Jell-o and let it harden. Cut the Jell-O on different angles—sideways, vertically, diagonally. Notice how the various pasta shapes look very different depending on how you slice the Jell-O.

Apple Angles For another illustration, cut up some apples at a variety different angles—sideways, vertically, diagonally. Notice how your view of the core and seeds changes.

▶ GLOBAL WARMING WARNING

One of the most controversial issues in the world today is the question of global warming and long-term climate change. As part of their study of Earth and space, eighth graders often explore the effects of various factors on climate and the consequences of various factors on climate and the consequences of climate change.

CONNECT THE KIDS

We must bring the power of the Information Age into all our schools. Last year [1996], I challenged America to connect every classroom and library to the Internet by the year 2000, so that, for the first time in history, a child in the most isolated rural town, the most comfortable suburb, the poorest inner-city school, will have the same access to the same universe of knowledge.
—from 1997 State of the Union Address, President Clinton

HELPLESS, CLUELESS

Successful students, on average, are more likely to attribute their academic accomplishments to hard work and their occasional failures to a lack of effort. Unsuccessful students, in contrast, are more likely to see their performance as due to factors that are beyond their personal control.
—from *Beyond the Classroom* by Laurence Steinberg, Ph.D. (Simon & Schuster, 1996)

Making the Grade

HOT STUFF

Greenhouse effect: A layer of atmospheric gases surrounding Earth holding in warmth from the sun heating up our world. It operates in much the same way as the glass structure of a greenhouse, which lets heat in but impedes its escape so that life inside the greenhouse gets hotter than normal.

PACING THE PROCESS

Education at home has to be done in a way that allows kids to learn at their own pace. They shouldn't be pushed. They should be allowed to develop and learn from where they're most comfortable.

You and your child can explore how these ideas hit close to home, increasing her awareness of how everyday activities can contribute to environmental global problems. And you can look for ways in which you and your family can contribute to improving Earth's environmental health.

At a Glance

Grade/Subject: 8th/Science—Earth and Space, Inquiry Skills
Skills: understanding how small atmospheric changes can cause climate change, exploring ways of responding to environmental problems
Materials: science notebook
Time: about 30–45 minutes of record keeping per day for one week of observation; variable times for follow-up activities

Getting Ready

Lay the groundwork for this activity by discussing the basic questions concerning global warming with your child:

- A number of human activities and natural processes increase the gases—mainly carbon dioxide—that create the "greenhouse effect."
- The normal greenhouse effect makes life on Earth possible. Increases in the amount of greenhouse gases in the atmosphere, however, are expected to raise average temperatures around the world.
- One major consequence would be the melting of polar ice caps causing a rise in sea level, which would cause the flooding of low-lying coastal areas.

Step One

Collaborate in keeping a one-week record of all the ways you and your family possibly contribute to the destructive greenhouse gases released everyday into Earth's atmosphere. Each of you can monitor and report your own uses, while your child also gathers and records those of other family members. Meet briefly once a day during the week to share and have him record the information in his science notebook.

Since carbon dioxide, the main greenhouse gas, is produced by the burning of fossil fuels such as gas, oil, and coal, you'll need to record items such as these:

- Number of miles driven in a car
- Hours of home heat and temperature set (if you heat with oil or coal)
- Hours of heat using wood in a stove or fireplace
- Cars or trucks with engines idling
- Use of gas-powered machinery like lawn mowers, snow or leaf blowers, etc.
- Recreational and other gas-powered machines like outboard motor, ski mobile, dirtbike, motorcycle, etc.

Unless your electric company uses water power, it is likely that your household electricity also comes from fossil fuels. Take a look at

- Hours of air-conditioning used and temperature set
- Hours of home electric heat and temperature set
- Appliances used and hours of use
- Rooms lighted, total watts and time lighted

Step Two

To add to your observations, look for other activities around you that also send greenhouse gases into the air. Here are things for you and your child to look for:

- Burning in open dumps
- Woodland being cut down and/or burned
- Burning vegetation such as leaves

Point out that living trees return huge amounts of oxygen to the atmosphere. Therefore, not only do burning trees increase the amounts of carbon dioxide, but simply killing them reduces the amount of oxygen that otherwise they would contribute to the atmosphere.

Step Three

At the end of the week, add up all the information you have collected. Discuss what other activities you and other family members might have been involved in but forgotten to tally. Decide how you want to tabulate all that you and your child have learned. You will have a lot of information and no "right" way to summarize it. Discussing how to make sense of it (and act on it) is the important thing. You will have succeeded in performing a major scientific activity if you have gathered information that poses questions and problems for further exploration!

WHAT'S MORE

Use library periodicals and the Internet to investigate current world conferences and treaties focused on the question of global warming.

Use a world map to study which low-lying areas—even whole island nations—that might be harmed if global warming caused a change in ocean level.

Make a poster that will encourage people to be globally responsible.

Use the library and the Internet to investigate a related problem: the apparent destruction by chemicals (mainly chlorofluorocarbons or CFCs) of Earth's ozone layer. What steps have already been taken to address this problem?

GRANDMA SAYS

Grandma's admonition, "Turn off lights when you leave the room," was never more timely, and she might want to add, "And don't run the hot water when you aren't using it!" Parents—and grandparents—should set good environmental examples for teens.

Step Four

Your child can also track more accurately the amount of fuel your family uses. Have him collect receipts for every gasoline purchase for a month from each trip to the fuel pump. He can then figure out from them the average amount of gasoline the family uses in a week. You can examine the family's electric bills together also. If possible, from the "fuel charges," estimate the amount of oil used to generate the electricity your household used in a week. Try contacting the electric company for more information.

Step Five

Hold a family meeting in which your child presents the results of his research. Discuss the information recorded in his science notebook.

Then brainstorm possible changes in family behaviors and alternatives that would help your family reduce the amount of carbon dioxide sent into the air.

For instance, in many households, driving the family car will be the largest item. Alternatives include walking, taking public transportation, and combining errands into one trip. Keeping the temperature a few degrees lower in cold seasons (and wearing a sweater) or a few degrees higher in hot seasons can mean a reduction in fuels burned to generate that energy.

▶ HARMONY IN MOTION

Making a harmonograph is really quite easy. Only very simple carpentry skills are needed. Besides being able to make beautiful designs that could be used for stationery or even framed pictures, it is a constant fascination to watch. Principles of pendulums, momentum, friction, and harmonic motion are all visually demonstrated by this wondrous device. It also will allow a child the opportunity to experiment with changing simple variables and graphically seeing the results.

At a Glance

Grade/Subject: 8th/Science—Physical Science, Inquiry Skills
Skills: changing variables, harmonic motion, friction, momentum
Materials: one paving slab (available at gardening supply stores)
plywood (just larger than the paving slab)

WHAT'S MORE

Experiment with a single pendulum. Get a stopwatch and see how long it takes for the pendulum to swing back and forth ten times. Then double the length of the rope and time ten swings again. What effect does changing the length of the rope have on the duration of the swing? Experiment with different lengths and see.

rope or clothes line

tape

mat board about the size of the paving slab

wood (see dimensions described in the diagram)

6 short screw (1 1/4")

2 long screws (2")

roller ball pen

small rock

3 hooks

paper (smooth surfaced, finger-painting paper works best—experiment!)

drill and 2 drill bits

weight

Time: 1 hour for construction

several hours as desired for experimentation and drawing

Getting Ready

Assemble all the materials. The exact measurements of the materials is not important—you can use items that are smaller or larger without affecting the final construction. One drill bit should be just smaller than the screws, to make it easier to attach them. The second drill bit should be large enough to drill a hole that will allow the pen to fit snugly in it.

Step One

Looking at the first diagram, help your child (only as needed) to construct the harmonograph. She should drill small holes in the four corners of the piece of plywood; then tie two lengths of rope to opposite corners. Attach one hook to the bottom of the plywood, in the middle. Attach two hooks from a beam or ceiling (or use an old swing set frame that already has two hooks). Loop the two ropes over the two hooks. Place the slab on top of the plywood. Tape the piece of mat board to the top of the slab to provide a smoother drawing surface.

WHAT'S MORE

Many variables that can be changed in the harmonograph: the length of the two hanging ropes, the length of the rope hanging from the bottom hook, and the weight hanging from the bottom. Experiment with changing each of these. Predict how the various changes will effect the designs and then talk about the results afterwards and your ideas about what caused them.

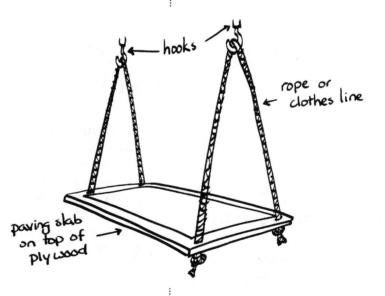

hooks

rope or clothes line

paving slab on top of plywood

Step Two

Next your child can construct the pivoting pen arm seen in the diagram. Attach the middle of the 36" wood piece to the middle of the 12" wood piece with short screws (drill small holes first). Drill small holes in the end of the 12" piece and screw the long screws through the wood, allowing about 1/2" of the screw to protrude. These screw points will be the pivoting points of the pen arm. Connect the two wooden blocks to the ends of the 16" piece of wood— the pivoting arm will rest on top of this. Drill a hole near the end of the 36" piece of wood and place the pen in it. Finally find a box, chair, table, etc. to place the pivoting pen-arm mechanism on, allowing the pen arm to be just barely above the slab harmonograph.

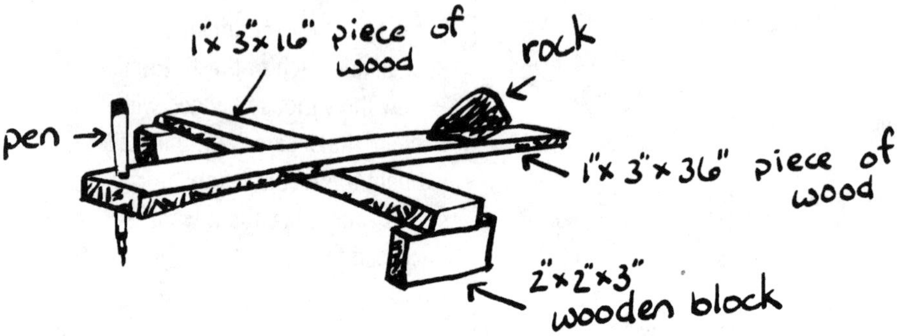

pen →

1" x 3" x 16" piece of wood

rock

1" x 3" x 36" piece of wood

2" x 2" x 3" wooden block

Step Three

She should now tape a piece of paper on top of the harmonograph and position the pen-arm so that the pen is directly above the middle of the paper. Start the slab moving in a circle, and then gently lower the pen down onto the paper as the harmonograph continues to swing. Experiment with the position of the rock so that the pen rests lightly (but not too lightly) on the paper. The heavy weight of the slab gives the harmonograph a lot of momentum to continue for a while. The greater the friction of the pen on the paper, the sooner the harmonograph will slow down.

Your child can try using different colored pens to create one design on top of another.

Step Four

After experimenting with the harmonograph as described above, try attaching a rope and weight to the hook on the bottom of the harmonograph. This will drastically affect the type of drawing that the harmonograph can make.

SAFETY IN GLASSES

We've said it before, but it needs repeating: When using hand tools it's a good idea for your child to get into the habit of wearing safety glasses, which are inexpensively available in hardware stores.

▶ CHANGING TECHNOLOGY

The twentieth century has seen immense and rapid technological change. Interviewing older people about how technology changed their lives is a fascinating way for your child to understand how technology has changed how we work and live. He can then present his findings to family and friends, leading to lively discussions about the pros and cons of technology!

Carrying out this research also provides your child an experience that can strengthen his relationships with older family members and acquaintances, giving him a better understanding of his elders, while they appreciate the interest he takes in the history they have lived and how their lives have changed, just as his life will change as technology continues its advance.

At a Glance

Grade/Subject: 8th/Science—Technology
Skills: look into the impact and speed of technological change
Materials:
paper and pencil
tape recorder (optional)
video camera and/or camera (optional)
Time: 15 minutes preparation
an hour or more for the interview
an hour or more for follow-up discussion and reporting

Getting Ready

Talk with your child about the changes in technology that have occurred in the past few decades, such as the rise of computers, television, commercial aviation, and atomic energy. Brainstorm with your child to figure out which family members have been affected the most by these changes. Help him decide which person has a good story to tell. An elderly person may have the most interesting observations, since they have seen so many changes.

Once your subject has agreed to be interviewed, have your child ask him or her to begin thinking back on everyday life from childhood and consider ways in which technology changed it.

Making the Grade

WHAT'S MORE

Look carefully at your own life to analyze what technologies you depend on. Write a description of how you would do things if modern technologies were not available to you.

What is the newest technology in your life. What are you doing differently this year because of some technology that was not available to you at some earlier time?

Follow up the report by comparing your subject's opinions with the observations of other elders. Use your interviewing and reporting skills to gather information from others, then compare the experiences of the group, looking for similarities and differences and reasons for them.

Research how the technology that your subject talked about has affected the country. Compare this experience with your subject's experience.

Step One

Help your child make arrangements with the person who will be interviewed and to plan the interview. Talk together about questions he might ask about how technology affect family, work, and personal life. Brainstorm together the beginnings of a list of technologies that have occurred during the lifetime of the person he will interview. Consider the role of technology in agriculture, manufacturing, family life, business, warfare, transportation, and communications. Have him make notes during your discussion.

Discuss also a variety of ways he can use for prompting his subject to reminisce about technology's effect on everyday life. For example, your child might encourage talk about the impact of a specific device, such as the television or airplanes. Another approach would be to seek memories and opinions about all the devices that have changed people's lives. Your child might plan questions about the effects of technology on the pace of life, on how people communicate, or on how work is done, and on what kinds of work are done?

He can then use his notes to prepare a list of questions and prompts he can use in his interview.

Step Two

Try to be present during the interview. You can support your child by jotting some notes and by helping the interview stay on the topic when necessary. (You may want to photograph or videotape parts of the interview—using today's technology, of course!)

As he talks with his interviewee, your child should make notes even if a tape recorder is available. If a tape recorder is used, make sure it is plugged in or has a strong battery and is working well. A 60-minute tape is probably sufficient, but once your child gets the elder going, you'd hate to run out of tape!

Step Three

Take the role of editorial supporter to your child's efforts to produce a special report on "Effects of Technology an Ordinary Life: a case study." Provide encouragement as your teen listens to the tape and makes more notes (if the interview was taped), organizes his notes, and plans his report. Spend some time together discussing what was learned in the interview.

When he has roughed out his first draft, read it and talk it over with him. You may be able to provide some family photos to supplement the story.

Step Four

When his report is ready, schedule a special time for him to present it to family members and interested friends. You can make this a special occasion, with your child and the interviewee as guests of honor. Plan enough time for the stimulating discussion about technology that the report is bound to trigger.

Then, with your child, conduct a technology follow-up rap session inviting everyone to give their opinions about subjects like

- Which technology has had the greatest effect on their own lives
- How they feel about the pace of technological change
- Examples of what they feel are negative effects of technology and why

How Can Our Family "Make the Grade"?

CHAPTER 18

What Should I Do About . . .?

HOMEWORK

Ah, homework—most of us dreaded doing it, and most of us wind up making sure that our children get it done! It's useful to keep in mind the two important functions that homework serves in education.

What we know of the process of long-term learning shows us that information needs to be processed several times for it to become a part of anyone's store of knowledge. Hearing something in the classroom is a first time and, if students don't think about it or use it a second or third time soon after, that first time becomes the last time. Homework is an opportunity to make a new piece of learning stick. Homework also helps to make teaching more efficient. When your child makes the effort to be prepared for a class, she and her teacher can then use their time together to expand on the knowledge, share insights, and move into new areas of learning.

How can I be sure my child does her homework?

Oh, if only we parents could just wave a homework wand! Without it, here are some guidelines that may help homework time be less stressful.

Establish a routine and help your child stick with it. This is likely to require some time from you at the beginning, but it's well worth the effort. Let your child know that you expect that she will do her homework in the same way you expect that she'll eat dinner, participate in sports, or go to bed at a certain hour. Even if you hear the cry, "But I don't have any," sit and spend some time talking about what she did that day at school. (Maybe your child's teacher requires students to keep an assignment notebook—wouldn't that be great!) Encourage her to write in a journal, do a little online research on nights when there isn't a real assignment to do, or do one of the Learning Adventure activities in this book. Your attention and involvement will help your child see that it is part of her day to think about school things at home.

Practice some time management with your child. Look at her other time commitments (sports, music lessons, that favorite and acceptable TV program, other family routines) and help her set out a schedule that she can maintain reasonably. A set time every day is the easiest to remember but may not always be feasible. The point is to have the homework schedule make life easier, not harder. Be sure to work in the extra time required for doing long-term research papers and special projects.

Create a study area. Make sure that it has few to no distractions and good lighting (stay outside of earshot of the TV if you can manage it). Going to a space that encourages your child to focus on work is an important part of the routine too. It might be where the computer is (as long as she has room to set out her books or papers and write), or it might be the table after supper is cleared. Keep homework items in a bag or box so they can be easily laid out and then picked up each night.

Make time in your own schedule. Those few moments you spend taking an interest in what your kid is doing, reviewing her progress, or giving a little help where needed make a big difference. (But resist the temptation to actually do the work for her!) Keeping in touch prevents your child from thinking she is banished to do her homework in solitary confinement. Some work should certainly be done alone, but a lot of problem solving and creative thinking can be done through dialogue. If you care about what she is doing, she'll care more too.

My child's math is way over my head. How can I be helpful?

This isn't an uncommon problem for parents. Some basic school content will always be the same, but emphasis, styles of teaching, and (particularly in the case of science and some areas of mathematics) new discoveries and teaching techniques mean changes in the standard curriculum. There are several things you can do.

- First, remember that you don't have to replace the teacher. What you can most easily provide is a comfortable and supportive environment for your child's homework. This may mean putting a firm hand on the television power switch. It may mean setting aside a space where your child can work quietly and without disturbance. At all times, respect your child's ability and express confidence in him. Reassure him that you will help in whatever way you can.

- Second, if the problems are with understanding specific material or just a general failure to be able to get and follow directions, consult with your child's teacher. Some children find it difficult to ask for help or information in the classroom. Work with the teacher to make it possible for your child to ask.

- Third, use the Learning Adventure activities in this book to turn potentially difficult subject matter into something both fun and understandable.

- Fourth, some communities sponsor call-in homework phone assistance. Others have programs to connect students with mentors or tutors. After-school programs like *SCORE!* provide subject matter remediation and enrichment for the community. Check with your school's principal and with other parents to find out what is available.

- Fifth, ask your child's teacher for suggestions about books, magazines, and other resources that you can use to stimulate an interest in the subject. Try the Resources section in this book for further ideas.

How much help should I give my child with grammar and spelling in his written work?

In this situation, you need to walk a fine line between answering your kid's questions and actually taking over what ought to be his practicing of the editing and proofreading steps of the writing process. Encourage him to do as much as he can on his own. Even when you answer a question, try to cast yourself as the last resort. For instance, the first response to, "Mom, how do you spell . . . ?" probably should be, "Have you tried finding it in the dictionary?" or it could be asking him about a spelling guideline. After that, you can give some guidance in finding the word and, finally, help with the actual spelling.

If you're not certain about grammar and usage questions, admit your uncertainty. See if you can look up the rule or explanation together. Turn your rusty skills into a positive opportunity for you both to learn something.

What can I do when my child doesn't do his homework?

While this is a familiar problem, it has many answers—depending mainly on what problems or issues stand between your child and his homework. If he doesn't have a place to work, if his time is taken up with family chores, or if he has a TV in his room, those problems need to be solved first.

If there are no outside reasons or interference, it may be just a question of his developing self-discipline. There should be a definite time set aside for doing whatever homework has been assigned: no TV, no phone calls. Make it clear that the faster the homework gets done, the sooner he can be on the phone or doing something else.

If there's a serious problem, he may try to convince you that he just doesn't have any homework. In most schools today, having no homework is unlikely. Try to find out the truth—from other parents or, if necessary, from the teacher. Then you'll have to impose discipline from the outside.

Making the Grade

TECHNOLOGY

Technology is a confusing and difficult area for both parents and educators. Although schools grew in size and complexity from the eighteenth century to the early twentieth century, the basic technology of education—blackboards, books, paper, and simple writing instruments—remained almost the same from decade to decade for almost 250 years.

Suddenly, following the Second World War, school equipment began changing, and they have been changing ever since. Technology like tape recorders, slide projectors, television, photo copiers, and film loop equipment became an increasingly regular part of school apparatus. But these additions were minor compared to the upheaval caused by computers. Today's information technology is so powerful, so full of promise, and so certain to alter how we work, play, and learn that schools and parents alike have to struggle to comprehend its implications.

Two problems stand out for parents and schools. One is trying to understand a technology that is still developing and whose implications for us are still unclear. The other is the enormous expense of this technology. Families and schools face hard economic and educational decisions as computer consumers and users.

How do I decide which computer to buy for my family?

Your decision will involve a combination of research and self-assessment; and unfortunately the answer may not be cut-and-dried for you. But here are the things to consider:

- Who will be using the computer?
- What programs will you want to use now? in the future?

If both you and your children will use the computer, you should consider checking into what your child's school has for hardware and software; kids tend to be pretty flexible when it comes to jumping from one program to another, but continuity is good if you can arrange it. (Many programs today can run on either a Windows™ or Macintosh® computer, so compatibility issues are less important than they used to be.) Depending on what you plan to do with the computer (word processing, telecommunicating), you may need to consider buying add-ons like a printer and a modem. As you consider what computer model to select, try to think ahead to what your computing needs will be a year or so from now. As with any electronic device, today's model may be outdated tomorrow; but if it meets your budget now and can meet your work plans for a couple years, then it is probably the right choice for your family.

How do I pick educational software that is good and that my kids will use?

It's sort of like picking out toys or books or clothes for children—some guesswork, some research, some sense of your child's likes and dislikes, and some luck. And after all that, they may still grow out of it in a year .... Given the number of new software titles that appear on store shelves every month, it is a bit daunting to go into a store or open a catalog and know what to buy. In general, your home software library should include a variety of programs (as your budget allows) in several main categories:

- Tools like a word processor (there are some very simple ones for even the youngest kids) and database or spreadsheet programs for older kids
- Creative programs like art, music, and card-making programs
- Academic programs that provide instruction and practice in areas like spelling or math
- Games that result in learning something like words, geography, or historical events (If you look around, you can find many that kids are motivated to play, but aren't the shoot-'em-up kind.)
- Simulation programs and other thinking-skill activity products (they involve kids in decision making, problem solving, anticipating outcomes)

Here are several solid ways to help you make your purchasing decision.

Find out what your kids are using at school. There may be a title that your child particularly enjoys or that the teachers think is great. This is a good opportunity to strengthen the home-school connection.

Talk to other parents. Someone may have done some research that can benefit you. Fellow parents can give you firsthand reports of what their kids are doing with products they have or why they like them. Recommendations from them about what not to buy can be helpful, too.

Subscribe to one of the many family-oriented periodicals with software reviews. New ones come on the newsstands every month (Another choice to make! See the Resources section for a few recommendations), and there are a bunch that specialize in home computing software. Reviews and articles are likely to talk about a range of issues like titles that are good for 5-year-olds but are also enjoyed by 2nd graders and safety tips for letting your kids use your home computer.

Make note of brand names that are usually good. When your kids have a really good time with a particular title, see what else the company makes.

Keep your eyes open for reviews. Software and multimedia reviews appear in lots of places: weekly news magazines, your daily newspaper, flyers that you pick up in a store, on the Internet, and on other online services.

What should I know about the World Wide Web?

To understand the World Wide Web (WWW), we need to start with the Internet, which is an immense linkage of computer networks all over the world. When it started in the 1950s, the Internet was used primarily by the government and universities to conduct and communicate research projects. It displayed only text (words, numbers, symbols) on-screen, and users had to type in commands to do anything. Since then, the Internet network of computers has expanded to include thousands of new users—business people, educators, and families like yours—and in ways that are extremely more friendly and easy to use.

Another major development in the Internet is the way in which you can see and use information on screen. You use one portion of the Internet—called the World Wide Web—by clicking on pictures and images rather than typing in words. Probably because of this ease of use, it is said to be the fastest growing part of the Internet.

Now, thanks to programs called Web browsers (perhaps you've heard of Netscape™ or Internet Explorer) you see screens that look like the colorful pages of a magazine, but besides text and images these pages also offer sounds and sometimes even video clips. Some of the graphics and text on these pages are highlighted. By clicking on highlighted items, you can jump to other places (sites) in the Web. (Think about the intricate arrangement of a spider's web and the name World Wide Web makes sense.) The first page of any Web site is called its home page—sort of like the contents page of a magazine. The home page usually contains a table of contents for the rest of the site.

Should I let my child have access to the Internet considering some of its bad press?

With some guidance, your child can use the Internet as a very beneficial tool. Our children live in a dynamic, video-oriented age; their daily worlds are filled with videotapes, music videos, cartoons, TV shows, and advertisements. The Internet can merge this video culture with traditional academic learning. Furthermore, it adds interactivity, which is not available in the passive surround of video and TV. To use the Internet, children have to get involved rather than just sit and watch. And their involvement can take place in the form of writing, critical thinking, math, conversation, or research—all with a level of excitement that you seldom see in other learning situations. In the same way that you monitor what TV your child watches (or where she goes or what she eats), you can

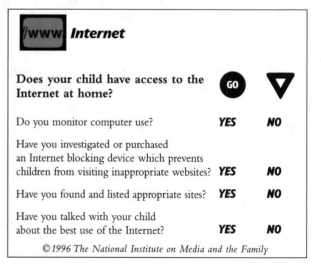

©1996 The National Institute on Media and the Family

set up guidelines for how and when your child uses your online service. You may also want to look into one of the many new software programs that allow you to restrict access to certain areas of the Internet.

What should I do about how much TV my child watches?

We can't ignore television. We all grew up with it and lived to tell the tale. But the degree to which TV can dominate the development of many children is much greater now than it was when there were fewer programs, channels, and TV sets in a home—and more scruples about what finds its way onto the screen. Sure, TV can be addictive and too many parents use it as a pacifier or baby-sitter, but it is also a powerful tool that can be turned to the advantage of valuable learning. Your challenge, as a parent, is to reduce the role of the television to one of educational support, supplemented with a small dash of recreation. Do not put a TV set in your child's room. Find some programs that are educational whether drama, science, history, the arts, or whatever. Watch *with* your child as often as possible and talk together about what you see. If you're not monitoring family TV viewing, your child may be spending too much time with TV. Show that you care about what and how your children learns by setting some serious goals (and examples), and follow through with them.

Should I regulate which TV shows or videos my child watches?

Yes, when possible—in much the same way that you make choices for her about what to eat, what books to read, and what language to use. Young children usually need clear guidance in the choices available to them and there are many lists available in print and online that provide guidelines for age-appropriate viewing. As they progress through elementary school, children can begin to make some of their own decisions well *if* you talk with them about what they are watching, what they think of it, and what alternative things might be as engaging for them as watching TV.

Here are some helpful ways to start such discussions. Ask for your child's ideas on:

- How to choose between two programs
  (If you could watch only *National Geographic* or *Friends,* but not both, which would you pick? Why?)
- How to distinguish between reality and fantasy programs
  (What did you think when the man jumped out of the window and didn't get hurt? What do you think would happen if someone you know tried it?)
- How commercials influence our behavior
  (Why do you want that toy, cereal, soda . . . ? Where did you hear about it? How do you know whether it is good or not or whether you would actually like it or not?)

- How to set a schedule for viewing
  (Let's pick some shows together for you to watch during your TV hour today. Let's figure out some fun things for you to do when TV time is over.)

THE PARENT-SCHOOL PARTNERSHIP

Forty years ago it would not have been unlikely for your 8th grade teacher to look you in the eye (in the way that only 8th grade teachers could) and say, "I remember when your father used to have the same trouble with square roots."

Today, such memories would be almost impossible. Teachers and students have become part of a highly mobile society. Everyone is on the move. Everyone is also working longer and longer, and two-paycheck families or single-parent families are common. Increased mobility and busier families mean extra strains on school and parent relationships, and this makes good communication between parents and teachers extremely important.

Should I worry about expecting too much of my child or when a teacher expects too little?

Children respond to their own expectations of what they can and cannot learn. If they believe they are able to learn something, whether solving equations or riding a bicycle, they usually make real headway. But when they lack confidence, learning eludes them. Children grow in self-confidence as they experience success in learning, just as they lose confidence in the face of repeated failure. Thus teachers and parents need to provide them with challenging but attainable learning tasks and help them experience success.

Research has shown that children's personal expectations are closely linked to what they perceive others think of them. Children, especially many girls, are quick to pick up the expectations of success or failure that others have for them. The positive and negative expectations shown by parents, counselors, principals, and peers affect students' expectations and hence their learning behavior.

In addition, we know that parents and teachers who expect a child to succeed tend to more effectively support that child's learning. If you suspect that your child's teacher has low expectations for her, address the problem head on before it becomes a self-fulfilling prophesy.

How can I make the most of parent-teacher conferences?

Preparation is the key to a good conference. Most teachers will have gathered up marks, thoughts, and examples of your child's work to bring to your conference. If you plan out beforehand what you want to ask about, you'll be able to get the most out of your meeting. Here are some suggestions:

- Ask your child if there is anything she wants you to talk over with her teacher.
- Think about what you want to cover and make a list of questions; then arrange them by putting the most important questions first.
- Check your list frequently during the conference so that if you and the teacher get sidetracked you can be sure to cover what is most important.
- Jot notes during the conference and then take a moment afterwards to fill in the notes enough so that you can follow up on comments and suggestions over the year.
- If there are problems, whether it's homework, classroom behavior, or social issues, ask for specific ways to help your child.
- After the conference, check back in with the teacher on a regular basis.

What can I do to support my child's teacher?

For starters, just keep in mind that teachers are people. We all tote around baggage left over from our own childhood as well as our present anxieties about our children. If feelings take over our relationship with a teacher, it's very hard to communicate anything.

It can be helpful to remember that teaching is an extremely demanding occupation and, considering the expectations we have of the profession, not a very well paid one (compare the starting salaries for the department of sanitation or public transport workers to those for teachers in your community). Classroom teachers are answerable to principals, superintendents, school boards, a large number of ever-changing parents, and their own desires to do the best they can for their students. In most schools, they work steadily, with few breaks and little opportunity to interact with other adults, and then they take work home with them in the evening.

So begin all interactions with a measure of patience. This doesn't mean you should not be firm and persistent, but you'll get off to a more productive start if you assume that you and your child's teacher have the same goal—to do what is best for your child.

Should I speak up if I disagree with how my child is being taught math, science, art . . . ?

Please do. Education is best conducted as a partnership between parents and schools. We rely on teachers to be skilled at running their classrooms and competent in their fields. That's a fair expectation. Teaching is a profession and most teachers, in addition to their regular work in school, take refresher courses, workshops, and pursue advanced degrees. Education, like other fields, changes, and new ways of presenting material, organizing classrooms, and evaluating students appear regularly. Sometimes these new ways of doing things baffle parents, particularly when they suddenly appear during a homework session at the kitchen table.

Teachers are usually eager to share what they have learned and what they are doing, so if you have questions about what kids are doing in the classroom, teachers are generally glad to meet with you and explain it. In the rare instance when a teacher is not performing up to the standards of the school system, it is important for you and other parents to speak up and work with the school administration to solve the problem.

Should I spend time finding out the details of our school's curriculum?

Absolutely. School conferences and open houses are times when you can ask questions about the specifics of classroom instruction as well as about the curriculum in general. If there isn't time to cover everything, ask your child's teacher for recommended books and periodicals. If enough parents are interested, a school may be willing to arrange an evening devoted to presenting information about curriculum specifics. If individual parents or parents working through a PTA or other parent-school organization offer to set up and arrange the meeting, they will probably be even more willing.

My child's teacher doesn't seem to like my child; what can I do?

Talk with your child's teacher. In almost all cases, and particularly with younger children, apparent slights or injured feelings are the result of misunderstandings. Most teachers have had years of experience with many children and families. They are happy to sift through the problems of communication to find ways to support your child and make him comfortable. In the rare case when a teacher has for some reason taken a dislike to your child, also begin by talking with the teacher. But don't be confrontational. The teacher who dislikes a child and acts upon it is behaving in an unprofessional way, even if unintentional. A gentle nudge may alert the teacher to an awareness of her actions, thereby prompting her to do whatever is necessary to correct the situation. If your effort is not successful, consult the principal, and then if necessary, talk with other parents.

Teachers here are big on "cooperative learning," but my child works best alone. What should I do?

It's a good idea at a parent-teacher conference to bring up any question like this that's troubling you and your child. It's true, there's a lot of emphasis today on cooperative projects that bring together students of varying abilities and skills. And it's also true that some kids—like yours—may be more comfortable with other approaches.

But before dismissing the idea of cooperative learning, take a look at what it's all about. One of the ideas behind cooperative learning is that it's good preparation for the real world, where interpersonal skills and teamwork are often required.

Genuine cooperative learning differs from traditional group projects, though, in the way it involves every member, not just the smartest kid or the strongest leader. The aim in cooperative learning is to develop youngsters' capacity for working as a real team. Most importantly, each member of the group is responsible for a specific part of the overall project or goal.

Those goals and ideals mean that cooperative learning may actually be a good experience for a kid like yours, who already knows how to work by herself (an equally valuable gift). At the same time, do bring this issue up at a conference. The teacher who is guiding the cooperative learning activity needs to keep such individual differences in mind when structuring the group and to keep watching for how each child participates and benefits.

SCHOOL SERVICES

It's part of every school's mandate to meet children's physical social and intellectual needs. Toward that end, school buildings are being modified for access by all mobility levels and are becoming increasingly equipped for a wider range of educational needs and activities. As budgets allow, school staff lists include both the core teachers and the specialists needed to meet students' group and individual needs.

What is Attention Deficit Disorder (ADD)?

Everyone can remember a few kids from their school years who never stayed in their seats, talked out of turn, threw spitballs, or turned in sloppy papers. And the teacher may have ignored them or sent them on an occasional trip to the principal's office. So what's all this recent fuss about kids who are hyperactive or have an attention problem? How is "hacking around a little" now considered a special need?

Well, we have a little more information to work with now. It is reported that approximately 3–5% of all American children—up to 3.5 million—have Attention Deficit Disorder. ADD is a neurologically based disability (that is, it has to do with the brain). Some researchers believe that ADD is due to altered brain biochemistry. Research has shown that the rate at which the brain uses glucose, its main energy source, is lower in persons with ADD—especially in the portions of the brain that are responsible for paying attention, handwriting, motor control, and inhibition responses.

Since the symptoms of ADD—among them being fidgety, talkative, bossy, and inattentive—are behaviors seen in most children at some point in their lives, the diagnosis and labeling of a child with ADD is often a subject of debate. Some kids who seem jumpy or act out now may simply grow out of it; others may need intervention to learn how to have more control. It is vitally important to put together a complete picture of a child's development and draw from many sources of information before rendering a diagnosis.

School is often where the characteristics of ADD may be more easily recorded, since the school setting requires the very skills that are difficult for kids with ADD—sustained attention to a task, waiting turns, and staying seated.

Making the Grade

A child suspected of having ADD should receive a comprehensive evaluation including medical, psychological, educational, and behavioral components.

Can I ask to meet separately with the special teachers who see my child?

This depends entirely on your local school system's policies and resources. Widespread reluctance to adequately fund education at both the local and national level means that the specialist teachers are frequently overburdened. Many are willing to work with parents, but they feel that their limited time is best spent with the children. If you have a special need, begin first with your child's regular teacher. She or he is in the best position to help get you the information you need. If this is not successful, consult with your school's principal.

How do I know if my child has a learning disability?

A big indicator is when you, as a parent, sense something is amiss. You may notice that your child, who generally seems smart, has no major physical problems, and does very well in some things, just can't cut it in some other basic areas. Your suspicions may be reinforced at parent-teacher conference time when you hear things like: "He's a good kid and does very well in math, but he doesn't apply himself, especially when it has to do with reading or following directions. He should be doing a lot better."

Putting a finger on a learning disability is tricky because there are as many combinations of problems as there are children who have them. But some familiar patterns can be identified. Basically, kids with a learning disability have trouble learning some things, but not all things. They may:

- Consume reading material like crazy, but not deal well with even simple social situations
- Be completely aware of current events and enjoy talking about them, but be completely frustrated by any attempt to put pen to paper
- Do academic subjects well but not be able to ever follow directions (especially oral ones) or do something that requires physical coordination

Success in school (and in life, for that matter) has to do with making sense of what we see and hear. Think of the brain as a big filing cabinet. If all the information is in neat files and in alphabetical order so we can get to it easily, then reading, writing, computing, and talking is generally pretty problem free. For kids with LD concerns, however, the information is there, but not neatly piled and alphabetized; it takes longer for these kids to figure some things out. One of the goals in providing them with special education services is to help them develop better information-processing skills.

The severity of an LD problem may seem to rise and fall over the years. That's usually because different classroom environments can either amplify what's hard for a child or support what he can do well. People don't generally grow out of a learning disability but rather learn to compensate for a weakness by focusing on the things they are very good at. (Lots of kids with learning disabilities even use their smarts to sidestep doing what's hard for them!)

It's definitely possible to be learning disabled and successful. Consider just a few famous examples: Winston Churchill, Albert Einstein, Beethoven, John F. Kennedy, Walt Disney, Whoopi Goldberg—there are lots more. With perseverance, they made it—so can your kid.

SCHOOL PROGRAMS AND CHOICES

It was simpler back then, wasn't it? Kids went to school and parents basically knew what was going on. Things were solid. It felt right. Now you overhear your kids' conversations, get flyers at home, read newspaper articles that talk about alternative classes and magnet schools. You can even choose to attend a school out of your neighborhood!

The school wants to put my daughter into the next higher grade. Is that a good idea?

Moving to a new community or changing schools can present this problem at least as often as having an especially bright child. Regardless of the reason, there are several factors to consider. One important one is your child's social and physical maturity—will it be obvious that she's younger? Might she be teased or bullied as a "baby" by her older and bigger classmates? Will she feel socially different or unprepared? Such problems could outweigh the benefits and cause lasting problems with social relationships.

On the other hand, if she's grown-up enough to fit in and deal with slightly older kids, it could be a good opportunity to challenge her intelligence and avoid her being bored by materials and skill lessons she may have already mastered. or learned in her old school.

What happens if my child works too far ahead of her class in some subjects? Will she be bored?

This can be a problem, particularly in classrooms that adhere closely to a standardized curriculum. When students have already accomplished the classroom goals, they are placed in a difficult position. Going over what they already know is boring, and they may either suffer in silence or get into trouble. Neither of these is a desirable alternative.

This doesn't mean that you should hold back on your child's academic development or that you shouldn't make an effort to extend her education. The best solution is to consult with your child's teacher. Together you can plan learning paths that supplement and extend the standard curriculum without overlapping what the whole class is doing together. Your child can forge ahead at her own pace, explore new material, and continue to be challenged. In the "What's More" sidebars with the Learning Adventure activities in this book, you will find sets of supplemental activities. These extend the skills practice or knowledge base of the activities and are an example of how a single learning activity can encompass a greater depth of learning.

Should I worry that there is less and less physical education in my daughter's school?

Yes, it should be a concern to all parents for two reasons. The most important is the physical well being of your child. Modern children lead increasingly sedentary lives, and this is probably related to the alarming increase in obesity throughout our country. C. Everett Koop, the former U.S. Surgeon General, and other health experts identify obesity as a major health problem and a contributing factor in a number of disease conditions ranging from diabetes to cancer. Removing any opportunity for movement and exercise should be protested by concerned parents. Try to enlist your local public health figures in efforts to maintain physical education programs.

The second (and more academic) reason is that children learn better when study time is broken up by the opportunity to move around and change environments. Japanese schools, often cited as models of intense academic pursuit by some educators, do have longer days and longer school years, but they also build in many more breaks for exercise, relaxation, and organized sports. All work (and sitting at a desk all day) does indeed make Jack a dull boy.

What is this America 2000 plan that people talk about?

The Goals 2000: Educate America Act was signed into law on March 31, 1994. This act serves as an outline for redefining our school systems in an attempt to ensure that all students are prepared for life in the twenty-first century. It targets areas that need to change, particularly in light of the developments in information processing and global connectivity. It talks about changing roles and expectations of teachers, functions of schools, and attitudes and behaviors of students. Here are the eight national goals. The actual document is over 200 pages long, so just highlights are included here:

1. School Readiness: By the year 2000, all children in America will start school ready to learn.
2. School Completion: By the year 2000, the high school graduation rate will increase to at least 90 percent.
3. Student Achievement and Citizenship: By the year 2000, all students will leave grades 4, 8, and 12 having demonstrated competency over challenging subject matter including English, mathematics, science, foreign languages, civics and government, economics, arts, history, and geography, and every school in America will ensure that all students learn to use their minds well, so they may be prepared for responsible citizenship, further learning, and productive employment in our nation's modern economy.
4. Teacher Education and Professional Development: By the year 2000, the Nation's teaching

force will have access to programs for the continued improvement of their professional skills and the opportunity to acquire the knowledge and skills needed to instruct and prepare all American students for the next century.

5. Mathematics and Science: By the year 2000, U. S. students will be first in the world in mathematics and science achievement.

6. Adult Literacy and Lifelong Learning: By the year 2000, every adult American will be literate and will possess the knowledge and skills necessary to compete in a global economy and exercise the rights and responsibilities of citizenship.

7. Safe, Disciplined, and Alcohol- and Drug-Free Schools: By the year 2000, every school in the United States will be free of drugs, violence, and the unauthorized presence of firearms and alcohol and will offer a disciplined environment conducive to learning.

8. Parental Participation: By the year 2000, every school will promote partnerships that will increase parental involvement and participation in promoting the social, emotional, and academic growth of children.

In the first two years of the plan, 46 states wrote school improvement plans and were granted Goals 2000 funds. Some states and communities are creating new schools—called charter schools—while others are revitalizing existing ones. Community participation in schools is a vital part of local reform efforts. If you are a parent who wants to make an impact in your school system, Goals 2000 may offer an opportunity for you. Check with your local school board to see what is happening in your area.

THE SOCIAL SIDE OF SCHOOL

School is a social setting and, like it or not, social issues play a large part in the success of the learning environment. It is a major challenge for us as parents to be aware of the moods and feelings of our children, and it's one of the challenges that gets more difficult as they mature. Sorting out the normal grumps and bumps from the unusual mood swings that signal a problem isn't easy, but it is important to keep checking. Most children, and probably yours, have days when they are reluctant to go to school, but have these suddenly increased? Has normal play outside of school diminished? Has your child's performance in school inexplicably dropped off? This is an area in which communication between you and your child's teacher will make a tremendous difference.

What should I do when my child is teased?

Differences in size or weight—even wearing glasses—can sometimes be cause for suffering among school children. Whatever the problem, your child needs you to be accepting of his feelings and to give him emotional support. At the same time, let him know that he is a strong and capable person. Bullying and teasing behavior comes from children who are bullied and teased themselves and, although they are the perpetrators rather than the victims, these children are also hurt by situations in which they act out unchecked. This information may not seem immediately helpful to your child, but it is useful to have. The point is not to minimize the emotional hurt your child receives, but to demystify the menace by putting it into perspective. Make contact with your child's teacher right away. A note or phone call will serve as an alert, and make an appointment to meet as soon as possible. Children can sometimes be cruel, but they can also be very supportive, and a good teacher who catches potentially hurtful situations in the early stages can turn them around. If you notice or hear of things going on before the school does, don't hesitate to speak up.

Should I worry that my kid, an only child, tends to be something of a loner?

Some of the world's most interesting and creative people have been loners. A lot depends on your definition of "loner." Is your kid simply self-reliant and self-sufficient, and good at being alone and entertaining herself? Many only children develop such valuable traits.

Since there are no other kids in your family, an only child may sometimes feel very much at home among adults. You can help her be more sociable with people her own age simply by facilitating visits to other kids' houses and having friends over. You also can encourage her to take part in activities with kids with similar interests.

On the other hand, some kids—and not just only children—seem to be loners to an extreme degree. If your kid is truly withdrawn and seriously moody or hostile, the situation probably demands stronger interest and intervention and some outside counseling.

TIME OUTSIDE OF SCHOOL

It has always been true that children receive a good share of their education outside of the schools. In fact, kids are always learning (aren't we all!), so it matters what they are learning during the majority of their time, which is spent away from school.

The quality and quantity of outside educational experiences is directly proportional to parental involvement. The more you put into it, the more they get out of it. Whether it's locating enrichment programs, supporting youth programs, doing a little teaching yourself, or just offering your support for your child's quest for knowledge, you make a tremendous difference.

I don't have much time or money to provide my child with after-school activities. Help!

You're not alone. Many parents have discovered that our schools have less and less to offer in the way of extracurricular activities. Even though they have less and less time, parents are having to do more and more. The Learning Adventure activities in this book have been designed for after-school fun with little or no cost to parents—so there's one place to start!

Other help is available. Established after-school or extended day programs, both commercial and community supported, are becoming more common. Shopping around isn't always possible, but if it is, look for programs that have a specific focus. Programs built around activity—whether it's sports, supplemental education, ethnic identity, the arts, or crafts—tend to be more stimulating and thoughtfully run, than those that are just places for kids to stay. But after-school centers simply designed for kids with nowhere else to go can include aspects of all such activities. And you can encourage these centers to offer more by making suggestions, helping think of places to visit, and the like.

Sometimes just beginning to look for opportunities for your child will help. As you look for programs and activities, people will suggest other resources and, more importantly, you will encounter other parents engaged in the same search. Connecting with other busy parents means you can share resources and information and pool your energy. Connecting can be as simple as talking about your search with other parents at the playground, church, or at a PTA meeting. A note on the local library bulletin board or a message in the school newsletter may be enough to organize other parents around a particular activity.

Is enrolling my child after school to learn our ethnic culture and language asking too much of her?

Being proud of one's heritage is an important component of every person's self esteem. Programs that support this are excellent supplements to regular schooling. Indeed, given the frequent cutbacks in school arts programs, these can be an important resource for your child's intellectual growth. The experience may even help her do well at school. Whether or not committing her time to such a program serves your child well depends entirely on your assessment of her abilities and needs.

Learning a second language is extremely valuable. Many of us forget how immigrants to North America, including those who've made major contributions on this continent, became bilingual and, not infrequently, trilingual. Having a second language and being intimate with another culture gives your child an educational advantage, particularly if it's also a source of pride.

What kinds of reference books should I get my child?

A quick answer: small ones! Thick atlases, massive encyclopedia sets, and other large reference books look impressive, but the old idea of encompassing all of human knowledge in an expensive shelf of books has gone out the window. Our body of knowledge continues to undergo rapid change (just look at the cartographic scramble when the Soviet Union came apart or the overnight shifts in thinking in the medical and biological sciences). Large atlases, encyclopedias, and other reference books themselves have changed, and most of them are available both at the library and electronically; many are capable of being rapidly and inexpensively updated on a regular basis.

Dictionaries, almanacs, field guides, and smaller reference books are a different story. These contain information that is more useful on a day-to-day basis, and they are inexpensive, portable, and worth buying. Besides, even if you have a computer-based encyclopedia program, you'll need something if the power goes off!

What books for kids does it make sense to buy?

Sometimes it seems like books for children are a little like their shoes, too expensive and too quickly outgrown. Most of us, however, have a cherished old book or two tucked away in the bottom of a box or bookcase. Good books are treasured—read and reread and worth the investment. That doesn't mean you have to buy every book that comes along. Use the school and public libraries to discover the particular books that will strike your child as wonderful. Read reviews of literature for children in newspapers and magazines. Check out lots of library books and encourage your child to participate in the selection. Not every one will be a hit; but over time, you will find books, authors, and subject matter that both suit and fascinate your child. This can be your guide to the occasional purchase.

If money is tight, think twice about spending money on fad toys. Toy makers and sellers spend vast sums on market research that, at its heart, only creates new ways to exploit children's gullibility and parental guilt. Stroll past any yard sale and add up the amazing amount of money that was spent on yesterday's gotta-have-it toy. And while you're there, check through the children's books—you may find some buys.

Birthdays and holidays are prime occasions for book buying. A gift list of books can add to your home library. Grandparents and relatives often ask for gift suggestions. If they don't, drop them a note with ideas before the holidays or birthdays roll around. This helps them with their gift buying and (sometimes) means you won't be getting that toy that you really don't want in the house! If you have a ready list of books, sharing it with others makes life easier.

How can I find good children's literature?

Check the Sunday papers around the winter holiday times. There are often articles or supplements that provide listings and reviews of what's new and recommended in children's literature. Cut these out and save them for future reference.

When you're in a library, wander around in the periodical section looking for articles on children's books in magazines for parents. Most libraries have bookmarks, pamphlets, or information from the American Library Association on their annual aware-winning books (ask for the Caldecott, Newberry, and Coretta Scott King awards). Periodicals as different as

Mothering and *The Scientific American* have book review sections that occasionally feature children's fiction and nonfiction books.

Subscribe to, or borrow from the library, children's story and special-interest magazines. Authors and illustrators usually do short pieces or excerpts from books for these periodicals. The magazines also make great bedtime reading for younger children, and you will find many authors whose style or subject matter appeals to your child. You can then go to the library together to search out this author's books.

How can I add to the educational resources in my home?

Start by being selfish. Think about what you would like to learn, and go for it. Even though we are constantly reminded by our children that they mimic us ("Where did you hear that, Sally?" "Dad said it when he dropped the microwave."), we forget that our children are modeling themselves on our good habits as well. Your enthusiasm for learning will be contagious.

First, recycle your own trash for craft and Learning Adventure activities—everything from egg cartons and milk jugs to shoe boxes and junk mail can be used for school and home educational projects.

Second, be a trash picker. You don't have to push a shopping cart down the street, but be alert to the value of other people's castoffs. We know a parent who scans the neighborhood on trash day. When a neighbor of his who coached a hockey team threw out an old goal net, our trash picker turned part of it into a climbing net hung from a tree branch, and part of it became a fantasy spider web for a child's school project on creepy crawlies. Somebody installing lots of carpet? Those long cardboard tubes can turn into alpenhorns, flag poles, and tunnels for rolling balls (and don't forget your hamster's love of tubes!). Some towns have a transfer station (today's incarnation of the town dump) where castoffs are set aside to look for new owners.

Be an advanced trash picker. A manufacturer of file folders and envelopes produces enormous amounts of cut ends and defects. These go straight to the shredder unless an alert parent or teacher gets there first, and the company is more than happy to get the good will that comes from giving away a treasure in paper. Offices are treasure troves of discarded memo and computer paper, envelopes, folders, and catalogs. The same is true for any small manufacturing concern that produces useful (to someone) waste material. Small electronic parts, metal stampings, bits of brightly colored plastic, and pieces of wood are all much better off as parts of collages, dioramas, and science or construction projects than they are as landfill.

How can I keep my child's education going during summer vacation?

Of course, you'll obviously find lots of great ideas in the Learning Adventure activities in this book! Once school is out, you can involve the whole family in some of them. Take time also to play board games such as Scrabble™ or Monopoly™ as a family. Monopoly, for example, is a subtle way of being sure your kid practices math skills as the banker or the rent-collecting proprietor of Atlantic Avenue and the Water Works. Scrabble challenges everyone's word knowledge.

When summer's here, you'll want to look at the outdoor resources in your community. Some city park systems or schools have summer programs that focus on nature study and the outdoors, augmenting your kid's science knowledge. Nature experiences are usually a part of camp life too. Summer projects can offer practice in both math and science. Carpentry projects, for instance, require careful measuring. Building a rabbit cage, remodeling projects, or redecorating involve measuring, figuring square footage, estimating costs, and other math challenges. To keep up your kid's interest in language arts, turn to your local library. It may have a summer reading program or, for younger children, story and reading hours. Look for free or low-cost summer theaters, which often present Shakespeare and other theater classics. Even without special programs, your kid can learn to revel in the summer joys of reading at the beach or in a hammock.

My child feels she's put down as "brainy." She worries she won't be popular if she seems smart. How can I help her?

First, by just listening. The first order of business is give your child the chance to let you know about the immediate hurt that she's experiencing. Your love, understanding, and basic trust in her as a person are communicated by being able to listen closely and carefully.

The years of early adolescence are a time of physical, intellectual, and emotional transition (and that's not to mention the social too!). Children at this age are often caught between relishing their newly developing abilities and wanting to blend into their peer group. For bright children, children who enjoy doing school work, or children gifted in some special way, this can be a rough time. They may be tempted to play dumb, they may try and avoid any situations where they will stand out.

Since this issue comes on top of the regular emotional see-saw that young adolescents ride, it is especially hard for parents to help. First you have to sort out the normal emotional bumps, then you have to figure out the facts of the situation, and finally you have to confront your own feelings because, let's be frank, we as parents are caught up in the same bind! We want our children to be outstanding, and we also want them to be relaxed, comfortable, and well liked among their peers.

Once you acknowledge that it is a difficult time for your kid, the next step is to provide honest information. Reading from books about development at this age can be useful, as well as frank and open discussions. Biographies of all kinds are a very important resource. Children, particularly bright ones, are not always too interested in their parent's experiences (no matter how relevant we may think they are), but they are curious about how other people grew up and will find that they are not alone in their struggles and feelings.

Some of the kids in my child's class are starting to date. I'm worried.

Welcome to the party! Your concern has been shared by parents from at least the days of Romeo and Juliet, and it probably caused anxiety around the cave campfires long ago. Many children at this age are not interested in dating at all, some are curious, and a few are wild to jump in. Setting limits (and sticking to them) will relieve the children in the first two categories and protect those in the third.

It's good for children in the middle school years to have lots of opportunities to socialize with members of the opposite sex. It is not so good, however, for them to engage in most kinds of dating. The uneven rates of physical development and the confused rush of new feelings experienced by middle schoolers make them poor candidates for the kinds of activity that steady (and out of the range of parents) dating implies. And frequently, attention spent on dating and its attendant issues diverts attention from school work and the pleasures to be gained in learning. Setting limits and expectations regarding social life is not easy, but it is necessary.

So, how do I set limits?

Clearly and with as much family discussion as needed. The good news is that children appreciate your firmness, although a decade may pass before you hear about that. While you're waiting for that appreciative word, there is a lot you and other parents can do. Arrange events that groups of children can enjoy together. Kids thrive in social activities of all kinds; youth functions through churches, synagogues, or mosques; festivals; dramatic presentations; community events, and play parties. Well supervised group activities, with spaces where the adult's can be nearby yet apart, give children the opportunity to move in and out of the social world, to mingle with friends, and explore relationships while they still have the safety of alert and caring grown-ups near at hand (which is really what they want).

Another area for social growth worth exploring is community service. Children at this age are putting their toes into the waters of the adult world for the first time. Movies, television, and, most of all, advertisements present a picture of adult life that consists largely of parties and sexually charged situations. Giving them opportunities to model real adult activity by participating in a food sharing program, working on a local campaign, or assisting in a charitable activity sponsored by a community or religious organization are wonderful ways to engage young people in positive group social situations.

I try to give supportive advice, but my child won't listen or tell me what's up. What can I do?

Keep trying, but gently. Seventh and eighth graders are exploring the world and, though they need and want a parent's support, they aren't always willing to say so. However, being there to back them up, offer advice (even if they don't wish to appear to need it), and provide emotional support is crucial. Not every child is like this, but if yours is, just remember that the yo-yo quality of early adolescence depends on having that string (still attached to you) to roll back up on.

CHAPTER 19

What Resources Should I Use?

Here's our nonexhaustive list of resources in print, on disc, and online. They cover various areas, including math, science, language arts, and parenting issues. A good starting place!

PARENTING

Books and Newsletters

Adolescence: The Survival Guide for Parents and Teenagers, by Elizabeth Fenwick and Dr. Tony Smith (New York: Dorling Kindersley, 1994). A guide for parents and teenagers covering such topics as sexuality, eating disorders, drugs, and suicide. Includes real-life case studies.

All Kinds of Minds, by Mel Levine (Cambridge and Toronto, Educational Publishing Service, 1993). A sympathetic, light-hearted, and extremely intelligent presentation of learning abilities, learning disorders, and other learning issues.

Beyond the Classroom: Why School Reform Has Failed and What Parents Need to Do, by Laurence Steinberg (New York: Simon & Schuster, 1996). Discusses authoritative parenting and the home environment, the power of peers, ethnicity, and more.

Child Safety on the Internet, by the Staff of Classroom Connect with Vince Distefano (Lancaster PA: Classroom Connect, Prentice Hall, 1997). A guide to protecting children from accessing inappropriate material on the Internet; includes "Kid Safe" Internet sites.

Education on the Internet: A Hands-On Book of Ideas, Resources, Projects, and Advice, by Jill H. Ellsworth (New York: Macmillan Publishing USA, 1996). A great way for parents to tune in to good material on the Net.

Helping Your Child Succeed in School: A Guide for Parents of 4 to 14 Year Olds, by Michael H. Popkin, et al. (Atlanta: Active Parenting Publishers, 1995). Fun, supportive, and creative ways to help your children learn, including working with the school system.

Parents' Choice
P.O. Box 185
Newton, MA 02168
(617) 965-5913
Quarterly newsletter that reviews books, toys, audiotapes, videotapes, catalogs and more.

Playing Smart: A Parent's Guide to Enriching, Offbeat Learning Activities for Ages 4–14, by Susan K. Perry (Minneapolis: Free Spirit Publishing, 1990). Hundreds of ideas for educating and entertaining kids while cultivating their creativity.

Positive Coaching: Building Character and Self-Esteem through Sports, by Jim Thompson (Portola Valley CA: Warde Publishers). Designed to be a helpful philosophical aid to all parents. Features 50 motivational stories that can be used to develop strong two-way communication.

Making the Grade

The Problem Solver: Activities for Learning Problem-Solving Strategies, by Shirley Hoogeboom and Judy Goodnow (Mountainview, CA: Creative Publications, 1987).

Quantum Learning, by Bobbi DePorter with Mike Hernacki (New York: Dell Publishing, 1992). Written for students, teachers, and parents, *Quantum Learning* helps students of all ages develop a personal learning style and a positive attitude toward learning new skills.

Stress Management and Self-Esteem Activities, by Patricia Rizzo Toner (Simon & Schuster/Center for Applied Research in Education). Ninety ready-to-use worksheets.

The Parents' Answer Book, by Gerald Deskin and Greg Steckler (Minneapolis: Fairview Press, 1995). User-friendly, comprehensive resource for child and adolescent development questions.

Why It's Great to Be a Girl: 50 Eye-Opening Things You Can Tell Your Daughter to Increase her Pride in Being Female, by Jacqueline Shannon (New York: Warner Books, 1994). The title says it all.

Catalogs

Active Parenting Publishers
810 Franklin Court, Suite B
Marietta, GA 30067
(800) 825-0060
Books, videos, games, and programs for workshops to help parents build academic success and overall parenting skills.

Fairview Press
2450 Riverside Avenue South
Minneapolis, MN 55454
(800) 544-8207
http://www.press.fairview.org
Fairview Press publishes books on a variety of family- and community-related issues.

Free Spirit Publishing
400 First Avenue North, suite 616
Minneapolis, MN 55401-1724
(800) 735-7323
Books, posters and products to build children's and teen's self-esteem, assist with homework, and help confront difficult topics.

National PTA Catalog
135 S. LaSalle St., Dept. 1860
Chicago, IL 60674-1860
http://www.pta.org
Resources for educators and parents on family involvement, child safety, and local PTA activities.

Internet Sites

Adolescence Directory On-Line
http://education.indiana.edu/cas/adol/adol.html
A guide to teen-related links, plus online support for teenagers, parents, and counselors.

Alt.parents-teens
news:alt.parents-teens
A newsgroup for parents of teenagers.

Association of Science-Technology Centers
http://www.astc.org/astc/
ASTC is a nonprofit organization of science centers and related institutions, including zoos, nature centers, aquaria, planetariums and space theaters, and natural history and children's museums. ASTC's membership includes nearly 400 science museums in 40 countries.

The Children's Literature Web Guide
http://www.ucalgary.ca/~dkbrown/index.html
Lists of juvenile bestsellers and great links.

Classroom Connect on the Net
http://www.classroom.net
Classroom Connect's Web site helps educators and students to locate and use the best K–12 educational resources the Internet has to offer. Includes its own search engine and a resource section.

Computer Curriculum Corporation
http://www.cccnet.com
A leading publisher of comprehensive curriculum-based educational software.

EdWeb Home Page
http://edweb.gsn.org
Find online educational resources around the world, learn about trends in education policy and information infrastructure development, and examine success stories of computers in the classroom.

ERIC—Educational Resources Information Center
http://www.accesseric.org
A vast clearinghouse of educational issues and links, plus a search engine.

Family Planet
http://family.go.com
An online magazine about education, legislation, health, and child-rearing issues, with advice and reviews of kids' products.

Global SchoolNet Foundation
http://www.gsn.org
Resources and links pertinent to integrating the Internet into K-12 classrooms
International Registry of K–12 Schools on the Web
http://web66.coled.umn.edu/schools.html
Links to school Web pages throughout the world.

National Center for Fathering
http://www.fathers.com
Resources for dads, including articles from *Today's Father* magazine, parenting tips, and humor.

National PTA
http://www.pta.org
The site for family involvement in education, for parents and educators.

Parent Soup
http://www.parentsoup.com
Online support and information on parenting, plus homework help.

Parenting Q&A
http://www.parenting-qa.com
A searchable database of parenting issues, with answers from experts in child development and behavior.

ParentsPlace.com
http://www.parentsplace.com/
A grab bag of information on parenting.

ParentTime
http://www.pathfinder.com/ParentTime/homepage/homepage.all.html
Chat and info on parenting, personalized for your child's age and interests.

HEALTH

Books

The Seventeen Guide to Sex and Your Body, by Sabrina Solin with Paula Elbirt (Simon & Schuster, 1996). Advice on serious topics in a hip, fun tone. Covers menstruation, birth control, eating disorders, HIV, and more.

STUDY AIDS

Software

Succeed in School
Kaplan Educational Centers
(800) KAP-ITEM
Mac and Windows CD
Learn how to organize and manage information, improve communication skills, improve reading speed and comprehension, and enhance your memory retention.

LANGUAGE ARTS

Books and Magazines

Totally Private and Personal: Journaling Ideas for Girls and Young Women, by Jessica Wilber (Minneapolis: Free Spirit Publishing., 1996). A 14-year-old writer gives an inside look at how keeping a journal can help young writers explore feelings and sort out issues pertinent to preteens and teens.

The 21st Century
Box 30
Newton, MA 02161
(617) 964-6800
http://www.teenpaper.org
Articles, stories, art, and interviews by and for teens around the United States.

The Young Person's Guide to Becoming a Writer, by Janet E. Grant (Minneapolis: Free Spirit Publishing, 1996). Tips for young writers on developing a personal writing style and getting work published.

Catalogs

Educational Software Catalog
Sanctuary Woods
2228 S. El Camino Real #223
San Mateo, CA 94403
(800) 943-3664
http://www.theatrix.com/index.html
A catalog of educational and entertaining language arts, social studies, math, science, and ESL software for kids of all ages.

Great Source Education Group
A Houghton Mifflin Company
181 Ballardvale Street
Wilmington, MA 01887
(800) 289-4490
http://www.greatsource.com
Intended for in-school use but handy for home-based learning as well, this catalog includes language arts and mathematics for students grades K–12.

Simon & Schuster Children's Publishing Division
(800) 223-2336
http://www.simonandschuster.com

Software

Alien Tales
Broderbund
(800) 521-6263
Mac and Windows CD
Zap extraterrestrials while you read passages from 30 classic books, answer questions and solve puzzles.

The 21st Century
Box 30
Newton, MA 02161
(617) 964-6800
http://www.teenpaper.org
Articles, stories, art, and interviews by and for teens around the United States.

Student Writing and Research Center
The Learning Company
(800) 852-2255
Windows CD
Everything you need to create reports or research papers: a full-featured word processor, plus *Compton's Concise Encyclopedia*.

Ultimate Writing and Creativity Center
The Learning Company
(800) 852-2255
Mac and Windows CD
A word processing program that teaches kids to write; includes online help for every step of the writing process, plus dictionary, thesaurus, and multimedia presentation theater.

Internet Sites

Complete Works of William Shakespeare
http://the-tech.mit.edu/Shakespeare
The place to find all of Shakespeare's plays and prose, as well as quotations, annotations, and definitions.

Cool Word of the Day Page
http://www.edu.yorku.ca/wotd/
A site to help students expand their vocabulary, or just have fun with words.

CyberKids
http://www.cyberkids.com
A quarterly online 'zine by and for kids ages 7–16.

KidZone
http://www.mckinley.com
Magellan's kids' site has lots and lots of great book-related links—explore!

The Human Languages Page
http://www.june29.com/HLP/
Dictionaries and sound files for more than 500 languages.

Yahooligans!
http://www.yahooligans.com
Yahoo's kids' directory, with lots of reading and language arts links.

MATH

Books

A Zebra Named Al, by Wendy Isdell (Minneapolis: Free Spirit Publishing, 1993). An adventure written by an 8th grader, designed to teach math basics in a fun and friendly way.

How Math Works, by Carol Vorderman (Pleasantville, NY: Reader's Digest, 1996). Subtitled *100 Ways Parents and Kids Can Share the Wonders of Mathematics,* this book contains activities intended to bring math to life.

Manipulatives

Algebra Lab Gear
Creative Publications
Mountainview, CA 94041
(415) 988-1000
Great for home use with 7th and 8th graders. A variety of plastic blocks that represent equation variables, spatial relationships, functions such as multiplication, etc., bring equations to life. Instruction book included in a three-ring binder. Catalog item #33340.

Holey Cards
3817 No. Pulaski
Chicago, Il 60641
(312) 588-5761
Kids have two minutes to get math questions right. Use the cards over and over again until the two-minute goal is reached. Multiplication, subtraction, and addition cards available.

Catalogs

Creative Publications
5623 W. 115th Street
Worth, IL 60482-9931
(800) 357-MATH
Books, manipulatives, and teacher resources to help teach everything from counting to algebra.

Educational Software Catalog
Sanctuary Woods
2228 S. El Camino Real #223
San Mateo, CA 94403
(800) 943-3664
http://www.sanctuary.com
A catalog of educational and entertaining language arts, social studies, math, science, and ESL software for kids of all ages.

Educational Toys and Games Catalog
American Educational Products Inc.
401 Hickory Street, P.O. Box 2121
Fort Collins, CO 80522

This supplier of educational toys and games for schools offers math and science products for parents and children to use at home.

Great Source Education Group
A Houghton Mifflin Company
181 Ballardvale Street
Wilmington, MA 01887
(800) 289-4490
http://www.greatsource.com
Intended for in-school use but useful for home-based learning as well, this catalog includes language arts and mathematics materials—workouts, games, and study plans—for students grades K-12.

MPH Catalog
P.O. Box 1125
Fairfield, CT 06432
Deck of 52 cards, all marked differently from 1 to 25. Fun card games for learning addition, subtraction, division, and multiplication.

Simon & Schuster Children's Publishing Division
(800) 223-2336
http://www.simonandschuster.com

Software

Geometry Blaster
Davidson & Associates
(800) 545-7677
Mac, Windows, and Windows 95 CD
Save Zoid's homeland from turning from 3-D to 2-D, and learn geometry in the process.

Major League Math
Sanctuary Woods
(800) 943-3664
Mac and Windows
Fun way to learn math via baseball.

Math Heads
Theatrix
(800) 955-8749
Mac and Windows CD
Kids act as contestants and create videos in games about fractions, decimals, percentages, and prealgebra, hosted by silly characters.

Making the Grade

Mystery Math Island
Lawrence Productions
(800) 421-4157
Mac and Windows
Teaches math skills in the form of a treasure hunt.

Internet Sites

Dr. Math
http://forum.swarthmore.edu/dr.math/dr-math.html
Swarthmore College math students act as "math doctors" and answer students' math questions from all over the world. E-mailed questions and answers are gathered into an archive, organized by grade level and topic. Includes search function.

The Math Forum
http://forum.swarthmore.edu
This site covers simple and advanced mathematics, offering help to both students and teachers.

Mathematics Resource Page
http://www.deakin.edu.au
Math links for teachers and students

Mega Mathematics
http://www.c3.lanl.gov/mega-math/welcome.html
Advanced mathematical concepts are explained here for elementary school children.

SAMI: Science and Math Initiatives
http://www.learner.org/k12/sami
A clearinghouse of information for science and math teachers, but appropriate for home learning as well.

SCIENCE

Books and Magazines

The Chemy Called Al, by Wendy Isdell (Minneapolis: Free Spirit Publishing, 1996). Challenging science basics are presented in an imaginative story; includes companion teacher's guide.

Girls and Young Women Inventing: 20 True Stories About Inventors Plus How You Can Be One Yourself, by Frances A. Karnes and Suzanne M. Bean (Minneapolis: Free Spirit Publishing, 1995). Inspiration for girls who love science and inventing.

National Geographic WORLD
National Geographic Society
(800) 647-5463
A monthly magazine containing the lush photos you'd expect from *National Geographic,* plus projects and facts.

Zero to Einstein in 60, by B. K. Hixson (Salt Lake City: The Wild Goose Company, 1989). Billed as "60 experiments guaranteed to cure science nincompoopitis," this fun book contains experiments for teachers and parents of children 8 and up.

Catalogs

Dacta
The Educational Division of the LEGO Group
555 Taylor Road
Enfield, CT 06083-1600
(800) 527-8339
http://www.lego.com/learn
Science, technology, and math kits for constructing simple machines, gears, levers, etcetera, out of LEGOs.

Educational Software Catalog
Sanctuary Woods
2228 S. El Camino Real #223
San Mateo, CA 94403
(800) 943-3664
http://www.sanctuary.com
A catalog of educational and entertaining language arts, social studies, math, science, and ESL software for kids of all ages.

Educational Toys and Games Catalog
American Educational Products Inc.
401 Hickory Street, P.O. Box 2121
Fort Collins, CO 80522
(800) 466-8767
This supplier of educational toys and games for schools now offers math and science products for parents and children to use at home.

MindWare
2720 Patton Road
Roseville, MN 55113
(800) 999-0398
A catalog that contains puzzles, games, and books intended to "tap the other 90 percent of your brain," MindWare products help kids and parents develop math, science, and reasoning skills.

Simon & Schuster Children's Publishing Division
(800) 223-2336
http://www.simonandschuster.com

The Wild Goose Co.
375 Whitney Avenue
Salt Lake City, UT 84115
(800) 373-1498
Kits, books, and science equipment and accessories for teachers and students for wacky and fun science experiments. Includes the *Newton's Apple* Science Kit series.

Software

Dr. Sulfur's Night Lab
McGraw-Hill Home Interactive
(800) 937-4663
Mac and Windows 95 CD
A virtual 3-D chemistry set lets kids conduct volatile experiments without destroying the house.

Inventor Labs
Houghton Mifflin Interactive
(800) 829-7962
Mac and Windows CD
Try experiments and check out machines in the labs of Thomas Edison, Alexander Bell, and James Watt.

Invention Studio
Discovery Channel Multimedia
(800) 678-3343
Mac and Windows CD
Develop your own invention in a 3-D lab, then test in real-world conditions.

Redshift 2
Maris Multimedia
(800) 526-2947
Mac and Windows CD
A virtual planetarium lets students view stars and planets from any location in the solar system.

The Way Things Work 2.0
DK Multimedia
(800) 356-6575
Mac and Windows CD
Based on the bestselling book, this multimedia disc of inventions and inventors includes an online link to *mammoth.net*, a site for young inventors.

Internet Sites

Animals Around the World
http://www.chicojr.chico.k12.ca.us/staff/gray/animals.html
A resource on every species of animal, with loads of links.

Ask An Expert
http://njnie.dl.stevenstech.edu/curriculum/aska.html
Send your science, technology, or math questions to these experts.

KidZone
http://www.mckinley.com
Magellan's kids' site has lots and lots of great science links—explore!

Liberty Science Center
http://www.lsc.org/
Homepage of one of the niftiest science museums around.

National Park Service
http://www.nps.gov
Explore the United States' national parks through pictures, maps, and lots of info.

New Scientist's Planet Science
http://www.newscientist.com/
Why don't penguins' feet freeze? How do mushrooms push their way up through cement? Why do banana skins turn brown faster in the refrigerator than at room temperature? The answers to these and other questions at this terrific magazines' site.

OER—Online Educational Resources
http://quest.arc.nasa.gov/oer/
Collection of links to many science-related educational sites, including: the "Star Child" page of K–12 astrophysics images/text; NASA K–12 Internet Project Home Page; "Virtually Hawaii" K–12 remote sensing data project; and ASU/NASA K–12 Mars program, among others.

Science Hobbyist
www.eskimo.com/~billb/
Cool science, weird science, amateur science: a fun page with experiments and lots of links.

Making the Grade

The Society for Amateur Scientists
http://www.thesphere.com/sas/
A nonprofit research and educational organization that helps people to follow their passion to take part in scientific adventures of all kinds.

The Why Files
http://whyfiles.news.wisc.edu/
Answers to all your science questions.

Yahooligans!
http://www.yahooligans.com
Yahoo's kids' directory, with lots of science links.

About

KAPLAN

Educational Centers

Kaplan Educational Centers is one of the nation's leading providers of premier education and career services. Kaplan is a wholly owned subsidiary of The Washington Post Company.

TEST PREPARATION & ADMISSIONS

Kaplan's nationally recognized test prep courses cover more than 20 standardized tests, including secondary school, college and graduate school entrance exams and foreign language and professional licensing exams. In addition, Kaplan offers private tutoring and comprehensive, one-to-one admissions and application advice for students applying to graduate programs. Kaplan also provides information and guidance on the financial aid process.

SCORE! EDUCATIONAL CENTERS

SCORE! after-school learning centers help K-8 students build confidence, academic and goal-setting skills in a motivating, sports-oriented environment. Its cutting-edge, interactive curriculum continually assesses and adapts to each child's academic needs and learning style. Enthusiastic Academic Coaches serve as positive role models, creating a high-energy atmosphere where learning is exciting and fun. SCORE! Prep provides in-home, one-on-one tutoring for high school academic subjects and standardized tests.

KAPLAN LEARNING SERVICES

Kaplan Learning Services provides customized assessment, education and professional development programs to K-12 schools and universities.

KAPLAN INTERNATIONAL PROGRAMS

Kaplan services international students and professionals in the U.S. through a series of intensive English language and test preparation programs. These programs are offered at Kaplan City Centers and four new campus-based centers in California, Washington and New York via Kaplan/LCP International Institute. Kaplan and Kaplan/LCP offer specialized services to sponsors including placement at top American universities, fellowship management, academic monitoring and reporting, and financial administration.

KAPLAN PUBLISHING

Kaplan Publishing produces books, software and online services. Kaplan Books, a joint imprint with Simon & Schuster, publishes titles in test preparation, admissions, education, career development and life skills; Kaplan and Newsweek jointly publish guides on getting into college, finding the right career, and helping your child succeed in school. Through an alliance with Knowledge Adventure, Kaplan publishes educational software for the K-12 retail and school markets.

KAPLAN PROFESSIONAL

Kaplan Professional provides recruitment and training services for corporate clients and individuals seeking to advance their careers. Member units include Kaplan Professional Career Services, the largest career fair provider in North America; Perfect Access/CRN, which delivers software education and consultation for law firms and businesses; HireSystems, which provides web-based hiring solutions; and Kaplan Professional Call Center Services, a total provider of services for the call center industry.

DISTANCE LEARNING DIVISION

Kaplan's distance learning programs include Concord School of Law, the nation's first online law school; and National Institute of Paralegal Arts and Sciences, a leading provider of degrees and certificates in paralegal studies and legal nurse consulting.

COMMUNITY OUTREACH

Kaplan provides educational resources to thousands of financially disadvantaged students annually, working closely with educational institutions, not-for-profit groups, government agencies and other grass roots organizations on a variety of national and local support programs. Kaplan enriches local communities by employing high school, college and graduate students, creating valuable work experiences for vast numbers of young people each year.

Want more information about our services, products, or the nearest Kaplan center?

1 **Call our nationwide toll-free numbers:**

1-800-KAP-TEST for information on our live courses, private tutoring and admissions consulting
1-800-KAP-ITEM for information on our products
1-888-KAP-LOAN* for information on student loans

(outside the U.S.A., call **1-212-262-4980**)

2 **Connect with us in cyberspace:**

On AOL, keyword:"Kaplan"
On the World Wide Web, go to: **http://www.kaplan.com**
Via e-mail: info@kaplan.com

3 **Write to:**

Kaplan Educational Centers
888 Seventh Avenue
New York, NY 10106

The Home Learning Quizzes

Your child learns in a unique way. In fact, all children vary greatly in learning style, level of maturity, individual personality, and how they learn on any given day. This is why single standardized tests

administered across a grade level are not always accurate indicators of what academic skills your child has mastered. What these tests can indicate are possible problem areas or concepts that your child may need further practice to understand and material your child has not yet been introduced to in school.

YOUR CHILD'S QUIZZES

As a bonus, we've added our pull-out *Making the Grade* Kids' Home Learning Quizzes (the last eight pages of this section) to help you and your child locate possible problem areas or gaps in learning in language arts, math, and science. The questions cover material which your child may have encountered in 7th and 8th grade. Each quiz starts with 7th grade work and progresses to 8th grade items (an equal number from each grade level).

After your child quizzes herself, use the grade- and subject-specific Learning Adventure activities in *Making the Grade* to help her practice and hone skills in particular subjects. The quizzes are not meant to serve as definitive tests of your child's intelligence or an indication of subject mastery; they only serve as a supplement to the Learning Adventure activities to help you and your child spend more time on specific activities that correspond to problem areas or brand new material. Keep the home learning focus on having fun and "serving the learning in welcome helpings"; never pressure your child to "score high" or "learn on command."

YOUR QUIZ

The first eight pages of this section are for parents only. They contain your *Making the Grade* Parents' Home Learning Quiz, explanations for the quiz, and the answer key for the kids' quizzes. Taking the parents' quiz will help you identify possible gaps in your own knowledge and awareness of your child's growth and educational development. Like the subject-specific quizzes for your child, the parents' assessment is not an all-encompassing evaluation of your parenting or home education skills; just take the assessment to acquaint yourself with the latest educational and development issues. As on the kids' quizzes, there is no emphasis on how you score. Approach it as just another chance to discover something new or reinforce previous knowledge.

USING THE QUIZZES

Your Parents' Home Learning Quiz is self-explanatory. Take it on your own, at your convenience. It's a little more complicated with the Kids' Home Learning Quizzes, but you can be sure that there is no right way for your child to take them. Take all the quizzes in a row, or take one quiz one day and save the others for different occasions. Your child can quiz himself—like taking a fun activity break with *BrainQuest*™—or you and your child can take the quizzes together for an exercise in finding out how much you both know about 7th and 8th grade subjects. Photocopy his pull-out quiz pages and time each section. Compare notes and answers when you finish.

Making the Grade

Have your child use a pencil to fill in the answer ovals and make scratch-note calculations; provide an eraser to change answers. Also discuss the purpose of the last two answer ovals. One oval (e) will indicate to both of you that a question covers skills your child hasn't learned in school yet; your child can mark this oval without selecting an answer (there's no point taking time to guess). The last oval, choice (f), signals that a certain question covers previously learned material that is still difficult for your child; this can be marked along with one of the answer choices to the question.

Here are some specific ideas for sitting down with your child after taking the quizzes:

- Praise your child's correct answers on the quizzes, and have him show you how he made his calculations or worked through the steps that led to the correct answer.

- If your child chose an incorrect answer and didn't indicate that the material was difficult, go through the answer with him and try to clear up any confusion with the skills covered. An appropriate Learning Adventure activity can clarify skills and reinforce learning.

- If your child scored correctly and indicated difficulty with the material, celebrate the correct answer and bolster your child's confidence! Perhaps your child is ready to tackle new material in a particular subject matter; use a Learning Adventure activity to introduce the new skills in an informal, enjoyable way.

- If your child indicates that a question covers new material not yet taught in school, you have the future option of introducing the new skills through a Learning Adventure activity—if and when your child is ready and open to the new material.

- You might want to review the quizzes with your child's teacher to verify the responses, learn when new skills will be covered, and develop a plan of action to help your child bolster weaknesses and fill in learning gaps.

USING THE LEARNING ADVENTURE ACTIVITIES

Work with your child on the Learning Adventure activities in this book. Pace the flow of activities from day to day and week to week. Never push the learning, but, instead, develop a natural pacing that meets your schedule and reinforces your belief in fostering learning at home. As you do these activities with your child, observe her progress. On-the-spot observations of a specific activity might even tell you more about what's really going on than the quizzes. You will be giving your child the individual attention, support, and encouragement that enhances any learning activity.

Build a picture of your child's learning style. Everyone learns in a unique way. Determine your child's learning style(s) by noting what goes on as she works on an activity. Does she learn more easily by reading the material or by listening to you as you direct the activity? Does she become more enthusiastic when drawing and performing other hands-on activities? Noting these subtleties can help you better suit the activities to your child's strength, as well as work on the weaker learning styles.

Assess what your child knows. Evaluation does not depend on tests alone. Observe your child working on an activity and assess how well he understands and handles information. Are there basic concepts that he needs to work on? In a math activity, does your child grasp the main idea but have trouble with the process, the basic math calculations? Does he write creatively but have trouble with quotation marks and punctuation? It's not necessary to grade the work or point out the deficiencies; just use these notes to select the activities, resources, and ways of supporting your child that will build competence and confidence.

LEARNING FROM THE QUIZZES AND ACTIVITIES

The *Making the Grade* Parents' Home Learning Quiz concludes with evaluations and suggestions to help you become even more knowledgeable and aware of your child's education and development. In addition, be aware of just three simple guidelines—Be Alert,

Be Patient, and Be Positive—to establish a successful learning environment in your home.

Be Alert There was once a master of the martial art t'ai chi who was so adept, a sparrow landing on his upraised arm was unable to fly off. The art of this master was neither speed nor strength, it was awareness. He was so alert that as soon as the sparrow crouched to take flight, he sensed it and lowered his arm just enough to interrupt the sparrow's upward spring. The goal of education is, of course, just the opposite. We want to encourage the upward spring of our young sparrows.

The technique, however, is the same. Being alert at the end of a long day is easier than you think. Being alert is really only enhanced relaxation. Just remind yourself, once in a while, to relax and be open to your child.

Watch for subtle cues. Children communicate with their bodies. Closely watch your child at work. Is she slouched over or poised and energetic, calm or fidgety, morose or happy? Is she easily distracted or attentive? Facial expressions and tone of voice are also key clues.

Allow for emotional needs. Some children tell their parents what is going well and what isn't, but many won't. Sometimes your child's issues surface at home in ways that have nothing to do with your home life. Tensions surrounding your child's friends and school often surface indirectly at home. Emotions will probably spring to the surface during some of the activities.

Tears may erupt over a broken pencil tip, or a sulk develop over a misunderstood word in a reading assignment. These reactions may often be much stronger than the situation warrants. Don't let these moments defeat either of you. Children generally feel safer about showing their feelings to their parents than they do to their teachers. They feel safer at home, and it's good that they do, but it sometimes makes your job a little harder. The trick, and it works most of the time, is to accept the feelings, acknowledge the hurt, and weather the emotional release. And weather is the key word. The storm passes, the sun comes out, and then, in most cases, you'll be able to move on. For the times when this doesn't work, heed the advice of the Kenny Rogers song, "know when to hold 'em and know when to fold 'em." There will always be another time to try a Learning Adventure activity.

Note lack of interest. Your child may show signs of boredom, whether physical or verbal. These are important to watch for, but they can be ambiguous. Boredom can mean a task is too hard; it can be your child's way of reacting to an activity that asks too much. But boredom can also mean that an activity is too easy. Figure out what your child is really communicating; don't react to the sometimes irritating signs of boredom itself.

Note signs of interest. One child's enthusiasm may be communicated with an exuberant, "Look at these earthworms!" Another may react with increased concentration and silence as she focuses on a task that excites her. Indications of interest are just as important as signs of boredom in helping you determine where to go next, whether or not to repeat an activity or move on to harder skills, etc.

Be Patient We all feel the pressure to achieve. It's there and it's real, but it doesn't belong in home learning situations. Communicating this pressure to children while they're engaged in academic work usually doesn't do much for the learning process. This doesn't mean that hard work and the desire to successfully learn something aren't important. They certainly are. However, external tensions, particularly those brought in from the adult world, can interfere with learning. The more you can relax and be your child's guide and supporter, the more successful you both will be.

Adjust to your child. Take your time doing the activities and pace yourself to allow your child to take his time. Each of us has our own style and pace for learning. Adjust the rate to which you start new activities to your child's natural pace. Remember that there are day-to-day events such as head colds, late evenings the night before, or the anticipation of birthday parties that affect your child's concentration and energy. Longer-range maturational changes also alter behavior and ability. Read (or browse through again) the essay on development in Section One.

Making the Grade

Focus on individual learning tasks. Enjoy each moment of learning with your child and don't worry about what is next or where it's all headed. The Learning Adventure activities are meant to function as building blocks. Each activity should give your child a taste of success—which you can both celebrate!

Be patient with yourself. No teacher or parent gets it right every time. Learn from any mistake, and don't let it derail you. You care enough to spend time on your child's education, so give yourself a pat on the back—and then figure out what to do differently next time.

Be Positive Each step in learning is important and deserves praise. The old "ruler on the knuckles" technique produced children who couldn't wait to get out of school. Help your child get the most out of staying in school and develop a lifetime love of learning.

Positive doesn't always equal fun. Some things are just plain old hard work. For some children, mastering the frustratingly inconsistent spelling of English is a chore. Others find it difficult to calculate sets of math facts such as the times tables. Effortless spelling and ease of computation will come, but the process is sometimes hard going. You can acknowledge this truth and yet regard the work in a positive light. The rewards are real. As different skills are mastered successfully, hard work and practice will pay off.

Use praise that works for both of you. Although children need positive reinforcement, they are able to see through transparent praise. Kids are the best spotters of what is phony. Specific praise for achievements, on the other hand, always works. Statements like, "You did that math problem very well," and "That graph explains things so that I can understand," are more useful than a general pat on the head because they tell your child that you have paid attention to just what she has done. If things aren't going well, that problem also needs to be acknowledged and, just like the praise, put in concrete terms. Focus on the positive (even in the problem) and draw upon that to tackle what might not be going well.

SIMON SAYS

Some recommended books for 7th and 8th graders:

SCIENCE
The Day the Sky Split Apart by Roy A. Gallant
Water: Almost Enough for Everyone by Stephanie Ocko
Your Brain: How You Got It and How It Works by Tabitha Powledge
"We Have Conquered Pain:" The Discovery of Anesthesia by Dennis Brindell Fradin

WRITING
Tears of a Tiger by Sharon Draper
Poetspeak: In Their Work, About Their Work by Paul B. Janeczko
Louisa May: The World and Works of Louisa May Alcott by Norma Johnston

READING
Tiger Eyes by Judy Blume
Abigail Adams: Witness to a Revolution by Natalie S. Bober
The White Mountains (The Tripods Trilogy) by John Christopher
Mary Wolf by Cynthia D. Grant
Hatchet by Gary Paulsen

These books can be found at your local bookstore or from Simon & Schuster Children's Publishing Division at (800) 223-2336. For a catalog of titles write: Simon and Schuster, Children's Marketing, 1230 Avenue of the Americas, New York, NY 10020.

Parents' Home Learning Quiz

How much do you know right now about your child's growth and educational development? Test your knowledge and awareness.

Directions: Mark Y (yes) or N (no) for each statement below, as it applies to you.

ⓨⓝ **(a)** I praise my child—even for small achievements.

ⓨⓝ **(b)** Doing well on weekly assignments is fine, but I think my child's test scores and grades are what really count.

ⓨⓝ **(c)** I talk to my child about school at least twice a week.

ⓨⓝ **(d)** I meet with my child's teacher(s) fewer than three times a year.

ⓨⓝ **(e)** I do not feel adequately prepared to help my child with homework.

ⓨⓝ **(f)** I attend my child's school-related programs most of the time.

ⓨⓝ **(g)** My child watches more than three hours of television per day.

ⓨⓝ **(h)** If my teenager came home one night after the agreed-upon curfew, I'd find out the reason and emphasize that next time, a phone call would be appropriate.

ⓨⓝ **(i)** If I learned my child was doing poorly in a particular subject at school, I'd handle the problem myself rather than going through school channels.

ⓨⓝ **(j)** I believe that my child's problems at school can be readily detected at home.

ⓨⓝ **(k)** I could easily describe my child's performance in school.

ⓨⓝ **(l)** I sometimes feel guilty about not providing more enriching experiences for my child.

ⓨⓝ **(m)** There have been incidents involving violence, harassment, or drug use at my child's school.

ⓨⓝ **(n)** I am a single parent.

Making the Grade

Explanations: Parents' Home Learning Quiz

That was relatively painless! Here's an explanation of the Yes and No responses for each statement:

(a) *I praise my child—even for small achievements.* If you chose *yes,* good for you! Even acknowledging small hurdles and achievements helps your child maintain a positive attitude about learning. Try coming up with creative, fun expressions of pride and celebration instead of giving him gifts or monetary rewards. A special meal you plan and cook together, an outing, going to the movies, playing one-on-one sports, or just hanging out together are rewards your child will appreciate. Spending some private time together works well, especially in families with several children.

(b) *Doing well on weekly assignments is fine, but I think my child's test scores and grades are what really count.* If you said *yes* to this statement, you're half right (the first part is positive). If your child practices solid learning skills and study habits, the good scores and grades will come in due course, and she will develop excellent skills for a lifetime of learning. Use test scores and grades as feedback to help your family focus on successes and problem areas, but also give your child praise for plugging away on those weekly assignments. Emphasizing the whole learning process is the right message to send to your child.

(c) *I talk to my child about school at least twice a week.* Great, if this applies to you! It's important that parents make their interest in education clear to their children. This is especially necessary given a recent survey by Dr. Laurence Steinberg, co-author of *Beyond the Classroom: Why School Reform Has Failed and What Parents Need to Do* (Simon & Schuster, 1996), which found that 72 percent of students aged ten to thirteen said they would prefer to talk more often to their parents about their homework, while only 40 percent of parents believe they are not attentive enough to their children's education. This discrepancy suggests that children would open up more about school-related issues or difficulties if they were given the opportunity to do so by their parents.

(d) *I meet my child's teacher(s) fewer than three times a year.* Meeting with your child's teachers has more educational value than you may be aware of. By offering insights about your child's home life and social habits, you help the teacher gain a fuller understanding of your child. You are also conveying to the teacher your interest in your child's education, and your willingness to collaborate to further his learning progress.

(e) *I do not feel adequately prepared to help my child with homework.* Even if you said *yes* to this, there are many ways to support your child's education, and all of them require only your energy and enthusiasm for learning. If you have a little time and willingness, you can use your feelings of inadequacy as motivation to learn with your child and test your skills together. In doing so, you'll be teaching your child an important lesson: Don't hesitate to undertake something that you may not do well. As a fellow student, you'll also be more sympathetic to your child's struggles, and he will appreciate the interest and attention. If time and other responsibilities do not allow for these sessions, you can still serve as your child's cheering section and keep in touch with his teacher.

(f) *I attend my child's school-related programs most of the time.* If you answered *yes* to this, good! Parents who attend school functions—extracurricular activities, teacher conferences, and "back to school" nights—are indicating that school is important to them and that, by extension, it should be equally important to their children. When parents don't get involved in some capacity with their child's activities, intended or not, they're sending a strong message that they're not interested. Make the time; your effort will not go unnoticed by your child.

(g) *My child watches more than three hours of television per day.* Educators generally agree that watching too much television can affect a child's emotional makeup. Without supervision, children will be disturbed by particular types of programs or news pieces, depending on their maturity level. TV is also a passive activity. Monitor your child's viewing habits. Watch TV with your child and carefully screen programs. Some TV shows have sound information and entertainment content, but offer more active ways to spend free time with the family (like after-school or community-based programs).

(h) *If my teenager came home one night after the agreed-upon curfew, I'd find out the reason and emphasize that* *next time, a phone call would be appropriate.* Excellent. Responsibility leads to maturity, and maturity makes a world of difference in a child. Mature children are self-confident, autonomous, persistent, and more likely to achieve the goals they set for themselves than children who rely on others to make and enforce rules and goals for them. You and your child are on a good track.

(i) *If I learned my child was doing poorly in a particular subject at school, I'd handle the problem myself rather than going through school channels.* The problem with trying to tackle these difficulties at home is that most children are taught subjects differently from how their parents learned, and this can make helping out more difficult. When a child doesn't understand a concept or a parent's explanation of it, no amount of increased study time is going to help. Try meeting with teachers and counselors and discussing ways in which the school can help. You do your child the service of getting involved in her education, and you do teachers and counselors a service by conveying that you have faith in their abilities. Set up an appointment with a teacher or counselor. Discuss how they can better serve your child, and offer your assistance. Exploring other strategies . . .

Punishment You could punish your child for his lack of diligence, but that doesn't mean that your child's performance will improve. In reality, punishment may help a child understand how important schoolwork is to his parents, but it will not help the child understand the material itself. Instead of alienating the child through punishment, parents should try to affect the learning process itself by getting involved, speaking and collaborating with teachers to isolate problem areas, and supporting their child's efforts.

Doing nothing You've never heard of your child having such problems before, so you're content to just let the kid tackle it on her own. Be careful! There are any number of reasons why your child's performance decreased: learning problems, increased social calendars, needing reading glasses, drug abuse, or emotional trauma (to name a few). Observe your child for indications of change, and arrange to speak with teachers.

(j) *I believe that my child's problems at school can be readily detected at home.* Parenthood is probably the most difficult job—you deal with every aspect of your child, including emotions that are either revealed or hidden. You can't expect yourself to know everything your child is feeling, thinking, and experiencing. What you can do is observe your child and pick up on warning signs. Look for changes, and discuss them openly and calmly. Your child may not know how to approach you with difficulties she may be experiencing, so reassure her of your love and support. Emphasize that if she has done something wrong or been hurt or confused, you want to know about it regardless of how it will make you feel.

(k) *I could easily describe my child's performance in school.* Good job if you said *yes* to this one! The concern that enough parents don't demonstrate an interest in their child's performance in school is warranted. According to a study published by Dr. Laurence Steinberg, co-author of *Beyond the Classroom: Why School Reform Has Failed and What Parents Need to Do* (Simon & Schuster, 1996), nearly one-third of students believe their parents have no idea how they're doing in school, one-sixth don't think their parents care whether they earn good grades in school, and more than half say they could bring home grades of C or worse without upsetting their parents. Regardless of whether these assessments pertain to you and your child, the fact that so many students believe them is an indication that both parents and children need to break some communication barriers.

(l) *I sometimes feel guilty about not providing more enriching experiences for my child.* Parents often feel guilty when they can't afford to spend enough money on their children's needs or take the time necessary to do all the things they'd like with their children. Instead of pressuring yourself, investigate the variety of quality, inexpensive opportunities offered in your community, namely after-school and community-based programs in art, music, dance, and sports. By encouraging your child to participate in these activities, you can engage him in worthwhile, rewarding experiences without having to expend energy or money that you don't have. Consider letting your child know that your family must prioritize purchases; by comfortably discussing your financial situation, you stand a better chance of raising a child who is more conscious of and responsible about money matters.

Making the Grade

(m) *There have been incidents involving violence, harassment, or drug use at my child's school.* It's sad if you had to answer *yes* to this statement. There's really no way to shield your child from being aware of these incidents, but you can stop your child from experiencing them directly by stunting their innocent curiosity with cold hard facts. If you need to get informed yourself, check out the resources listed in the back of *Making the Grade,* or check out your local library. Don't wait for schools to teach your child about these issues. Schools may address them, but schools are not administrators of social service—they are administrators of curriculum-based education. A parent is the only reliable resource a child has on these and other developmental issues. Please make yourself available!

(n) *I am a single parent.* Single parenthood can prove to be an extremely hectic lifestyle. Time is a rare commodity, and single parents find they must budget it wisely just to complete day-to-day responsibilities. Under these circumstances, you may not be able to spend as much time with your child as you would like. But even two-parent families experience time crunches and hectic lifestyles. Whether you're a single parent or not, allow your child to handle some of the responsibilities, preferably those that could be finished faster with two individuals. This way, you and your child can talk and bond while you work. Hopefully, handing over some of the responsibilities will also free up some time that you can spend with your child in more entertaining and educational activities. Try preparing in advance so you can attend meetings with your child's teachers and school programs in which your child is participating. And don't feel guilty for putting your child to work; by letting your child help you out, you're actually teaching good values and responsibility. Success at school and success at home—that's what "making the grade" is all about!

FOR PARENTS ONLY: ANSWERS TO THE KIDS' HOME LEARNING QUIZZES

Language Arts

1. (c)	11. (c)
2. (c)	12. (b)
3. (a)	13. (d)
4. (a)	14. (c)
5. (c)	15. (a)
6. (b)	16. (b)
7. (d)	17. (a)
8. (a)	18. (c)
9. (b)	19. (b)
10. (a)	

Math

1. (d)	14. (a)
2. (b)	15. (d)
3. (d)	16. (a)
4. (a)	17. (c)
5. (c)	18. (b)
6. (b)	19. (c)
7. (a)	20. (b)
8. (d)	21. (b)
9. (b)	22. (c)
10. (a)	23. (d)
11. (c)	24. (b)
12. (d)	25. (a)
13. (b)	

Science

1. (b)	9. (a)
2. (d)	10. (b)
3. (c)	11. (d)
4. (a)	12. (c)
5. (d)	13. (b)
6. (b)	14. (c)
7. (c)	15. (d)
8. (d)	16. (b)

Kids' Home Learning Quizzes

Language Arts See how many questions you can get right! Follow the directions for each question. Read everything carefully before filling in one answer oval. Fill in the (e) oval if you haven't been taught something in the question. Fill in the (f) if you've learned this already in school, but it's still pretty hard for you.

1. Which sentence is an example of a compound sentence?
   - (a) Francis Ford Coppola directed the film *Apocalypse Now.*
   - (b) He directed *The Godfather,* which became one of the biggest money-making films of all time, and its sequel, *The Godfather Part II,* which raked in seven Academy Awards.
   - (c) Coppola spent his early years working on B-movie horror films, but he became popular after winning an Academy Award for best screenplay for the 1969 film, *Patton.*
   - (d) Depending on your perspective, he could be called one of the greatest filmmakers of all time.
   - (e) We haven't studied this in school yet.
   - (f) We've studied this, but it's still hard for me.
     - ⓐ ⓑ ⓒ ⓓ ⓔ ⓕ

2. Which sentence does not contain an adverb?
   - (a) Sara modestly bowed at the curtain call.
   - (b) She had been very nervous about her performance.
   - (c) Her fears were unwarranted.
   - (d) Her acting was absolutely error free.
   - (e) We haven't studied this in school yet.
   - (f) We've studied this, but it's still hard for me.
     - ⓐ ⓑ ⓒ ⓓ ⓔ ⓕ

3. Which sentence uses a verb in the passive voice?
   - (a) A glove had been left in Mrs. Johnson's room.
   - (b) The next day, Mrs. Johnson told everyone about it.
   - (c) "The owner of the glove can reclaim it after class," she said.
   - (d) Danny stopped by her desk before leaving and got his glove back.
   - (e) We haven't studied this in school yet.
   - (f) We've studied this, but it's still hard for me.
     - ⓐ ⓑ ⓒ ⓓ ⓔ ⓕ

4. Which is an example of a past progressive verb?
   - (a) I was talking to Hannah.
   - (b) We decided to take a walk.
   - (c) Hannah's mom had taken us out for lunch.
   - (d) We were really full.
   - (e) We haven't studied this in school yet.
   - (f) We've studied this, but it's still hard for me.
     - ⓐ ⓑ ⓒ ⓓ ⓔ ⓕ

5. Which is a run-on sentence?
   - (a) Jazz trumpeter Miles Davis was a musical pioneer.
   - (b) Widely admired by his contemporaries.
   - (c) He created "cool jazz," in the 1960s he fused jazz and rock.
   - (d) contributing his own albums, like *Birth of the Cool* and *Sketches of Spain.*
   - (e) We haven't studied this in school yet.
   - (f) We've studied this, but it's still hard for me.
     - ⓐ ⓑ ⓒ ⓓ ⓔ ⓕ

6. Which sentence does not use homophones correctly?
   - (a) You're going to the play with me tonight.
   - (b) I don't know if I should. Its getting late.
   - (c) There's going to be quite a production.
   - (d) I'll go because you're trying hard to persuade me.
   - (e) We haven't studied this in school yet.
   - (f) We've studied this, but it's still hard for me.
     - ⓐ ⓑ ⓒ ⓓ ⓔ ⓕ

7. Which sentence uses the underlined word correctly?
   - (a) It was <u>real</u> hot and balmy outside.
   - (b) The sun had a blinding <u>affect</u> on my eyes.
   - (c) I wasn't feeling very <u>good</u>.
   - (d) I went to my room and <u>lay</u> down.
   - (e) We haven't studied this in school yet.
   - (f) We've studied this, but it's still hard for me.

   ⓐ ⓑ ⓒ ⓓ ⓔ ⓕ

8. Which sentence uses correct punctuation and capitalization?
   - (a) Gary bought some bread on his way home; his wife loved having bread with dinner.
   - (b) At 8:00 P.M., the President began his speech, it was televised nationally.
   - (c) Dad forgot his keys in the Car (that's the second time this month!) so he asked mom to bring him his spare set.
   - (d) George Pataki is currently the governor of the State of New york.
   - (e) We haven't studied this in school yet.
   - (f) We've studied this, but it's still hard for me.

   ⓐ ⓑ ⓒ ⓓ ⓔ ⓕ

9. The roots *astro* and *aster,* found in words like *astronomy, asterisk, asteroid,* and *disaster,* most likely mean _____.
   - (a) rock
   - (b) star
   - (c) pen
   - (d) between
   - (e) We haven't studied this in school yet.
   - (f) We've studied this, but it's still hard for me.

   ⓐ ⓑ ⓒ ⓓ ⓔ ⓕ

10. Which of the following could be the theme of a work of literature?
   - (a) Love has no boundaries.
   - (b) Catherine's sister is about to be married.
   - (c) As it turned out, the butler was the villain.
   - (d) It was a dark and stormy night.
   - (e) We haven't studied this in school yet.
   - (f) We've studied this, but it's still hard for me.

   ⓐ ⓑ ⓒ ⓓ ⓔ ⓕ

11. Which of the following could introduce the setting of a work of literature?
   - (a) Holcomb was the mayor of the town, a rosy-cheeked, robust fellow who carried his cane with a distinctive swagger.
   - (b) A human being utterly overcome by obsession makes a frightful sight.
   - (c) The windows on the house were as dark as eyes filled with sleep.
   - (d) The doctor's grave eyes betrayed his calm countenance.
   - (e) We haven't studied this in school yet.
   - (f) We've studied this, but it's still hard for me.

   ⓐ ⓑ ⓒ ⓓ ⓔ ⓕ

12. "The child's face revealed a lamblike innocence" utilizes which figure of speech?
   - (a) repetition
   - (b) simile
   - (c) irony
   - (d) metaphor
   - (e) We haven't studied this in school yet.
   - (f) We've studied this, but it's still hard for me.

13. In which literary genre does a biography of Princess Diana belong?
   - (a) contemporary fiction
   - (b) folklore
   - (c) Victorian literature
   - (d) nonfiction
   - (e) We haven't studied this in school yet.
   - (f) We've studied this, but it's still hard for me.

   ⓐ ⓑ ⓒ ⓓ ⓔ ⓕ

Questions 14–16: Read the paragraph below and select the best answer to each question.

(1) The English king, Richard III, was a tyrannical ogre, an evil man whose veins must have held poison instead of blood. (2) In addition to killing his brother, Clarence, and his nephew, Edward V, Richard committed a number of other horrendous, manipulative crimes en route to the throne. (3) It is hard to believe that he actually distinguished himself in the Wars of the Roses, that is, the civil wars in England between the houses of Lancaster and York. (4) Fortunately, Henry, Earl of Richmond, raised a rebellion in which Richard III was killed.

14. Based on the tone and content of this passage, how would you characterize the narrator?
    (a) The narrator is allied with Richard III's enemies.
    (b) The narrator is well versed in English history.
    (c) The narrator is extremely critical of Richard III.
    (d) The narrator writes clearly and without bias.
(e) We haven't studied this in school yet.
(f) We've studied this, but it's still hard for me.
ⓐ ⓑ ⓒ ⓓ ⓔ ⓕ

15. Which sentence contains an exaggeration?
    (a) 1
    (b) 2
    (c) 3
    (d) 4
(e) We haven't studied this in school yet.
(f) We've studied this, but it's still hard for me.
ⓐ ⓑ ⓒ ⓓ ⓔ ⓕ

16. Which sentence contains an overly general statement?
    (a) 1
    (b) 2
    (c) 3
    (d) 4
(e) We haven't studied this in school yet.
(f) We've studied this, but it's still hard for me.
ⓐ ⓑ ⓒ ⓓ ⓔ ⓕ

Questions 17–19: Use the following encyclopedia entries to select the best answer for each question.

fable A story with a moral, either in verse or prose, in which animals or inanimate objects think and speak like human beings. Some famous writers of fables include Aesop, Phaedrus, and La Fontaine.

falsificationism In the philosophy of science, the belief that a scientific theory must be proved again and again and subjected to constant scrutiny in order to have merit.

Fates In Greek mythology, the three female spinners, Clotho, Lachesis, and Atropos, who determined the llength of human life.

Faulkner, William 1897–1962 U.S. novelist who was awarded the Nobel Prize for Literature in 1949 and is often considered the greatest American writer of the 20th century. He primarily wrote in a stream-of-consciousness style, and his major works include *The Sound and the Fury, As I Lay Dying, Light in August,* and *The Unvanquished.*

17. If you were doing a report about a story in which a dog convinces a boy to forgive his parents, which entry would be of interest to you?
    (a) fable
    (b) falsificationism
    (c) Fates
    (d) Faulkner
(e) We haven't studied this in school yet.
(f) We've studied this, but it's still hard for me.
ⓐ ⓑ ⓒ ⓓ ⓔ ⓕ

18. The entry for falsificationism would be instrumental for someone who was _____.
    (a) studying Pavlov's theories on conditioning and experiments with dogs
    (b) using repetition as a literary device in an original poem
    (c) writing an essay about the different beliefs concerning scientific theory
    (d) none of the above
(e) We haven't studied this in school yet.
(f) We've studied this, but it's still hard for me.
ⓐ ⓑ ⓒ ⓓ ⓔ ⓕ

19. Someone who was studying Greek mythology might be interested in reading _____.
    (a) some of Faulkner's works
    (b) about Fates
    (c) a few of Aesop's fables
    (d) none of the above
(e) We haven't studied this in school yet.
(f) We've studied this, but it's still hard for me.
ⓐ ⓑ ⓒ ⓓ ⓔ ⓕ

You're done! Now look up the answers and see how many questions you got right.

Making the Grade

Math See how many questions you can get right! Follow the directions for each question. Read everything carefully before filling in one answer oval. Fill in the (e) oval if you haven't been taught something in the question. Fill in the (f) if you've learned this already in school, but it's still pretty hard for you.

1. Which of the following is not a rational number?
    (a) 483/23
    (b) $\sqrt{241,964}$
    (c) −1
    (d) π
   (e) We haven't studied this in school yet.
   (f) We've studied this, but it's still hard for me.
   ⓐ ⓑ ⓒ ⓓ ⓔ ⓕ

2. Which of the following is not a real number?
    (a) 0
    (b) $\sqrt{2}$
    (c) π
    (d) $\sqrt{361}$
   (e) We haven't studied this in school yet.
   (f) We've studied this, but it's still hard for me.
   ⓐ ⓑ ⓒ ⓓ ⓔ ⓕ

3. $23^0 = $ _____
    (a) −23
    (b) 0
    (c) 23
    (d) 1
   (e) We haven't studied this in school yet.
   (f) We've studied this, but it's still hard for me.
   ⓐ ⓑ ⓒ ⓓ ⓔ ⓕ

4. $0^{-21} = $ _____
    (a) 0
    (b) 1
    (c) −21
    (d) −1
   (e) We haven't studied this in school yet.
   (f) We've studied this, but it's still hard for me.
   ⓐ ⓑ ⓒ ⓓ ⓔ ⓕ

5. $1.1 \times 10^{-14} = $ _____
    (a) 110,000,000,000,000
    (b) −110,000,000,000,000
    (c) .000000000000011
    (d) −.000000000000011
   (e) We haven't studied this in school yet.
   (f) We've studied this, but it's still hard for me.
   ⓐ ⓑ ⓒ ⓓ ⓔ ⓕ

6. $|-21| = $ _____
    (a) 11
    (b) 21
    (c) − 11
    (d) −121
   (e) We haven't studied this in school yet.
   (f) We've studied this, but it's still hard for me.
   ⓐ ⓑ ⓒ ⓓ ⓔ ⓕ

7. $16.17 \times 4.59 = $ _____
    (a) 74.2203
    (b) 7322.03
    (c) 7422.03
    (d) 73.2203
   (e) We haven't studied this in school yet.
   (f) We've studied this, but it's still hard for me.
   ⓐ ⓑ ⓒ ⓓ ⓔ ⓕ

Questions 8–9: Use the following display to determine the best answer to each question.

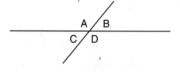

8. Which of the above angles are vertical angles?
    (a) A and B
    (b) B and D
    (c) A and C
    (d) A and D
   (e) We haven't studied this in school yet.
   (f) We've studied this, but it's still hard for me.
   ⓐ ⓑ ⓒ ⓓ ⓔ ⓕ

9. If $\angle B = 43°$, then $D = $ _____
    (a) 47°
    (b) 137°
    (c) 43°
    (d) 317°
   (e) We haven't studied this in school yet.
   (f) We've studied this, but it's still hard for me.
   ⓐ ⓑ ⓒ ⓓ ⓔ ⓕ

Questions 10–11: Use the following display to determine the best answer to each question.

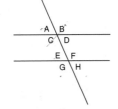

10. Which of the following are corresponding angles?
    (a) *B* and *F*
    (b) *C* and *E*
    (c) *D* and *G*
    (d) *A* and *G*
(e) We haven't studied this in school yet.
(f) We've studied this, but it's still hard for me.
ⓐ ⓑ ⓒ ⓓ ⓔ ⓕ

11. ∠*D* and ∠*E* are examples of _____.
    (a) alternate exterior angles
    (b) adjacent angles
    (c) alternate interior angles
    (d) nonadjacent exterior angles
(e) We haven't studied this in school yet.
(f) We've studied this, but it's still hard for me.
ⓐ ⓑ ⓒ ⓓ ⓔ ⓕ

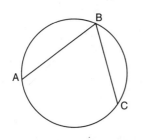

12. ∠*ABC* is _____.
    (a) an alternate interior angle
    (b) a transversal
    (c) an interior angle
    (d) an inscribed angle
(e) We haven't studied this in school yet.
(f) We've studied this, but it's still hard for me.
ⓐ ⓑ ⓒ ⓓ ⓔ ⓕ

13. Which of the following is true?
    (a) An equilateral triangle is one in which two sides are the same length.
    (b) A scalene triangle is one whose sides have different lengths.
    (c) An isosceles triangle is one in which all three sides have the same length.
    (d) all of the above
(e) We haven't studied this in school yet.
(f) We've studied this, but it's still hard for me.
ⓐ ⓑ ⓒ ⓓ ⓔ ⓕ

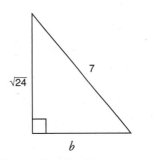

14. According to the triangle measurements, what must side *b* equal?
    (a) 5
    (b) 25
    (c) 5
    (d) 1
(e) We haven't studied this in school yet.
(f) We've studied this, but it's still hard for me.
ⓐ ⓑ ⓒ ⓓ ⓔ ⓕ

15. If a sphere's radius is 2 centimeters, what is its surface area?
    (a) 4π cm^2
    (b) 6π cm^2
    (c) 8π cm^2
    (d) 16π cm^2
(e) We haven't studied this in school yet.
(f) We've studied this, but it's still hard for me.
ⓐ ⓑ ⓒ ⓓ ⓔ ⓕ

16. Beverly spends 20% of her salary on her car payment and 40% on rent for her apartment. If she pays $450 a month on her car, how much of her salary does she have left after making car and rent payments each month?
    (a) $900
    (b) $1,350
    (c) $450
    (d) $1,800
(e) We haven't studied this in school yet.
(f) We've studied this, but it's still hard for me.
ⓐ ⓑ ⓒ ⓓ ⓔ ⓕ

Making the Grade

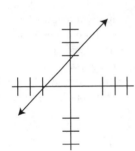

(5,7)

17. The graph displays which of the following equations?
    (a) $y = x - 1$
    (b) $1 = x - y$
    (c) $x = y - 1$
    (d) $x = y + 1$
    (e) We haven't studied this in school yet.
    (f) We've studied this, but it's still hard for me.
    ⓐ ⓑ ⓒ ⓓ ⓔ ⓕ

18. 5! = _____
    (a)   5
    (b)   120
    (c)   15
    (d)   25
    (e) We haven't studied this in school yet.
    (f) We've studied this, but it's still hard for me.
    ⓐ ⓑ ⓒ ⓓ ⓔ ⓕ

19. If $-19x - 4 \leq 61$, then which of the following is true?
    (a) $x \leq -3$
    (b) $x \leq 3$
    (c) $x \geq -3$
    (d) $x \geq 3$
    (e) We haven't studied this in school yet.
    (f) We've studied this, but it's still hard for me.
    ⓐ ⓑ ⓒ ⓓ ⓔ ⓕ

20. What is the next number in the following sequence?
    $3, 2, 5/3, 3/2, 7/5, 4/3, \_\_$
    (a) 3/7
    (b) 9/7
    (c) 5/7
    (d) 6/7
    (e) We haven't studied this in school yet.
    (f) We've studied this, but it's still hard for me.
    ⓐ ⓑ ⓒ ⓓ ⓔ ⓕ

21. What is the next number in the following sequence?
    $-1, 0, 1/3, 1/2, 3/5, 2/3, 5/7, \_\_$
    (a) 7/9
    (b) 3/4
    (c) 1
    (d) 6/7
    (e) We haven't studied this in school yet.
    (f) We've studied this, but it's still hard for me.
    ⓐ ⓑ ⓒ ⓓ ⓔ ⓕ

22. If $x^2 + 5x - 98 = 6$, then $x = \_\_$.
    (a) -4
    (b) 4/5
    (c) 8
    (d) $-.254$
    (e) We haven't studied this in school yet.
    (f) We've studied this, but it's still hard for me.
    ⓐ ⓑ ⓒ ⓓ ⓔ ⓕ

23. If $x = 2y + 5$ in the equation $y = 5x + 15$, then $y = \_\_$.
    (a) -2
    (b)   4/5
    (c)   2
    (d) -4
    (e) We haven't studied this in school yet.
    (f) We've studied this, but it's still hard for me.
    ⓐ ⓑ ⓒ ⓓ ⓔ ⓕ

24. $\{1, 2, 6, 7, 8\} \cup \{1, 3, 5, 7, 9\}$ is _____.
    (a) 1
    (b) $\{1, 2, 3, 5, 6, 7, 8, 9\}$
    (c) $\{2, 5, 11, 14, 17\}$
    (d) $\{1 + 2 + 3 + 5 + 6 + 7 + 8 + 9\}$
    (e) We haven't studied this in school yet.
    (f) We've studied this, but it's still hard for me.
    ⓐ ⓑ ⓒ ⓓ ⓔ ⓕ

25. What is the intersection of the two sets $\{1, 2, 6, 7, 8\}$ and $\{1, 3, 5, 7, 9\}$?
    (a) $\{1, 7\}$
    (b) $\{1, 2, 3, 5, 6, 7, 8, 9\}$
    (c) $(5, 6)$
    (d) $\{2, 5, 11, 14, 17\}$
    (e) We haven't studied this in school yet.
    (f) We've studied this, but it's still hard for me.
    ⓐ ⓑ ⓒ ⓓ ⓔ ⓕ

You're done! Now look up the answers and see how many questions you got right.

Science See how many questions you can get right! Follow the directions for each question. Read everything carefully before filling in one answer oval. Fill in the (e) oval if you haven't been taught something in the question. Fill in the (f) if you've learned this already in school, but it's still pretty hard for you.

1.   A gene is _____.
   (a) the process by which animals digest food
   (b) the part of a cell that controls hereditary traits
   (c) any animal that a parasite lives off of
   (d) a taxonomic classification
(e) We haven't studied this in school yet.
(f) We've studied this, but it's still hard for me.
   ⓐ ⓑ ⓒ ⓓ ⓔ ⓕ

2.   When a car cruises down a road, which of the following energy transfers takes place?
   (a) kinetic energy to nuclear energy
   (b) electrical energy to nuclear energy
   (c) heat energy to nuclear energy
   (d) potential energy to kinetic energy
(e) We haven't studied this in school yet.
(f) We've studied this, but it's still hard for me.
   ⓐ ⓑ ⓒ ⓓ ⓔ ⓕ

3.   Kinetic energy is _____.
   (a) the energy that powers nuclear plants
   (b) the energy that lights lamps
   (c) the energy of motion
   (d) the energy stored in an object
(e) We haven't studied this in school yet.
(f) We've studied this, but it's still hard for me.
   ⓐ ⓑ ⓒ ⓓ ⓔ ⓕ

4.   Which of the following is a true statement about energy?
   (a) Energy is never lost.
   (b) Energy never changes form.
   (c) Energy only comes from the sun.
   (d) Energy doesn't make rain fall.
(e) We haven't studied this in school yet.
(f) We've studied this, but it's still hard for me.
   ⓐ ⓑ ⓒ ⓓ ⓔ ⓕ

5.   Which of the following is not a conductor of heat?
   (a) silver
   (b) wood
   (c) water
   (d) rubber
(e) We haven't studied this in school yet.
(f) We've studied this, but it's still hard for me.
   ⓐ ⓑ ⓒ ⓓ ⓔ ⓕ

6.   Which of the following is not a true statement?
   (a) Every object exerts a force of attraction on every other object.
   (b) Inertia is the tendency of an object to succumb to changes in motion.
   (c) Heat is not the same as temperature.
   (d) A magnet is what makes a compass always point north.
(e) We haven't studied this in school yet.
(f) We've studied this, but it's still hard for me.
   ⓐ ⓑ ⓒ ⓓ ⓔ ⓕ

7.   Acceleration is _____.
   (a) a change in a moving object's direction
   (b) an equal and opposite force
   (c) a change in the motion of an object
   (d) an unbalanced force in action
(e) We haven't studied this in school yet.
(f) We've studied this, but it's still hard for me.
   ⓐ ⓑ ⓒ ⓓ ⓔ ⓕ

8.   What holds the earth and planets in their orbits?
   (a) electromagnetic energy
   (b) the earth's gravity
   (c) centripetal force
   (d) the Sun's gravity
(e) We haven't studied this in school yet.
(f) We've studied this, but it's still hard for me.
   ⓐ ⓑ ⓒ ⓓ ⓔ ⓕ

Making the Grade

9. What distinguishes Saturn from the other planets in the solar system?
    (a) It is encircled by rings made up of dust, rocks, and ice.
    (b) Recent findings indicate that it could have supported forms of life thousands of years ago.
    (c) It has no moon.
    (d) Its mass is more than twice the mass of all the other planets combined.
(e) We haven't studied this in school yet.
(f) We've studied this, but it's still hard for me.
ⓐ ⓑ ⓒ ⓓ ⓔ ⓕ

10. What causes seasons?
    (a) global warming
    (b) the tilt of the earth's axis
    (c) the phases of the moon
    (d) all of the above
(e) We haven't studied this in school yet.
(f) We've studied this, but it's still hard for me.
ⓐ ⓑ ⓒ ⓓ ⓔ ⓕ

11. Which of the following could cause climate change?
    (a) meteors
    (b) volcanic eruptions
    (c) the direction of an ocean current
    (d) all of the above
(e) We haven't studied this in school yet.
(f) We've studied this, but it's still hard for me.
ⓐ ⓑ ⓒ ⓓ ⓔ ⓕ

12. The smallest unit of an element that still has all the properties of the element is called _____.
    (a) a proton
    (b) a neutron
    (c) an atom
    (d) an electron
(e) We haven't studied this in school yet.
(f) We've studied this, but it's still hard for me.
ⓐ ⓑ ⓒ ⓓ ⓔ ⓕ

13. A molecule is _____.
    (a) an atomic classification
    (b) the basic unit of a compound
    (c) a metallic characteristic
    (d) an element with a proton, neutron, and electron

(e) We haven't studied this in school yet.
(f) We've studied this, but it's still hard for me.
ⓐ ⓑ ⓒ ⓓ ⓔ ⓕ

14. Which of the following is not a true statement?
    (a) Changing the volume of a gas changes its pressure and temperature.
    (b) Water is the compound of one oxygen atom and two atoms of hydrogen.
    (c) At warmer temperatures, atoms and molecules move slower.
    (d) No atoms are created or lost if they are in a reaction that takes place in a closed system.
(e) We haven't studied this in school yet.
(f) We've studied this, but it's still hard for me.
ⓐ ⓑ ⓒ ⓓ ⓔ ⓕ

15. Which of the following is not true about single-celled organisms?
    (a) They have the same basic life functions as multicellular organisms.
    (b) Yeast is a unicellular organism.
    (c) They produce new cells by asexual reproduction.
    (d) none of the above
(e) We haven't studied this in school yet.
(f) We've studied this, but it's still hard for me.
ⓐ ⓑ ⓒ ⓓ ⓔ ⓕ

16. The water cycle is an essential process to sustain life. Which of the following is not part of the cycle?
    (a) Water from the earth's surface increases in temperature and rises as vapor.
    (b) Water vapor combines with other particles in the air.
    (c) Heavier, the vapor floats or falls back to the earth
    (d) Falling on land or ocean, the liquid water turns back into water through evaporation.
(e) We haven't studied this in school yet.
(f) We've studied this, but it's still hard for me.
ⓐ ⓑ ⓒ ⓓ ⓔ ⓕ

You're done! Now look up the answers and see how many questions you got right.

How Did We Do? Grade Us.

Thank you for choosing a Kaplan book. Your comments and suggestions are very useful to us. Please answer the following questions to assist us in our continued development of high-quality resources to meet your needs.

The Kaplan book I read was: _____

My name is: _____

My address is: _____

_____

My e-mail address is: _____

What overall grade would you give this book?   Ⓐ Ⓑ Ⓒ Ⓓ Ⓕ

How relevant was the information to your goals?   Ⓐ Ⓑ Ⓒ Ⓓ Ⓕ

How comprehensive was the information in this book?   Ⓐ Ⓑ Ⓒ Ⓓ Ⓕ

How accurate was the information in this book?   Ⓐ Ⓑ Ⓒ Ⓓ Ⓕ

How easy was the book to use?   Ⓐ Ⓑ Ⓒ Ⓓ Ⓕ

How appealing was the book's design?   Ⓐ Ⓑ Ⓒ Ⓓ Ⓕ

What were the book's strong points? _____

How could this book be improved? _____

Is there anything that we left out that you wanted to know more about?

Would you recommend this book to others?   ☐ YES   ☐ NO

Other comments: _____

_____

_____

Do we have permission to quote you?   ☐ YES   ☐ NO

Thank you for your help. Please tear out this page and mail it to:

Dave Chipps, Managing Editor
Kaplan Educational Centers
888 Seventh Avenue
New York, NY 10106

Or, you can answer these questions online at www.kaplan.com/talkback.

Thanks!